Praise for *Foundations of Deep Reinforcement Learning*

"This book provides an accessible introduction to deep reinforcement learning covering the mathematical concepts behind popular algorithms as well as their practical implementation. I think the book will be a valuable resource for anyone looking to apply deep reinforcement learning in practice."
—*Volodymyr Mnih, lead developer of DQN*

"An excellent book to quickly develop expertise in the theory, language, and practical implementation of deep reinforcement learning algorithms. A limpid exposition which uses familiar notation; all the most recent techniques explained with concise, readable code, and not a page wasted in irrelevant detours: it is the perfect way to develop a solid foundation on the topic."
—*Vincent Vanhoucke, principal scientist, Google*

"As someone who spends their days trying to make deep reinforcement learning methods more useful for the general public, I can say that Laura and Keng's book is a welcome addition to the literature. It provides both a readable introduction to the fundamental concepts in reinforcement learning as well as intuitive explanations and code for many of the major algorithms in the field. I imagine this will become an invaluable resource for individuals interested in learning about deep reinforcement learning for years to come."
—*Arthur Juliani, senior machine learning engineer, Unity Technologies*

"Until now, the only way to get to grips with deep reinforcement learning was to slowly accumulate knowledge from dozens of different sources. Finally, we have a book bringing everything together in one place."
—*Matthew Rahtz, ML researcher, ETH Zürich*

D1551817

Foundations of Deep Reinforcement Learning

The Pearson Addison-Wesley Data & Analytics Series

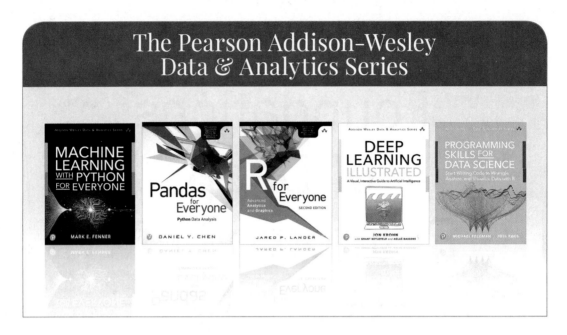

Visit **informit.com/awdataseries** for a complete list of available publications.

The **Pearson Addison-Wesley Data & Analytics Series** provides readers with practical knowledge for solving problems and answering questions with data. Titles in this series primarily focus on three areas:

1. **Infrastructure:** how to store, move, and manage data
2. **Algorithms:** how to mine intelligence or make predictions based on data
3. **Visualizations:** how to represent data and insights in a meaningful and compelling way

The series aims to tie all three of these areas together to help the reader build end-to-end systems for fighting spam; making recommendations; building personalization; detecting trends, patterns, or problems; and gaining insight from the data exhaust of systems and user interactions.

Make sure to connect with us!
informit.com/socialconnect

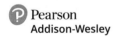

Foundations of Deep Reinforcement Learning

Theory and Practice in Python

Laura Graesser
Wah Loon Keng

✦✦ Addison-Wesley

Boston • Columbus • New York • San Francisco • Amsterdam • Cape Town
Dubai • London • Madrid • Milan • Munich • Paris • Montreal • Toronto • Delhi • Mexico City
São Paulo • Sydney • Hong Kong • Seoul • Singapore • Taipei • Tokyo

For those people who make me feel that anything is possible
—Laura

For my wife Daniela
—Keng

Contents

Foreword

In April of 2019, OpenAI's Five bots played in a Dota 2 competition match against 2018 human world champions, OG. Dota 2 is a complex, multiplayer battle arena game where players can choose different characters. Winning a game requires strategy, teamwork, and quick decisions. Building an artificial intelligence to compete in this game, with so many variables and a seemingly infinite search space for optimization, seems like an insurmountable challenge. Yet OpenAI's bots won handily and, soon after, went on to win over 99% of their matches against public players. The innovation underlying this achievement was deep reinforcement learning.

Although this development is recent, reinforcement learning and deep learning have both been around for decades. However, a significant amount of new research combined with the increasing power of GPUs have pushed the state of the art forward. This book gives the reader an introduction to deep reinforcement learning and distills the work done over the last six years into a cohesive whole.

While training a computer to beat a video game may not be the most practical thing to do, it's only a starting point. Reinforcement learning is an area of machine learning that is useful for solving sequential decision-making problems—that is, problems that are solved over time. This applies to almost any endeavor—be it playing a video game, walking down the street, or driving a car.

Laura Graesser and Wah Loon Keng have put together an approachable introduction to a complicated topic that is at the forefront of what is new in machine learning. Not only have they brought to bear their research into many papers on the topic; they created an open source library, SLM Lab, to help others get up and running quickly with deep reinforcement learning. SLM Lab is written in Python on top of PyTorch, but readers only need familiarity with Python. Readers intending to use TensorFlow or some other library as their deep learning framework of choice will still get value from this book as it introduces the concepts and problem formulations for deep reinforcement learning solutions.

This book brings together the most recent research in deep reinforcement learning along with examples and code that the readers can work with. Their library also works with OpenAI's Gym, Roboschool, and the Unity ML-Agents toolkit, which makes this book a perfect jumping-off point for readers looking to work with those systems.

—*Paul Dix, Series Editor*

Preface

We first discovered deep reinforcement learning (deep RL) when DeepMind achieved breakthrough performance in the Atari arcade games. Using only images and no prior knowledge, artificial agents reached human-level performance for the first time.

The idea of an artificial agent learning by itself, through trial and error, without supervision, sparked something in our imaginations. It was a new and exciting approach to machine learning, and it was quite different from the more familiar field of supervised learning.

We decided to work together to learn about this topic. We read books and papers, followed online courses, studied code, and tried to implement the core algorithms. We realized that not only is deep RL conceptually challenging, but that implementation requires as much effort as a large software engineering project.

As we progressed, we learned more about the landscape of deep RL—how algorithms relate to each other and what their different characteristics are. Forming a mental model of this was hard because deep RL is a new area of research and the theoretical knowledge had not yet been distilled into a book. We had to learn directly from research papers and online lectures.

Another challenge was the large gap between theory and implementation. Often, a deep RL algorithm has many components and tunable hyperparameters that make it sensitive and fragile. For it to succeed, all the components need to work together correctly and with appropriate hyperparameter values. The implementation details required to get this right are not immediately clear from the theory, but are just as important. A resource that integrated theory and implementation would have been invaluable when we were learning.

We felt that the journey from theory to implementation could have been simpler than we found it, and we wanted to contribute to making deep RL easier to learn. This book is our attempt to do that. It takes an end-to-end approach to introducing deep RL—starting with intuition, then explaining the theory and algorithms, and finishing with implementations and practical tips. This is also why the book comes with a companion software library, SLM Lab, which contains implementations of all the algorithms discussed in it. In short, this is the book we wished existed when we were starting to learn about this topic.

Deep RL belongs to the larger field of reinforcement learning. At the core of reinforcement learning is function approximation; in deep RL, functions are learned using deep neural networks. Reinforcement learning, along with supervised and unsupervised learning, make up the three core machine learning techniques, and each technique differs in how problems are formulated and how algorithms learn from data.

In this book we focus exclusively on deep RL because the challenges we experienced are specific to this subfield of reinforcement learning. This bounds the scope of the book in two ways. First, it excludes all other techniques that can be used to learn functions in reinforcement learning. Second, it emphasizes developments between 2013 and 2019 even though reinforcement learning has existed since the 1950s. Many of the recent developments build from older research, so we felt it was important to trace the development of the main ideas. However, we do not intend to give a comprehensive history of the field.

This book is aimed at undergraduate computer science students and software engineers. It is intended to be an introduction to deep RL and no prior knowledge of the subject is required. However, we do assume that readers have a basic familiarity with machine learning and deep learning as well as an intermediate level of Python programming. Some experience with PyTorch is also useful but not necessary.

The book is organized as follows. Chapter 1 introduces the different aspects of a deep reinforcement learning problem and gives an overview of deep reinforcement learning algorithms.

Part I is concerned with policy-based and value-based algorithms. Chapter 2 introduces the first Policy Gradient method known as REINFORCE. Chapter 3 introduces the first value-based method known as SARSA. Chapter 4 discusses the Deep Q-Networks (DQN) algorithm and Chapter 5 focuses on techniques for improving it—target networks, the Double DQN algorithm, and Prioritized Experience Replay.

Part II focuses on algorithms which combine policy-based and value-based methods. Chapter 6 introduces the Actor-Critic algorithm which extends REINFORCE. Chapter 7 introduces Proximal Policy Optimization (PPO) which can extend Actor-Critic. Chapter 8 discusses synchronous and asynchronous parallelization techniques that are applicable to any of the algorithms in this book. Finally, all the algorithms are summarized in Chapter 9.

Each algorithm chapter is structured in the same way. First, we introduce the main concepts and work through the relevant mathematical formulations. Then we describe the algorithm and discuss an implementation in Python. Finally, we provide a configured algorithm with tuned hyperparameters which can be run in SLM Lab, and illustrate the main characteristics of the algorithm with graphs.

Part III focuses on the practical details of implementing deep RL algorithms. Chapter 10 covers engineering and debugging practices and includes an almanac of hyperparameters and results. Chapter 11 provides a usage reference for the companion library, SLM Lab. Chapter 12 looks at neural network design and Chapter 13 discusses hardware.

The final part of book, Part IV, is about environment design. It consists of Chapters 14, 15, 16, and 17 which treat the design of states, actions, rewards, and transition functions respectively.

The book is intended to be read linearly from Chapter 1 to Chapter 10. These chapters introduce all of the algorithms in the book and provide practical tips for getting them to work. The next three chapters, 11 to 13, focus on more specialized topics and can be read in any order. For readers that do not wish to go into as much depth, Chapters 1, 2, 3, 4, 6, and 10 are a coherent subset of the book that focuses on a few of the algorithms. Finally, Part IV contains a standalone set of chapters intended for readers with a particular interest in understanding environments in more depth or building their own.

SLM Lab [67], this book's companion software library, is a modular deep RL framework built using PyTorch [114]. SLM stands for Strange Loop Machine, in homage to Hofstadter's iconic book *Gödel, Escher, Bach: An Eternal Golden Braid* [53]. The specific examples from SLM Lab that we include use PyTorch's syntax and features for training neural networks. However, the underlying principles for implementing deep RL algorithms are applicable to other deep learning frameworks such as TensorFlow [1].

The design of SLM Lab is intended to help new students learn deep RL by organizing its components into conceptually clear pieces. These components also align with how deep RL is discussed in the academic literature to make it easier to translate from theory to code.

Another important aspect of learning deep RL is experimentation. To facilitate this, SLM Lab also provides an experimentation framework to help new students design and test their own hypotheses.

The SLM Lab library is released as an open source project on Github. We encourage readers to install it (on a Linux or MacOS machine) and run the first demo by following the instructions on the repository website https://github.com/kengz/SLM-Lab. A dedicated git branch "book" has been created with a version of code compatible with this book. A short installation instruction copied from the repository website is shown in Code 0.1.

Code 0.1   Installing SLM-Lab from the book git branch

```
1  # clone the repository
2  git clone https://github.com/kengz/SLM-Lab.git
3  cd SLM-Lab
4  # checkout the dedicated branch for this book
5  git checkout book
6  # install dependencies
7  ./bin/setup
8  # next, follow the demo instructions on the repository website
```

We recommend you set this up first so you can train agents with algorithms as they are introduced in this book. Beyond installation and running the demo, it is not necessary to be familiar with SLM Lab before reading the algorithm chapters (Parts I and II)—we give all the commands to train agents where needed. We also discuss SLM Lab more extensively in Chapter 11 after shifting focus from algorithms to more practical aspects of deep reinforcement learning.

Register your copy of *Foundations of Deep Reinforcement Learning* on the InformIT site for convenient access to updates and/or corrections as they become available. To start the registration process, go to informit.com/register and log in or create an account. Enter the product ISBN (9780135172384) and click Submit. Look on the Registered Products tab for an Access Bonus Content link next to this product, and follow that link to access any available bonus materials. If you would like to be notified of exclusive offers on new editions and updates, please check the box to receive email from us.

Acknowledgments

There are many people who have helped us finish this project. We thank Milan Cvitkovic, Alex Leeds, Navdeep Jaitly, Jon Krohn, Katya Vasilaky, and Katelyn Gleason for supporting and encouraging us. We are grateful to OpenAI, PyTorch, Ilya Kostrikov, and Jamromir Janisch for providing high-quality open source implementations of different components of deep RL algorithms. We also thank Arthur Juliani for early discussions on environment design. These resources and discussions were invaluable as we were building SLM Lab.

A number of people provided thoughtful and insightful feedback on earlier drafts of this book. We would like to thank Alexandre Sablayrolles, Anant Gupta, Brandon Strickland, Chong Li, Jon Krohn, Jordi Frank, Karthik Jayasurya, Matthew Rahtz, Pidong Wang, Raymond Chua, Regina R. Monaco, Rico Jonschkowski, Sophie Tabac, and Utku Evci for the time and effort you put into this. The book is better as a result.

We are very grateful to the Pearson production team—Alina Kirsanova, Chris Zahn, Dmitry Kirsanov, and Julie Nahil. Thanks to your thoughtfulness, care, and attention to detail the text has been greatly improved.

Finally, this book would not exist without our editor Debra Williams Cauley. Thank you for your patience and encouragement, and for helping us to see that writing a book was possible.

About the Authors

Laura Graesser is a research software engineer working in robotics at Google. She has a masters in computer science from New York University where she specialized in machine learning.

Wah Loon Keng is an AI engineer who applies deep reinforcement learning to industrial problems at Machine Zone. He has a background in theoretical physics and computer science.

Together, they have developed two deep reinforcement learning software libraries and have given a number of talks and tutorials on the subject.

Introduction to Reinforcement Learning

In this chapter we introduce the main concepts in reinforcement learning. We start by looking at some simple examples to build intuitions about the core components of a reinforcement learning problem—namely, an agent and an environment.

In particular, we will look at how an agent interacts with an environment to optimize an objective. We will then define these more formally and define reinforcement learning as a Markov Decision Process. This is the theoretical foundation of reinforcement learning.

Next, we introduce the three primary functions an agent can learn—a *policy*, *value functions*, and a *model*. We then see how learning these functions gives rise to different families of deep reinforcement learning algorithms.

Finally, we give a brief overview of deep learning, which is the function approximation technique used throughout this book, and discuss the main differences between reinforcement learning and supervised learning.

1.1 Reinforcement Learning

Reinforcement learning (RL) is concerned with solving sequential decision-making problems. Many real-world problems—playing video games, sports, driving, optimizing inventory, robotic control—can be framed in this way. These are things that humans and machines do.

When solving these problems, we have an objective or goal—such as winning the game, arriving safely at our destination, or minimizing the cost of building products. We take actions and get feedback from the world about how close we are to achieving the objective—the current score, distance to our destination, or price per unit. Reaching our goal typically involves taking many actions in sequence, each action changing the world around us. We observe these changes in the world as well as the feedback we receive before deciding on the next action to take as a response.

Imagine the following scenario: you are at a party where a friend brings out a flag pole and challenges you to balance it on your hand for as long as possible. If you have never held a flag pole before, your initial attempts will not be very successful. You may spend the first few moments trying to get a feel of the flag pole via trial and error—as it keeps falling over.

These mistakes allow you to collect valuable information and gain some intuition about how to balance the flag pole—where its center of gravity is, how fast it tilts over, how quickly you should adjust, at what angle it falls over, etc. You use this information to make corrections in your next attempts, improve, make further adjustments—and, before you know it, you can start balancing it for 5 seconds, 10 seconds, 30 seconds, 1 minute, and so on.

This process illustrates how reinforcement learning works. In reinforcement learning, you are what is called the "agent," and the flag pole and your surroundings are called an "environment." In fact, the first environment we will learn to solve with reinforcement learning is a toy version of this scenario called CartPole, shown in Figure 1.1. An agent controls a cart sliding along an axis in order to balance a pole upright for a given time. In reality, a human does much more—for example, you may apply your existing intuition about physics, or transfer skills from similar tasks such as balancing a tray full of drinks—but the problems are essentially the same in formulation.

Figure 1.1   `CartPole-v0` is a simple toy environment. The objective is to balance a pole for 200 time steps by controlling the left-right motion of a cart.

Reinforcement learning studies problems of this form and methods by which artificial agents learn to solve them. It is a subfield of artificial intelligence that dates back to the optimal control theory and Markov decision processes (MDPs). It was first worked on by Richard Bellman in the 1950s in the context of dynamic programming and quasilinear equations [15]. We will see this name again when we study a famous equation in reinforcement learning—the Bellman equation.

RL problems can be expressed as a system consisting of an agent and an environment. An environment produces information which describes the state of the system. This is known as a *state*. An agent interacts with an environment by observing the state and using this information to select an *action*. The environment accepts the action and transitions into the next state. It then returns the next state and a *reward* to the agent. When the cycle of (*state* → *action* → *reward*) completes, we say that one *time step* has passed. The cycle repeats until the environment terminates, for example when the problem is solved. This entire process is described by the control loop diagram in Figure 1.2.

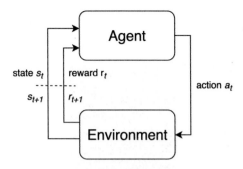

Figure 1.2   The reinforcement learning control loop

We call an agent's action-producing function a *policy*. Formally, a policy is a function which maps states to actions. An action will change the environment and affect what an agent observes and does next. The exchange between an agent and an environment unfolds in time—therefore it can be thought of as a sequential decision-making process.

RL problems have an *objective*, which is the sum of rewards received by an agent. An agent's goal is to maximize the objective by selecting good actions. It *learns* to do this by interacting with the environment in a process of trial and error, and uses the reward signals it receives to *reinforce* good actions.

Agent and environment are defined to be mutually exclusive, so that the boundaries between the exchange of the state, action, and reward are unambiguous. We can consider the environment to be anything that is not the agent. For example, when riding a bike, we can have multiple but equally valid definitions of an agent and an environment. If we consider our entire body to be the agent that observes our surroundings and produces muscle movements as actions, then the environment is the bicycle and the road. If we consider our mental processes to be the agent, then the environment is our physical body, the bicycle, and the road, with actions being the neural signals sent from our brain to the muscles and states being the sensory inputs sent back to our brain.

Essentially, a reinforcement learning system is a feedback control loop where an agent and an environment interact and exchange signals, while the agent tries to maximize the objective. The signals exchanged are (s_t, a_t, r_t), which stand for state, action, and reward, respectively, and t denotes the time step in which these signals occurred. The (s_t, a_t, r_t) tuple is called an *experience*. The control loop can repeat forever[1] or terminate by reaching either a terminal state or a maximum time step $t = T$. The time horizon from $t = 0$ to when the environment terminates is called an *episode*. A *trajectory* is a sequence of experiences over an episode, $\tau = (s_0, a_0, r_0), (s_1, a_1, r_1), \ldots$. An agent typically needs many episodes to learn a good policy, ranging from hundreds to millions depending on the complexity of the problem.

Let's look at the three example reinforcement learning environments, shown in Figure 1.3, and how the states, actions, and rewards are defined. All the environments are

---

1. Infinite control loops exist in theory but not in practice. Typically, we assign a maximum time step T to an environment.

available through the OpenAI Gym [18] which is an open source library that provides a standardized set of environments.

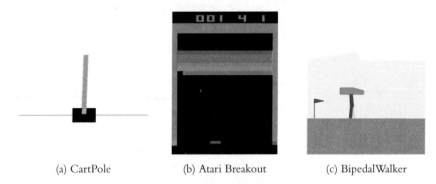

(a) CartPole   (b) Atari Breakout   (c) BipedalWalker

Figure 1.3   Three example environments with different states, actions, and rewards. These environments are available in OpenAI Gym.

CartPole (Figure 1.3a) is one of the simplest reinforcement learning environments, first described by Barto, Sutton, and Anderson [11] in 1983. In this environment, a pole is attached to a cart that can be moved along a frictionless track. The main features of the environment are summarized below:

1. **Objective:** Keep the pole upright for 200 time steps.

2. **State:** An array of length 4 which represents: [cart position, cart velocity, pole angle, pole angular velocity]. For example, [−0.034, 0.032, −0.031, 0.036].

3. **Action:** An integer, either 0 to move the cart a fixed distance to the left, or 1 to move the cart a fixed distance to the right.

4. **Reward:** +1 for every time step the pole remains upright.

5. **Termination:** When the pole falls over (greater than 12 degrees from vertical), or when the cart moves out of the screen, or when the maximum time step of 200 is reached.

Atari Breakout (Figure 1.3b) is a retro arcade game that consists of a ball, a bottom paddle controlled by an agent, and bricks. The goal is to hit and destroy all the bricks by bouncing the ball off the paddle. A player starts with five game lives, and a life is lost every time the ball falls off the screen from the bottom.

1. **Objective:** Maximize the game score.

2. **State:** An RGB digital image with resolution 160×210 pixels—that is, what we see on the game screen.

3. **Action:** An integer from the set {0, 1, 2, 3} which maps to the game controller actions {no-action, launch the ball, move right, move left}.

4. **Reward:** The game score difference between consecutive states.

5. **Termination:** When all game lives are lost.

BipedalWalker (Figure 1.3c) is a continuous control problem where an agent uses a robot's lidar sensor to sense its surroundings and walk to the right without falling.

1. **Objective:** Walk to the right without falling.

2. **State:** An array of length 24 which represents: [hull angle, hull angular velocity, x-velocity, y-velocity, hip 1 joint angle, hip 1 joint speed, knee 1 joint angle, knee 1 joint speed, leg 1 ground contact, hip 2 joint angle, hip 2 joint speed, knee 2 joint angle, knee 2 joint speed, leg 2 ground contact, ..., 10 lidar readings]. For example, [2.745e−03, 1.180e−05, −1.539e−03, −1.600e−02, ..., 7.091e−01, 8.859e−01, 1.000e+00, 1.000e+00].

3. **Action:** A vector of four floating point numbers in the interval $[-1.0, 1.0]$ which represents: [hip 1 torque and velocity, knee 1 torque and velocity, hip 2 torque and velocity, knee 2 torque and velocity]. For example, [0.097, 0.430, 0.205, 0.089].

4. **Reward:** Reward for moving forward to the right, up to a maximum of +300. −100 if the robot falls. Additionally, there is a small negative reward (movement cost) at every time step, proportional to the absolute torque applied.

5. **Termination:** When the robot body touches the ground or reaches the goal on the right side, or after the maximum time step of 1600.

These environments demonstrate some of the different forms that states and actions can take. In CartPole and BipedalWalker, the states are vectors describing properties such as positions and velocities. In Atari Breakout, the state is an image from the game screen. In CartPole and Atari Breakout, actions are single, discrete integers, whereas in BipedalWalker, an action is a continuous vector of four floating-point numbers. Rewards are always a scalar, but the range varies from task to task.

Having seen some examples, let's now formally describe states, actions, and rewards.

$$s_t \in \mathcal{S} \text{ is the state, } \mathcal{S} \text{ is the state space.} \tag{1.1}$$

$$a_t \in \mathcal{A} \text{ is the action, } \mathcal{A} \text{ is the action space.} \tag{1.2}$$

$$r_t = \mathcal{R}(s_t, a_t, s_{t+1}) \text{ is the reward, } \mathcal{R} \text{ is the reward function.} \tag{1.3}$$

The state space $\mathcal{S}$ is the set of all possible states in an environment. Depending on the environment, it can be defined in many different ways—as integers, real numbers, vectors, matrices, structured or unstructured data. Similarly, the action space $\mathcal{A}$ is the set of all possible actions defined by an environment. It can also take many forms, but is commonly defined as either a scalar or a vector. The reward function $\mathcal{R}(s_t, a_t, s_{t+1})$ assigns a positive, negative, or zero scalar to each transition (s_t, a_t, s_{t+1}). The state space, action space, and reward function are specified by the environment. Together, they define the (s, a, r) tuples which are the basic unit of information describing a reinforcement learning system.

1.2   Reinforcement Learning as MDP

Now, consider how an environment transitions from one state to the next using what is known as the *transition function*. In reinforcement learning, a transition function is formulated as a Markov decision process (MDP) which is a mathematical framework that models sequential decision making.

To understand why transition functions are represented as MDPs, consider a general formulation shown in Equation 1.4.

$$s_{t+1} \sim P\big(s_{t+1} \,|\, (s_0, a_0), (s_1, a_1), \ldots, (s_t, a_t)\big) \tag{1.4}$$

Equation 1.4 says that at time step t, the next state s_{t+1} is sampled from a probability distribution P conditioned on the entire history. The probability of an environment transitioning from state s_t to s_{t+1} depends on all of the preceding states s and actions a that have occurred so far in an episode. It is challenging to model a transition function in this form, particularly if episodes last for many time steps. Any transition function that we design would need to be able to account for a vast combination of effects that occurred at any point in the past. Additionally, this formulation makes an agent's action-producing function—its *policy*—significantly more complex. Since the entire history of states and actions is relevant for understanding how an action might change the future state of the world, an agent would need to take into account all of this information when deciding how to act.

To make the environment transition function more practical, we turn it into an MDP by adding the assumption that the transition to the next state s_{t+1} only depends on the previous state s_t and action a_t. This is known as the *Markov property*. With this assumption, the new transition function becomes the following:

$$s_{t+1} \sim P\big(s_{t+1} \,|\, s_t, a_t\big) \tag{1.5}$$

Equation 1.5 says that the next state s_{t+1} is sampled from a probability distribution $P(s_{t+1} \,|\, s_t, a_t)$. This is a simpler form of the original transition function. The Markov property implies that the current state and action at time step t contain sufficient information to fully determine the transition probability for the next state at $t + 1$.

Despite the simplicity of this formulation, it is still quite powerful. A lot of processes can be expressed in this form, including games, robotic control, and planning. This is because a state can be defined to include any necessary information required to make the transition function Markov.

For example, consider the Fibonacci sequence described by the formula $s_{t+1} = s_t + s_{t-1}$, where each term s_t is considered a state. To make the function Markov, we redefine the state as $s'_t = [s_t, s_{t-1}]$. Now the state contains sufficient information to compute the next element in the sequence. This strategy can be applied more generally to any system in which a finite set of k consecutive states contains sufficient information to transition to the next state. Box 1.1 contains more details on how states are defined in an MDP and in its generalization, an POMDP. Note that throughout this book, Boxes serve to provide in-depth details that may be skipped on first reading without a loss of understanding of the main subject.

Box 1.1 MDP and POMDP

So far, the concept of state has appeared in two places. First, the state is what is produced by an environment and observed by an agent. Let's call this the *observed state* s_t. Second, the state is what is used by transition function. Let's call this the environment's *internal state* s_t^{int}.

In an MDP, $s_t = s_t^{\text{int}}$, that is, the observed state is identical to the environment's internal state. The same state information that is used to transition an environment into the next state is also made available to an agent.

This is not always the case. The observed state may differ from the environment's internal state, $s_t \neq s_t^{\text{int}}$. In this case, the environment is described as a *partially observable MDP* (POMDP) because the state s_t exposed to the agent only contains partial information about the state of the environment.

In this book, for the most part, we forget about this distinction and assume that $s_t = s_t^{\text{int}}$. However, it is important to be aware of POMDPs for two reasons. First, some of the example environments we consider are not perfect MDPs. For example, in the Atari environment, the observed state s_t is a single RGB image which conveys information about object positions, lives, etc., but not object velocities. Velocities would be included in the environment's internal state since they are required to determine the next state given an action. In these cases, to achieve good performance, we will have to modify s_t to include more information. This is discussed in Chapter 5.

Second, many interesting real-world problems are POMDPs for many reasons, including sensor or data limitations, model error, and environment noise. A detailed discussion of POMDPs is beyond the scope of this book, but we will touch on them briefly when discussing network architecture in Chapter 12.

Finally, when discussing state design in Chapter 14, the distinction between s_t and s_t^{int} will be important because an agent learns from s_t. The information that is included in s_t and the extent to which it differs from s_t^{int} contributes to making a problem harder or easier to solve.

We are now in a position to present the MDP formulation of a reinforcement learning problem. An MDP is defined by a 4-tuple $\mathcal{S}, \mathcal{A}, P(.), \mathcal{R}(.)$, where

- $\mathcal{S}$ is the set of states.
- $\mathcal{A}$ is the set of actions.
- $P(s_{t+1} \mid s_t, a_t)$ is the state transition function of the environment.
- $\mathcal{R}(s_t, a_t, s_{t+1})$ is the reward function of the environment.

One important assumption underlying the reinforcement learning problems discussed in this book is that agents do not have access to the transition function, $P(s_{t+1} \mid s_t, a_t)$, or the reward function, $\mathcal{R}(s_t, a_t, s_{t+1})$. The only way an agent can get information about these functions is through the states, actions, and rewards it actually experiences in the environment—that is, the tuples (s_t, a_t, r_t).

To complete the formulation of the problem, we also need to formalize the concept of an objective which an agent maximizes. First, let's define the *return*[2] $R(\tau)$ using a trajectory from an episode, $\tau = (s_0, a_0, r_0), \ldots, (s_T, a_T, r_T)$:

$$R(\tau) = r_0 + \gamma r_1 + \gamma^2 r_2 + \cdots + \gamma^T r_T = \sum_{t=0}^{T} \gamma^t r_t \tag{1.6}$$

Equation 1.6 defines the return as a discounted sum of the rewards in a trajectory, where $\gamma \in [0, 1]$ is the discount factor.

Then, the *objective* $J(\tau)$ is simply the expectation of the returns over many trajectories, shown in Equation 1.7.

$$J(\tau) = \mathbb{E}_{\tau \sim \pi}[R(\tau)] = \mathbb{E}_{\tau} \left[\sum_{t=0}^{T} \gamma^t r_t \right] \tag{1.7}$$

The return $R(\tau)$ is the sum of discounted rewards $\gamma^t r_t$ over all time steps $t = 0, \ldots, T$. The objective $J(\tau)$ is the return averaged over many episodes. The expectation accounts for stochasticity in the actions and the environment—that is, in repeated runs, the return may not always end up the same. Maximizing the objective is the same as maximizing the return.

The discount factor $\gamma \in [0, 1]$ is an important variable which changes the way future rewards are valued. The smaller γ, the less weight is given to rewards in future time steps, making it "shortsighted." In the extreme case with $\gamma = 0$, the objective only considers the initial reward r_0, as shown in Equation 1.8.

$$R(\tau)_{\gamma=0} = \sum_{t=0}^{T} \gamma^t r_t = r_0 \tag{1.8}$$

The larger γ, the more weight is given to rewards in future time steps: the objective becomes more "farsighted." If $\gamma = 1$, rewards from every time step are weighted equally, as shown in Equation 1.9.

$$R(\tau)_{\gamma=1} = \sum_{t=0}^{T} \gamma^t r_t = \sum_{t=0}^{T} r_t \tag{1.9}$$

For problems with *infinite* time horizon, we need to set $\gamma < 1$ to prevent the objective from becoming unbounded. For *finite* time horizon problems, γ is an important parameter as a problem may become more or less difficult to solve depending on the discount factor we use. We'll look at an example of this at the end of Chapter 2.

Having defined reinforcement learning as an MDP and the objective, we can now express the reinforcement learning control loop from Figure 1.2 as an MDP control loop in Algorithm 1.1.

---

2. We use R to denote return and reserve $\mathcal{R}$ for the reward function.

Algorithm 1.1   MDP control loop

1: Given an env (environment) and an agent:
2: **for** *episode* = 0, . . . , *MAX_EPISODE* **do**
3:      state = env.reset()
4:      agent.reset()
5:      **for** $t = 0, \ldots, T$ **do**
6:          action = agent.act(state)
7:          state, reward = env.step(action)
8:          agent.update(action, state, reward)
9:          **if** env.done() **then**
10:             break
11:         **end if**
12:     **end for**
13: **end for**

Algorithm 1.1 expresses the interactions between an agent and an environment over many episodes and time steps. At the beginning of each episode, the environment and the agent are reset (lines 3–4). On reset, the environment produces an initial state. Then they begin interacting—an agent produces an action given a state (line 6), then the environment produces the next state and reward given the action (line 7), stepping into the next time step. The agent.act-env.step cycle continues until the maximum time step T is reached or the environment terminates. Here we also see a new component, agent.update (line 8), which encapsulates an agent's learning algorithm. Over multiple time steps and episodes, this method collects data and performs learning internally to maximize the objective.

This algorithm is generic to all reinforcement learning problems as it defines a consistent interface between an agent and an environment. The interface serves as a foundation for implementing many reinforcement learning algorithms under a unified framework, as we will see in SLM Lab, the companion library to this book.

1.3 Learnable Functions in Reinforcement Learning

With reinforcement learning formulated as an MDP, the natural question to ask is, what should an agent learn?

We have seen that an agent can learn an action-producing function known as a *policy*. However, there are other properties of an environment that can be useful to an agent. In particular, there are *three primary functions* to learn in reinforcement learning:

1. A policy, π, which maps state to action: $a \sim \pi(s)$

2. A value function, $V^\pi(s)$ or $Q^\pi(s, a)$, to estimate the expected return $\mathbb{E}_\tau[R(\tau)]$

3. The environment model,[3] $P(s' \mid s, a)$

A policy π is how an agent produces actions in the environment to maximize the objective. Given the reinforcement learning control loop, an agent must produce an action at every time step after observing a state s. A policy is fundamental to this control loop, since it generates the actions to make it run.

A policy can be stochastic. That is, it may probabilistically output different actions for the same state. We can write this as $\pi(a \mid s)$ to denote the probability of an action a given a state s. An action sampled from a policy is written as $a \sim \pi(s)$.

The value functions provide information about the objective. They help an agent understand how good the states and available actions are in terms of the expected future return. They come in two forms—the $V^\pi(s)$ and $Q^\pi(s, a)$ functions.

$$V^\pi(s) = \mathbb{E}_{s_0=s, \tau \sim \pi}\left[\sum_{t=0}^{T} \gamma^t r_t\right] \tag{1.10}$$

$$Q^\pi(s, a) = \mathbb{E}_{s_0=s, a_0=a, \tau \sim \pi}\left[\sum_{t=0}^{T} \gamma^t r_t\right] \tag{1.11}$$

The value function V^π shown in Equation 1.10 evaluates how good or bad a state is. V^π measures the expected return from being in state s, assuming the agent continues to act according to its current policy π. The return $R(\tau) = \sum_{t=0}^{T} \gamma^t r_t$ is measured from the current state s to the end of an episode. It is a forward-looking measure, since all rewards received before state s are ignored.

To give some intuition for the value function V^π, let's consider a simple example. Figure 1.4 depicts a grid-world environment in which an agent can move from cell to cell vertically or horizontally. Each cell is a state with an associate reward, as shown on the left of the figure. The environment terminates when the agent reaches the goal state with reward $r = +1$.

On the right, we show the value $V^\pi(s)$ calculated for each state from the rewards using Equation 1.10, with $\gamma = 0.9$. The value function V^π always depends on a particular policy π. In this example, we chose a policy π which always takes the shortest path to the goal state. If we had chosen another policy—for example, one that always moves right—then the values would be different.

Here we can see the forward-looking property of the value function and its ability to help an agent differentiate between states that give the same reward. The closer an agent is to the goal state, the higher the value.

---

3. To make notation more compact, it is customary to write a successive pair of tuples (s_t, a_t, r_t), $(s_{t+1}, a_{t+1}, r_{t+1})$ as (s, a, r), (s', a', r'), where the prime symbol $'$ represents the next time step. We will see this throughout the book.

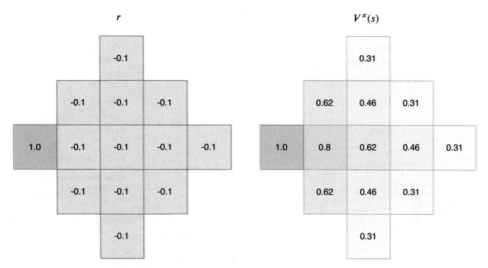

Figure 1.4   Rewards r and values $V^\pi(s)$ for each state s in a simple grid-world environment. The value of a state is calculated from the rewards using Equation 1.10 with $\gamma = 0.9$ while using a policy π that always takes the shortest path to the goal state with $r = +1$.

The Q-value function Q^π shown in Equation 1.11 evaluates how good or bad a state–action pair is. Q^π measures the expected return from taking action a in state s assuming that the agent continues to act according to its current policy, π. In the same manner as V^π, the return is measured from the current state s to the end of an episode. It is also a forward-looking measure, since all rewards received before state s are ignored.

We discuss the V^π and Q^π functions in more detail in Chapter 3. For the moment, you just need to know that these functions exist and can be used by agents to solve reinforcement learning problems.

The transition function $P(s' \mid s, a)$ provides information about the environment. If an agent learns this function, it is able to predict the next state s' that the environment will transition into after taking action a in state s. By applying the learned transition function, an agent can "imagine" the consequences of its actions without actually touching the environment. It can then use this information to plan good actions.

1.4 Deep Reinforcement Learning Algorithms

In RL, an agent learns functions to help it act and maximize the objective. This book is concerned with *deep* reinforcement learning (deep RL). This means that we use deep neural networks as the function approximation method.

In Section 1.3, we saw the three primary learnable functions in reinforcement learning. Correspondingly, there are three major families of deep reinforcement learning algorithms—*policy-based*, *value-based*, and *model-based* methods which learn policies, value functions, and models, respectively. There are also combined methods in which agents learn more than one of these functions—for instance, a policy and a value function, or a value function and a model. Figure 1.5 gives an overview of the major deep reinforcement learning algorithms in each family and how they are related.

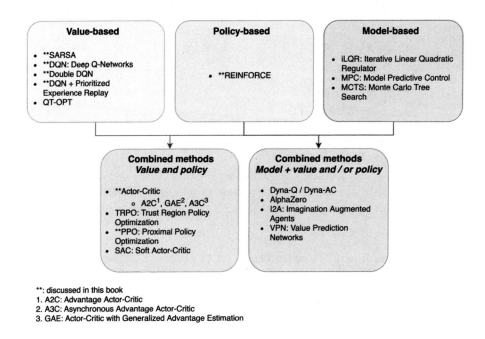

Figure 1.5 Deep reinforcement learning algorithm families

1.4.1 Policy-Based Algorithms

Algorithms in this family learn a policy π. Good policies should generate actions which produce trajectories τ that maximize an agent's objective, $J(\tau) = \mathbb{E}_{\tau \sim \pi} \left[\sum_{t=0}^{T} \gamma^t r_t \right]$. This approach is quite intuitive—if an agent needs to act in an environment, it makes sense to learn a policy. What constitutes a good action at a given moment depends on the state, so a policy function π takes a state s as input to produce an action $a \sim \pi(s)$. This means an agent can make good decisions in different contexts. REINFORCE [148], discussed in Chapter 2, is the most well known policy-based algorithm that forms the foundation of many subsequent algorithms.

A major advantage of policy-based algorithms is that they are a very general class of optimization methods. They can be applied to problems with any type of actions—discrete, continuous, or a mixture (multiactions). They also directly optimize for the thing an agent cares most about—the objective $J(\tau)$. Additionally, this class of methods is guaranteed to converge to a locally[4] optimal policy, as proven by Sutton et al. with the Policy Gradient Theorem [133]. One disadvantage of these methods is that they have high variance and are sample-inefficient.

1.4.2 Value-Based Algorithms

An agent learns either $V^\pi(s)$ or $Q^\pi(s, a)$. It uses the learned value function to evaluate (s, a) pairs and generate a policy. For example, an agent's policy could be to always select the action a in state s with the highest estimated $Q^\pi(s, a)$. Learning $Q^\pi(s, a)$ is far more common than $V^\pi(s)$ for pure value-based approaches because it is easier to convert into a policy. This is because $Q^\pi(s, a)$ contains information about paired states and actions whereas $V^\pi(s)$ just contains information about states.

SARSA [118], discussed in Chapter 3, is one of the older reinforcement learning algorithms. Despite its simplicity, SARSA incorporates many of the core ideas of value-based methods, so it is a good algorithm to study first in this family. However, it is not commonly used today due to its high variance and sample inefficiency during training. Deep Q-Networks (DQN) [88] and its descendants, such as Double DQN [141] and DQN with Prioritized Experience Replay (PER) [121], are much more popular and effective algorithms. These are the subjects of Chapters 4 and 5.

Value-based algorithms are typically more sample-efficient than policy-based algorithms. This is because they have lower variance and make better use of data gathered from the environment. However, there are no guarantees that these algorithms will converge to an optimum. In their standard formulation, they are also only applicable to environments with discrete action spaces. This has historically been a major limitation, but with more recent advances, such as QT-OPT [64], they can be effectively applied to environments with continuous action spaces.

1.4.3 Model-Based Algorithms

Algorithms in this family either learn a model of an environment's transition dynamics or make use of a known dynamics model. Once an agent has a model of the environment, $P(s' \mid s, a)$, it can "imagine" what will happen in the future by predicting the trajectory for a few time steps. If the environment is in state s, an agent can estimate how the state will change if it makes a sequence of actions $a_1, a_2, \ldots, a_n$ by repeatedly applying $P(s' \mid s, a)$, all without actually producing an action to change the environment. Hence, the predicted trajectory occurs in the agent's "head" using a model. An agent can complete many different trajectory predictions with different actions sequences, then examine these options to decide on the best action a to actually take.

Purely model-based approaches are most commonly applied to games with a target state, such as winning or losing in a game of chess, or navigation tasks with a goal state s^*.

---

4. Global convergence guarantee is still an open problem. Recently, it was proven for a subclass of problems known as linearized control. See the paper "Global Convergence of Policy Gradient Methods for Linearized Control Problems" by Fazel et al. (2018) [38].

This is because their transition functions do not model any rewards. In order to use it to plan actions, some information about an agent's objective needs to be encoded in the states themselves.

Monte Carlo Tree Search (MCTS) is a well-known model-based method that can be applied to problems with deterministic discrete state spaces with known transition functions. Many board games such as chess and Go fall into this category, and until recently MCTS powered many computer Go programs [125]. It does not use any machine learning but randomly samples sequences of actions, known as Monte Carlo rollouts, to explore a game's states and estimate their value [125]. There have been a number of improvements to this algorithm, but this is the essential idea.

Other methods, such as iterative Linear Quadratic Regulators (iLQR) [79] or Model Predictive Control (MPC), involve learning the transition dynamics, often under quite restrictive assumptions.[5] To learn the dynamics, an agent will need to act in an environment to gather examples of actual transitions (s, a, r, s').

Model-based algorithms are very appealing because a perfect model endows an agent with foresight—it can play out scenarios and understand the consequences of its actions without having to actually act in an environment. This can be a significant advantage in situations where it is very time-consuming or expensive to gather experiences from the environment—for example, in robotics. Compared to policy-based or value-based methods, these algorithms also tend to require many fewer samples of data to learn good policies since having a model enables an agent to supplement its actual experiences with imagined ones.

However, for most problems, models are hard to come by. Many environments are stochastic, and their transition dynamics are not known. In these cases, the model must be learned. This approach is still in early development, and it faces a number of challenges. First, an environment with a large state space and action space can be very difficult to model; doing so may even be intractable, especially if the transitions are extremely complex. Second, models are only useful when they can accurately predict the transitions of an environment many steps into the future. Depending on the accuracy of the model, prediction errors may compound for every time step and quickly grow to make the model unreliable.

The lack of good models is currently a major limitation for the applicability of model-based approaches. However, model-based methods can be very powerful. When they work, they are often 1 or 2 orders of magnitude more sample-efficient than model-free methods.

The distinction between *model-based* and *model-free* is also used to classify reinforcement learning algorithms. A model-based algorithm is simply any algorithm that makes use of the transition dynamics of an environment, whether learned or known in advance. Model-free algorithms are those that don't explicitly make use of the environment transition dynamics.

---

5. For example, in iLQR the transition dynamics are assumed to be a linear function of states and actions and the reward function is assumed to be quadratic.

1.4.4 Combined Methods

These algorithms learn two or more of the primary reinforcement learning functions. Given the strengths and weaknesses of each of the three methods discussed so far, it is natural to try to combine them to get the best of each. One widely used group of algorithms learns a policy and a value function. These are aptly named Actor-Critic algorithms because the policy *acts* and the value function *critiques* the actions. This is the subject of Chapter 6. The key idea is that during training, a learned value function can provide a more informative feedback signal to a policy than the sequence of rewards available from the environment. The policy learns using information provided by the learned value function. The policy is then used to generate actions, as in policy-based methods.

Actor-Critic algorithms are an active area of research and there have been many interesting developments in recent years — Trust Region Policy Optimization (TRPO) [122], Proximal Policy Optimization (PPO) [124], Deep Deterministic Policy Gradients (DDPG) [81], and Soft Actor-Critic (SAC) [47], to name a few. Of these, PPO is currently the most widely used; we discuss it in Chapter 7.

Algorithms may also use a model of the environment transition dynamics in combination with a value function and/or a policy. In 2016, researchers from DeepMind developed AlphaZero, which combined MCTS with learning V^{π} and a policy π to master the game of Go [127]. Dyna-Q [130] is another well-known algorithm which iteratively learns a model using real data from the environment, then uses the imagined data generated by a learned model to learn the Q-function.

The examples given in this section are just a few of the many deep reinforcement learning algorithms. It is by no means an exhaustive list; instead, our intention was to give an overview of the main ideas in deep reinforcement learning and the ways in which policies, value functions, and models can be used and combined. Deep reinforcement learning is a very active area of research, and it seems like every few months there is an exciting new development in the field.

1.4.5 Algorithms Covered in This Book

This book focuses on methods that are policy-based, value-based, and a combination of the two. We cover REINFORCE (Chapter 2), SARSA (Chapter 3), DQN (Chapter 4) and its extensions (Chapter 5), Actor-Critic (Chapter 6), and PPO (Chapter 7). Chapter 8 covers parallelization methods that are applicable to all of them.

We do not cover model-based algorithms. This book aims to be a practical guide; model-free methods are more well developed and more applicable to a wider range of problems because of their generality. With minimal changes, the same algorithm (for example, PPO) can be applied to play a video game such as Dota 2 [104] or to control a robotic hand [101]. Essentially, one can use a policy- or a value-based algorithm by placing it in an environment and letting it learn without any extra context required.

In contrast, model-based methods typically require more knowledge about the environment—that is, a model of the transition dynamics—in order to work. For problems such as chess or Go, the model is simply the game's rules which can easily be programmed. Even then, getting a model to work with a reinforcement learning algorithm is nontrivial, as seen in DeepMind's AlphaZero [127]. Often, models are not known and need to be learned, but this is a difficult task.

Our coverage of policy- and value-based algorithms is also not exhaustive. We include algorithms that are widely known and applied, and at the same time also illustrate the key concepts in deep reinforcement learning. Our goal is to help readers establish a solid foundation in this subject. We hope that after understanding the algorithms covered in this book, readers will be well equipped to follow current research and applications in deep reinforcement learning.

1.4.6   On-Policy and Off-Policy Algorithms

A final important distinction between deep reinforcement learning algorithms is whether they are *on-policy* or *off-policy*. This affects how training iterations make use of data.

An algorithm is *on-policy* if it learns on the policy—that is, training can only utilize data generated from the current policy π. This implies that as training iterates through versions of policies, $\pi_1, \pi_2, \pi_3, \ldots$, each training iteration only uses the current policy at that time to generate training data. As a result, all the data must be discarded after training, since it becomes unusable. This makes on-policy methods sample-inefficient—they require more training data. The on-policy methods discussed in this book are REINFORCE (Chapter 2), SARSA (Chapter 3), and the combined methods Actor-Critic (Chapter 6) and PPO (Chapter 7).

In contrast, an algorithm is *off-policy* if it does not have this requirement. Any data collected can be reused in training. Consequently, off-policy methods are more sample-efficient, but this may require much more memory to store the data. The off-policy methods we will look at are DQN (Chapter 4) and its extensions (Chapter 5).

1.4.7   Summary

We have introduced the main families of deep reinforcement learning algorithms and discussed a number of ways to classify them. Each way of looking at deep reinforcement learning algorithms highlights different characteristics, and there is no one best approach. These distinction can be summarized as follows:

- Policy-based, value-based, model-based, or combined methods: Which of the three primary reinforcement learning functions an algorithm learns

- Model-based or model-free: Whether an algorithm uses a model of an environment's transition dynamics

- On-policy or off-policy: Whether an algorithm learns with data gathered using just the current policy

1.5 Deep Learning for Reinforcement Learning

In this section we give a very brief overview of deep learning and the training workflow for learning the parameters of a neural network.

Deep neural networks excel at complex nonlinear function approximation. They are structured as alternating layers of parameters and nonlinear activation functions, and it is this structure that makes them so expressive. In their modern form, neural networks have existed since the 1980s when LeCun et al. successfully trained a convolutional neural network to recognize handwritten zip codes [70]. Since 2012, deep learning has been successfully applied to many different problems and has contributed to state-of-the-art results in a wide range of fields including computer vision, machine translation, natural language understanding, and speech synthesis. At the time of writing, deep learning is the most powerful function approximation technique available to us.

Neural networks were first combined with reinforcement learning to great effect in 1991 when Gerald Tesauro trained a neural network using reinforcement learning to play master-level backgammon [135]. However, it wasn't until 2015 when DeepMind achieved human-level performance on many of the Atari games that they became widely adopted in this field as the underlying function approximation technique. Since then all of the major breakthroughs in reinforcement learning have used neural networks to approximate functions. This is why we focus solely on deep reinforcement learning in this book.

Neural networks learn functions, which are simply mappings of inputs to outputs. They perform sequential computations on an input to produce an output; this process is known as a *forward pass*. A function is represented by a particular set of values of the of parameters θ of a network; we say that "the function is parametrized by θ." Different values of the parameters correspond to different functions.

To learn a function, we need a method to acquire or generate a sufficiently representative dataset of inputs and a way of evaluating the outputs that a network produces. Evaluating the outputs can mean one of two things. The first way is to generate the "correct" output, or target value, for each input and define a loss function which measures the error between the target and the network-predicted output. This loss should be minimized. The second way is to directly provide feedback for each input in the form of a scalar value, such as a reward or return. This scalar represents how good or bad the network's output is, and it should be maximized (for goodness). When negated, this value can also be considered a loss function to be minimized.

Given a loss function which evaluates a network's outputs, it is possible to change the values of a network's parameters to minimize the loss and improve performance. This is known as gradient descent because we change the parameters in the direction of steepest descent on the loss surface in search of a global minimum.

Changing the parameters of a network to minimize a loss is also known as *training* a neural network. To give an example, suppose the function $f(x)$ being learned is parametrized with network weights θ as $f(x; \theta)$, with x, y as the input-output data, and let $L(f(x; \theta), y)$ be the predefined loss function. A training step can be summarized as follows:

1. Sample a random batch (x, y) from dataset, where the batch size is significantly smaller than the total size of the dataset.

2. Compute a forward pass with the network using the inputs x to produce predicted outputs, $\hat{y} = f(x; \theta)$.

3. Compute the loss $L(\hat{y}, y)$ using $\hat{y}$ predicted by the network and y from the sampled batch.

4. Calculate the gradient (partial derivative) of the loss $\nabla_\theta L$ with respect to the parameters of the network. Modern neural network libraries such as PyTorch [114] or TensorFlow [1] handle this automatically using the backpropagation [117] algorithm (a.k.a. "autograd").

5. Use an optimizer to update the network parameters using the gradient. For example, a *stochastic gradient descent* (SGD) optimizer makes the following update: $\theta \leftarrow \theta - \alpha \nabla_\theta L$, where α is a scalar learning rate. However, there are many other optimization techniques available in neural network libraries.

This training step is repeated until the network's outputs stop changing or the loss has minimized and plateaued—that is, the network has converged.

In reinforcement learning, neither the network inputs x nor the correct outputs y are given in advance. Instead, these values are obtained through agent interactions with an environment—from the states and rewards it observes. This represents a particular challenge for training neural networks in reinforcement learning, and will be the subject of much discussion throughout this book.

The difficulties in data generation and evaluation are due to the fact that the functions that we try to learn are tightly coupled with the MDP loop. The data exchange between an agent and an environment is interactive and the process is inherently limited by the time needed for an agent to act and for an environment to transition. There is no shortcut to generating data for training—an agent has to experience every time step. The data collection and training cycle runs repeatedly, with every training step (potentially) waiting for new data to be collected.

Furthermore, since the current state of an environment and the actions an agent takes affect the future states it experiences, states and rewards at any given point in time are not independent of states and rewards at previous time steps. This violates an assumption of gradient descent—that data is identically and independently distributed (i.i.d.). The speed at which a network converges and the quality of the final result can be adversely affected. Significant research effort has gone into minimizing this effect, and some techniques are discussed later in this book.

Despite these challenges, deep learning is a powerful technique for function approximation. It is worth persevering to overcome the difficulties of applying it to reinforcement learning, as the benefits greatly outweigh the costs.

---

6. The AI community loves abbreviations. We will see many more later—nearly all of the algorithms and component names have abbreviations.

1.6 Reinforcement Learning and Supervised Learning

At the core of deep reinforcement learning is function approximation. This is something it shares with supervised learning (SL).[6] However, reinforcement learning is unlike supervised learning in a number of ways. There are three main differences:

- Lack of an oracle[7]
- Sparsity of feedback
- Data generated during training

1.6.1 Lack of an Oracle

A major difference between reinforcement learning and supervised learning is that for reinforcement learning problems, the "correct" answer for each model input is not available, whereas in supervised learning we have access to the correct or optimal answer for each example. In reinforcement learning, the equivalent of the correct answer would be access to an "oracle" which tells us the optimal action to take at every time step so as to maximize the objective.

The correct answer can convey a lot of information about a data point. For example, the correct answer for classification problems contains many bits of information. It not only tells us the right class for each training example, but also implies that the example does not belong to any of the other classes. If a particular classification problem has 1000 classes (as in the ImageNet dataset [32]), an answer contains 1000 bits of information per example (1 positive and 999 negative). Furthermore, the correct answer does not have to be a category or a real number. It can be a bounding box, or a semantic segmentation, each of which contains many bits of information about the example at hand.

In reinforcement learning, after an agent takes action a in state s, it only has access to the reward it receives. The agent is not told what the best action to take was. Instead, it is only given an indication, via the reward, of how good or bad a was. Not only does this convey less information than the right answer would have provided, but the agent only learns about rewards for the states it experiences. To learn about (s, a, r), an agent must experience the transition (s, a, r, s'). An agent may have no knowledge about important parts of the state and action spaces because it hasn't experienced them.

One way to deal with this problem is to initialize episodes to start in the states we want an agent to learn about. However, it is not always possible to do this, for two reasons. First, we may not have full control over an environment. Second, states can be easy to describe but difficult to specify. Consider a simulation of a humanoid robot learning to do a backflip. To help an agent learn about the reward for successful landing, we can initialize an environment to start just as the robot's feet make contact with the floor after a "good" flip. The reward function in this part of the state space is critical to learn about, since this is

---

7. In computer science, an oracle is a hypothetical black box that provides the correct answers to questions asked.

where the robot may either retain its balance and successfully execute the flip, or fall over and fail. However, it is not straightforward to define the precise numerical position and velocity of each of the robot's joint angles, or the force being exerted, to initialize the robot in this position. In practice, to reach this state, an agent needs to execute a long, very specific sequence of actions to first flip and then almost land. There is no guarantee that an agent will learn to do this, so this part of the state space may never be explored.

1.6.2   Sparsity of Feedback

In reinforcement learning, a reward function may be sparse, so the scalar reward is often 0. This means that most of the time, an agent is receiving no information about how to change the parameters of the network so as to improve performance. Consider again the backflipping robot and suppose an agent only receives a nonzero reward of $+1$ after successfully executing a backflip. Almost all actions that it takes will result in the same reward signal of 0 from the environment. Under these circumstances, learning is extremely challenging because an agent receives no guidance about whether its intermediate actions help reach the goal. Supervised learning doesn't have this problem; all input examples are paired with a desired output which conveys some information about how a network should perform.

The combination of sparse feedback and the lack of an oracle means that in reinforcement learning, much less information per time step is received from the environment, compared to the training examples in supervised learning [72]. As a result, all reinforcement learning algorithms tend to be significantly less sample-efficient.

1.6.3   Data Generation

In supervised learning, data is typically generated independently from algorithm training. Indeed, the first step in applying supervised learning to a problem is often to find or construct a good dataset. In reinforcement learning, data must be generated by an agent interacting with an environment. In many cases, this data is generated as training progresses in an iterative manner, with alternating phases of data gathering and training. Data and algorithm are coupled. The quality of an algorithm affects the data it is trained on, which in turn affects the algorithm's performance. This circularity and bootstrapping requirement does not occur in supervised learning.

RL is also interactive—actions made by the agent actually change the environment, which then changes the agent's decisions, which change the data the agent sees, and so on. This feedback loop is the hallmark of reinforcement learning. In supervised learning problems, there is no such loop and no equivalent notion of an agent which could change the data that an algorithm is trained on.

A final, more minor difference between reinforcement learning and supervised learning is that in reinforcement learning, neural networks are not always trained using a recognizable loss function. Instead of minimizing the error of the loss between a network's outputs and a desired target, rewards from the environment are used to construct an objective, then the network is trained so as to maximize this objective. Coming from a supervised learning background, this may seem a little strange at first, but the optimization mechanism is essentially the same. In both cases, the parameters of a network are adjusted to maximize or minimize a function.

1.7 Summary

This chapter described reinforcement learning problems as systems consisting of an agent and an environment interacting and exchanging information in the form of states, actions, and rewards. Agents learn how to act in an environment using a *policy* in order to maximize the expected sum of rewards. This is their objective. Using these concepts, we then showed how reinforcement learning can be formulated as an MDP by assuming that the environment's transition function has the Markov property.

An agent's experiences in an environment can be used to learn functions that help it maximize the objective. In particular, we looked at the three primary learnable functions in reinforcement learning, *policies* $\pi(s)$, *value functions* $V^{\pi}(S)$ and $Q^{\pi}(s, a)$, and *models* $P(s' \mid s, a)$. Deep reinforcement learning algorithms can be categorized, according to which of these functions an agent learns, as policy-based, value-based, model-based, or a combination. They can also be categorized according to the how the training data is generated. On-policy algorithms only use data generated by the current policy; off-policy algorithms may use data generated by any policy.

We also looked briefly at the deep learning training workflow and discussed some of the differences between reinforcement learning and supervised learning.

Part I

Policy–Based and Value–Based Algorithms

2

REINFORCE

This chapter introduces the first algorithm of the book, REINFORCE.

The REINFORCE algorithm, invented by Ronald J. Williams in 1992 in his paper "Simple Statistical Gradient-Following Algorithms for Connectionist Reinforcement Learning" [148], learns a parametrized policy which produces action probabilities from states. Agents use this policy directly to act in an environment.

The key idea is that during learning, actions that resulted in good outcomes should become more probable—these actions are positively *reinforced*. Conversely, actions which resulted in bad outcomes should become less probable. If learning is successful, over the course of many iterations action probabilities produced by the policy shift to distribution that results in good performance in an environment. Action probabilities are changed by following the *policy gradient*, therefore REINFORCE is known as a policy gradient algorithm.

The algorithm needs three components:

1. A parametrized policy

2. An objective to be maximized

3. A method for updating the policy parameters

Section 2.1 introduces parametrized policies. Then, in Section 2.2 we discuss the objective function which defines how to evaluate outcomes. Section 2.3 contains the core of the REINFORCE algorithm—the policy gradient. The policy gradient provides a way to estimate the gradient of the objective with respect to the policy parameters. This is a crucial step since the policy gradient is used to modify the policy parameters so as to maximize the objective.

After introducing the algorithm in Section 2.5, we discuss some limitations and introduce some strategies for improving performance. This is the subject of Section 2.5.1.

The chapter ends with two implementations of the algorithm. The first is minimal and self-contained. The second shows how it is implemented in SLM Lab.

2.1 Policy

A policy π is a function, mapping states to action probabilities, which is used to sample an action $a \sim \pi(s)$. In REINFORCE, an agent learns a policy and uses this to act in an environment.

A good policy is one which maximizes the cumulative discounted rewards. The key idea of the algorithm is to learn a good policy, and this means doing function approximation. Neural networks are powerful and flexible function approximators, so we can represent a policy using a deep neural network consisting of learnable parameters θ. This is often referred to as a policy network π_θ. We say that the policy is parametrized by θ.

Each specific set of values of the parameters of the policy network represents a particular policy. To see why, consider $\theta_1 \neq \theta_2$. For any given state s, different policy networks may output different sets of action probabilities, that is, $\pi_{\theta_1}(s) \neq \pi_{\theta_2}(s)$. The mappings from states to action probabilities are different so we say that π_{θ_1} and π_{θ_2} are different policies. A single neural network is therefore capable of representing many different policies.

Formulated in this way, the process of learning a good policy corresponds to searching for a good set of values for θ. For this reason, it is important that the policy network is differentiable. We will see in Section 2.3 that the mechanism by which the policy is improved is through gradient ascent in parameter space.

2.2 The Objective Function

In this section, we define the objective that is maximized by an agent in the REINFORCE algorithm. An objective can be understood as an agent's goal, such as winning a game or getting the highest score possible. First, we introduce the concept of a *return*, which is calculated using a trajectory. We then use this to formulate the objective.

Recall from Chapter 1 that an agent acting in an environment generates a trajectory, which contains a sequence of rewards along with the states and actions. A trajectory is denoted $\tau = s_0, a_0, r_0, \ldots, s_T, a_T, r_T$.

The *return* of a trajectory $R_t(\tau)$ is defined as a discounted sum of rewards from time step t to the end of a trajectory, as shown in Equation 2.1.

$$R_t(\tau) = \sum_{t'=t}^{T} \gamma^{t'-t} r'_t \tag{2.1}$$

Note that the sum starts from time step t, but the power that the discount factor γ is raised to, when summing for the return, starts from 0, so we need to offset the power by the starting time step t using $t' - t$.

When $t = 0$, the return is simply the return of the complete trajectory. This is also written as $R_0(\tau) = R(\tau)$ for brevity. The *objective* is the expected return over all complete trajectories generated by an agent. This is defined in Equation 2.2.

$$J(\pi_\theta) = \mathbb{E}_{\tau \sim \pi_\theta}[R(\tau)] = \mathbb{E}_{\tau \sim \pi_\theta}\left[\sum_{t=0}^{T} \gamma^t r_t\right] \tag{2.2}$$

Equation 2.2 says that the expectation is calculated over many trajectories sampled from a policy, that is, $\tau \sim \pi_\theta$. This expectation approaches the true value as more samples are gathered, and it is tied to the specific policy π_θ used.

2.3 The Policy Gradient

We have now defined the policy π_θ and the objective $J(\pi_\theta)$ which are two crucial ingredients for deriving the policy gradient algorithm. The policy provides a way for an agent to act, and the objective provides a target to maximize.

The final component of the algorithm is the policy gradient. Formally, we say a policy gradient algorithm solves the following problem:

$$\max_\theta J(\pi_\theta) = \mathbb{E}_{\tau \sim \pi_\theta}[R(\tau)] \tag{2.3}$$

To maximize the objective, we perform gradient ascent on the policy parameters θ. Recall from calculus that the gradient points in the direction of steepest ascent. To improve on the objective,[1] compute the gradient and use it to update the parameters as shown in Equation 2.4.[2]

$$\theta \leftarrow \theta + \alpha \nabla_\theta J(\pi_\theta) \tag{2.4}$$

α is a scalar, known as the learning rate, which controls the size of the parameter update. The term $\nabla_\theta J(\pi_\theta)$ is known as the *policy gradient*. It is defined in Equation 2.5.

$$\nabla_\theta J(\pi_\theta) = \mathbb{E}_{\tau \sim \pi_\theta}\left[\sum_{t=0}^{T} R_t(\tau)\nabla_\theta \log \pi_\theta(a_t \mid s_t)\right] \tag{2.5}$$

The term $\pi_\theta(a_t \mid s_t)$ is the probability of the action taken by the agent at time step t. The action is sampled from the policy, $a_t \sim \pi_\theta(s_t)$. The right-hand side of the equation states that the gradient of the log probability of the action with respect to θ is multiplied by return $R_t(\tau)$.

Equation 2.5 states that the gradient of the objective is equivalent to the expected sum of the gradients of the log probabilities of the actions a_t multiplied by the corresponding returns $R_t(\tau)$. The full derivation is shown in Section 2.3.1.

The policy gradient is the mechanism by which action probabilities produced by the policy are changed. If the return $R_t(\tau) > 0$, then the probability of the action $\pi_\theta(a_t \mid s_t)$ is increased; conversely, if the return $R_t(\tau) < 0$, then the probability of the action

1. The objective $J(\pi_\theta)$ can be thought of as an abstract hypersurface on which we try to find the maximum point with θ as the variables. A hypersurface is a generalization of an ordinary 2D surface residing in 3D space into higher dimensions. A hypersurface residing in N-dimensional space is an object with $(N-1)$ dimensions.
2. Note that the parameter update can be done with any suitable optimizer that takes a $\nabla_\theta J(\pi_\theta)$ as input.

$\pi_\theta(a_t \mid s_t)$ is decreased. Over the course of many updates (Equation 2.4), the policy will learn to produce actions which result in high $R_t(\tau)$.

Equation 2.5 is the foundation of all policy gradient methods. REINFORCE was the first algorithm to use it in its simplest form. Newer algorithms build on top of this by modifying the function to improve performance, as we will see in Chapters 6 and 7. However, a final question remains—how does one implement and estimate the ideal policy gradient equation?

2.3.1   Policy Gradient Derivation

Here we derive the policy gradient (Equation 2.5) from the gradient of the objective shown in Equation 2.6. Note that this section can be skipped on a first reading.

$$\nabla_\theta J(\pi_\theta) = \nabla_\theta \mathbb{E}_{\tau \sim \pi_\theta}[R(\tau)] \tag{2.6}$$

Equation 2.6 presents a problem because we cannot differentiate $R(\tau) = \sum_{t=0}^{T} \gamma^t r_t$ with respect to θ.[3] The rewards r_t are generated by an unknown reward function $\mathcal{R}(s_t, a_t, s_{t+1})$ which cannot be differentiated. The only way for the policy variables θ to influence $R(\tau)$ is by changing the state and action distributions which, in turn, change the rewards received by an agent.

We therefore need to transform Equation 2.6 into a form where we can take a gradient with respect to θ. To do so, we'll use some handy identities.

Given a function $f(x)$, a parametrized probability distribution $p(x \mid \theta)$, and its expectation $\mathbb{E}_{x \sim p(x \mid \theta)}[f(x)]$, the gradient of the expectation can be rewritten as follows:

$$\nabla_\theta \mathbb{E}_{x \sim p(x \mid \theta)}[f(x)]$$

$$= \nabla_\theta \int dx\ f(x) p(x \mid \theta) \qquad \textit{(definition of expectation)} \tag{2.7}$$

$$= \int dx\ \nabla_\theta \big(p(x \mid \theta) f(x)\big) \qquad \textit{(bring in } \nabla_\theta\textit{)} \tag{2.8}$$

$$= \int dx\ \big(f(x) \nabla_\theta p(x \mid \theta) + p(x \mid \theta) \nabla_\theta f(x)\big) \qquad \textit{(chain-rule)} \tag{2.9}$$

$$= \int dx\ f(x) \nabla_\theta p(x \mid \theta) \qquad \textit{(}\nabla_\theta f(x) = 0\textit{)} \tag{2.10}$$

$$= \int dx\ f(x) p(x \mid \theta) \frac{\nabla_\theta p(x \mid \theta)}{p(x \mid \theta)} \qquad \left(\textit{multiply } \frac{p(x \mid \theta)}{p(x \mid \theta)}\right) \tag{2.11}$$

$$= \int dx\ f(x) p(x \mid \theta) \nabla_\theta \log p(x \mid \theta) \qquad \textit{(substitute Equation 2.14)} \tag{2.12}$$

$$= \mathbb{E}_x[f(x) \nabla_\theta \log p(x \mid \theta)] \qquad \textit{(definition of expectation)} \tag{2.13}$$

---

3. However, the gradient can be estimated using black-box optimization techniques, such as Augmented Random Search [83]. This is beyond the scope of this book.

This identity says that the gradient of an expectation is equivalent to the expectation of the gradient of log probability multiplied by the original function. The first line is simply the definition of an expectation. An integral form is used for generality by considering $f(x)$ to be a continuous function, but it equally applies to a summation form for a discrete function. The next three lines follow from basic calculus.

Notice that Equation 2.10 has solved our initial problem since we can take the gradient of $p(x \mid \theta)$, but $f(x)$ is a black-box function which cannot be integrated. To deal with this, we need to convert the equation into an expectation so that it can be estimated through sampling. First, multiply it identically by $\frac{p(x\mid\theta)}{p(x\mid\theta)}$ in Equation 2.11. The resulting fraction $\frac{\nabla_\theta p(x\mid\theta)}{p(x\mid\theta)}$ can be rewritten with the *log-derivative trick* in Equation 2.14.

$$\nabla_\theta \log p(x \mid \theta) = \frac{\nabla_\theta p(x \mid \theta)}{p(x \mid \theta)} \tag{2.14}$$

Substituting Equation 2.14 into 2.11 gives Equation 2.12. This can be written as an expectation to give Equation 2.13. Finally, we simply rewrite the expression as an expectation.

Now, it should be apparent that this identity can be applied to our objective. By substituting $x = \tau, f(x) = R(\tau), p(x \mid \theta) = p(\tau \mid \theta)$, Equation 2.6 can be written as

$$\nabla_\theta J(\pi_\theta) = \mathbb{E}_{\tau \sim \pi_\theta}[R(\tau)\nabla_\theta \log p(\tau \mid \theta)] \tag{2.15}$$

However, the term $p(\tau \mid \theta)$ in Equation 2.15 needs to relate to the policy π_θ, which we have control over. Therefore, it needs to be expanded further.

Observe that the trajectory τ is just a sequence of interleaved events, a_t and s_{t+1}, sampled, respectively, from the agent's action probability $\pi_\theta(a_t \mid s_t)$ and the environment's transition probability $p(s_{t+1} \mid s_t, a_t)$. Since the probabilities are conditionally independent, the probability of the entire trajectory is the product of the individual probabilities, as shown in Equation 2.16.

$$p(\tau \mid \theta) = \prod_{t \geq 0} p(s_{t+1} \mid s_t, a_t)\pi_\theta(a_t \mid s_t) \tag{2.16}$$

Apply logarithms[4] to both sides to match Equation 2.16 with Equation 2.15.

$$\log p(\tau \mid \theta) = \log \prod_{t \geq 0} p(s_{t+1} \mid s_t, a_t)\pi_\theta(a_t \mid s_t) \tag{2.17}$$

$$\log p(\tau \mid \theta) = \sum_{t \geq 0} \big(\log p(s_{t+1} \mid s_t, a_t) + \log \pi_\theta(a_t \mid s_t)\big) \tag{2.18}$$

---

4. One benefit from using log probabilities is that they are numerically stabler than plain probabilities. Certain operations also become faster to compute. As a quick exercise, try to figure out the reasons for both these benefits.

$$\nabla_\theta \log p(\tau \mid \theta) = \nabla_\theta \sum_{t \geq 0} \Big(\log p(s_{t+1} \mid s_t, a_t) + \log \pi_\theta(a_t \mid s_t) \Big) \qquad (2.19)$$

$$\nabla_\theta \log p(\tau \mid \theta) = \nabla_\theta \sum_{t \geq 0} \log \pi_\theta(a_t \mid s_t) \qquad (2.20)$$

Equation 2.18 follows from the fact that logarithm of product equals the sum of logarithms of its components. From there, we can apply the gradient ∇_θ to both sides to get Equation 2.19. The gradient can be moved inside the summation terms. Since $\log p(s_{t+1} \mid s_t, a_t)$ is independent of θ, its gradient is zero, and it can be dropped. This yields Equation 2.20 that expresses the probability $p(\tau \mid \theta)$ in terms of $\pi_\theta(a_t \mid s_t)$. Also, note that the trajectory τ on the left corresponds to a summation of its individual time steps t on the right.

With this, we are finally ready to rewrite $\nabla_\theta J(\pi_\theta)$ from Equation 2.6 in a form that can be differentiated. By substituting Equation 2.20 into 2.15 and bringing in the multiplier $R(\tau)$, we obtain

$$\nabla_\theta J(\pi_\theta) = \mathbb{E}_{\tau \sim \pi_\theta} \left[\sum_{t=0}^{T} R_t(\tau) \nabla_\theta \log \pi_\theta(a_t \mid s_t) \right] \qquad (2.21)$$

Our problem was that Equation 2.6 contained a function that was not differentiable. After a series of transformations, we arrived at Equation 2.20. This can be estimated quite easily using a policy network π_θ, with the gradient calculation handled by the automatic differentiation feature available in neural network libraries.

2.4 Monte Carlo Sampling

The REINFORCE algorithm numerically estimates the policy gradient using Monte Carlo sampling.

Monte Carlo sampling refers to any method that uses random sampling to generate data used to approximate a function. In essence, it is just "approximation with random sampling." It is a technique which became popular thanks to Stanislaw Ulam, a mathematician who worked at the Los Alamos research lab in the 1940s.

To see how Monte Carlo works, let's work through an example of how it can be used to estimate the value of π (the mathematical constant)—the ratio of a circle's circumference to its diameter.[5] A Monte Carlo approach to solving this problem is to take a circle of radius $r = 1$ centered at the origin and inscribe it in a square. Their areas are πr^2 and $(2r)^2$, respectively. Hence, the ratio of these areas is simply

$$\frac{\textit{area of circle}}{\textit{area of square}} = \frac{\pi r^2}{(2r)^2} = \frac{\pi}{4} \qquad (2.22)$$

---

5. Just for this example, we stop using π for policy, but that usage will resume after this.

Numerically, the square has an area of 4, but since we do not yet know π, so the area of the circle is unknown. Let's consider one quadrant. To obtain an estimation for π, sample many points within the square using a uniformly random distribution. A point (x, y) that lands in the circle has distance less than 1 from the origin—that is, $\sqrt{(x-0)^2 + (y-0)^2} \leq 1$. This is shown in Figure 2.1. Using this, if we count the number of points in the circle, then count the number of points sampled in total, their ratio roughly equals to Equation 2.22. By iteratively sampling more points and updating the ratio, our estimation will get closer to the precise value. Multiplying this ratio by 4 gives us the estimated value of $\pi \approx 3.14159$.

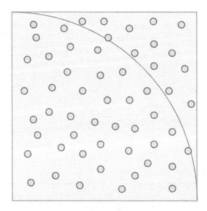

Figure 2.1   Monte Carlo sampling used to estimate π

Now, let's return to deep RL and look at how Monte Carlo can be used to numerically estimate the policy gradient in Equation 2.5. It is very straightforward. The expectation $\mathbb{E}_{\tau \sim \pi_\theta}$ implies that as more trajectories τs are sampled using a policy π_θ and averaged, it approaches the actual policy gradient $\nabla_\theta J(\pi_\theta)$. Instead of sampling many trajectories per policy, we can sample just one as shown in Equation 2.23.

$$\nabla_\theta J(\pi_\theta) \approx \sum_{t=0}^{T} R_t(\tau) \nabla_\theta \log \pi_\theta(a_t \mid s_t) \qquad (2.23)$$

This is how policy gradient is implemented—as a Monte Carlo estimate over sampled trajectories.

With all the components now in place, let's look at the REINFORCE algorithm.

2.5 REINFORCE Algorithm

This section discusses the REINFORCE algorithm and introduces the concept of an on-policy algorithm. We then look at some of its limitations and introduce a baseline to improve performance.

The algorithm is shown in Algorithm 2.1. It is very simple. First, initialize the learning rate α and construct a policy network π_θ with randomly initialized weights.

Next, iterate for multiple episodes as follows: use the policy network π_θ to generate a trajectory $\tau = s_0, a_0, r_0, \ldots, s_T, a_T, r_T$ for an episode. Then, for each time step t in the trajectory, compute the return $R_t(\tau)$. Use $R_t(\tau)$ to estimate the policy gradient. Sum the policy gradients for all time steps, then use the result to update the policy network parameters θ.

Algorithm 2.1   REINFORCE algorithm

1: Initialize learning rate α
2: Initialize weights θ of a policy network π_θ
3: **for** *episode* $= 0, \ldots, MAX\_EPISODE$ **do**
4:      Sample a trajectory $\tau = s_0, a_0, r_0, \ldots, s_T, a_T, r_T$
5:      Set $\nabla_\theta J(\pi_\theta) = 0$
6:      **for** $t = 0, \ldots, T$ **do**
7:          $R_t(\tau) = \sum_{t'=t}^{T} \gamma^{t'-t} r'_t$
8:          $\nabla_\theta J(\pi_\theta) = \nabla_\theta J(\pi_\theta) + R_t(\tau) \nabla_\theta \log \pi_\theta(a_t \mid s_t)$
9:      **end for**
10:     $\theta = \theta + \alpha \nabla_\theta J(\pi_\theta)$
11: **end for**

It is important that a trajectory is discarded after each parameter update—it cannot be reused. This is because REINFORCE is an *on-policy* algorithm. Recall from Section 1.4 that an algorithm is on-policy if the parameter update equation depends on the current policy. This is clear from line 8 since the policy gradient directly depends on action probabilities $\pi_\theta(a_t \mid s_t)$ generated by the current policy π_θ, but not some past policy $\pi_{\theta'}$. Correspondingly, the return $R_t(\tau)$ where $\tau \sim \pi_\theta$ must also be generated from π_θ, otherwise the action probabilities will be adjusted based on returns that the policy wouldn't have generated.

2.5.1 Improving REINFORCE

Our formulation of the REINFORCE algorithm estimates the policy gradient using Monte Carlo sampling with a single trajectory. This is an unbiased estimate of the policy gradient, but one disadvantage of this approach is that it has a high variance. In this section, we introduce a baseline to reduce the variance of the estimate. Following this, we will also discuss reward normalization to address the issue of reward scaling.

When using Monte Carlo sampling, the policy gradient estimate may have high variance because the returns can vary significantly from trajectory to trajectory. This is due to three factors. First, actions have some randomness because they are sampled from a probability distribution. Second, the starting state may vary per episode. Third, the environment transition function may be stochastic.

One way to reduce the variance of the estimate is to modify the returns by subtracting a suitable action–independent baseline, as shown in Equation 2.24.

$$\nabla_\theta J(\pi_\theta) \approx \sum_{t=0}^{T} \big(R_t(\tau) - b(s_t)\big)\nabla_\theta \log \pi_\theta(a_t \mid s_t) \tag{2.24}$$

One option for the baseline is the value function V^π. This choice of baseline motivates the Actor-Critic algorithm. We leave the discussion of this to Chapter 6.

An alternative is to use the mean returns over the trajectory. Let $b = \frac{1}{T}\sum_{t=0}^{T} R_t(\tau)$. Note that this is a constant baseline per trajectory that does not vary with state s_t. It has the effect of centering the returns for each trajectory around 0. For each trajectory, on average, the best 50% of the actions will be encouraged, and the others discouraged.

To see why this is useful, consider the case where all the rewards for an environment are negative. Without a baseline, even when an agent produces a very good action, it gets discouraged because the returns are always negative. Over time, this can still result in good policies since worse actions will get discouraged even more, thus indirectly increasing the probabilities of better actions. However, it can lead to slower learning because probability adjustments can only be made in one direction. The converse happens for environments where all the rewards are positive. Learning is more effective when we can both increase and decrease the action probabilities. This requires having both positive and negative returns.

2.6 Implementing REINFORCE

In this section we present two implementations. The first is a minimal, self-contained implementation. The second shows how the algorithm is implemented in SLM Lab; this is a slightly more advanced version that is integrated with the lab components.

2.6.1 A Minimal REINFORCE Implementation

A minimal implementation is useful as it closely corresponds to Algorithm 2.1. This is good practice for translating theory into code. REINFORCE is a good candidate for this because it is the simplest RL algorithm which can easily be implemented in a few lines of code (see Code 2.1).

Other RL algorithms are more complex and so benefit from being implemented within a common framework with reusable modular components. For this reason, to be consistent with the remaining algorithms in this book, we also present an implementation in SLM Lab. This serves as an introduction to the lab's algorithm API.

Code 2.1   A standalone working implementation of REINFORCE to solve `CartPole-v0`

```
1  from torch.distributions import Categorical
2  import gym
```

```
3   import numpy as np
4   import torch
5   import torch.nn as nn
6   import torch.optim as optim
7
8   gamma = 0.99
9
10  class Pi(nn.Module):
11      def __init__(self, in_dim, out_dim):
12          super(Pi, self).__init__()
13          layers = [
14              nn.Linear(in_dim, 64),
15              nn.ReLU(),
16              nn.Linear(64, out_dim),
17          ]
18          self.model = nn.Sequential(*layers)
19          self.onpolicy_reset()
20          self.train()  # set training mode
21
22      def onpolicy_reset(self):
23          self.log_probs = []
24          self.rewards = []
25
26      def forward(self, x):
27          pdparam = self.model(x)
28          return pdparam
29
30      def act(self, state):
31          x = torch.from_numpy(state.astype(np.float32))  # to tensor
32          pdparam = self.forward(x)  # forward pass
33          pd = Categorical(logits=pdparam)  # probability distribution
34          action = pd.sample()  # pi(a|s) in action via pd
35          log_prob = pd.log_prob(action)  # log_prob of pi(a|s)
36          self.log_probs.append(log_prob)  # store for training
37          return action.item()
38
39  def train(pi, optimizer):
40      # Inner gradient-ascent loop of REINFORCE algorithm
41      T = len(pi.rewards)
42      rets = np.empty(T, dtype=np.float32)  # the returns
43      future_ret = 0.0
44      # compute the returns efficiently
45      for t in reversed(range(T)):
46          future_ret = pi.rewards[t] + gamma * future_ret
```

```
47          rets[t] = future_ret
48      rets = torch.tensor(rets)
49      log_probs = torch.stack(pi.log_probs)
50      loss = - log_probs * rets  # gradient term; Negative for maximizing
51      loss = torch.sum(loss)
52      optimizer.zero_grad()
53      loss.backward()  # backpropagate, compute gradients
54      optimizer.step()  # gradient-ascent, update the weights
55      return loss
56
57  def main():
58      env = gym.make('CartPole-v0')
59      in_dim = env.observation_space.shape[0]  # 4
60      out_dim = env.action_space.n  # 2
61      pi = Pi(in_dim, out_dim)  # policy pi_theta for REINFORCE
62      optimizer = optim.Adam(pi.parameters(), lr=0.01)
63      for epi in range(300):
64          state = env.reset()
65          for t in range(200):  # cartpole max timestep is 200
66              action = pi.act(state)
67              state, reward, done, _ = env.step(action)
68              pi.rewards.append(reward)
69              env.render()
70              if done:
71                  break
72          loss = train(pi, optimizer)  # train per episode
73          total_reward = sum(pi.rewards)
74          solved = total_reward > 195.0
75          pi.onpolicy_reset()  # onpolicy: clear memory after training
76          print(f'Episode {epi}, loss: {loss}, \
77          total_reward: {total_reward}, solved: {solved}')
78
79  if __name__ == '__main__':
80      main()
```

Let's walk through the minimal implementation.

1. Pi constructs the policy network that is a a simple one-layer MLP with 64 hidden units (lines 10–20).

2. act defines the method to produce action (lines 30–37).

3. train implements the update steps in Algorithm 2.1. Note that the loss is expressed as the sum of the negative log probabilities multiplied by the returns (lines 50–51). The negative sign is necessary because by default, PyTorch's optimizer minimizes the loss, whereas we want to maximize the objective. Furthermore, we formulate the

loss in this way to utilize PyTorch's automatic differentiation feature. When we call `loss.backward()`, this computes the gradient of the loss (line 53), which is equal to the policy gradient. Finally, we update the policy parameters by calling `optimizer.step()` (line 54).

4. `main` is the main loop. It constructs a CartPole environment, the policy network `Pi`, and an optimizer. Then, it runs the training loop for 300 episodes. As training progresses, the total reward per episode should increase towards 200. The environment is solved when the total reward is above 195.

2.6.2   Constructing Policies with PyTorch

The implementation of a policy π_θ deserves a closer look. In this section, we will show how the outputs from a neural network are transformed into an action probability distribution that is used to sample an action, $a \sim \pi_\theta(s)$.

The key idea is that probability distributions can be parametrized, either by enumerating the full probabilities for a discrete distribution or by specifying the mean and standard deviation[6] of a continuous distribution such as the normal distribution. These probability distribution parameters can be learned and output by a neural network.

To output an action, we first use a policy network to compute the probability distribution parameters from a state. Then, we use these parameters to construct an action probability distribution. Finally, we use the action probability distribution to sample an action and compute the action log probability.

Let's see how this works in pseudocode. Algorithm 2.2 constructs a discrete-action probability distribution and uses it to compute the log probability. It constructs a categorical (multinomial) distribution, although other discrete distributions may be used. Since the network output is not necessarily normalized, the distribution parameters are treated as logits instead of probabilities. Algorithm 2.2 also closely corresponds to the PyTorch implementation of the policy in Code 2.1 (lines 31–35).

Algorithm 2.2   Constructing a discrete policy

1: Given a policy network `net`, a `Categorical` distribution class, and a *state*
2: Compute the output `pdparams = net(state)`
3: Construct an instance of an action probability distribution
    ↪   `pd = Categorical(logits=pdparams)`
4: Use pd to sample an action, `action = pd.sample()`
5: Use pd and `action` to compute the action log probability,
    ↪   `log_prob = pd.log_prob(action)`

A simple implementation of Algorithm 2.2 using PyTorch is shown in Code 2.2 with closely corresponding steps. For simplicity, we use a dummy policy network output. Inside

---

6. Some probability distributions require special parameters, but the same idea still applies.

the Categorial constructor, PyTorch will transform specified logits to probabilities when constructing a categorical distribution.

Code 2.2   A discrete policy implemented using categorical distribution

```
1  from torch.distributions import Categorical
2  import torch
3
4  # suppose for 2 actions (CartPole: move left, move right)
5  # we obtain their logit probabilities from a policy network
6  policy_net_output = torch.tensor([-1.6094, -0.2231])
7  # the pdparams are logits, equivalent to probs = [0.2, 0.8]
8  pdparams = policy_net_output
9  pd = Categorical(logits=pdparams)
10
11 # sample an action
12 action = pd.sample()
13 # => tensor(1), or 'move right'
14
15 # compute the action log probability
16 pd.log_prob(action)
17 # => tensor(-0.2231), log probability of 'move right'
```

Similarly, a continuous-action policy is constructed the same way. Algorithm 2.3 shows an example using a normal distribution. The normal distribution, like many other continuous distributions, is parametrized by a mean and standard deviation. In many scientific computing libraries, they are known, respectively, as loc and scale in code, to imply adjusting the location and scale of a distribution. Once the action probability distribution is constructed, the remaining steps for computing the action log probability are the same as in Algorithm 2.2.

Algorithm 2.3   Constructing a continuous policy

1: Given a policy network net, a Normal distribution class, and a *state*
2: Compute the output pdparams = net(state)
3: Construct an instance of an action probability distribution
    ↪   pd = Normal(loc=pdparams[0], scale=pdparams[1])
4: Use pd to sample an action, action = pd.sample()
5: Use pd and action to compute the action log probability,
    ↪   log_prob = pd.log_prob(action)

For completeness, Algorithm 2.3 is also implemented with PyTorch in Code 2.3.

Code 2.3 A continuous policy implemented using normal distribution

```
1   from torch.distributions import Normal
2   import torch
3
4   # suppose for 1 action (Pendulum: torque)
5   # we obtain its mean and std from a policy network
6   policy_net_output = torch.tensor([1.0, 0.2])
7   # the pdparams are (mean, std), or (loc, scale)
8   pdparams = policy_net_output
9   pd = Normal(loc=pdparams[0], scale=pdparams[1])
10
11  # sample an action
12  action = pd.sample()
13  # => tensor(1.0295), the amount of torque
14
15  # compute the action log probability
16  pd.log_prob(action)
17  # => tensor(0.6796), log probability of this torque
```

The generality of the policy construction workflow implies that it can be applied easily to both discrete and continuous-action environments. Its simplicity is also one of the strengths of a policy-based algorithm.

SLM Lab implements Algorithms 2.2 and 2.3 generally, for all policy-based algorithms, in a modular and reusable manner. Additionally, these implementations are also optimized for efficiency. For instance, the action log probabilities are computed all at once and only during training to speed up computation.

Having seen how REINFORCE can be implemented very simply, we now discuss the REINFORCE implementation in SLM Lab integrated with its components. This serves as an introduction to algorithm implementation using the SLM Lab framework. This REINFORCE code is used as the parent class which we will extend to implement more complex algorithms later in this book. As we use SLM Lab to run all the experiments discussed later, it's time to start becoming familiar with the framework.

In what follows, we discuss only the algorithm-specific methods and leave their integration into the lab framework for hands-on code exploration. The full code along with all the components required to run an RL training session can be found in the companion SLM Lab code repository.

2.6.3 Sampling Actions

Let's go through the action sampling methods of the `Reinforce` class shown in Code 2.4. Note that throughout this book, for clarity of exposition, some lines of code that are not essential to explaining the functionality of a method are omitted and replaced with

"...". Also note that methods tagged with @lab_api are standard API methods of an algorithm in SLM Lab.

calc_pdparam calculates the parameters for the action distribution. calc_pdparam is called by self.action_policy (line 15) which produces an action (this is described in more detail in Section 2.6.2). act samples an action from the algorithm's action policy, which can be a discrete or continuous distribution, for example Categorical and Normal.

Code 2.4 REINFORCE implementation: sampling actions from the policy network

```
1   # slm_lab/agent/algorithm/reinforce.py
2
3   class Reinforce(Algorithm):
4       ...
5
6       @lab_api
7       def calc_pdparam(self, x, net=None):
8           net = self.net if net is None else net
9           pdparam = net(x)
10          return pdparam
11
12      @lab_api
13      def act(self, state):
14          body = self.body
15          action = self.action_policy(state, self, body)
16          return action.cpu().squeeze().numpy()  # squeeze to handle scalar
```

2.6.4 Calculating Policy Loss

Code 2.5 shows the methods for calculating the policy loss. There are two components. First, we need to calculate the reinforcing signal. This is handled by the method calc_ret_advs which calculates the returns for each element in the batch. Optionally, we subtract the baseline from the returns. In this example, it is simply the mean returns over the batch.

Once we have the returns, we can calculate the policy loss. In calc_policy_loss, we first obtain the action probability distribution (line 15) needed to calculate the action log probabilities (line 18). Next, we combine the returns (denoted advs) with the log probabilities to form the policy loss (line 19). This has the same form as seen in Code 2.1 (lines 50–51), so that we can utilize PyTorch's automatic differentiation feature.

An optional addition to the loss is an entropy term to encourage exploration (lines 20–23). This is discussed in more detail in Section 6.3.

Code 2.5   REINFORCE implementation: calculating the policy loss

```
1   # slm_lab/agent/algorithm/reinforce.py
2
3   class Reinforce(Algorithm):
4       ...
5
6       def calc_ret_advs(self, batch):
7           rets = math_util.calc_returns(batch['rewards'], batch['dones'],
            ↪  self.gamma)
8           if self.center_return:
9               rets = math_util.center_mean(rets)
10          advs = rets
11          ...
12          return advs
13
14      def calc_policy_loss(self, batch, pdparams, advs):
15          action_pd = policy_util.init_action_pd(self.body.ActionPD, pdparams)
16          actions = batch['actions']
17          ...
18          log_probs = action_pd.log_prob(actions)
19          policy_loss = - self.policy_loss_coef * (log_probs * advs).mean()
20          if self.entropy_coef_spec:
21              entropy = action_pd.entropy().mean()
22              self.body.mean_entropy = entropy  # update logging variable
23              policy_loss += (-self.body.entropy_coef * entropy)
24          return policy_loss
```

2.6.5   REINFORCE Training Loop

Code 2.6 shows the training loop and associated memory sampling method. train makes one parameter update to the policy network using a batch of collected trajectories. Training will only be triggered once sufficient data has been collected. The trajectories are obtained from the agent's memory by calling sample (line 17).

After sampling a batch of data, we compute the action probability distribution parameters pdparams and the returns advs used to calculate the policy loss (lines 19–21). Then, we update the policy network parameters using the loss (line 22).

Code 2.6   REINFORCE implementation: training method

```
1   # slm_lab/agent/algorithm/reinforce.py
2
3   class Reinforce(Algorithm):
4       ...
```

```
 5
 6      @lab_api
 7      def sample(self):
 8          batch = self.body.memory.sample()
 9          batch = util.to_torch_batch(batch, self.net.device,
              ↪  self.body.memory.is_episodic)
10          return batch
11
12      @lab_api
13      def train(self):
14          ...
15          clock = self.body.env.clock
16          if self.to_train == 1:
17              batch = self.sample()
18              ...
19              pdparams = self.calc_pdparam_batch(batch)
20              advs = self.calc_ret_advs(batch)
21              loss = self.calc_policy_loss(batch, pdparams, advs)
22              self.net.train_step(loss, self.optim, self.lr_scheduler,
                  ↪  clock=clock, global_net=self.global_net)
23              # reset
24              self.to_train = 0
25              return loss.item()
26          else:
27              return np.nan
```

2.6.6 On-Policy Replay Memory

This section looks at a memory class which implements on-policy sampling. We can see on line 17 of Code 2.6 that a memory object is called to produce trajectories for training. Since REINFORCE is an *on-policy* algorithm, trajectories sampled by the algorithm should be stored in a Memory class for learning, then flushed after each training step.

Readers uninterested in the details of memory classes can skip this section without loss of understanding of the REINFORCE algorithm. It is sufficient to know what information is stored in memory and how it is used in the training loop.

Let's look at the OnPolicyReplay class which implements this logic. It contains the API methods:

1. reset clears and resets the memory class variables.

2. update adds an experience to the memory.

3. sample samples a batch of data for training.

Memory Initialization and Reset   __init__ initializes the class variables, including the storage keys on line 15. It then calls reset to construct empty data structures.

reset in Code 2.7 is used to clear the memory after each training step. This is specific to an on-policy memory because trajectories cannot be reused for later training.

The memory class can store trajectories from multiple episodes in the attributes initialized in lines 21–22. Individual episodes are constructed by storing experiences in the current episode data dictionary self.cur_epi_data, which is reset on line 23.

Code 2.7   OnPolicyReplay: reset

```
1   # slm_lab/agent/memory/onpolicy.py
2
3   class OnPolicyReplay(Memory):
4       ...
5
6       def __init__(self, memory_spec, body):
7           super().__init__(memory_spec, body)
8           # NOTE for OnPolicy replay, frequency = episode; for other classes
            ↪   below frequency = frames
9           util.set_attr(self, self.body.agent.agent_spec['algorithm'],
            ↪   ['training_frequency'])
10          # Don't want total experiences reset when memory is
11          self.is_episodic = True
12          self.size = 0  # total experiences stored
13          self.seen_size = 0  # total experiences seen cumulatively
14          # declare what data keys to store
15          self.data_keys = ['states', 'actions', 'rewards', 'next_states',
            ↪   'dones']
16          self.reset()
17
18      @lab_api
19      def reset(self):
20          '''Resets the memory. Also used to initialize memory vars'''
21          for k in self.data_keys:
22              setattr(self, k, [])
23          self.cur_epi_data = {k: [] for k in self.data_keys}
24          self.most_recent = (None,) * len(self.data_keys)
25          self.size = 0
```

Memory Update   The update function serves as an API method to the memory class. Adding an experience to memory is mostly straightforward. The only tricky part is keeping track of the episode boundaries. The steps in Code 2.8 can be broken down as follows:

1. Add the experience to the current episode (lines 14–15).

2. Check if the episode is finished (line 17). This is given by the `done` variable which will be `1` if the episode is finished, `0` otherwise.

3. If the episode is finished, add the entire set of experiences for the episode to the main containers in the memory class (lines 18–19).

4. If the episode is finished, clear the current episode dictionary (line 20) so that the memory class is ready to store the next episode.

5. If the desired number of episodes has been collected, set the `train` flag to `1` in the agent (lines 23–24). This signals that the agent should train this time step.

Code 2.8 OnPolicyReplay: add experience

```
1    # slm_lab/agent/memory/onpolicy.py
2
3    class OnPolicyReplay(Memory):
4        ...
5
6        @lab_api
7        def update(self, state, action, reward, next_state, done):
8            '''Interface method to update memory'''
9            self.add_experience(state, action, reward, next_state, done)
10
11       def add_experience(self, state, action, reward, next_state, done):
12           '''Interface helper method for update() to add experience to memory'''
13           self.most_recent = (state, action, reward, next_state, done)
14           for idx, k in enumerate(self.data_keys):
15               self.cur_epi_data[k].append(self.most_recent[idx])
16           # If episode ended, add to memory and clear cur_epi_data
17           if util.epi_done(done):
18               for k in self.data_keys:
19                   getattr(self, k).append(self.cur_epi_data[k])
20               self.cur_epi_data = {k: [] for k in self.data_keys}
21               # If agent has collected the desired number of episodes, it is
                 ↪  ready to train
22               # length is num of epis due to nested structure
23               if len(self.states) ==
                 ↪  self.body.agent.algorithm.training_frequency:
24                   self.body.agent.algorithm.to_train = 1
25           # Track memory size and num experiences
26           self.size += 1
27           self.seen_size += 1
```

Memory Sample   `sample` in Code 2.9 simply returns all of the completed episodes packaged into a batch dictionary (line 6). Then it resets the memory (line 7) as the stored experiences will no longer be valid once the agent has completed a training step.

Code 2.9   OnPolicyReplay: sample

```python
1  # slm_lab/agent/memory/onpolicy.py
2
3  class OnPolicyReplay(Memory):
4
5      def sample(self):
6          batch = {k: getattr(self, k) for k in self.data_keys}
7          self.reset()
8          return batch
```

2.7 Training a REINFORCE Agent

Deep RL algorithms often have many hyperparameters. For example, the network type, architecture, activation functions, optimizer, and learning rate need to be specified. More advanced neural network functionality can involve gradient clipping and learning rate decay schedules. This is only the "deep" part! RL algorithms also involve hyperparameter choices, such as the discount rate, γ, and how frequently to train an agent. To make this more manageable, all of the hyperparameter choices are specified in a JSON file in SLM Lab known as a `spec` (i.e., "specification"); for more details on the `spec` file, see Chapter 11.

Code 2.10 contains an example spec file for REINFORCE. The file is also available in SLM Lab at `slm_lab/spec/benchmark/reinforce/reinforce_cartpole.json`.

Code 2.10   A simple REINFORCE cartpole spec file

```json
1  # slm_lab/spec/benchmark/reinforce/reinforce_cartpole.json
2
3  {
4    "reinforce_cartpole": {
5      "agent": [{
6        "name": "Reinforce",
7        "algorithm": {
8          "name": "Reinforce",
9          "action_pdtype": "default",
10         "action_policy": "default",
11         "center_return": true,
12         "explore_var_spec": null,
13         "gamma": 0.99,
14         "entropy_coef_spec": {
```

```
15          "name": "linear_decay",
16          "start_val": 0.01,
17          "end_val": 0.001,
18          "start_step": 0,
19          "end_step": 20000,
20        },
21        "training_frequency": 1
22      },
23      "memory": {
24        "name": "OnPolicyReplay"
25      },
26      "net": {
27        "type": "MLPNet",
28        "hid_layers": [64],
29        "hid_layers_activation": "selu",
30        "clip_grad_val": null,
31        "loss_spec": {
32          "name": "MSELoss"
33        },
34        "optim_spec": {
35          "name": "Adam",
36          "lr": 0.002
37        },
38        "lr_scheduler_spec": null
39      }
40    }],
41    "env": [{
42      "name": "CartPole-v0",
43      "max_t": null,
44      "max_frame": 100000,
45    }],
46    "body": {
47      "product": "outer",
48      "num": 1
49    },
50    "meta": {
51      "distributed": false,
52      "eval_frequency": 2000,
53      "max_session": 4,
54      "max_trial": 1,
55    },
56    ...
57  }
58 }
```

This may seem like a lot to configure, so it is worth walking through the main components.

- **Algorithm:** The algorithm is REINFORCE (line 8). γ is set on line 13, and we use a baseline for the reinforcing signal by enabling `center_return` on line 11. We add entropy with a linear decay schedule to the loss to encourage exploration (lines 14–20).

- **Network architecture:** Multilayer perceptron with one hidden layer of 64 units and SeLU activation function (lines 27–29).

- **Optimizer:** The optimizer is Adam [68] with a learning rate of 0.002 (lines 34–37). The learning rate is constant throughout because we have specified a `null` learning rate scheduler (line 38).

- **Training frequency:** Training is episodic because we have selected `OnPolicyReplay` memory (line 24) and the agent is trained at the end of every episode. This is controlled by the `training_frequency` parameter (line 21) since it means the network will be trained every 1 episodes.

- **Environment:** The environment is OpenAI Gym's CartPole [18] (line 42).

- **Training length:** Training consists of 100,000 time steps (line 44).

- **Evaluation:** The agent is evaluated every 2,000 time steps (line 52). During evaluation, four episodes are run, then the mean total rewards are calculated and reported.

To train this REINFORCE agent using SLM Lab, run the commands shown in Code 2.11 in a terminal.

Code 2.11   Training a REINFORCE agent

```
1  conda activate lab
2  python run_lab.py slm_lab/spec/benchmark/reinforce/reinforce_cartpole.json
   ↪  reinforce_cartpole train
```

This will use the specified spec file to run a training `Trial` consisting of four repeated `Sessions`[7] to obtain an average result, which is then plotted as a trial graph with an error band. Additionally, the trial graph is also plotted with a moving average over a window of 100 evaluation checkpoints to provide a smoothed curve. Both graphs are shown in Figure 2.2.[8]

---

7. A `Trial` should be run with many `Sessions` using the same spec and different random seeds. This is taken care of automatically in SLM Lab.

8. Total rewards are denoted `mean_returns` in the graphs. For evaluation, `mean_returns` are computed without discounting.

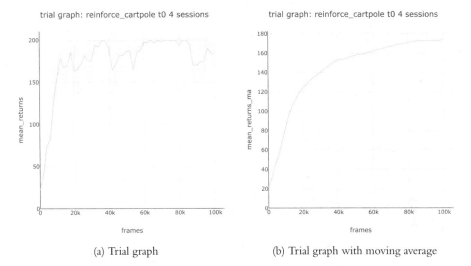

(a) Trial graph   (b) Trial graph with moving average

Figure 2.2   REINFORCE trial graphs from SLM Lab, plotted by averaging four repeated sessions. The vertical axis shows the total rewards (denoted `mean_returns`) averaged over eight episodes during checkpoints, and the horizontal axis shows the total training frames. The graph on the right is a smoothed version which plots the moving average with a window of 100 evaluation checkpoints. Note that the maximum total reward for CartPole is 200.

2.8   Experimental Results

In this section, we use the experimentation feature of SLM Lab to study the effects of some components of the algorithm. The first experiment compares the effect of different values of the discount factor γ; the second shows the improvement from using a baseline in the reinforcing signal.

2.8.1   Experiment: The Effect of Discount Factor γ

The discount factor γ controls the weight of future rewards when calculating the return $R(\tau)$ that is used as reinforcing signal. The higher the discount factor, the more weight is placed on future rewards. The optimal value of γ is problem-specific. For problems where an agent needs to consider the effect of its actions on future rewards over a longer time horizon, γ should be larger.

To study the effects of the discount factor, we can run the REINFORCE algorithm and search over different values of γ. To do this, modify the spec file from Code 2.10 by adding a `search` spec for γ. This is shown in Code 2.12, where line 15 specifies a grid search over the `gamma` hyperparameter. The full spec file is already available in SLM Lab at `slm_lab/spec/benchmark/reinforce/reinforce_cartpole.json`.

Code 2.12   REINFORCE spec file with search spec for different gamma values

```
1   # slm_lab/spec/benchmark/reinforce/reinforce_cartpole.json
2
3   {
4     "reinforce_cartpole": {
5       ...
6       "meta": {
7         "distributed": false,
8         "eval_frequency": 2000,
9         "max_session": 4,
10        "max_trial": 1,
11      },
12      "search": {
13        "agent": [{
14          "algorithm": {
15            "gamma__grid_search": [0.1, 0.5, 0.7, 0.8, 0.90, 0.99, 0.999]
16          }
17        }]
18      }
19    }
20  }
```

To run the experiment in SLM Lab, use the commands shown in Code 2.13. This is not very different from training an agent—we simply reuse the same spec file and substitute the mode `train` with `search`.

Code 2.13   Run an experiment to search over different gamma values as defined in the spec file.

```
1   conda activate lab
2   python run_lab.py slm_lab/spec/benchmark/reinforce/reinforce_cartpole.json
    ↪  reinforce_cartpole search
```

This will run an `Experiment` which spawns multiple `Trials`, each with a different value of `gamma` substituted into the original REINFORCE spec. Each `Trial` runs four repeated `Sessions` to obtain an average along with an error band. This is used to plot a multitrial graph. A smoothed plot with moving average over 100 evaluation checkpoints is also provided for easier comparison. These are shown in Figure 2.3.

Figure 2.3 shows that γ values above 0.90 perform better, with $\gamma = 0.999$ from trial 6 giving the best result. When γ is too low, the algorithm fails to learn a policy that solves the problem, and the learning curve stays flat.

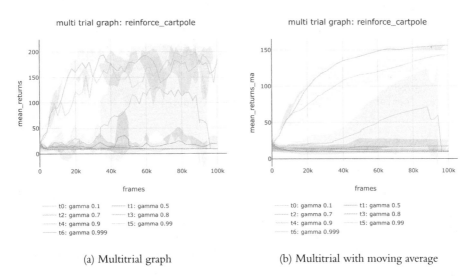

(a) Multitrial graph   (b) Multitrial with moving average

Figure 2.3   The effect of setting the discount factor γ to different values. For CartPole, a lower γ performs worse, and $\gamma = 0.999$ from trial 6 performs best. In general, different problems may have different optimal values for γ.

2.8.2 Experiment: The Effect of Baseline

We learned in this chapter that using a baseline can help reduce the variance of the Monte Carlo policy gradient estimate. Let's run an experiment to compare the performance of REINFORCE with and without a baseline. The baseline can be toggled on or off with the algorithm spec hyperparameter `center_return`.

To run an experiment, we copy the original REINFORCE spec and rename it to `reinforce_baseline_cartpole`. This spec is shown partly in Code 2.14. Then, add a search spec to perform a grid search by toggling `center_return` on and off (line 15). The spec file is also available in SLM Lab at `slm_lab/spec/benchmark/reinforce /reinforce_cartpole.json`.

Code 2.14   REINFORCE spec file with search spec for toggling baseline (`center_return`) on and off

```
1   # slm_lab/spec/benchmark/reinforce/reinforce_cartpole.json
2
3   {
4     "reinforce_baseline_cartpole": {
5       ...
6       "meta": {
7         "distributed": false,
8         "eval_frequency": 2000,
9         "max_session": 4,
```

```
10        "max_trial": 1,
11      },
12      "search": {
13        "agent": [{
14          "algorithm": {
15            "center_return__grid_search": [true, false]
16          }
17        }]
18      }
19    }
20  }
```

To run the experiment in SLM Lab, use the commands shown in Code 2.15.

Code 2.15   Run an experiment to compare performance with and without baseline as defined in the spec file.

```
1  conda activate lab
2  python run_lab.py slm_lab/spec/benchmark/reinforce/reinforce_cartpole.json
   ↪  reinforce_baseline_cartpole search
```

This will run an Experiment with two Trials with four Sessions each. The multitrial graph and its moving average over 100 evaluation checkpoints are shown in Figure 2.4.

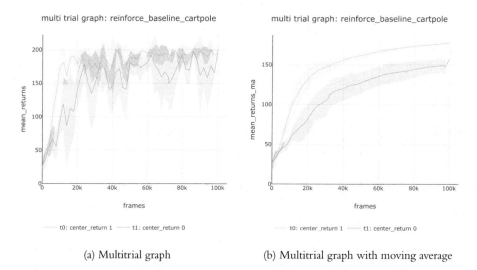

(a) Multitrial graph   (b) Multitrial graph with moving average

Figure 2.4   These graphs show that when a baseline is used to reduce the variance of policy gradient estimates, performance is improved.

As expected, REINFORCE with a baseline outperforms its variant without a baseline by reducing the variance of policy gradient estimates. Figure 2.4 shows that the baseline variant from trial 0 learns faster and obtains higher total rewards.

This section was a minimal introduction to show how we can run specific experiments using the experimentation feature in SLM Lab. Chapter 11 goes into more detail on experiment design with SLM Lab. We will only need to understand this feature with more advanced use cases, and it is not necessary for understanding the algorithms discussed in this book.

2.9 Summary

This chapter introduced REINFORCE, a policy gradient algorithm. The key idea is that the parameters of a policy network are adjusted to maximize the objective, which is the expected return $J(\pi_\theta) = \mathbb{E}_{\tau \sim \pi_\theta}[R(\tau)]$ for an agent.

We introduced and derived the policy gradient. It is an elegant expression which allows us to adjust the policy action probabilities to encourage good actions and discourage bad ones. In REINFORCE, the policy gradient is estimated using Monte Carlo sampling. This estimate can have high variance, and one common method to reduce it is by introducing a baseline.

The algorithm can be implemented quite simply as shown in Code 2.1. We also discussed its implementation in SLM Lab as an introduction to the algorithm API used throughout this book.

2.10 Further Reading

- "Sep 6: Policy gradients introduction, Lecture 4," *CS 294: Deep Reinforcement Learning, Fall 2017*, Levine [74].

- "Lecture 14: Reinforcement Learning," *CS231n: Convolutional Neural Networks for Visual Recognition, Spring 2017* [39].

- "The Beginning of the Monte Carlo Method," Metropolis, 1987. [85]

2.11 History

Monte Carlo was popularized by Stanislaw Ulam who was working at the Los Alamos research lab in the 1940s. The name "Monte Carlo" does not carry any special connotations; it is simply a memorable alternative to "random estimation." Still, it does have an entertaining origin. It was suggested by Nicholas Metropolis, a physicist and computer designer, responsible for the wryly named MANIAC computer [5]. Metropolis heard about Ulam's uncle who borrowed money from relatives because he "just had to go to Monte Carlo." After that, the name just seemed obvious [85].

During the same period, the ENIAC computer had been developed at the University of Pennsylvania in Philadelphia. A vast machine, consisting of more than 18,000 vacuum tubes, it was one of the earliest general-purpose electronic computers. Ulam was impressed by the computational power and flexibility of the ENIAC, and contemplated that it would be an appropriate tool for the many tedious calculations needed to make use of statistical techniques in function evaluation. John von Neumann, a brilliant polymath and Los Alamos colleague, immediately saw the value of the Monte Carlo approach and in 1947 outlined the technique in a note to the head of the Theoretical Division at Los Alamos [85]. For more information on the emergence of Monte Carlo methods, see "The Beginning of the Monte Carlo Method," N. Metropolis, *Los Alamos Science* Special Issue, 1987.

3

SARSA

In this chapter we look at SARSA, our first value-based algorithm. It was invented by Rummery and Niranjan in their 1994 paper "On-Line Q-Learning Using Connectionist Systems" [118] and was given its name because "you need to know State-Action-Reward-State-Action before performing an update."[1]

Value-based algorithms evaluate state-action pairs (s, a) by learning one of the value functions—$V^\pi(s)$ or $Q^\pi(s, a)$—and use these evaluations to select actions. Learning value functions stands in contrast to REINFORCE (Chapter 2) in which an agent directly learns a policy which maps states to actions. The SARSA algorithm learns $Q^\pi(s, a)$ whereas other algorithms, such as the Actor-Critic algorithm, learn $V^\pi(s)$. Section 3.1 discusses why learning $Q^\pi(s, a)$ is a good choice in this case.

The SARSA algorithm consists of two core ideas. The first is a technique for learning the Q-function known as temporal difference (TD) learning. It is an alternative to Monte Carlo sampling for estimating state or state-action values from the experiences an agent gathers in an environment. TD learning is the subject of Section 3.2.

The second core idea is a method for generating actions using the Q-function. This raises the question of how agents discover good actions. One of the fundamental challenges in RL is achieving a good balance between exploiting what an agent knows and exploring the environment in order to learn more. This is known as the *exploration-exploitation tradeoff* covered in Section 3.3. We also introduce a simple approach for solving this problem—an ε-greedy policy.

Having introduced the main ideas behind SARSA, Section 3.4 covers the algorithm and Section 3.5 contains an implementation. The chapter ends with instructions for training a SARSA agent.

---

1. SARSA was not actually called SARSA by Rummery and Niranjan in their 1994 paper "On-Line Q-Learning Using Connectionist Systems" [118]. The authors preferred "Modified Connectionist Q-Learning." The alternative was suggested by Richard Sutton and it appears that SARSA stuck.

3.1 The Q- and V-Functions

In this section, we give motivation for why SARSA learns the Q-function instead of the V-function. We will review their definitions and give an intuitive explanation for what each function measures, then describe the advantages of Q.

Section 1.3 introduced the two value functions, $V^\pi(s)$ and $Q^\pi(s,a)$. The Q-function measures the value of state-action pairs (s,a) under a particular policy π, as defined in Equation 3.1. The value of (s,a) is the expected cumulative discounted reward from taking action a in state s, and then continuing to act under the policy π.

$$Q^\pi(s,a) = \mathbb{E}_{s_0=s,a_0=a,\tau\sim\pi}\left[\sum_{t=0}^{T}\gamma^t r_t\right] \tag{3.1}$$

Value functions are always defined with respect to a particular policy π, which is why they are denoted with the π superscript. To see why, suppose we are evaluating (s,a). $Q^\pi(s,a)$ depends on the sequences of rewards an agent can expect to experience after taking action a in state s. These rewards depend on the future sequences of states and actions, and these depend on a policy. Different policies may generate different future action sequences given (s,a), which may result in different rewards.

$V^\pi(s)$ measures the value of state s under a particular policy π and is defined in Equation 3.2. The value of a state, $V^\pi(s)$, is the expected cumulative discounted reward from that state s onwards under a specific policy π.

$$V^\pi(s) = \mathbb{E}_{s_0=s,\tau\sim\pi}\left[\sum_{t=0}^{T}\gamma^t r_t\right] \tag{3.2}$$

$Q^\pi(s,a)$ is closely related to $V^\pi(s)$. $V^\pi(s)$ is the expectation over the Q-values for all of the actions a available in a particular state s under the policy π.

$$V^\pi(s) = \mathbb{E}_{a\sim\pi(s)}[Q^\pi(s,a)] \tag{3.3}$$

Which function is it better for an agent to learn, $Q^\pi(s,a)$ or $V^\pi(s)$?

Let's first put this in context by considering the game of chess from one player's perspective. This player can be represented as a policy π. A certain configuration of the chessboard pieces is a state s. A good chess player will have an intuition about whether certain chess positions are good or bad. $V^\pi(s)$ is this intuition expressed quantitatively with a number—for example, between 0 and 1. When the game begins, $V^\pi(s)$ is equal to 0.5, since both sides start out equal. As it progresses, our player makes gains or losses, and $V^\pi(s)$ goes up or down with each move. If our player develops a huge upside, then $V^\pi(s)$ becomes close to 1. In this particular case, $V^\pi(s)$ is akin to our player's probability of winning, evaluated at every position of the game. However, the range of $V^\pi(s)$ depends on the definition of the reward signal r, so in general it is not necessarily equal to the winning probability. Furthermore, for single-player games there is no notion of winning probability.

In addition to evaluating positions, a chess player will also consider a number of alternative moves and the likely consequences of making each move. $Q^\pi(s, a)$ provides a quantitative value for each move. This value can be used to decide on the best move (action) to make in a particular position (state). Another way to evaluate a chess move using just $V^\pi(s)$ is to consider the next state s' from each legal move a, calculate $V^\pi(s')$ for each of these next states, and select the action leading to the best s'. However, this is time-consuming and relies on knowing the transition function, which is available in chess but not in many other environments.

$Q^\pi(s, a)$ has the benefit of giving agents a direct method for acting. Agents can calculate $Q^\pi(s, a)$ for each of the actions $a \in A_s$ available in a particular state s, and select the action with the maximum value. In the optimal case, $Q^\pi(s, a)$ represents the optimal expected value from taking action a in state s, denoted by $Q^*(s, a)$. It represents the best you could possibly do if you acted optimally in all subsequent states. Knowing $Q^*(s, a)$ therefore yields an optimal policy.

The disadvantage of learning $Q^\pi(s, a)$ is that the function approximation is more computationally complex and requires more data to learn from compared to $V^\pi(s)$. Learning a good estimate for $V^\pi(s)$ requires that the data covers the state space reasonably well, whereas learning a good estimate for $Q^\pi(s, a)$ requires that data covers all (s, a) pairs, not just all states s [76, 132]. The combined state-action space is often significantly larger than the state space, so more data is needed to learn a good Q-function estimate. To make this more concrete, suppose there are 100 possible actions in state s and an agent tried each action once. If we are learning $V^\pi(s)$, then each of these 100 data points can contribute to learning the value of s. However, if we are learning $Q^\pi(s, a)$, then we only have one datapoint for each (s, a) pair. Typically, the more data we have, the better the function approximation. For the same quantity of data, the V-function estimate will likely be better than the Q-function estimate.

$V^\pi(s)$ may be a simpler function to approximate but it has one significant disadvantage. To use $V^\pi(s)$ to choose actions, agents need to be able to take each of the actions $a \in A_s$ available in a state s and observe s', the next state the environment transitions to,[2] along with the next reward r. Then an agent can act optimally by selecting the action which led to the largest expected cumulative discounted rewards $\mathbb{E}[r + V^\pi(s')]$. However, if state transitions are stochastic (taking action a in state s can result in different next states s'), the agent may need to repeat this process many times to get a good estimation of the expected value of taking a particular action. This is a potentially computationally expensive process.

Consider the following example. Suppose that taking action a in state s leads to state s_1' with reward $r_1' = 1$ half the time, and state s_2' with reward $r_2' = 2$ the other half of the time. Furthermore, suppose the values of states s_1' and s_2' are known and are $V^\pi(s_1') = 10$ and $V^\pi(s_2') = -10$, respectively. We get

$$r_1' + V^\pi(s_1') = 1 + 10 = 11 \tag{3.4}$$
$$r_2' + V^\pi(s_2') = 2 - 10 = -8 \tag{3.5}$$

---

2. At this point, for simplicity, we drop the time step subscript and adopt the standard notation of (s, a, r, s', a', r') to denote the tuples (s, a, r) at the current time step t and (s', a', r') at the next time step $t + 1$.

Then, the expected value is $\mathbb{E}[r + V^\pi(s')] = 1.5$, as shown in Equation 3.6.

$$\mathbb{E}[r + V^\pi(s')] = \frac{1}{2}\left(r'_1 + V^\pi(s'_1) + r'_2 + V^\pi(s'_2)\right) = \frac{1}{2}(11 - 8) = 1.5 \qquad (3.6)$$

However, a single sample would yield for $\mathbb{E}[r + V^\pi(s')]$ an estimate of 11 or -8, both of which are far from the expected value of 1.5.

This *one-step lookahead* requirement for $V^\pi(s)$ is often a problem. For example, it might not be possible to restart the agent in any state in order to try out every available action, or the restarting process might be expensive. $Q^\pi(s, a)$ avoids this problem because it directly learns the value of (s, a). It can be thought of as storing the one-step lookahead for every action a in every state s [132]. As a result, RL algorithms which select actions using a learned value function tend to approximate $Q^\pi(s, a)$.

3.2   Temporal Difference Learning

In this section we discuss how to learn the Q-function using temporal difference (TD) learning. The main idea is to use a neural network which produces Q-value estimates given (s, a) pairs as inputs. This is known as *value network*.

The workflow for learning the value network parameters goes as follows. We generate trajectories τs and predict a $\hat{Q}$-value for each (s, a) pair. Then, we use the trajectories to generate target Q-values Q_{tar}. Finally, we minimize the distance between $\hat{Q}$ and Q_{tar} using a standard regression loss such as *MSE* (mean squared error). We repeat this process many times. This is similar to the supervised learning workflow in which each prediction is associated with a target value. However, in this case we need a way of generating them for each trajectory, whereas in supervised learning the target values are given in advance.

TD learning is how we will produce the target values Q_{tar} in SARSA. To motivate this, it is helpful to consider how it can be done with Monte Carlo sampling which we discussed in Section 2.4.

Given N trajectories $\tau_i, i \in \{1, \ldots, N\}$ starting in state s where the agent took action a, the Monte Carlo (MC) estimate of $Q^\pi_{\text{tar}}(s, a)$ is the average of all the trajectories' returns, shown in Equation 3.7. Note that Equation 3.7 can also be applied to any set of trajectories with any starting (s, a) pair.

$$Q^\pi_{\text{tar:MC}}(s, a) = \frac{1}{N} \sum_{i=1}^{N} R(\tau_i) \qquad (3.7)$$

If we have access to an entire trajectory τ_i, it is possible to calculate the actual Q-value the agent received in that particular case for each (s, a) pair in τ_i. This follows from the definition of the Q-function (Equation 3.1), since the expectation of future cumulative discounted rewards from a single example is just the cumulative discounted reward from the current time step to the end of the episode for that example. Equation 3.7 shows that this is also the Monte Carlo estimate for $Q^\pi(s, a)$ where the number of trajectories used in the estimate is $N = 1$.

Now, each (s, a) pair in the dataset is associated with a target Q-value. The dataset can be said to be "labeled" since each datapoint (s, a) has a corresponding target value $Q_{\text{tar}}^{\pi}(s, a)$.

One disadvantage of Monte Carlo sampling is that an agent has to wait for episodes to end before any of the data from that episode can be used to learn from. This is evident from Equation 3.7. To calculate $Q_{\text{tar:MC}}^{\pi}(s, a)$, we need the rewards for the remainder of the trajectory starting from (s, a). Episodes might have many time steps as measured by T, which delays training. This motivates an alternative approach to learning Q-values—TD learning.

The key insight in TD learning is that Q-values for the current time step can be defined in terms of Q-values of the next time step. That is, $Q^{\pi}(s, a)$ is defined recursively, as shown in Equation 3.8.

$$Q^{\pi}(s, a) = \mathbb{E}_{s' \sim p(s'|s,a), r \sim \mathcal{R}(s,a,s')} \left[r + \gamma \mathbb{E}_{a' \sim \pi(s')} [Q^{\pi}(s', a')] \right] \qquad (3.8)$$

Equation 3.8 is known as the Bellman equation. If the Q-function is correct for the policy π, Equation 3.8 holds exactly. It also suggests a way of learning Q-values. We just saw how Monte Carlo sampling can be used to learn $Q^{\pi}(s, a)$ given many trajectories of experiences. The same idea can be applied here, using TD learning to derive the target value $Q_{\text{tar}}^{\pi}(s, a)$ for each (s, a) pair.

Assume we have a neural network to represent the Q-function, Q_{θ}. In TD learning, $Q_{\text{tar}}^{\pi}(s_t, a_t)$ is derived by estimating the right-hand side of Equation 3.8 using Q_{θ}. At each training iteration, $\hat{Q}^{\pi}(s_t, a_t)$ is updated to bring it closer to $Q_{\text{tar}}^{\pi}(s_t, a_t)$.

If $Q_{\text{tar}}^{\pi}(s_t, a_t)$ is derived using the same neural network which produces $\hat{Q}^{\pi}(s_t, a_t)$, then why does this work? Why can it result in a good approximation of the Q-function after many steps? This is discussed in more detail in Section 3.2.1, but in brief, $Q_{\text{tar}}^{\pi}(s_t, a_t)$ uses information one time step into the future when compared with $\hat{Q}^{\pi}(s_t, a_t)$ and thus has access to the reward r from the next state s'. Consequently, $Q_{\text{tar}}^{\pi}(s_t, a_t)$ is slightly more informative about how the trajectory will ultimately turn out. Underlying this formulation is the assumption that information about the objective—maximizing cumulative rewards—is revealed as the trajectory progresses and is not available at the start of an episode. This is a fundamental characteristic of RL problems.

However, there are two problems with Equation 3.8 if it is to be used to construct $Q_{\text{tar}}^{\pi}(s_t, a_t)$—the two expectations. The first problem is the outer expectation $\mathbb{E}_{s' \sim p(s'|s,a), r \sim \mathcal{R}(s,a,s')}[\ldots]$ due to the next state and reward. This can be illustrated by supposing we have a collection of trajectories, $\{\tau_1, \tau_2, \ldots, \tau_M\}$. Each trajectory τ_i contains (s, a, r, s') tuples. For each tuple (s, a, r, s'), only one example of the next state s' is available given the action selected.

If the environment is deterministic, then it is correct to only consider the actual next state when calculating the expectation over the next states. However, if the environment is stochastic, this breaks down. Taking action a in states s could transition the environment into a number of different next states, but only one next state was actually observed at each step. This problem can be overcome by considering only one example—the one that actually happened. This does mean that the Q-value estimate may have high variance if the environment is stochastic, but it helps make the estimation more tractable. Using just one example to estimate the distribution over next states s' and rewards r, we can take the outer expectation out and the Bellman equation can be rewritten as shown in Equation 3.9.

$$Q^\pi(s, a) = r + \gamma \mathbb{E}_{a' \sim \pi(s')}[Q^\pi(s', a')] \tag{3.9}$$

The second problem is the inner expectation $\mathbb{E}_{a' \sim \pi(s')}[\ldots]$ of Equation 3.8 over the actions. We have access to the Q-value estimates for all of the actions in the next state s', because we are using the current estimate of the Q-function to calculate the values. The problem arises from not knowing the probability distribution over actions which is needed to calculate the expectation. There are two ways to solve this, each corresponding to a different algorithm—SARSA and DQN (Chapter 4).

SARSA's solution is to use the action actually taken in the next state, a' (Equation 3.10). Over the course of many examples, the proportion of actions selected should approximate the probability distribution over actions, given states. DQN's solution is to use the maximum Q-value (Equation 3.11). This corresponds to an implicit policy of selecting the action with the maximum Q-value with probability 1. As we will see in Chapter 4, the implicit policy in Q-learning is greedy with respect to Q-values, and so the transformation of the equation is valid.[3]

$$\text{SARSA: } Q^\pi(s, a) \approx r + \gamma Q^\pi(s', a') = Q^\pi_{\text{tar:SARSA}}(s, a) \tag{3.10}$$

$$\text{DQN: } Q^\pi(s, a) \approx r + \gamma \max_{a'_i} Q^\pi(s', a'_i) = Q^\pi_{\text{tar:DQN}}(s, a) \tag{3.11}$$

Now $Q^\pi_{\text{tar}}(s, a)$ can be calculated using the right-hand side Equation 3.10 for each tuple (s, a, r, s', a').[4] As in Monte Carlo sampling, each (s, a) pair in the dataset is associated with a Q-value, so the same supervised learning techniques can be used to train the neural network function approximator for $Q^\pi(s, a)$. Notice that only the information from the next step in the environment was required to calculate the target Q-values, instead of a whole episode's trajectory. This makes it possible to update the Q-function in a batched (after a few examples) or online (after one example) manner when using TD learning instead of having to wait for an entire trajectory to finish.

TD learning is a bootstrapped learning method because the existing estimates of Q-values for a (s, a) pair are used when calculating $Q^\pi_{\text{tar}}(s, a)$. This has the advantage of lowering the variance of the estimate as compared to Monte Carlo sampling. TD learning only uses the actual reward r from the next state s' and combines it with Q-value estimates to approximate the remaining part of the value. The Q-function represents an expectation over different trajectories and so typically has lower variance than the whole trajectory used by Monte Carlo sampling. However, it also introduces bias into the learning approach since the Q-function approximator is not perfect.

---

3. A third alternative is to derive the probability distribution over actions from the policy and calculate the expectation. This algorithm is known as Expected SARSA. For more information, see Chapter 6 of "Reinforcement Learning, An Introduction" by Sutton and Barto, 2nd Edition [132].

4. The SARSA Bellman equation (Equation 3.10) requires knowing the action that was actually taken by an agent in the next state s', denoted a'. Consequently, each experience tuple for SARSA includes an additional element a' to make (s, a, r, s', a'). DQN, in contrast, only needs to know the next state s', so an experience tuple is (s, a, r, s').

3.2.1 Intuition for Temporal Difference Learning

To build some intuition for how TD learning works, let's consider an example. Suppose an agent is learning to play the toy environment shown in Figure 3.1. This is a essentially a corridor and the agent has to learn to navigate to the end of the corridor to the good terminal state s_{T2}, denoted with a star. There are five states in total—s_1, s_2, s_3 and two terminal states s_{T1}, s_{T2}. There are only two actions, a_{UP} and a_{DOWN}. Choosing a_{UP} moves the agent one cell up the corridor; choosing a_{DOWN} moves the agent one cell down the corridor. The agent always starts the game in state s_1, denoted **S**, and the game ends if the agent reaches either of the terminal states. s_{T2} is the goal state—the agent receives a reward of 1 if it reaches this state. The agent receives rewards of 0 in all other states. The agent's discount rate γ is 0.9. The game is therefore optimally solved by a policy which reaches s_{T2} in the smallest number of steps because an agent values rewards received sooner more than rewards received later in time. In this case, the smallest number of steps an agent can take to optimally solve the environment is 3.

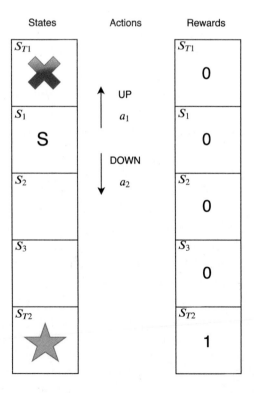

Figure 3.1   Simple environment: five states, two actions per state

For this very simple environment, the Q-function can be represented by a table, known at a tabular Q-function, with one cell per (s, a) pair. This makes six pairs in total since the agent cannot act once it has moved to the terminal states. The optimal Q-function is defined as the expected cumulative discounted rewards from taking action a in state s and thereafter following the optimal policy. For this environment, the optimal policy is to select the action a_{DOWN} in all states since this is the quickest way to reach s_{T2} from any of the other states. The optimal Q-function for this environment is shown in tabular form in Figure 3.2.

$$Q^*(s, a)$$

	UP	DOWN
S_1	0	0.81
S_2	0.73	0.9
S_3	0.81	1.0

Figure 3.2   Optimal Q-values for the simple environment from Figure 3.1, $\gamma = 0.9$

The optimal Q-values are derived from the definition of the Q-function. Let's consider some examples.

- (s_0, a_{UP}): The agent moves out of the corridor, receives a reward of 0, and the episode terminates, so $Q^*(s_0, a_{\text{UP}}) = 0$.
- (s_3, a_{DOWN}): The agent reaches the terminal state, receives a reward of 1, and the episode terminates, so $Q^*(s_3, a_{\text{DOWN}}) = 1$.
- (s_2, a_{DOWN}): The agent receives a reward of 0 and moves to s_3, so $Q^*(s_2, a_{\text{DOWN}}) = r_2 + 0.9\, Q^*(s_3, a_{\text{DOWN}}) = 0 + 0.9 * 1.0 = 0.9$.
- (s_3, a_{UP}): The agent receives a reward of 0 and moves to s_2, so $Q^*(s_3, a_{\text{UP}}) = r_3 + 0.9\, Q^*(s_2, a_{\text{DOWN}}) = 0 + 0.9(0 + 0.9 * 1.0) = 0.81$.

How can we learn the optimal Q-function using TD learning? Suppose we initialize the Q-value table to 0 for every cell. The process of learning the Q-function involves randomly sampling a set of trajectories and, every time the agent experiences a (s, a, r, s') tuple, updating the Q-value table using the Bellman equation. That is, set:

$$Q^*(s, a) = r + \gamma Q^*(s', a') \qquad (3.12)$$
$$= r + 0.9\, Q^*(s', a_{\text{DOWN}}) \qquad (3.13)$$

Figure 3.3 illustrates the process of learning the optimal Q-function in tabular form using a set of five trajectories from the environment. The diagram is split into five blocks from top to bottom. Each block corresponds to a single episode of experiences in the environment; the first block corresponds to the first episode, the second block the second episode, and so on. Each block contains a number of columns. They are interpreted from left to right as follows:

- **Q-function episode start:** The value of the Q-function at the start of the episode. At the beginning of episode 1, all of the values are initialized to 0 since we have no information yet about the function.

- **Episode:** The episode number.

- **Time step:** Each block contains a variable number of experiences. For example, there are three experiences in episode 2 and seven experiences in episode 4. The time index of each experience within the block is indicated by the time step.

- **Action:** The action the agent took at each time step.

- (s, a, r, s')**:** The agent's experience at each time step. This consists of the current state s, the action the agent took a, the reward received r, and the next state the environment transitioned into s'.

- $r + \gamma Q^*(s', a)$**:** The target value (i.e., the right-hand side of the equation) to use in the Bellman update: $Q^*(s, a) = r + \gamma Q^*(s', a')$.

- **Q-function episode end:** The value of Q-function at the end of the episode. The Bellman update has been applied for each experience of the episode in time step order. This means that the Bellman update was applied first for the experience corresponding to time step 1, then time step 2, and so on. The table shows the final result after all of the Bellman updates have been applied for the episode.

After five trajectories consisting of 21 time steps in total, the tabular Q-function has the same values as the optimal Q-function shown in Figure 3.2. That is, it has *converged* to the optimal Q-function.

The TD update makes use of the actual reward received in the following state. This has the effect of gradually backing up reward signals from future time steps to earlier time steps by one time step each update. Each time there is a TD backup, the Q-function incorporates information about an additional time step in the future. Over the course of many backups, more information about the future is incorporated into the Q-function estimate at time t. This mechanism makes it possible for the Q-function to incorporate long-term information.

The number of time steps that the Q-function will take to converge depends on both the environment and the actions an agent takes, as they both affect the experiences that are used to learn the Q-function. If, for example, the agent didn't select the UP action until the sixth episode, then the Q-function would have taken longer (in terms of episodes) to converge because we would not have any information about the left-hand side of the Q-table until episode 6.

The value of the discount factor γ affects the optimal Q-values. Figure 3.4 shows the optimal Q-values for the extreme values of γ, 0 or 1. If $\gamma = 0$, the agent becomes myopic, only caring about the reward it receives in the current state. In this case, the only (s, a)

Q-function episode start			Episode	Time step	Action	(s, a, r, s')	$r + \gamma Q^*(s', a)$	Q-function episode end		

Episode 1

Q-function episode start:

	UP	DOWN
S_1	0	0
S_2	0	0
S_3	0	0

Episode	Time step	Action	(s,a,r,s')	$r + \gamma Q^*(s',a)$
1	1	↓	$(S_1, D, 0, S_2)$	$0 + 0.9 \times 0 = 0$
1	2	↑	$(S_2, U, 0, S_1)$	$0 + 0.9 \times 0 = 0$
1	3	↓	$(S_1, D, 0, S_2)$	$0 + 0.9 \times 0 = 0$
1	4	↓	$(S_2, D, 0, S_3)$	$0 + 0.9 \times 0 = 0$
1	5	↓	$(S_3, D, 1, S_{T2})$	1

Q-function episode end:

	UP	DOWN
S_1	0	0
S_2	0	0
S_3	0	1

Episode 2

Q-function episode start:

	UP	DOWN
S_1	0	0
S_2	0	0
S_3	0	1

Episode	Time step	Action	(s,a,r,s')	$r + \gamma Q^*(s',a)$
2	1	↓	$(S_1, D, 0, S_2)$	$0 + 0.9 \times 0 = 0$
2	2	↓	$(S_2, D, 0, S_3)$	$0 + 0.9 \times 1 = 0.9$
2	3	↓	$(S_3, D, 1, S_{T2})$	1

Q-function episode end:

	UP	DOWN
S_1	0	0
S_2	0	0.9
S_3	0	1

Episode 3

Q-function episode start:

	UP	DOWN
S_1	0	0
S_2	0	0.9
S_3	0	1

Episode	Time step	Action	(s,a,r,s')	$r + \gamma Q^*(s',a)$
3	1	↓	$(S_1, D, 0, S_2)$	$0 + 0.9 \times 0.9 = 0.81$
3	2	↓	$(S_2, D, 0, S_3)$	$0 + 0.9 \times 1 = 0.9$
3	3	↑	$(S_3, U, 0, S_2)$	$0 + 0.9 \times 0.9 = 0.81$
3	4	↓	$(S_2, D, 0, S_3)$	$0 + 0.9 \times 1 = 0.9$
3	5	↓	$(S_3, D, 1, S_{T2})$	1

Q-function episode end:

	UP	DOWN
S_1	0	0.81
S_2	0	0.9
S_3	0.81	1

Episode 4

Q-function episode start:

	UP	DOWN
S_1	0	0.81
S_2	0	0.9
S_3	0.81	1

Episode	Time step	Action	(s,a,r,s')	$r + \gamma Q^*(s',a)$
4	1	↓	$(S_1, D, 0, S_2)$	$0 + 0.9 \times 0.9 = 0.81$
4	2	↑	$(S_2, U, 0, S_1)$	$0 + 0.9 \times 0.81 = 0.73$
4	3	↓	$(S_1, D, 0, S_2)$	$0 + 0.9 \times 0.9 = 0.81$
4	4	↑	$(S_2, U, 0, S_1)$	$0 + 0.9 \times 0.81 = 0.73$
4	5	↓	$(S_1, D, 0, S_2)$	$0 + 0.9 + 0.9 = 0.81$
4	6	↓	$(S_2, D, 0, S_3)$	$0 + 0.9 \times 1 = 0.9$
4	7	↓	$(S_3, D, 1, S_{T2})$	1

Q-function episode end:

	UP	DOWN
S_1	0	0.81
S_2	0.73	0.9
S_3	0.81	1

Episode 5

Q-function episode start:

	UP	DOWN
S_1	0	0.81
S_2	0.73	0.9
S_3	0.81	1

Episode	Time step	Action	(s,a,r,s')	$r + \gamma Q^*(s',a)$
5	1	↑	$(S_1, U, 0, S_{T1})$	0

Q-function episode end:

	UP	DOWN
S_1	0	0.81
S_2	0.73	0.9
S_3	0.81	1

Figure 3.3 Learning the $Q^*(s, a)$ for the simple environment from Figure 3.1

pair with a nonzero Q-value is (s_3, DOWN). This is not very useful because information about the reward in future time steps is no longer incorporated in the Q-values. Consequently, the agent doesn't get any clues about how to act in s_1 and s_2. If $\gamma = 1$,

$$Q^*(s, a) \qquad\qquad Q^*(s, a)$$
$$\gamma = 0 \qquad\qquad\qquad \gamma = 1$$

	UP	DOWN		UP	DOWN
S_1	0	0	S_1	0	1.0
S_2	0	0	S_2	1.0	1.0
S_3	0	1.0	S_3	1.0	1.0

Figure 3.4   Optimal Q-values for the simple environment from Figure 3.1,
γ = 0 (left), γ = 1 (right)

then all (s, a) pairs except (s_1, UP) (which leads to the game ending with no reward) have a Q-value of 1 because the agent does not care about receiving the reward for reaching s_{T2} sooner rather than later.

Another way to think about γ is to consider how it affects the speed at which the Q-function can be learned. Small values of γ correspond to the agent having a short time horizon—it only cares about a few time steps into the future, so the Q-values will only need to be backed up for a few steps. It will likely be faster to learn the Q-function under these circumstances. However, there may be important information about rewards further into the future that is not captured by this Q-function, thus negatively affecting an agent's performance. If γ is large, then the Q-function may take much longer to learn because there are many time steps of information to back up, but the resulting function may be much more useful to the agent. Consequently, the optimal value of γ depends on the environment; we will see examples of specific values for γ throughout this book. Box 3.1 discusses the role of γ in more detail.

Box 3.1   Problem Horizon

The discount factor γ controls the problem horizon of an agent. It is such a crucial parameter affecting all algorithms that it is worth showing the time horizon that is implied by different values of γ.

γ determines how much an agent weights rewards received in the future compared to the current time step. Consequently, changing γ transforms the nature of a RL problem as perceived by an agent. If γ is small, then an agent will only care about the rewards received in the current time step and just a few steps in the future. This effectively reduces the length of the RL problem to a few time steps and can drastically simplify the credit assignment problem. Learning may be faster with a small γ, since it either takes fewer time steps to back up the Q-value over the horizon the agent cares about, or reduces the length of a trajectory needed for policy gradient updates. Whether this will lead to good performance depends on the nature of the problem since an agent will learn to maximize rewards received in the near future.

Table 3.1 shows the discount applied to a reward received k time steps into the future for different values of γ. This gives an idea of the problem horizon for an agent under different γs. For example, if γ is 0.8, the effective problem horizon is around 10 steps, whereas if γ is 0.99, it is around 200–500 steps.

Table 3.1   Discount applied to rewards after k time steps

	Time step						
γ	**10**	**50**	**100**	**200**	**500**	**1000**	**2000**
0.8	0.11	0.00	0.00	0.00	0.00	0.00	0.00
0.9	0.35	0.01	0.00	0.00	0.00	0.00	0.00
0.95	0.60	0.08	0.01	0.00	0.00	0.00	0.00
0.99	0.90	0.61	0.37	0.13	0.07	0.00	0.00
0.995	0.95	0.78	0.61	0.37	0.08	0.01	0.00
0.999	0.99	0.95	0.90	0.82	0.61	0.37	0.14
0.9997	0.997	0.985	0.970	0.942	0.861	0.741	0.549

A good value for γ depends on how delayed rewards typically are in an environment. This may be tens, hundreds, or thousands of steps. Fortunately, γ tends to require less tuning; 0.99 is a good default value to use for a wide range of problems. For example, 0.99 was used in this book in the training examples for Atari games.

One simple datapoint that can be useful is the maximum length of an episode. Some environments have maximum time steps. For example, CartPole has a maximum length of 200 by default. If an environment only lasts for 200 steps, then there is not much point in using a large γ which implies caring about rewards many hundreds of time steps into the future. In contrast, when learning to play the game of Dota 2, which has around 80,000 time steps per game, OpenAI found it helpful to gradually increase γ during training from 0.998 to 0.9997 [104].

Most environments in deep RL (and the associated optimal Q-functions) are much more complex than the simple environment we have discussed in this section. In more complex cases, the Q-function cannot be represented in tabular form. Instead, we will use neural networks to represent them. One consequence of this is that the backup of information through time will be slower. $\hat{Q}^\pi(s, a)$ is not fully updated to $r + \gamma Q^\pi(s', a)$

for each experience because neural networks learn gradually, using gradient descent. Each update only moves $\hat{Q}^\pi(s, a)$ partially towards $r + \gamma Q^\pi(s', a)$. However, despite the simplicity of the example we worked through, it illustrates a fundamental concept—that TD learning is a mechanism for backing up information about an environment's reward function through time, from later to earlier time steps.

3.3 Action Selection in SARSA

Now we return to the open question from the previous section. How can a technique for learning a good approximation of the Q-function be transformed into an algorithm for learning a good policy? TD learning gives us a method for learning how to evaluate actions. What is missing is a policy—a mechanism for selecting actions.

Suppose we had already learned the optimal Q-function. Then the value of each state-action pair will represent the best possible expected value from taking that action. This gives us a way to reverse-engineer the optimal way of acting. If the agent always selects the action which corresponds to the maximum Q-value in each state—that is, if the agent acts *greedily* with respect to the Q-values—then it will be acting optimally. This also implies that the SARSA algorithm is limited to discrete action spaces, as explained in Box 3.2.

Box 3.2   SARSA Is Limited to Discrete Action Spaces

To identify the maximum Q-value in state s, we need to compute the Q-values for all the possible actions in that state. When actions are discrete, this is straightforward because we can list all the possible actions and compute their Q-values. However, when actions are continuous, the actions cannot be fully enumerated, and this becomes a problem. For this reason, SARSA and other value-based methods such as DQN (Chapters 4 and 5) are generally restricted to discrete action spaces. However, there are methods, such as *QT-Opt* [64], which approximate the maximum Q-value by sampling from a continuous action space. These are beyond the scope of this book.

Unfortunately, the optimal Q-function is typically not known. However, the relationship between the optimal Q-function and acting optimally tells us that if we have a good Q-function, then we can derive a good policy. It also suggests an iterative approach to improving the Q-value.

First, randomly initialize a neural network with parameters θ to represent the Q-function, denoted $Q^\pi(s, a; \theta)$. Then, repeat the following steps until the agent stops improving, as evaluated by the total undiscounted[5] cumulative rewards received during an episode:

---

5. Reward discounting is only used by the agent. Evaluation of agent performance is typically done with undiscounted cumulative rewards.

1. Use $Q^\pi(s, a; \theta)$ to act in the environment, by acting greedily with respect to the Q-values. Store all of the (s, a, r, s') experiences.

2. Use the stored experiences to update $Q^\pi(s, a; \theta)$ using the SARSA Bellman equation (Equation 3.10). This improves the Q-function estimate which, in turn, improves the policy, since the Q-value estimates are now better.

3.3.1   Exploration and Exploitation

One issue with acting greedily with respect to the Q-values is that this strategy is deterministic, which means an agent may not explore the entire state-action space sufficiently. If an agent always selects the same action a in state s, then there may be many (s, a) pairs that an agent never experiences. As a result, the Q-function estimates for some (s, a) pairs may be inaccurate since they were randomly initialized and there were no actual experiences of (s, a). There was no opportunity for a network to learn about this part of the state-action space—so the agent may make suboptimal actions and get stuck in a local minimum.

To mitigate this issue, it is common to use an ε-greedy[6] policy, instead of a purely greedy policy, for the agent. Under this policy, an agent selects the greedy action with probability $1 - \varepsilon$ and acts randomly with probability ε, which is known as the exploration probability since acting randomly $\varepsilon \times 100\%$ of the time helps an agent explore the state-action space. Unfortunately, this comes at a cost: such a policy may not be as good as the greedy policy because the agent is taking random actions with nonzero probability, instead of the Q-value maximizing action.

The tension between the potential value of exploring during training and taking the best actions based on the information available to an agent (Q-values) is known as the *exploration-exploitation* tradeoff. Should the agent *exploit* its current knowledge to perform as best it can, or *explore* by acting randomly? Exploring risks poor performance for some time, but it also opens up the possibility of discovering better states and ways of acting. Another way of expressing this is that if the agent had access to the optimal Q-function, it should be acting greedily, but while it is learning the Q-function, acting greedily can prevent it from getting better.

A common approach to managing this tradeoff is to start with high ε, 1.0 or close to this, so that the agent acts almost randomly and rapidly explores the state-action space. As the agent has not yet learned anything at the beginning of training, there is nothing to exploit. Over time, ε is gradually decayed, so that after many steps the policy, hopefully, approaches the optimal policy. As the agent learns better Q-functions, and so better policies, there is less benefit to exploring and the agent should act more greedily.

In the ideal case, after some time the agent will have discovered the optimal Q-function, so ε can then be reduced to 0. In practice, due to limited time, continuous or high-dimensional discrete state spaces, and nonlinear function approximators, the learned Q-function does not fully converge to the optimal policy. Therefore, ε is typically

---

6. Pronounced "epsilon-greedy."

annealed to a small value, for example 0.1–0.001, and fixed to allow a small amount of continued exploration.

TD learning has been proven to converge to the optimal Q-function for linear function approximators [131, 137]. However, much of the recent progress in reinforcement learning has been driven by the introduction of complex nonlinear function approximators, such as neural networks, because they can represent much more complex Q-functions. Unfortunately, the move to nonlinear function approximation means that there are no guarantees that TD learning will converge. A complete explanation of this is beyond the scope of this book; interested readers should watch Sergey Levine's excellent lecture on the theory of value function learning given as part of UC Berkeley's CS294 course.[7] Fortunately, in practice it has been shown that good results can be achieved [88, 135] even without this guarantee.

3.4 SARSA Algorithm

We now describe the SARSA algorithm and discuss why it is on-policy.

The pseudocode for SARSA with an ε-greedy policy is given in Algorithm 3.1. The Q-function estimate $\hat{Q}^{\pi}(s, a)$ is parameterized by a network with parameters θ, denoted Q^{π_θ}, so we have $\hat{Q}^{\pi}(s, a) = Q^{\pi_\theta}(s, a)$. Note that the good start and minimum values for ε, as well as the rate at which we decay ε, depend on the environment.

Algorithm 3.1 SARSA

1: Initialize learning rate α
2: Initialize ε
3: Randomly initialize the network parameters θ
4: **for** $m = 1 \dots MAX\_STEPS$ **do**
5:      Gather N experiences $(s_i, a_i, r_i, s_i', a_i')$ using the current ε-greedy policy
6:      **for** $i = 1 \dots N$ **do**
7:          # Calculate target Q-values for each example
8:          $y_i = r_i + \delta_{s_i'} \gamma \, Q^{\pi_\theta}(s_i', a_i')$ where $\delta_{s_i'} = 0$ if s_i' is terminal, 1 otherwise
9:      **end for**
10:     # Calculate the loss, for example using MSE
11:     $L(\theta) = \frac{1}{N} \sum_i (y_i - Q^{\pi_\theta}(s_i, a_i))^2$
12:     # Update the network's parameters
13:     $\theta = \theta - \alpha \nabla_\theta J(\theta)$
14:     Decay ε
15: **end for**

---
7. The video is publicly available at https://youtu.be/k1vNh4rNYec [76].

3.4.1 On-Policy Algorithms

An important feature of SARSA is that it is an *on-policy* algorithm. Recall from Chapter 2 that an algorithm is on-policy if the information used to improve the current policy depends on the policy used to gather data. This can happen in two ways.

First, the target value used to train the Q-function can depend on the policy that was used to generate experiences. SARSA is an example, as shown in Algorithm 3.1 (line 7). The target value y_i depends on the actual action a' taken in the next state s'. The actual action taken depends on the experience-generating policy—that is, the current ε-greedy policy.

The second way in which an algorithm can be on-policy is if the policy is being learned directly. Learning a policy involves changing it so as to make good actions more likely and poor actions less likely. To make this improvement, it is necessary to have access to the probabilities that the current policy assigned to the actions taken. REINFORCE (Chapter 2) is an example of an on-policy algorithm where the policy is directly learned.

The fact that SARSA is an on-policy algorithm has implications for the type of experiences that can be used to train the Q-function approximator over time. Only experiences collected using the current policy can be used in each training iteration. Once the parameters of the function approximator have been updated once, all of the experiences must be discarded and the experience-collection process must begin again. This holds even if the update to the parameters is small, as is typically the case for a single parameter update when training neural networks, since this changes the policy. Algorithm 3.1 makes this explicit since new experiences are collected for each training iteration m.

Why does it matter that only experiences collected with the current policy are used to update the Q-function in each iteration? Let's revisit the SARSA TD update in Equation 3.14.

$$Q^{\pi_1}(s, a) \approx r + \gamma Q^{\pi_1}(s', a_1') \tag{3.14}$$

The second term of the update, $\gamma Q^{\pi_1}(s', a_1')$, assumes that a' has been selected using the policy π_1. This follows from the definition of the Q-function, which is the expected future value of (s, a) assuming that the agent acts according to policy π_1. There is no place for experiences generated using a different policy.

Suppose we have an example (s, a, r, s', a_2') generated using a different policy π_2, for example from an earlier iteration during training with different values for θ (the parameters of the Q-function approximator). a_2' is not necessarily the same as a_1'. The action taken in s' by π_2 might not be the same as the action that the current policy π_1 takes. If this is the case, then $Q^{\pi_1}(s, a)$ will not reflect the expected cumulative future discounted rewards from taking action a in state s under π_1.

$$Q_{\text{tar}}^{\pi_1}(s, a) = r + \gamma Q^{\pi_1}(s', a_1') \neq r + \gamma Q^{\pi_1}(s', a_2') \tag{3.15}$$

Equation 3.15 shows that if (s, a, r, s', a_2') was used instead of (s, a, r, s', a_1'), then $Q^{\pi_1}(s, a)$ will have been updated incorrectly. This is because it uses Q-value estimates derived from a course of action different to the one that the current policy would have taken.

3.5 Implementing SARSA

This section walks you through an implementation of the SARSA algorithm. First, we look at the `epsilon_greedy` code. This determines how the SARSA agent acts in an environment. Next, we review the method for calculating the target Q-value. The section ends with the network training loop and a discussion of `Memory` classes for SARSA.

3.5.1 Action Function: ε-Greedy

An action function returns the action a an agent should carry out in state s. Every action function takes in a `state`, an `algorithm` from which the neural network function approximator can be accessed, and an agent's `body` which stores information about the exploration variable (e.g., ε) and the action space. Action functions return the action selected by the agent and the probability distribution from which the action was sampled. In the case of SARSA, the distribution is degenerate. All the probability mass is assigned to the Q-value-maximizing action.

`epsilon_greedy` in Code 3.1 has three elements:

- The agent decides whether to act randomly or greedily (line 5). This depends on the current value of ε (line 4).

- If acting randomly, call the `random` action function (line 6). This returns an action from the action space by sampling from a random uniform distribution over the actions.

- If acting greedily, estimate the Q-value for each action in `state`. Choose the action which corresponds to the maximum Q-value. This is handled by the call to the `default` action function (lines 11–14).

One important implementation detail for the Q-function approximator is that it outputs all of the Q-values for a particular state at the same time. Structuring a neural network to approximate the Q-function in this way is more efficient than the alternative of taking a state and an action as input and outputting a single value. It only requires one forward pass through the network instead of `action_dim` forward passes. For more details on building and initializing different types of networks, see Chapter 12.

Code 3.1 SARSA implementation: ε-greedy action function

```
1  # slm_lab/agent/algorithm/policy_util.py
2
3  def epsilon_greedy(state, algorithm, body):
4      epsilon = body.explore_var
5      if epsilon > np.random.rand():
6          return random(state, algorithm, body)
7      else:
8          # Returns the action with the maximum Q-value
9          return default(state, algorithm, body)
```

```
10
11   def default(state, algorithm, body):
12       pdparam = calc_pdparam(state, algorithm, body)
13       action = sample_action(body.ActionPD, pdparam)
14       return action
```

3.5.2 Calculating the Q-Loss

The next step in the SARSA algorithm is to calculate the Q-loss. This value is used to update the parameters of the Q-function approximator.

In Code 3.2, first, $\hat{Q}^\pi(s, a)$ is calculated for the action a taken by the agent in the current state s for each experience in the batch. This involves a forward pass through the value network to obtain the Q-value estimates for all of the (s, a) pairs (line 11). Recall that in the SARSA version of the Bellman equation, we use the action actually taken by the agent in the next state to calculate $Q_{\text{tar}}^\pi(s, a)$.

$$\hat{Q}^\pi(s, a) = r + \gamma \hat{Q}^\pi(s', a') = Q_{\text{tar}}^\pi(s, a) \tag{3.16}$$

So we repeat the same step with next states instead of the current states (lines 12–13). Note that we treat the target Q-values as fixed, so we do not compute the gradient for this step. Hence, the forward pass is called under a `torch.no_grad()` context to prevent PyTorch from tracking the gradient.

Next, we extract the Q-value estimate for the action actually taken in both cases (lines 15–16). With this, we can estimate $Q_{\text{tar}}^\pi(s, a)$ using `act_next_q_preds` (line 17). Care is taken to handle terminal states for which $Q_{\text{tar}}^\pi(s, a)$ is just the reward received. This is achieved by multiplying $\hat{Q}^\pi(s', a')$ (`act_next_q_preds`) with a one-hot vector `1 - batch['dones']`, which is 0 if the state is terminal and 1 otherwise. Once we have the current and target Q-value estimates (`q_preds` and `act_q_targets`, respectively), calculating the loss is straightforward (line 18).

One important element to be aware of is that for each experience, the agent only receives information about the action actually taken. Consequently, it can only learn something about this action, not the other actions available. This is why the loss is only calculated using values that correspond to the actions taken in the current and next states.

Code 3.2   SARSA implementation: calculating Q-targets and the corresponding loss

```
1    # slm_lab/agent/algorithms/sarsa.py
2
3    class SARSA(Algorithm):
4        ...
5
6        def calc_q_loss(self, batch):
7            '''Compute the Q value loss using predicted and target Q values from
             ↪   the appropriate networks'''
```

```
8        states = batch['states']
9        next_states = batch['next_states']
10       ...
11       q_preds = self.net(states)
12       with torch.no_grad():
13           next_q_preds = self.net(next_states)
14       ...
15       act_q_preds = q_preds.gather(-1,
         ↪ batch['actions'].long().unsqueeze(-1)).squeeze(-1)
16       act_next_q_preds = next_q_preds.gather(-1,
         ↪ batch['next_actions'].long().unsqueeze(-1)).squeeze(-1)
17       act_q_targets = batch['rewards'] + self.gamma * (1 - batch['dones']) *
         ↪ act_next_q_preds
18       q_loss = self.net.loss_fn(act_q_preds, act_q_targets)
19       return q_loss
```

3.5.3 SARSA Training Loop

The training loop in Code 3.3 proceeds as follows:

1. At each time step, `train` is called and the agent checks if it is ready to train (line 10). The `self.to_train` flag is set by the memory class discussed in the following section.

2. If it is time to train, then the agent samples the data from memory by calling `self.sample()` (line 11). For the SARSA algorithm, a batch is all of the experiences collected since the last time the agent was trained.

3. Calculate the Q-loss for the `batch` (line 13).

4. Use the Q-loss to make a single update of the value network parameters (line 14). With the loss defined, PyTorch conveniently handles the parameter update using automatic differentiation.

5. Reset `self.to_train` to 0 to ensure that the agent is not trained until it is ready again (line 16)—that is, it has gathered a sufficient number of new experiences.

6. Update ε (`explore_var`) (line 23) with a chosen strategy, such as linear decay.

Code 3.3 SARSA implementation: training loop

```
1    # slm_lab/agent/algorithm/sarsa.py
2
3    class SARSA(Algorithm):
4        ...
5
6        @lab_api
```

```
7      def train(self):
8          ...
9          clock = self.body.env.clock
10         if self.to_train == 1:
11             batch = self.sample()
12             ...
13             loss = self.calc_q_loss(batch)
14             self.net.train_step(loss, self.optim, self.lr_scheduler,
               ↪   clock=clock, global_net=self.global_net)
15             # reset
16             self.to_train = 0
17             return loss.item()
18         else:
19             return np.nan
20
21     @lab_api
22     def update(self):
23         self.body.explore_var = self.explore_var_scheduler.update(self,
           ↪   self.body.env.clock)
24         return self.body.explore_var
```

Summary   At a high level, an implementation of SARSA has three main components.

1. epsilon_greedy: Define a method for acting in the environment using the current policy.

2. calc_q_loss: Use the experiences collected to calculate Q-targets and the corresponding loss.

3. train: Make one parameter update of the value network parameters using the Q-loss. Update any relevant variables such as explore_var (ε).

3.5.4 On-Policy Batched Replay Memory

The code in the previous section assumed that when it was time to train the agent, a set of examples containing the relevant experiences was available to the agent.

We saw this through self.sample() in the train() function of the SARSA algorithm class. This section walks you through storing experiences and providing them to agents when they need them to train.

The mechanism for storing and retrieving experiences—(s, a, r, s', a') tuples—is abstracted into the Memory classes introduced in Chapter 2. The type of experiences that can be used to train function approximators is shared by on-policy algorithms. These are experiences collected using the current policy. Recall that each memory class must implement an update function which adds an agent's experiences to the memory, a sample function which returns a batch of data for training, and a reset function which clears the memory.

SARSA is a temporal difference learning algorithm, so it is only necessary to wait until the next time step before the algorithm's parameters can be updated using a single (s, a, r, s', a') tuple. This makes it possible for SARSA to be an *online* algorithm. However, using just one example per update can be very noisy, so it is common to wait for a number of steps and update the algorithm's parameters using the average loss computed over multiple experiences. This is known as batch training. An alternative strategy is to gather one or more full episodes of experiences and update the algorithm's parameters using all of this data at once. This is known as episodic training.

The different choices reflect a tradeoff between speed and variance. Data from multiple episodes typically has the least variance, but the algorithm may learn more slowly, since the parameters are updated infrequently. Updates using a single experience have the highest variance but can lead to rapid learning. The choice of how many experiences to use in each update depends on the environment and the algorithm. Some environments may result in extremely high-variance data, in which case many experiences may be needed to reduce the variance sufficiently for the agent to learn. Other environments may result in low-variance data; in this case the number of examples per update can be quite small, increasing the potential learning speed.

Two `Memory` classes provide this spectrum of functionality—from online to batch to episodic learning. `OnPolicyReplay` implements episodic training, and `OnPolicyBatchReplay`, which inherits from `OnPolicyReplay`, implements batch training. Online training is also covered in this class by setting a batch size to 1. Note that for SARSA, at least two steps in the environment are needed for online training so that the next state and action are known, corresponding to a batch size of 2.

`OnPolicyReplay` was introduced in Chapter 2, so here we just focus on `OnPolicyBatchReplay`.

Batch Memory Update   It is easy to adapt the episodic memory to batch by using class inheritance and overriding the `add_experience` function, as shown in Code 3.4.

Batch memory does not require the nested structure of the episodic memory, so the current experience is added directly to the main memory containers in Code 3.4 (lines 8–9). If enough examples have been collected, the memory sets the agent's train flag (lines 14–15).

Code 3.4   `OnPolicyBatchReplay`: add experience

```
1   # slm_lab/agent/memory/onpolicy.py
2
3   class OnPolicyBatchReplay(OnPolicyReplay):
4       ...
5
6       def add_experience(self, state, action, reward, next_state, done):
7           self.most_recent = [state, action, reward, next_state, done]
8           for idx, k in enumerate(self.data_keys):
9               getattr(self, k).append(self.most_recent[idx])
```

```
10          # Track memory size and num experiences
11          self.size += 1
12          self.seen_size += 1
13          # Decide if agent is to train
14          if len(self.states) == self.body.agent.algorithm.training_frequency:
15              self.body.agent.algorithm.to_train = 1
```

3.6   Training a SARSA Agent

We configure a SARSA agent using a spec file shown in Code 3.5. The file is also available in SLM Lab at `slm_lab/spec/benchmark/sarsa/sarsa_cartpole.json`.

Code 3.5   A simple SARSA CartPole spec file

```
1   # slm_lab/spec/benchmark/sarsa/sarsa_cartpole.json
2
3   {
4     "sarsa_epsilon_greedy_cartpole": {
5       "agent": [{
6         "name": "SARSA",
7         "algorithm": {
8           "name": "SARSA",
9           "action_pdtype": "Argmax",
10          "action_policy": "epsilon_greedy",
11          "explore_var_spec": {
12            "name": "linear_decay",
13            "start_val": 1.0,
14            "end_val": 0.05,
15            "start_step": 0,
16            "end_step": 10000
17          },
18          "gamma": 0.99,
19          "training_frequency": 32
20        },
21        "memory": {
22          "name": "OnPolicyBatchReplay"
23        },
24        "net": {
25          "type": "MLPNet",
26          "hid_layers": [64],
27          "hid_layers_activation": "selu",
28          "clip_grad_val": 0.5,
29          "loss_spec": {
```

```
30          "name": "MSELoss"
31        },
32        "optim_spec": {
33          "name": "RMSprop",
34          "lr": 0.01
35        },
36        "lr_scheduler_spec": null
37      }
38    }],
39    "env": [{
40      "name": "CartPole-v0",
41      "max_t": null,
42      "max_frame": 100000
43    }],
44    "body": {
45      "product": "outer",
46      "num": 1
47    },
48    "meta": {
49      "distributed": false,
50      "eval_frequency": 2000,
51      "max_trial": 1,
52      "max_session": 4
53    },
54    ...
55  }
56 }
```

Let's walk through the main components.

- **Algorithm:** The algorithm is SARSA (line 6), the action policy is ε-greedy (line 10) with linear decay (lines 11–17) of the exploration variable ε, and γ is set on line 18.

- **Network architecture:** Multilayer perceptron with one hidden layer of 64 units and SeLU activation function (lines 25–27).

- **Optimizer:** The optimizer is RMSprop [50] with a learning rate of 0.01 (lines 32–35).

- **Training frequency:** Training is batch-wise because we have selected `OnPolicyBatchReplay` memory (line 22) and the batch size is 32 (line 19). This is controlled by the `training_frequency` parameter (line 19) since it means the network will be trained every 32 steps.

- **Environment:** The environment is OpenAI Gym's CartPole [18] (line 40).

- **Training length:** Training consists of 100,000 time steps (line 42).

■ **Evaluation:** The agent is evaluated every 2000 time steps (line 50). During evaluation, ε is set to its final value (line 14). Four episodes are run, then the mean total rewards are calculated and reported.

To train this SARSA agent using SLM Lab, run the commands shown in Code 3.6 in a terminal.

Code 3.6   Training a SARSA agent

```
1  conda activate lab
2  python run_lab.py slm_lab/spec/benchmark/sarsa/sarsa_cartpole.json
   ↪   sarsa_epsilon_greedy_cartpole train
```

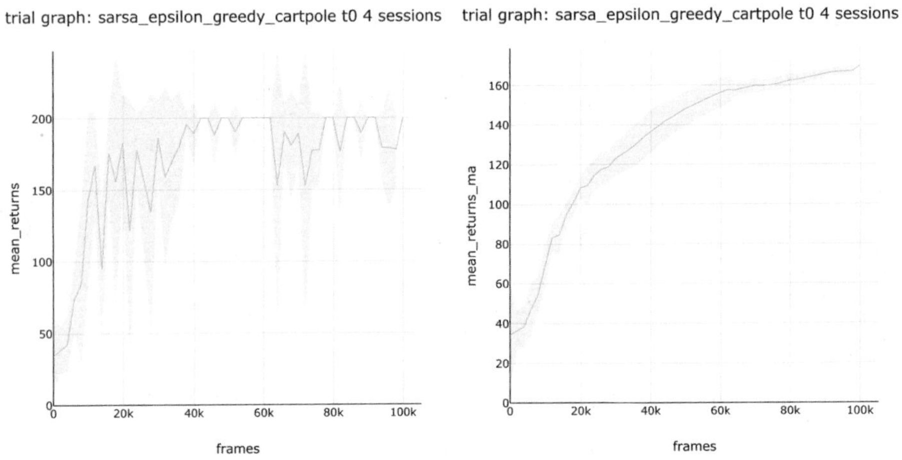

(a) Trial graph   (b) Trial graph with moving average

Figure 3.5   SARSA trial graphs from SLM Lab averaged over four sessions. The vertical axis shows the total rewards (`mean_return` for evaluation is computed without discount) averaged over eight episodes during checkpoints, and the horizontal axis shows the total training frames. The graph on the right is a moving average with a window of 100 evaluation checkpoints.

This will use the spec file to run a training `Trial` with four `Sessions` to obtain an average result. The result is then plotted with an error band. A moving average version with a window of 100 evaluations is also generated. Both graphs are shown in Figure 3.5.

3.7 Experimental Results

This section will look at the effect of learning rate on the performance of SARSA in the CartPole environment. We use the experimentation feature of SLM Lab to perform a grid search over the learning rates, then plot and compare them.

3.7.1 Experiment: The Effect of Learning Rate

The learning rate controls the size of the parameter update of a network. Higher learning rate can make learning faster, but it may also overshoot in parameter space if parameter updates are too large. Conversely, small learning rate is less likely to overshoot, but may take longer to converge. To find an optimal learning rate, we often use hyperparameter tuning.

In this experiment, we look at the effect of using different learning rates on SARSA by performing a grid search over multiple learning rates. To do so, use the spec file from Code 3.5 to add a search spec, as shown in Code 3.7. Line 10 specifies a grid search over a list of learning rate lr values. The full spec file is already available in SLM Lab at slm_lab/spec/benchmark/sarsa/sarsa_cartpole.json.

Code 3.7 SARSA spec file with search spec for different learning rate values

```
1   # slm_lab/spec/benchmark/sarsa/sarsa_cartpole.json
2
3   {
4     "sarsa_epsilon_greedy_cartpole": {
5       ...
6       "search": {
7         "agent": [{
8           "net": {
9             "optim_spec": {
10              "lr__grid_search": [0.0005, 0.001, 0.001, 0.005, 0.01, 0.05, 0.1]
11            }
12          }
13        }]
14      }
15    }
16  }
```

To run the experiment in SLM Lab, use the commands shown in Code 3.8.

Code 3.8 Run an experiment to search over different learning rates as defined in the spec file.

```
1   conda activate lab
2   python run_lab.py slm_lab/spec/benchmark/sarsa/sarsa_cartpole.json
    ↪   sarsa_epsilon_greedy_cartpole search
```

This will run an Experiment which spawns multiple Trials, each with a different value of lr substituted in the original SARSA spec. Each Trial runs four Sessions to obtain an average. The multitrial graph and its moving average over a window of 100 evaluation checkpoints are shown in Figure 3.6.

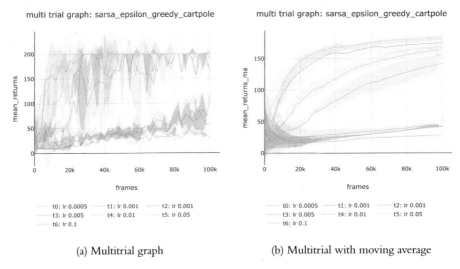

(a) Multitrial graph   (b) Multitrial with moving average

Figure 3.6   The effect of higher learning rates on the performance of SARSA. As expected, the agent learns faster with a higher learning rate.

Figure 3.6 shows a clear effect of increasing the learning rate on the learning curve of SARSA, as long as the learning rate is not too high. In trials 5 and 6, SARSA quickly obtains the maximum total reward of 200 for CartPole. In contrast, when learning rate is low, the agent learns too slowly, as shown in trials $0, 1, 2$.

3.8 Summary

The SARSA algorithm has two main elements—learning the Q-function with TD learning and a method for acting using the Q-value estimates.

First, we discussed why the Q-function is a good choice of value function to learn for SARSA. The Q-function is approximated with TD learning which seeks to minimize the difference between two formulations of the Q-function based on the Bellman equation. A crucial idea behind TD learning is that rewards are revealed over time in RL problems. It takes advantage of this to back up information from future time steps to earlier ones in the Q-function estimates.

After we learned the Q-function, we saw that a good policy can be derived by acting ε-greedily with respect to the Q-values. This means that the agent acts randomly with probability ε, otherwise it selects the action corresponding to the maximum Q-value estimate. The ε-greedy policy is a simple way to address the *exploration-exploitation* problem in RL. Agents need to balance exploiting what they know with exploring the environment to discover better solutions.

When implementing the SARSA algorithm, the most important components are the action function—a function for calculating the Q-values and the associated loss—and the training loop. These were implemented through `epsilon_greedy`, `calc_q_loss`, and the `train` methods. The experiences a SARSA agent collects are stored in an agent's `Memory`. These experiences are provided by the `Memory` to the agent each time training occurs. We saw that SARSA is an on-policy algorithm because $Q_{\text{tar}}^{\pi}(s, a)$, which is used to train the value network, depends on the experience-gathering policy. Using experiences that were not gathered under the current policy would lead to incorrect Q-values. Consequently, the `Memory` is cleared each time an agent trains.

Monte Carlo sampling and TD learning can be interpreted as occupying two ends of a spectrum of the tradeoff between bias and variance. The SARSA algorithm can be extended to incorporate this tradeoff by parameterizing the number of steps of actual rewards an agent uses before estimating the remaining value with the value network. This stands in contrast to the single step of actual rewards used in the standard SARSA algorithm. "Reinforcement Learning, An Introduction" [132] contains more details on this topic, as well as the related, more computationally efficient, approach involving eligibility traces.

3.9 Further Reading

- Chapters 4 and 5, *Reinforcement Learning: An Introduction, Second Edition*, Sutton and Barto, 2018 [132].

- *On-Line Q-Learning Using Connectionist Systems*, Rummery and Niranjan, 1994 [118].

- "Temporal Difference Learning and TD-Gammon," Tesauro, 1995, pp. 58–68 [135].

3.10 History

Temporal difference (TD) techniques were first used almost sixty years ago by Arthur Samuel in his checkers-playing algorithm [119, 120]. Thirty years later, Richard Sutton provided the first formal results [131], proving the convergence of a subset of linear TD algorithms. In 1997, Tsitsiklis and Van Roy [137] extended this, proving the convergence of TD algorithms in general with linear function approximators. TD learning is also behind the earliest deep reinforcement learning algorithm, TD-Gammon [135]. Gerald Tesauro's algorithm combined a multilayer perceptron with TD learning and self-play to achieve master-level performance in 1991. The assessment was conducted by Bill Robertie, a backgammon grandmaster and former world champion [135]. For more information, see "Temporal Difference Learning and TD-Gammon," Gerald Tesauro, originally published in *Communications of the ACM*, March 1995.

The Bellman equation was named after Richard Bellman, a renowned mathematician who invented dynamic programming [34]. The Bellman equation incorporates the "Principle of Optimality" [16] which states that "an optimal policy has the property that whatever the initial state and initial decisions are, the remaining decisions must constitute an optimal policy with regard to the state resulting from the first decision." It can be summarized as follows. Suppose you knew how to act perfectly in for all future states except the current state. Then the optimal action in the current state reduces to comparing the outcomes from all the possible actions in the current state, incorporating your knowledge about the value of actions in all of the following states, and selecting the best one. That is, the value of the current state can be defined recursively in terms of the value of future states. See "Richard Bellman on the Birth of Dynamic Programming" by Stuart Dreyfus [34] for a brief and charming history, in Bellman's own words, of the emergence of dynamic programming.

4

Deep Q-Networks (DQN)

This chapter introduces the Deep Q-Networks algorithm (DQN) proposed by Mnih et al. [88] in 2013. Like SARSA, DQN is a value-based temporal difference (TD) algorithm that approximates the Q-function. The learned Q-function is then used by an agent to select actions. DQN is only applicable to environments with discrete action spaces. However, DQN learns a different Q-function compared to SARSA—the *optimal* Q-function instead of the Q-function for the current policy. This small but crucial change improves the stability and speed of learning.

In Section 4.1, we first discuss why DQN learns the optimal Q-function by looking at the Bellman equation for DQN. One important implication is that this makes DQN an *off-policy* algorithm. This optimal Q-function does not depend on the data-gathering policy, which means DQN can learn from experiences gathered by any agent.

In theory, any policy can be used to generate training data for DQN. In practice, however, some policies are more appropriate than others. Section 4.2 looks at the characteristics of a good data-gathering policy and introduces the Boltzmann policy as an alternative to the ε-greedy policy discussed in Section 3.4.

In Section 4.3, we consider how to use the fact that DQN is off-policy to improve its sample efficiency compared to SARSA. During training, the experiences gathered by older policies are stored in an experience replay [82] memory and are reused.

Section 4.4 presents the DQN algorithm and in Section 4.5 we discuss an example implementation. The chapter ends with a comparison of DQN agent performance in the CartPole environment from OpenAI Gym as we vary the network architecture.

We will see in this chapter that it only takes a small change to the Q-function update to transform SARSA into DQN, but the result is an algorithm which addresses many of SARSA's limitations. DQN makes it possible to decorrelate and reuse experiences by sampling random batches from a large experience replay memory, and allows for multiple parameter updates using the same batch. These ideas, which significantly improve DQN's efficiency relative to SARSA, are the subject of this chapter.

4.1   Learning the Q-Function in DQN

DQN, like SARSA, learns the Q-function using TD learning. Where the two algorithms differ is in how $Q_{\text{tar}}^{\pi}(s, a)$ is constructed.

Equations 4.1 and 4.2 show the Bellman equation for DQN and SARSA, respectively.

$$Q_{\text{DQN}}^{\pi}(s, a) \approx r + \gamma \max_{a'} Q^{\pi}(s', a') \tag{4.1}$$

$$Q_{\text{SARSA}}^{\pi}(s, a) \approx r + \gamma Q^{\pi}(s', a') \tag{4.2}$$

Correspondingly, Equations 4.3 and 4.4 show how $Q_{\text{tar}}^{\pi}(s, a)$ is constructed in each algorithm.

$$Q_{\text{tar:DQN}}^{\pi}(s, a) = r + \gamma \max_{a'} Q^{\pi}(s', a') \tag{4.3}$$

$$Q_{\text{tar:SARSA}}^{\pi}(s, a) = r + \gamma Q^{\pi}(s', a') \tag{4.4}$$

Instead of using the action a' actually taken in the next state s' to estimate $Q_{\text{tar}}^{\pi}(s, a)$, DQN uses the maximum Q-value over all of the potential actions available in that state.

In DQN, the Q-value that is used in the next state s' doesn't depend on the policy used to gather experiences. Since the reward r and the next state s' are produced by the environment given the current state s and action a, this means that no part of the $Q_{\text{tar:DQN}}^{\pi}(s, a)$ estimation depends on the data-gathering policy. This makes DQN an *off-policy* algorithm because the function being learned is independent of the policy being followed to act in the environment and gather experiences [132]. In contrast, SARSA is on-policy because it uses the action a' taken by the current policy in state s' to calculate the Q-value for the next state. It directly depends on the policy used to gather experiences.

Suppose we have two policies π^1 and π^2 and let $\hat{Q}^{\pi^1}(s, a)$ and $\hat{Q}^{\pi^2}(s, a)$ be the Q-functions which correspond to these policies. Let (s, a, r, s', a_1') be a sequence of data generated using π^1, and (s, a, r, s', a_2'), by π^2. If π^1 is the current policy and π^2 is an older policy from an earlier point in the training process, then Section 3.4.1 showed how using (s, a, r, s', a_2') to update the parameters of $\hat{Q}^{\pi^1}(s, a)$ would be incorrect.

However, if we are using DQN, then neither a_1' or a_2' are used when calculating $Q_{\text{tar:DQN}}^{\pi}(s, a)$. Since the next state s' is the same in both cases, each experience results in the same value for $Q_{\text{tar:DQN}}^{\pi}(s, a) = r + \gamma \max_{a'} Q^{\pi}(s', a')$, and so both are valid. Even though different policies were used to gather each sequence of data, $Q_{\text{tar:DQN}}^{\pi}(s, a)$ is the same.

If the transition and reward functions are stochastic, then choosing action a in state s multiple times may result in a different r and a different s'. Q^{π} accounts for this because it is defined as the *expected* future return from taking action a in state s, so it is still valid to use (s, a, r, s', a_2') to update $\hat{Q}^{\pi^1}(s, a)$. Another way of looking at this is that the environment is responsible for the reward r and transition into the next state s'. This is external to the agent and the agent's policy, so $Q_{\text{tar:DQN}}^{\pi}(s, a)$ is still independent of the policy used to gather experiences.

If $Q^{\pi}_{\text{tar:DQN}}(s, a)$ does not depend on the policy used to gather the data, then what policy does it correspond to? It is the optimal policy as defined by Sutton and Barto [132]:

> A policy π' is defined to be better than or equal to a policy π if its expected return is greater than or equal to that of π for all states. In other words, $\pi' \geq \pi$ if and only if $V^{\pi'}(s) \geq V^{\pi}(s)$ for all $s \in \mathcal{S}$. There is always at least one policy that is better than or equal to all other policies. This is an optimal policy, π^*.

The optimal Q-function is defined as taking action a in state s and afterwards following the optimal policy π^*. This is shown in Equation 4.5.

$$Q^*(s, a) = \max_{\pi} Q^{\pi}(s, a) = Q^{\pi^*}(s, a) \tag{4.5}$$

Let's reconsider $Q^{\pi}_{\text{tar:DQN}}(s, a)$ in light of Equation 4.5. If the estimates for Q^{π} were correct, then selecting the action which maximizes $Q^{\pi}(s', a')$ would be optimal. It is the best an agent could possibly do. This implies that the policy that $Q^{\pi}_{\text{tar:DQN}}(s, a)$ corresponds to is the optimal policy π^*.

It is important to note that just because DQN's objective is to learn the optimal Q-function doesn't mean it will. There may be many reasons for this. For example, the hypothesis space represented by the neural network may not actually contain the optimal Q-function; nonconvex optimization methods are imperfect and might not find a global minimum; and computation and time constraints place a limit on how long we can train an agent. However, we can say that the upper bound on performance with DQN is optimal, compared to a potentially suboptimal upper bound for SARSA resulting from learning the Q-function under an ε-greedy policy.

4.2 Action Selection in DQN

Even though DQN is an off-policy algorithm, how a DQN agent gathers experiences still matters. There are two important factors to consider.

First, an agent still faces the exploration-exploitation tradeoff discussed in Chapter 3. An agent should rapidly explore the state-action space at the beginning of training to increase the chances of discovering good ways to act in an environment. As training progresses and the agent learns more, it should gradually decrease the rate of exploration and spend more time exploiting what it has learned. This improves the efficiency of training as the agent focuses on better actions.

Second, if the state-action space is very large because it consists of continuous values or is discrete with high dimensionality,[1] then it will be intractable to experience all (s, a) pairs, even once. In this case, Q-values for the unvisited (s, a) pairs may be no better than random guessing.

---

1. For example, the state space might be described via digital representations of images. Pixels values are typically discrete, such as between 0 and 255 for a grayscale image, but a single image can have thousands or millions of such pixels.

Fortunately, function approximation with neural networks mitigates this problem because they are able generalize from visited (s, a) pairs to similar[2] states and actions, as discussed in Box 4.1. However, this does not completely solve the problem. There may still be parts of the state-action space that are far away and very different to the states and actions an agent has experienced. A neural network is unlikely to generalize well in these cases and the estimated Q-values may be inaccurate.

Box 4.1 Generalization and Neural Networks

An important property of function-approximation methods is how well they generalize to unseen inputs. For example, how good is a Q-function estimate for unvisited (s, a) pairs? Linear (e.g., linear regression) and nonlinear (e.g., neural networks) function approximation methods are both capable of some generalization, whereas tabular methods are not.

Let's consider a tabular representation for $\hat{Q}^\pi(s, a)$. Suppose the state-action space is very large, with millions of (s, a) pairs, and at the beginning of training each cell representing a particular $\hat{Q}^\pi(s, a)$ is initialized to 0. During training, an agent visits (s, a) pairs and the table is updated, but the unvisited (s, a) pairs continue to have $\hat{Q}^\pi(s, a) = 0$. Since the state-action space is large, many (s, a) pairs will remain unvisited and their Q-value estimates will remain at 0 even if (s, a) is desirable, with $Q^\pi(s, a) \gg 0$. The main issue is that a tabular function representation does not learn anything about how different states and actions relate to each other.

In contrast, neural networks can extrapolate from Q-values for known (s, a) to unknown (s', a') because they learn how different states and actions are related to each other. This is very useful when (s, a) is large or has infinitely many elements because it means an agent does not have to visit all (s, a) to learn a good estimate of the Q-function. An agent only needs to visit a representative subset of the state-action space.

There are limitations to how well a network will generalize, and there are two common cases where it often fails. First, if a network receives inputs that are significantly different to the inputs it has been trained on, it is unlikely to produce good outputs. Generalization is typically much better in small neighborhoods of the input space surrounding the training data. Second, neural networks are likely to generalize poorly if the function they are approximating has sharp discontinuities. This is because neural networks implicitly assume that the input

---

2. There are many ways to define what a similar state or action means; this is a large topic in its own right. A simple measure of similarity is the L2 distance. The smaller the distance, the more similar two states or actions are. However, for high-dimensional states such as images, the L2 distance in pixel space may not capture important similarities—for example, similar game states may look visually different. Other approaches try to deal with this problem, for instance, by first learning a lower-dimensional representation of states and then measuring the L2 distance between state representations.

space is locally smooth. If the inputs x and x' are similar, then the corresponding outputs y and y' should also be similar.

Consider the example shown in Figure 4.1. It represents a one-dimensional environment in which an agent can walk on a flat mountain top. The state is the agent's position on the x-axis, the action is the change in x per time step δx, and the reward is shown on the y-axis. There is a cliff in this environment—a vertical drop in the reward when the agent reaches state $s = x = 1$. "Falling off" the cliff by moving from $s = x = 0.99$ to $s' = x' = 1.0$ will lead to a sharp drop in the reward received even though s and s' are close to each other. Moving the same distance in other parts of the state space does not produce such a significant change in reward.

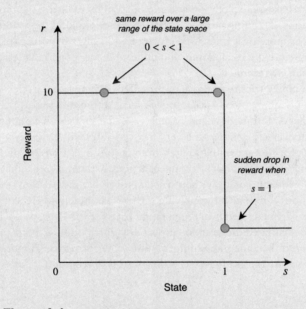

Figure 4.1   Cliff environment with a discontinuous reward function

If an environment has a large state–action space, it is unlikely that an agent will be able to learn good Q-value estimates for all parts of this space. It is still possible to achieve good performance in such environments if an agent focuses learning on the states and actions that a good policy is likely to visit often. When this strategy is combined with neural networks, the Q-function approximation is likely to be good in local regions surrounding the commonly visited parts of the state–action space.

The policy used by a DQN agent should therefore visit states and select actions that are reasonably similar to those that would be visited by acting greedily with respect to the agent's current Q-function estimate, which is the current estimate of the optimal policy. We say that the two policies should generate similar data distributions.

In practice, this can be achieved by using the ε-greedy policy discussed in Chapter 3 or the Boltzmann policy introduced in the next section. Using either of these policies helps focus the agent on learning from data it would likely experience when using its estimate of the optimal policy.[3]

4.2.1   The Boltzmann Policy

A greedy or an ε-greedy policy are not the only options available to a DQN or SARSA agent. In this section we discuss a third option—the Boltzmann policy, named after the Boltzmann probability distribution.

Good policies should strike a balance between exploring the state-action space and exploiting knowledge learned by an agent.

ε-greedy policies balance exploration and exploitation by reducing the probability ε of taking random actions as training progresses. Such a policy explores more at the start of training, and exploits more over time. One problem with this is that the exploration strategy is naive. Agents explore randomly and do not use any previously learned knowledge about the environment.

The Boltzmann policy tries to improve over random exploration by selecting actions using their relative Q-values. The Q-value-maximizing action a in state s will be selected most often, but other actions with relatively high Q-values will also have a high probability of being chosen. Conversely, actions with very low Q-values will hardly ever be taken. This has the effect of focusing exploration on more promising actions off the Q-value-maximizing path instead of selecting all actions with equal probability.

To produce a Boltzmann policy, we construct a probability distribution over the Q-values for all actions a in state s by applying the softmax function (Equation 4.6). The softmax function is parameterized by a temperature parameter $\tau \in (0, \infty)$, which controls how uniform or concentrated the resulting probability distribution is. High values of τ push the distribution to become more uniform, low values of τ make it more concentrated. Actions are then sampled according to this distribution, as shown in Equation 4.7.

$$p_{\text{softmax}}(a \mid s) = \frac{e^{Q^{\pi}(s,a)}}{\sum\limits_{a'} e^{Q^{\pi}(s,a')}} \tag{4.6}$$

$$p_{\text{boltzmann}}(a \mid s) = \frac{e^{Q^{\pi}(s,a)/\tau}}{\sum\limits_{a'} e^{Q^{\pi}(s,a')/\tau}} \tag{4.7}$$

The role of the temperature parameter τ in the Boltzmann policy is analogous to that of ε in the ε-greedy policy. It encourages exploration of the state-action space. To see why, let's look at the examples shown in Equation 4.8.

---

3. The challenges of learning a Q-function for a large state-action space also apply to SARSA. However, since SARSA is on-policy, learning is automatically focused on the area of the state-action space that is frequently visited by the policy.

$$\begin{aligned}
\text{Softmax:} \qquad & x : [1,2] \to p(x) : [0.27, 0.73] \\
\text{Boltzmann, } \tau = 5: \qquad & x : [1,2] \to p(x) : [0.45, 0.55] \\
\text{Boltzmann, } \tau = 2: \qquad & x : [1,2] \to p(x) : [0.38, 0.62] \\
\text{Boltzmann, } \tau = 0.5: \qquad & x : [1,2] \to p(x) : [0.12, 0.88] \\
\text{Boltzmann, } \tau = 0.1: \qquad & x : [1,2] \to p(x) : [0.00, 1.00]
\end{aligned} \qquad (4.8)$$

High values of τ (e.g., $\tau = 5$) move the probability distribution closer to a uniform distribution. This results in an agent acting very randomly. Low values of τ (e.g., 0.1) increase the probability of the action corresponding to the largest Q-value, so the agent will act more greedily. $\tau = 1$ reduces to the softmax function. Adjusting the value of τ during training balances exploration and exploitation: high values of τ at the beginning of training will encourage exploration; as τ is decreased over time, the policy will approach the greedy policy.

The main advantage of the Boltzmann policy when compared to the ε-greedy policy is that it explores the environment less randomly. Each time an agent selects an action, it samples a from the probability distribution over the actions generated by the Boltzmann policy. Instead of acting randomly with probability ε, the agent selects action a with probability $p_{\text{boltzmann}}(a \mid s)$, so actions with higher Q-values are more likely to be chosen. Even if an agent does not select the Q-maximizing action, it is more likely to select the second than the third or fourth best action as measured by $\hat{Q}^{\pi}(s, a)$.

A Boltzmann policy also results in a smoother relationship between Q-value estimates and action probabilities compared to an ε-greedy policy. Consider the example shown in Table 4.1. There are two available actions, a_1 and a_2, in state s. Table 4.1 compares the probability of selecting a_1 and a_2 in state s under the ε-greedy and Boltzmann policies as we vary $Q^{\pi}(s, a_1)$ and $Q^{\pi}(s, a_2)$. In this example, $\tau = 1$ and $\varepsilon = 0.1$.

Table 4.1   Action probabilities: this table compares the probabilities of selecting a_1 and a_2 in s when using an ε-greedy and a Boltzmann policy as $Q^{\pi}(s, a)$ is varied, with $\tau = 1$ and $\varepsilon = 0.1$.

$Q^{\pi}(s, a_1)$	$Q^{\pi}(s, a_2)$	$p_{\varepsilon}(a_1 \mid s)$	$p_{\varepsilon}(a_2 \mid s)$	$p_B(a_1 \mid s)$	$p_B(a_2 \mid s)$
1.00	9.00	0.05	0.95	0.00	1.00
4.00	6.00	0.05	0.95	0.12	0.88
4.90	5.10	0.05	0.95	0.45	0.55
5.05	4.95	0.95	0.05	0.53	0.48
7.00	3.00	0.95	0.05	0.98	0.02
8.00	2.00	0.95	0.05	1.00	0.00

The two leftmost columns show the Q-values for a_1 and a_2. When these values are very different—for example, when $Q^{\pi}(s, a_1) = 1$ and $Q^{\pi}(s, a_2) = 9$—both policies assign low probability to a_1. However, when these values are similar—for example, when $Q^{\pi}(s, a_1) = 5.05$ and $Q^{\pi}(s, a_2) = 4.95$—the ε-greedy policy assigns most of the probability to a_2 since it corresponds to the maximum Q-value. In contrast, the Boltzmann policy assigns almost equal probability to both actions, $p(a_1) = 0.53$ and $p(a_2) = 0.48$.

Intuitively, this seems better than the ε-greedy policy. Actions a_1 and a_2 are approximately equivalent to take in s because they have very similar Q-values, so they should be selected with roughly equal probability. This is what the Boltzmann policy does. ε-greedy policies lead to more extreme behavior. If one of the Q-values is a fraction higher than the other, an ε-greedy policy will assign all of the nonrandom probability $(1 - \varepsilon)$ to that action. If in the next iteration the other Q-value becomes slightly higher, ε-greedy will immediately switch and assign all of the nonrandom probability to the other action. An ε-greedy policy can therefore be more unstable than a Boltzmann policy, which can make it more difficult for an agent to learn.

A Boltzmann policy can cause an agent to get stuck in a local minimum if the Q-function estimate is inaccurate for some parts of the state space. Consider again two actions, a_1 and a_2, available in s. Let $Q^*(s, a_1) = 2$ and $Q^*(s, a_2) = 10$, and suppose the current estimate is $\hat{Q}^\pi(s, a_1) = 2.5$ and $\hat{Q}^\pi(s, a_2) = -3$. The optimal action is a_2, but the Boltzmann policy will have an extremely low probability of selecting a_2 ($< 0.5\%$ if $\tau = 1$). This leaves very few opportunities for the agent to try a_2 and discover that it is better. The agent is likely to remain stuck taking a_1 in s. In contrast, an ε-greedy policy will select a_2 with probability $p = \varepsilon/2$ regardless of the Q-value estimates. This makes it more likely that the Q-value estimate will be corrected over time.

One way to tackle this problem with the Boltzmann policy is to use a large value of τ at the beginning of training so that the action probability distribution is more uniform. As training progresses and the agent learns more, τ can be decayed, allowing the agent to exploit what it has learned. However, care must be taken not to decay τ too quickly, otherwise a policy may get stuck in a local minimum.

4.3 Experience Replay

In this section we discuss how DQN improves on the sample efficiency of SARSA by using an *experience replay* memory [82]. Let's first look at two things that make on-policy algorithms sample-inefficient.

First, we have seen that on-policy algorithms can only use data gathered by the current policy to update the policy parameters. Each experience is used just once. This is problematic when combined with function approximation methods which learn using gradient descent, such as neural networks. Each parameter update must be small, because the gradient only conveys meaningful information about a descent direction in a small area around the current parameter values. However, the optimal parameter update for some experiences may be large—for example, if there is a large difference between the Q-value a network predicts, $\hat{Q}^\pi(s, a_1)$ and $Q^\pi(s, a_1)$. In these cases, a network's parameters may need to be updated many times, using the experiences, to make use of all of the information conveyed in them. On-policy algorithms cannot do this.

Second, the experiences used to train on-policy algorithms are highly correlated. This is because the data used to compute a single parameter update is often from a single episode, whereas future states and rewards depend on previous states and actions.[4] This can lead to high variance in parameter updates.

Off-policy algorithms such as DQN do not have to discard experiences once they have been used. Long-Ji Lin [82] first made this observation in 1992 and proposed an augmentation to Q-learning called *experience replay*. He observed that TD learning could be slow due to the trial-and-error mechanism for gathering data inherent in RL and the need to propagate information backwards through time. Speeding up TD learning amounts to either speeding up the credit assignment process or shortening the trial-and-error process [82]. Experience replay focuses on the latter by facilitating the reuse of experiences.

An experience replay memory stores the k most recent experiences an agent has gathered. If memory is full, the oldest experience is discarded to make space for the latest one. Each time an agent trains, one or more batches of data are sampled random-uniformly from the experience replay memory. Each of these batches is used in turn to update the parameters of the Q-function network. k is typically quite large, between 10,000 and 1,000,000, whereas the number of elements in a batch is much smaller, typically between 32 and 2048.

The size of the memory should be large enough to contain many episodes of experiences. Each batch will typically contain experiences from different episodes and different policies, which decorrelates the experiences used to train an agent. In turn, this reduces the variance of the parameter updates, helping to stabilize training. However, the memory should also be small enough so that each experience is likely to be sampled more than once before being discarded, which makes learning more efficient.

Discarding the oldest experiences is also important. As an agent learns, the distribution of (s, a) pairs that an agent experiences changes. Older experiences become less useful because an agent is less likely to visit the older states. With finite time and computational resources, it is preferable for an agent to focus on learning from the more recently gathered experiences, since these tend to be more relevant. Storing just the k most recent experiences in the memory implements this idea.

4.4   DQN Algorithm

Having introduced all of the components of DQN, we now describe the algorithm. The pseudocode for DQN with a Boltzmann policy is given in Algorithm 4.1. The Q-function estimate $\hat{Q}^{\pi}(s, a)$ is parameterized by a network with parameters θ, denoted Q^{π_θ}, so we have $\hat{Q}^{\pi}(s, a) = Q^{\pi_\theta}(s, a)$.

---

4. It is possible to collect multiple episodes of data. However, this delays learning and the experiences within each episode are still highly correlated.

Algorithm 4.1   DQN

 1: Initialize learning rate α
 2: Initialize τ
 3: Initialize number of batches per training step, B
 4: Initialize number of updates per batch, U
 5: Initialize batch size N
 6: Initialize experience replay memory with max size K
 7: Randomly initialize the network parameters θ
 8: **for** $m = 1 \ldots MAX\_STEPS$ **do**
 9:     Gather and store h experiences (s_i, a_i, r_i, s_i') using the current policy
10:     **for** $b = 1 \ldots B$ **do**
11:         Sample a batch b of experiences from the experience replay memory
12:         **for** $u = 1 \ldots U$ **do**
13:             **for** $i = 1 \ldots N$ **do**
14:                 # Calculate target Q-values for each example
15:                 $y_i = r_i + \delta_{s_i'} \gamma \max_{a_i'} Q^{\pi_\theta}(s_i', a_i')$ where $\delta_{s_i'} = 0$ if s_i' is terminal,
                    $\hookrightarrow$ 1 otherwise
16:             **end for**
17:             # Calculate the loss, for example using MSE
18:             $L(\theta) = \frac{1}{N} \sum_i (y_i - Q^{\pi_\theta}(s_i, a_i))^2$
19:             # Update the network's parameters
20:             $\theta = \theta - \alpha \nabla_\theta L(\theta)$
21:         **end for**
22:     **end for**
23:     Decay τ
24: **end for**

We start by gathering and storing some data (line 9) using the Boltzmann policy with Q-values generating using the current Q^{π_θ}. Note that we could also use an ε-greedy policy. To train an agent, sample B batches of experiences from the experience replay memory (lines 10–11). For each batch of data, complete U parameter updates as follows. First, we calculate the target Q-values for each element in the batch (line 15). Notice that this calculation involves selecting the Q-value-maximizing action in the next state s'. This is one reason why DQN is only applicable to environments with discrete action spaces. When the action space is discrete, this calculation is straightforward—we simply calculate the Q-values for all the actions and select the maximum. However, when the action space is continuous, there are infinitely many possible actions—we cannot calculate the Q-value for every action. The other reason is the same as we saw for SARSA: the Q-value-maximizing action is required for the ε-greedy policy.

Then, we calculate the loss (line 18). Finally, calculate the gradient of the loss and update the network parameters θ (line 20). After a full training step has been completed (lines 10–22), update τ (line 23).

Algorithm 4.1 demonstrates two practical consequences of DQN being an off-policy algorithm. First, in each training iteration we can use more than one batch of experiences to update the Q-function estimate. Second, the agent is not limited to one parameter update per batch. If desired, the Q-function approximator can be trained to convergence for each batch. These steps increase the computational burden per training iteration when compared to SARSA, but they can also make learning significantly faster. There is a tradeoff between learning more from the experiences the agent has currently gathered and using the improved Q-function to gather better experiences to learn from. The number of parameter updates per batch, U, and the number of batches per training step, B, reflect this tradeoff. Good values for these parameters depend on the problem and computational resources available; however, 1 to 5 batches and parameter updates per batch are common.

4.5   Implementing DQN

DQN can be understood as a modification to the SARSA algorithm. In this section, we will see how DQN can be implemented as an extension to the SARSA class in SLM Lab.

VanillaDQN extends SARSA and reuses most of its methods. Since the Q-function estimate in DQN is different, we need to override calc_q_loss. train also needs to be changed to reflect the additional choices of the number of batches and parameter updates per batch. Finally, we need to implement experience replay. This is handled through a new Memory class, Replay.

4.5.1   Calculating the Q-Loss

DQN's calc_q_loss method is shown in Code 4.1. Its form is very similar to SARSA's.

First, $\hat{Q}^{\pi}(s, a)$ is calculated for all the actions for each state s in the batch (line 9). We repeat the same step for the next state s' but without tracking the gradient (lines 10–11).

Then, we select the Q-value estimate for the action a taken by the agent in the current state s for each experience in the batch (line 12). Line 13 selects the maximum Q-value estimate for each of the next states and this is used to calculate $Q^{\pi}_{\text{tar:DQN}}(s, a)$ (line 14). Finally, we calculate the loss using $\hat{Q}^{\pi}(s, a)$ and $Q^{\pi}_{\text{tar:DQN}}(s, a)$ (act_q_preds and max_q_targets, respectively).

Code 4.1   DQN implementation: calculating Q-targets and the corresponding loss

```
1   # slm_lab/agent/algorithms/dqn.py
2
3   class VanillaDQN(SARSA):
4       ...
5
6       def calc_q_loss(self, batch):
7           states = batch['states']
8           next_states = batch['next_states']
```

```
9         q_preds = self.net(states)
10        with torch.no_grad():
11            next_q_preds = self.net(next_states)
12        act_q_preds = q_preds.gather(-1,
          ↪ batch['actions'].long().unsqueeze(-1)).squeeze(-1)
13        max_next_q_preds, _ = next_q_preds.max(dim=-1, keepdim=False)
14        max_q_targets = batch['rewards'] + self.gamma * (1 - batch['dones']) *
          ↪ max_next_q_preds
15        q_loss = self.net.loss_fn(act_q_preds, max_q_targets)
16        ...
17        return q_loss
```

4.5.2 DQN Training Loop

The training loop in Code 4.2 proceeds as follows:

1. At each time step, `train` is called and the agent checks if it is ready to train (line 10). The `self.to_train` flag is set by the memory class.

2. If it is time to train, the agent samples `self.training_iter` batches from memory (line 12) by calling `self.sample()` (line 13).

3. Each batch is used to make `self.training_batch_iter` parameter updates (lines 15–18). Each parameter update proceeds as follows.

4. Calculate the Q-loss for the `batch` (line 16).

5. Use the Q-loss to make a single update of the value network parameters (line 17). With the loss defined, PyTorch conveniently handles the parameter update using automatic differentiation.

6. Accumulate the loss (line 18).

7. After all of the parameter updates have been completed, compute the average loss for logging (line 19).

8. Reset `self.to_train` to 0 to ensure that the agent is not trained until it is ready again (line 20).

Code 4.2   DQN implementation: training method

```
1   # slm_lab/agent/algorithms/dqn.py
2
3   class VanillaDQN(SARSA):
4       ...
5
6       @lab_api
```

```
7      def train(self):
8          ...
9          clock = self.body.env.clock
10         if self.to_train == 1:
11             total_loss = torch.tensor(0.0)
12             for _ in range(self.training_iter):
13                 batch = self.sample()
14                 ...
15                 for _ in range(self.training_batch_iter):
16                     loss = self.calc_q_loss(batch)
17                     self.net.train_step(loss, self.optim, self.lr_scheduler,
                     ↪ clock=clock, global_net=self.global_net)
18                     total_loss += loss
19             loss = total_loss / (self.training_iter *
                 ↪ self.training_batch_iter)
20             self.to_train = 0
21             return loss.item()
22         else:
23             return np.nan
```

4.5.3 Replay Memory

This section looks at the Replay memory class which implements experience replay. This section can be skipped on a first reading without loss of understanding of the DQN algorithm. It is sufficient to understand the main ideas behind experience replay discussed in Section 4.3.

Replay memory conforms to the Memory API in SLM Lab, and has three core methods—memory reset, adding an experience, and sampling a batch.

Replay Memory Initialization and Reset   __init__ in Code 4.3 initializes the class variables, including the storage keys in line 20. In Replay memory, we need to keep track of the current size of the memory (self.size) and the location of the most recent experience (self.head). It then calls reset to construct empty data structures.

reset is used to create the data structures. In Replay memory all the experience data is stored in lists. Unlike OnPolicyReplay from Section 2.6.6, this is only called once when the memory is initialized. The memory is retained across training steps so that experiences can be reused.

Code 4.3   Replay: init and reset

```
1   # slm_lab/agent/memory/replay.py
2
3   class Replay(Memory):
```

```
4          ...
5
6        def __init__(self, memory_spec, body):
7            super().__init__(memory_spec, body)
8            util.set_attr(self, self.memory_spec, [
9                'batch_size',
10               'max_size',
11               'use_cer',
12           ])
13           self.is_episodic = False
14           self.batch_idxs = None
15           self.size = 0  # total experiences stored
16           self.seen_size = 0  # total experiences seen cumulatively
17           self.head = -1  # index of most recent experience
18           self.ns_idx_offset = self.body.env.num_envs if body.env.is_venv else 1
19           self.ns_buffer = deque(maxlen=self.ns_idx_offset)
20           self.data_keys = ['states', 'actions', 'rewards', 'next_states',
                 ↪ 'dones']
21           self.reset()
22
23       def reset(self):
24           for k in self.data_keys:
25               if k != 'next_states':  # reuse self.states
26                   setattr(self, k, [None] * self.max_size)
27           self.size = 0
28           self.head = -1
29           self.ns_buffer.clear()
```

Replay Memory Update   add_experience in Replay memory (Code 4.4) behaves differently from the on-policy memory classes.

To add an experience, increment self.head, the index of the most recent experience, wrapping around back to 0 if the index is incremented out of bounds (line 13). If the memory is not full, it will point to a blank slot in the memory. If it is full, it will point to the oldest experience, which will be replaced. This way, Replay stores the self.max_size most recent experiences. Next, the experience is added to memory (lines 14–18) by setting the values of the elements in the storage lists indexed by self.head to the elements of the current experience. Lines 20–22 track the actual size of the memory and the total number of experiences gathered by the agent, and lines 23–24 set the training flag, algorithm.to_train.

Code 4.4 Replay: add experience

```
1   # slm_lab/agent/memory/replay.py
2
3   class Replay(Memory):
4       ...
5
6       @lab_api
7       def update(self, state, action, reward, next_state, done):
8           ...
9           self.add_experience(state, action, reward, next_state, done)
10
11      def add_experience(self, state, action, reward, next_state, done):
12          # Move head pointer. Wrap around if necessary
13          self.head = (self.head + 1) % self.max_size
14          self.states[self.head] = state.astype(np.float16)
15          self.actions[self.head] = action
16          self.rewards[self.head] = reward
17          self.ns_buffer.append(next_state.astype(np.float16))
18          self.dones[self.head] = done
19          # Actually occupied size of memory
20          if self.size < self.max_size:
21              self.size += 1
22          self.seen_size += 1
23          algorithm = self.body.agent.algorithm
24          algorithm.to_train = algorithm.to_train or (self.seen_size >
              ↪ algorithm.training_start_step and self.head %
              ↪ algorithm.training_frequency == 0)
```

Replay Memory Sample Sampling a batch involves sampling a set of valid indices and using these indices to extract the relevant examples from each of the memory storage lists to build a batch (see Code 4.5). First, `batch_size` indices are selected by calling the `sample_idxs` function (line 8). The indices are sampled random-uniformly with replacement from a list of indices $\in \{0, \ldots, \texttt{self.size}\}$ (line 18). If `self.size == self.max_size`, the memory is full, and this corresponds to sampling indices from the entire memory store. The batch is then assembled using these indices (lines 9–14).

One further detail regarding sampling is worth mentioning. To save space in memory (RAM), the next states are not explicitly stored. They already exist in the state buffer, with the exception of the very latest next state. Consequently, assembling the batch of next states is a little more involved and is handled by the `sample_next_states` function called in line 12. Interested readers can look at the implementation in SLM Lab at `slm_lab/agent/memory/replay.py`.

Code 4.5   Replay: sample

```
1   # slm_lab/agent/memory/replay.py
2
3   class Replay(Memory):
4       ...
5
6       @lab_api
7       def sample(self):
8           self.batch_idxs = self.sample_idxs(self.batch_size)
9           batch = {}
10          for k in self.data_keys:
11              if k == 'next_states':
12                  batch[k] = sample_next_states(self.head, self.max_size,
                    ↪ self.ns_idx_offset, self.batch_idxs, self.states,
                    ↪ self.ns_buffer)
13              else:
14                  batch[k] = util.batch_get(getattr(self, k), self.batch_idxs)
15          return batch
16
17      def sample_idxs(self, batch_size):
18          batch_idxs = np.random.randint(self.size, size=batch_size)
19          ...
20          return batch_idxs
```

4.6   Training a DQN Agent

Code 4.6 is an example spec file which trains a DQN agent. The file is available in SLM Lab at slm_lab/spec/benchmark/dqn/dqn_cartpole.json.

Code 4.6   A DQN spec file

```
1   # slm_lab/spec/benchmark/dqn/dqn_cartpole.json
2
3   {
4     "vanilla_dqn_boltzmann_cartpole": {
5       "agent": [{
6         "name": "VanillaDQN",
7         "algorithm": {
8           "name": "VanillaDQN",
9           "action_pdtype": "Categorical",
10          "action_policy": "boltzmann",
11          "explore_var_spec": {
12            "name": "linear_decay",
```

```
13              "start_val": 5.0,
14              "end_val": 0.5,
15              "start_step": 0,
16              "end_step": 4000,
17            },
18            "gamma": 0.99,
19            "training_batch_iter": 8,
20            "training_iter": 4,
21            "training_frequency": 4,
22            "training_start_step": 32
23          },
24          "memory": {
25            "name": "Replay",
26            "batch_size": 32,
27            "max_size": 10000,
28            "use_cer": false
29          },
30          "net": {
31            "type": "MLPNet",
32            "hid_layers": [64],
33            "hid_layers_activation": "selu",
34            "clip_grad_val": 0.5,
35            "loss_spec": {
36              "name": "MSELoss"
37            },
38            "optim_spec": {
39              "name": "Adam",
40              "lr": 0.01
41            },
42            "lr_scheduler_spec": {
43              "name": "LinearToZero",
44              "frame": 10000
45            },
46            "gpu": false
47          }
48        }],
49        "env": [{
50          "name": "CartPole-v0",
51          "max_t": null,
52          "max_frame": 10000
53        }],
54        "body": {
55          "product": "outer",
56          "num": 1
```

```
57        },
58        "meta": {
59          "distributed": false,
60          "eval_frequency": 500,
61          "max_session": 4,
62          "max_trial": 1
63        },
64        . . .
65      }
66    }
```

As with SARSA, there are several components. All line numbers refer to Code 4.6.

- **Algorithm:** The algorithm is `"VanillaDQN"` (line 8), to distinguish from `"DQN"` with target network from Chapter 5. The action policy is the Boltzmann policy (lines 9–10) with linear decay (lines 11–17) of the temperature parameter τ known as exploration variable `explore_var` (line 11). γ is set on line 18.

- **Network architecture:** Multilayer perceptron with one hidden layer of 64 units (line 32) and SeLU activation functions (line 33).

- **Optimizer:** The optimizer is Adam [68] with a learning rate of 0.01 (lines 38–41). The learning rate is specified to decay linearly to zero over the course of training (lines 42–45).

- **Training frequency:** Training starts after the agent has made 32 steps in the environment (line 22) and occurs every 4 steps from then on (line 21). At each training step, 4 batches are sampled from the `Replay` memory (line 20) and used to make 8 parameter updates (line 19). Each batch has 32 elements (line 26).

- **Memory:** A maximum of 10,000 most recent experiences are stored in the `Replay` memory (line 27).

- **Environment:** The environment is OpenAI Gym's CartPole [18] (line 50).

- **Training length:** Training consists of 10,000 time steps (line 52).

- **Checkpointing:** The agent is evaluated every 500 time steps (line 60).

When training with Boltzmann policies, it is important to set `action_pdtype` to `Categorical` so that the agent samples actions from the categorical probability distribution generated by the Boltzmann action policy. This is different to ε-greedy policies which have an argmax "distribution." That is, the agent will select the action with the maximum Q-value with probability 1.0.

Notice also that the maximum value for τ in the Boltzmann policy (line 14) is not constrained to 1 as it is for ε-greedy policies. The exploration variable in this case, τ, does not represent a probability but a temperature, so it can take any positive value. However, it should never be zero, as this will lead to division-by-0 numerical errors.

To train this DQN agent using SLM Lab, run the commands shown in Code 4.7 in a terminal.

Code 4.7   Training a DQN agent to play CartPole

```
1   conda activate lab
2   python run_lab.py slm_lab/spec/benchmark/dqn/dqn_cartpole.json
↪       vanilla_dqn_boltzmann_cartpole train
```

This will use the spec file to run a training `Trial` with four `Sessions` to obtain an average result and plot the trial graphs shown in Figure 4.2.

trial graph: vanilla_dqn_boltzmann_cartpole t0 4 sessions trial graph: vanilla_dqn_boltzmann_cartpole t0 4 sessions

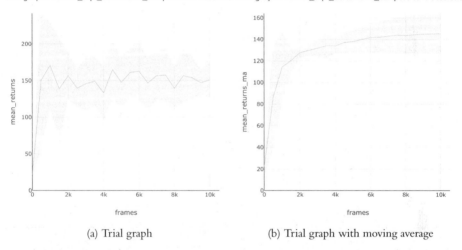

(a) Trial graph   (b) Trial graph with moving average

Figure 4.2   DQN trial graphs from SLM Lab averaged over four sessions. The vertical axis shows the total rewards (`mean_return` for evaluation is computed without discount) averaged over eight episodes during checkpoints, and the horizontal axis shows the total training frames. The graph on the right is a moving average with a window of 100 evaluation checkpoints.

4.7   Experimental Results

This section will look at how changing the neural network architecture affects the performance of DQN on CartPole. We will use the experimentation feature of SLM Lab to perform a grid search over network architecture parameters.

4.7.1   Experiment: The Effect of Network Architecture

The architecture of neural networks affects their capability to approximate functions. In this experiment, we will perform a simple grid search over a number of hidden layer configurations, then plot and compare their performance. The experiment spec file, extended from Code 4.6, is shown in Code 4.8. Lines 8–15 specify a grid search over the

architecture of the Q-network's hidden layers `net.hid_layers`. The full spec file is
available in SLM Lab at `slm_lab/spec/benchmark/dqn/dqn_cartpole.json`.

Code 4.8   DQN spec file with search spec over different network architectures

```
1   # slm_lab/spec/benchmark/dqn/dqn_cartpole.json
2
3   {
4     "vanilla_dqn_boltzmann_cartpole": {
5       ...
6       "search": {
7         "agent": [{
8           "net": {
9             "hid_layers__grid_search": [
10               [32],
11               [64],
12               [32, 16],
13               [64, 32]
14             ]
15           }
16         }]
17       }
18     }
19   }
```

Code 4.9 shows the command to run this experiment. Note that we are using the same
spec file as training, but now we replace the mode `train` with `search`.

Code 4.9   Run an experiment to search over different network architectures as defined in the
spec file.

```
1   conda activate lab
2   python run_lab.py slm_lab/spec/benchmark/dqn/dqn_cartpole.json
    ↪  vanilla_dqn_boltzmann_cartpole search
```

This will run an `Experiment` which spawns four `Trials` by substituting different values
of `net.hid_layers` into the original spec of DQN with a Boltzmann policy. Each `Trial`
runs four repeated `Sessions` to obtain an average. Figure 4.3 shows the multitrial graphs
plotted from this experiment.

Figure 4.3 shows that networks with two hidden layers (trials 2 and 3) perform better
than networks with a single layer (trials 0 and 1) thanks to their increased learning capacity.
When the number of layers is the same, networks with fewer units (trials 0 and 2),

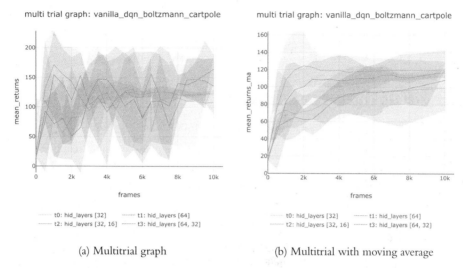

(a) Multitrial graph   (b) Multitrial with moving average

Figure 4.3 The effect of different network architectures. Networks with two hidden layers and therefore a greater learning capacity perform slightly better than networks with a single hidden layer.

provided they have sufficient learning capacity, learn slightly faster because there are fewer parameters to tune. Neural network architecture design is the subject of Chapter 12.

We can see from the training trial and experiment that the plain DQN algorithm can be unstable and not too performant, as seen from the large error envelopes in the learning curves and the total rewards of less than 200 for CartPole. In the next chapter, we will look at methods to improve DQN and make it powerful enough to solve Atari problems.

4.8 Summary

This chapter introduced the DQN algorithm. We saw that DQN is very similar to SARSA, with one critical difference. DQN uses the maximum Q-value in the next state to calculate Q-target values. As a result, DQN learns the optimal Q-function instead of the Q-function corresponding to the current policy. This makes DQN an off-policy algorithm in which the learned Q-function is independent of the experience-gathering policy.

Consequently, a DQN agent can reuse experiences gathered previously that are stored in an experience replay memory. At each training iteration, one or more batches are randomly sampled for learning the Q-function. Additionally, this also helps to decorrelate the experiences used during training. The combination of data-reuse and decorrelation significantly improves the sample efficiency of DQN when compared with SARSA.

We saw that the experience gathering policy in DQN should have two characteristics—it should facilitate exploration of the state space and approximate the optimal policy over time. ε-greedy is one such policy, but this chapter also introduced an alternative known as the Boltzmann policy. The two main advantages of this policy are that it explores the state-action space less randomly than ε-greedy policy and that it samples actions from a probability distribution that varies smoothly with Q-values.

4.9   Further Reading

- *Playing Atari with Deep Reinforcement Learning*, Mnih et al., 2013 [88].

- "Self-Improving Reactive Agents Based on Reinforcement Learning, Planning and Teaching," Lin, 1992 [82].

- Chapters 6 and 7, *Reinforcement Learning: An Introduction, Second Edition*, Sutton and Barto, 2018 [132].

- "Sep 13: Value functions introduction, Lecture 6," *CS 294: Deep Reinforcement Learning, Fall 2017*, Levine [76].

- "Sep 18: Advanced Q-learning algorithms, Lecture 7," *CS 294: Deep Reinforcement Learning, Fall 2017*, Levine [77].

4.10   History

The Q-learning component of DQN was invented in 1989 by Christopher Watkins in his PhD thesis titled "Learning from Delayed Rewards" [145]. Experience replay quickly followed, invented by Long-Ji Lin in 1992 [82]. This played a major role in improving the efficiency of Q-learning. In the years that followed, however, there were no major success stories involving deep Q-learning. This is perhaps not surprising given the combination of limited computational power in the 1990s and early 2000s, data-hungry deep learning architectures, and the sparse, noisy, and delayed feedback signals experienced in RL. Progress had to wait for the emergence of general-purpose GPU programming, for example with the launch of CUDA in 2006 [96], and the reignition of interest in deep learning within the machine learning community that began in the mid-2000s and rapidly accelerated after 2012.

2013 saw a major breakthrough with the paper from DeepMind, "Playing Atari with Deep Reinforcement Learning" [88]. The authors coined the term DQN or "Deep Q-Networks" and demonstrated the first example of learning a control policy directly from high-dimensional image data using RL. Improvements quickly followed; Double DQN [141] and Prioritized Experience Replay [121] were both developed in 2015. However, the fundamental breakthrough was the algorithm presented in this chapter combined with a simple convolutional neural network, state processing, and GPU training. See Chapter 5 for a more detailed discussion of the "Playing Atari with Deep Reinforcement Learning" paper [88].

5

Improving DQN

In this chapter, we will look at three modifications to the DQN algorithm—target networks, Double DQN [141], and Prioritized Experience Replay [121]. Each modification addresses a separate issue with DQN, so they can be combined to yield significant performance improvements.

In Section 5.1 we discuss target networks which are lagged copies of $\hat{Q}^{\pi}(s, a)$. The target network is then used to generate the maximum Q-value in the next state s' when calculating Q_{tar}^{π}, in contrast to the DQN algorithm from Chapter 4 which used $\hat{Q}^{\pi}(s, a)$ when calculating Q_{tar}^{π}. This helps to stabilize training by reducing the speed at which Q_{tar}^{π} changes.

Next, we discuss the Double DQN algorithm in Section 5.2. Double DQN uses two Q-networks to calculate Q_{tar}^{π}. The first network selects the action which corresponds to its estimate of maximum Q-value. The second network produces the Q-value for the action selected by the first network. The value produced by the second network is used in the Q_{tar}^{π} calculation. This modification addresses the fact that DQN systematically overestimates the true Q-values, which may lead to slower training and weaker policies.

DQN can be further improved by changing how batches are sampled from experience replay. Instead of sampling random-uniformly, experiences can be prioritized according to how informative they currently are to an agent. Known as *Prioritized Experience Replay*, experiences that an agent can learn more from are sampled more frequently than those an agent can learn little from. This is discussed in Section 5.3.

Having introduced the main ideas behind each modification, in Section 4.5 we look at an implementation which incorporates these changes.

The chapter ends by putting together all of the different elements discussed in Chapters 4 and 5 and training a DQN agent to play the Atari games Pong and Breakout. The implementations, network architecture, and hyperparameters are based on the algorithms described in three papers: "Human-Level Control through Deep Reinforcement Learning" [89], "Deep Reinforcement Learning with Double Q-Learning" [141], and "Prioritized Experience Replay" [121].

5.1 Target Networks

The first adjustment to the DQN algorithm is to use a target network to calculate Q_{tar}^{π}. It was introduced by Mnih et al. in "Human-Level Control through Deep Reinforcement Learning" [89] and helps to stabilize training. It motivated by the fact that in the original DQN algorithm, Q_{tar}^{π} is constantly changing because it depends on $\hat{Q}^{\pi}(s, a)$. During training, the Q-network parameters θ are adjusted to minimize the difference between $\hat{Q}^{\pi}(s, a) = Q^{\pi_\theta}(s, a)$ and Q_{tar}^{π}, but this is difficult when Q_{tar}^{π} changes at each training step.

To reduce the changes in Q_{tar}^{π} between training steps, we use a target network. A target network is a second network with parameters φ which is a lagged copy of the Q-network $Q^{\pi_\theta}(s, a)$. The target network $Q^{\pi_\varphi}(s, a)$ is used to calculate Q_{tar}^{π}, as shown in the modified Bellman update shown in Equation 5.2. The original DQN update is shown in Equation 5.1 for ease of comparison.

$$Q_{\text{tar}}^{\pi_\theta}(s, a) = r + \gamma \max_{a'} Q^{\pi_\theta}(s', a') \tag{5.1}$$

$$Q_{\text{tar}}^{\pi_\varphi}(s, a) = r + \gamma \max_{a'} Q^{\pi_\varphi}(s', a') \tag{5.2}$$

Periodically, φ is updated to the current values for θ. This is known as a *replacement update*. The update frequency for φ is problem-dependent. For example, in the Atari games φ is updated every 1,000–10,000 environment steps. For simpler problems it may not be necessary to wait so long; updating φ every 100–1,000 steps will be sufficient.

Why does this help to stabilize training? Every time $Q_{\text{tar}}^{\pi_\theta}(s, a)$ is calculated, the Q-function represented by the parameters θ will be slightly different, so $Q_{\text{tar}}^{\pi_\theta}(s, a)$ may be different for the same (s, a). It is possible that between one training step and the next, $Q_{\text{tar}}^{\pi_\theta}(s, a)$ differs significantly from the previous estimate. This "moving target" can destabilize training because it makes it much less clear what values a network should be trying to approach. Introducing a target network literally stops the target from moving. In between updating φ to θ, φ is fixed, so the Q-function represented by φ doesn't change. This transforms the problem into a standard supervised regression [77]. Whilst this does not fundamentally change the underlying optimization problem, a target network helps stabilize training and makes divergence or oscillation of the policy less likely [77, 89, 141].

The algorithm for DQN with a target network is given in Algorithm 5.1. The differences when compared with the original DQN algorithm (Algorithm 4.1) are as follows:

- The target update frequency F is an additional hyperparameter that needs to be chosen (line 7).

- In line 8 we initialize an additional network as the target network and set its parameters φ to θ.

- In line 17, y_i is calculated using the target network $Q_{\text{tar}}^{\pi_\varphi}$.

- The target network is periodically updated (lines 26–29).

Note that it is the network parameters θ that are used to calculate $Q^{\pi_\theta}(s, a)$ (line 20) and are updated during training (line 22). This is the same as in the original DQN algorithm.

Algorithm 5.1   DQN with a target network

1: Initialize learning rate α
2: Initialize τ
3: Initialize number of batches per training step, B
4: Initialize number of updates per batch, U
5: Initialize batch size N
6: Initialize experience replay memory with max size K
7: Initialize target network update frequency F
8: Randomly initialize the network parameters θ
9: Initialize the target network parameters $\varphi = \theta$
10: **for** $m = 1 \ldots MAX\_STEPS$ **do**
11:     Gather and store h experiences (s_i, a_i, r_i, s_i') using the current policy
12:     **for** $b = 1 \ldots B$ **do**
13:        Sample a batch of experiences b from the experience replay memory
14:        **for** $u = 1 \ldots U$ **do**
15:           **for** $i = 1 \ldots N$ **do**
16:              # Calculate target Q-values for each example
17:              $y_i = r_i + \delta_{s_i'} \gamma \max_{a_i'} Q^{\pi_\varphi}(s_i', a_i')$ where $\delta_{s_i'} = 0$ if s_i' is terminal,
                 $\hookrightarrow$ 1 otherwise
18:           **end for**
19:           # Calculate the loss, for example using MSE
20:           $L(\theta) = \frac{1}{N} \sum_i (y_i - Q^{\pi_\theta}(s_i, a_i))^2$
21:           # Update the network's parameters
22:           $\theta = \theta - \alpha \nabla_\theta L(\theta)$
23:        **end for**
24:     **end for**
25:     Decay τ
26:     **if** $(m \mod F) == 0$ **then**
27:        # Update the target network
28:        $\varphi = \theta$
29:     **end if**
30: **end for**

Periodically replacing the target network parameters φ with a copy of the network parameters θ is a common way to perform the update. Alternatively, at each time step, φ can be set to a weighted average of φ and θ, as shown in Equation 5.4. This is known as a *Polyak update* and can be thought of as a "soft update": at each step, the parameters φ and θ are mixed to produce a new target network. In contrast to a *replacement update* (Equation 5.3), φ changes each time step, but more slowly than the training network θ.

The hyperparameter β controls the speed at which φ changes by specifying how much of the old target network φ is kept at each update. The larger β, the more slowly φ changes.

$$\text{Replacement update:} \quad \varphi \leftarrow \theta \tag{5.3}$$

$$\text{Polyak update:} \quad \varphi \leftarrow \beta\varphi + (1 - \beta)\theta \tag{5.4}$$

Each approach has its advantages and neither one is clearly better than the other. The main advantage of a replacement update is that φ is fixed for a number of steps, which temporarily eliminates the "moving target." In contrast, when using a Polyak update, φ still changes each training iteration but more gradually than θ. However, a replacement update has a dynamic lag between φ and θ which depends on the number of time steps since the last update of φ; a Polyak update doesn't have this quirk as the mix between φ and θ remains constant.

One disadvantage of target networks is that they can slow down training, since $Q_{\text{tar}}^\pi(s, a)$ is generated from the older target network. If φ and θ are too close, then training may be unstable, but if φ changes too slowly then training may be unnecessarily slow. The hyperparameter which controls how fast φ changes (the update frequency or β) needs to be tuned to find a good balance between stability and training speed. In Section 5.6 we show the effect of varying the update frequency for a DQN agent trained to play Atari Pong.

5.2 Double DQN

The second adjustment to DQN is to use *double estimation* to calculate $Q_{\text{tar}}^\pi(s, a)$. Known as the *Double DQN* algorithm [140, 141], this modification addresses the problem of overestimating Q-values. Let's first look at why the original DQN algorithm overestimates Q-values and why this is a problem, then describe how to address that using Double DQN.

In DQN, we construct $Q_{\text{tar}}^\pi(s, a)$ by selecting the maximum Q-value estimate in state s' as shown in Equation 5.5.

$$\begin{aligned} Q_{\text{tar}}^{\pi_\theta}(s, a) &= r + \gamma \max_{a'} Q^{\pi_\theta}(s', a') \\ &= r + \max \left(Q^{\pi_\theta}(s', a_1'), Q^{\pi_\theta}(s', a_2'), \dots, Q^{\pi_\theta}(s', a_n') \right) \end{aligned} \tag{5.5}$$

Q-values are the expected future return from taking action a in state s, so calculating $\max_{a'} Q^{\pi_\theta}(s', a')$ involves selecting the maximum from a set of expected values, $\left(Q^{\pi_\theta}(s', a_1'), Q^{\pi_\theta}(s', a_2'), \dots, Q^{\pi_\theta}(s', a_n') \right)$.

In the paper "Deep Reinforcement Learning with Double Q-Learning" [141], van Hasselt et al. showed that if $Q^{\pi_\theta}(s', a')$ contain any errors, then $\max_{a'} Q^{\pi_\theta}(s', a')$ will be positively biased and the resulting Q-values will be overestimated. Unfortunately, there are many reasons why $Q^{\pi_\theta}(s', a')$ will not be exactly correct. Function approximation using neural networks is not perfect, an agent may not fully explore the environment, and the environment itself may be noisy. We should therefore expect $Q^{\pi_\theta}(s', a')$ to contain some error, so the Q-values will be overestimated. Furthermore, the more actions are there to choose from in state s', the greater the overestimation is likely to be. We show a concrete example in Box 5.1.

Box 5.1   Estimating the Maximum Expected Value

Q-value overestimation is a specific instance of a more general and well-known problem: the expected maximum value of a set of estimated values is positively biased when the value estimates contain some noise [128]. In DQN, the maximum expected value is $\mathbb{E}\left[\max_a Q^\pi(s,a)\right]$ and the noisy estimates are generated from Q^{π_θ}.

As a way to build intuition for how this issue emerges, consider a state s in which $Q^{\pi^*}(s,a) = 0$ for all the available actions a and suppose that our Q-value estimates are noisy but unbiased. This can be simulated by assuming that the Q-values are drawn from a standard normal distribution with mean 0 and standard deviation of 1.

The extent to which $\max_{a'} Q^\pi(s',a')$ will be overestimated can be seen by sampling k values from the standard normal distribution and selecting the maximum. In this case, k represents the number of actions a' in state s'. We repeat this process many times and calculate the average of all of the maximum values to estimate the expected maximum value for each k.

Table 5.1 shows the expected maximum value for $k = 1 \ldots 10$, with 10,000 samples for each k. The correct value for $\max_{a'} Q^\pi(s',a') = 0$ and, when $k = 1$, the estimation is correct in expectation. However, as k increases, the estimation becomes more positively biased. For example, when $k = 2$, $\mathbb{E}\left[\max_a Q^\pi(s,a)\right] = 0.56$ and when $k = 10$, $\mathbb{E}\left[\max_a Q^\pi(s,a)\right] = 1.53$.

Table 5.1   Expected value of $\max_a Q^\pi(s,a)$ when the estimates for $Q^\pi(s,a)$ are unbiased but noisy and $Q^\pi(s,a) = 0$ for all a. This is a reproduction of Smith and Winkler's experiment from "The Optimizer's Curse" [128].

Number of actions	$\mathbb{E}[\max_a Q^\pi(s,a)]$	Number of actions	$\mathbb{E}[\max_a Q^\pi(s,a)]$
1	0.00	6	1.27
2	0.56	7	1.34
3	0.86	8	1.43
4	1.03	9	1.48
5	1.16	10	1.53

It is not immediately obvious to what extent Q-value overestimation is a problem. For example, if all of the Q-values were uniformly overestimated, then the agent would still select the correct action a in state s and we can expect no drop in performance. Furthermore, overestimation in the face of uncertainty can be useful [61]. For example, at the beginning of training it can be helpful to overestimate $Q^\pi(s, a)$ for unvisited or rarely visited (s, a) pairs because this increases the likelihood that these states will be visited, allowing an agent to gain experience about how good or bad they are.

However, DQN overestimates $Q^\pi(s, a)$ for the (s, a) pairs that have been visited often. This becomes a problem if an agent does not explore (s, a) uniformly. Then the overestimation of $Q^\pi(s, a)$ will also be nonuniform and this may incorrectly change the rank of actions as measured by $Q^\pi(s, a)$. Under these circumstances, the a an agent thinks is best in s is in fact not the best action to take. When overestimating $Q^\pi(s, a)$ is combined with bootstrapped learning (as in DQN), the incorrect relative Q-values will be propagated backwards in time to earlier (s, a) pairs and add error to those estimates as well. It is therefore beneficial to reduce the overestimation of Q-values.

The Double DQN algorithm reduces the overestimation of Q-values by learning two Q-function estimates using different experiences. The Q-maximizing action a' is selected using the first estimate, and the Q-value that is used to calculate $Q_{\text{tar}}^\pi(s, a)$ is generated by the second estimate using the action a selected by the first estimate. The use of a second Q-function trained with different experiences removes the positive bias in the estimation.

Modifying DQN into Double DQN is simple. The required change is made clearer by rewriting $Q_{\text{tar}}^\pi(s, a)$ as shown in Equation 5.6.

$$
\begin{aligned}
Q_{\text{tar:DQN}}^\pi(s, a) &= r + \gamma \max_{a'} Q^{\pi_\theta}(s', a') \\
&= r + \gamma Q^{\pi_\theta}\left(s', \max_{a'} Q^{\pi_\theta}(s', a')\right)
\end{aligned}
\tag{5.6}
$$

The DQN algorithm uses the same network θ to select action a' and to evaluate the Q-function for that action. Double DQN uses two different networks, θ and φ. θ is used to select a', and φ is used to calculate the Q-value for (s', a'), as shown in Equation 5.7.

$$
Q_{\text{tar:DoubleDQN}}^\pi(s, a) r + \gamma Q^{\pi_\varphi}\left(s', \max_{a'} Q^{\pi_\theta}(s', a')\right)
\tag{5.7}
$$

After introducing target networks in Section 5.1, we already have two networks: the training network θ and the target network φ. These two networks have been trained with overlapping experiences, but if the number of time steps between setting $\varphi = \theta$ is large enough, then in practice they are sufficiently different to work as the two different networks for Double DQN.

The training network θ is used to select the action. It is important to ensure that we are still learning the optimal policy after introducing the Double DQN modification [141]. The target network φ is used to evaluate that action. Note that if there is no lag between φ and θ—that is, if $\varphi = \theta$, then Equation 5.7 reduces to the original DQN.

Double DQN with a target network is shown in Algorithm 5.2. In line 17, y_i is calculated using both networks θ and φ. This is the only difference when compared with Algorithm 5.1.

Algorithm 5.2 Double DQN with a target network

1: Initialize learning rate α
2: Initialize τ
3: Initialize number of batches per training step, B
4: Initialize number of updates per batch, U
5: Initialize batch size N
6: Initialize experience replay memory with max size K
7: Initialize target network update frequency F
8: Randomly initialize the network parameters θ
9: Initialize the target network parameters $\varphi = \theta$
10: **for** $m = 1 \ldots MAX\_STEPS$ **do**
11:      Gather and store h experiences (s_i, a_i, r_i, s_i') using the current policy
12:      **for** $b = 1 \ldots B$ **do**
13:          Sample a batch, b, of experiences from the experience replay memory
14:          **for** $u = 1 \ldots U$ **do**
15:              **for** $i = 1 \ldots N$ **do**
16:                  # Calculate target Q-values for each example
17:                  $y_i = r_i + \delta_{s_i'} \gamma Q^{\pi_\varphi}(s_i', \max_{a_i'} Q^{\pi_\theta}(s_i', a_i'))$ where $\delta_{s_i'} = 0$

                     $\hookrightarrow$ if s_i' is terminal, 1 otherwise
18:              **end for**
19:              # Calculate the loss, for example using MSE
20:              $L(\theta) = \frac{1}{N} \sum_i (y_i - Q^{\pi_\theta}(s_i, a_i))^2$
21:              # Update the network's parameters
22:              $\theta = \theta - \alpha \nabla_\theta L(\theta)$
23:          **end for**
24:      **end for**
25:      Decay τ
26:      **if** $(m \mod F) == 0$ **then**
27:          # Update the target network
28:          $\varphi = \theta$
29:      **end if**
30: **end for**

5.3 Prioritized Experience Replay (PER)

The final modification to DQN is to use a *Prioritized Experience Replay* memory introduced by Schaul et al. in 2015 [121]. The main idea is that some experiences in the replay memory are more informative than others. If we can train an agent by sampling informative experiences more frequently than uninformative ones, the agent may learn faster.

Intuitively, when learning a new task, we can imagine that some experiences are more informative than others. Consider, for example, a humanoid agent trying to learn how to stand up. At the beginning of each episode, the agent is always initialized sitting on the floor. Initially, most actions will result in the agent flailing around on the ground, and only a few experiences will convey meaningful information about how to combine joint movements so as to balance and stand up. These experiences are more important for learning how to stand than those in which the agent is stuck on the ground. They help the agent learn what to do right instead of the many things it can do wrong. An alternative way to look at this is to consider the experiences in which $Q^{\pi_\theta}(s,a)$ deviates most significantly from $Q^{\pi}_{\text{tar}}(s,a)$. These are the experiences that are most "surprising" to an agent—they can be thought of as the experiences it has the most to learn from. An agent might learn faster if it is trained with these experiences relatively more often than with the experiences for which it can accurately predict $Q^{\pi}_{\text{tar}}(s,a)$. In light of these considerations, can we do better than sampling experiences uniformly from replay memory—can we, instead, have the agent *prioritize* learning from some experiences over others?

Prioritized Experience Replay is based on this simple and intuitive idea, but it presents two implementation challenges. First, how can we automatically assign each experience a priority? Second, how to sample efficiently from the replay memory using these priorities?

A natural solution to the first problem is for the priority to be derived from the absolute difference between $Q^{\pi_\theta}(s,a)$ and $Q^{\pi}_{\text{tar}}(s,a)$, known as the TD error. The larger the difference between these two values, the larger the mismatch between an agent's expectations and what happened in the next step, and the more an agent should correct $Q^{\pi_\theta}(s,a)$. Additionally, the TD error is available for each experience as part of the DQN or Double DQN algorithms with very little computation and implementation effort. The only remaining issue is what priority to assign to experiences initially when there is no TD error available. Typically, this is solved by setting the score to a large constant value to encourage each experience to be sampled at least once.

Schaul et al. propose two different options for sampling using the scores: rank-based and proportional prioritization. Both approaches are based on an interpolation between greedy prioritization (always picking the experiences with the top n scores) and uniform random sampling. This ensures that experiences with higher scores are sampled more often but that each experience has a nonzero probability of being sampled. We consider only the proportional prioritization method here; for details on rank-based prioritization, refer to the "Prioritized Experienced Replay" [121] paper. If ω_i is the TD error for experience i, ε is a small positive number,[1] and $\eta \in [0,\infty)$, then the priority of an experience is shown in Equation 5.8.

$$P(i) = \frac{(|\omega_i| + \varepsilon)^\eta}{\sum_j (|\omega_j| + \varepsilon)^\eta} \tag{5.8}$$

ε prevents experiences from never being sampled if $\omega_i = 0$. η determines how much to prioritize. $\eta = 0$ corresponds to uniform sampling, since all experiences will have a priority of 1. The larger η, the greater the prioritization, as shown in Equation 5.9.

---

1. This ε is not related to the ε-greedy policy—it's a different constant.

$$\eta = 0.0: \quad (\omega_1 = 2.0, \omega_2 = 3.5) \rightarrow \big(P(1) = 0.50, P(2) = 0.50\big)$$
$$\eta = 0.5: \quad (\omega_1 = 2.0, \omega_2 = 3.5) \rightarrow \big(P(1) = 0.43, P(2) = 0.57\big)$$
$$\eta = 1.0: \quad (\omega_1 = 2.0, \omega_2 = 3.5) \rightarrow \big(P(1) = 0.36, P(2) = 0.64\big) \quad (5.9)$$
$$\eta = 1.5: \quad (\omega_1 = 2.0, \omega_2 = 3.5) \rightarrow \big(P(1) = 0.30, P(2) = 0.70\big)$$
$$\eta = 2.0: \quad (\omega_1 = 2.0, \omega_2 = 3.5) \rightarrow \big(P(1) = 0.25, P(2) = 0.75\big)$$

5.3.1 Importance Sampling

Prioritizing certain examples changes the expectation of the entire data distribution, which introduces bias into the training process. This can be corrected by multiplying the TD error for each example by a set of weights—this is known as *importance sampling*. If the bias is small, it is unclear how effective importance sampling is because there are other factors, such as action noise or a highly nonstationary data distribution, that may dominate the effect of a small bias, especially in the early stages of learning. Schaul et al. [121] hypothesize that correcting for the bias is only likely to matter towards the end of training, and show that the effect of making the correction is mixed. In some cases, adding importance sampling led to improved performance; in others, it made little difference or caused performance to deteriorate. For simplicity, importance sampling has been omitted from the implementation discussed in this chapter; we refer readers to the "Prioritized Experience Replay" paper [121] and Lecture 4 (https://youtu.be/tWNpiNzWu08) from Sergey Levine's Deep Reinforcement Learning class [74] for more details.

It is conceptually straightforward to extend the Double DQN with target networks algorithm to include PER, as shown in Algorithm 5.3. Four modifications are needed:

1. The replay memory needs to store an additional element per experience—the priority of that experience (line 14).

2. When batches are sampled from memory, experiences are sampled in proportion to their priority (line 16).

3. The TD error per training experience needs to be calculated and stored (line 22).

4. Finally, the TD errors are used to update the priorities of the corresponding examples in memory (lines 29–30).

Algorithm 5.3   Double DQN with a target network and Prioritized Experience Replay

---

1: Initialize learning rate α
2: Initialize τ
3: Initialize number of batches per training step, B
4: Initialize number of updates per batch, U
5: Initialize batch size N
6: Initialize experience replay memory with max size K
7: Initialize target network update frequency F
8: Initialize maximum priority P
9: Initialize ε

10: Initialize prioritization parameter η

11: Randomly initialize the network parameters θ

12: Initialize the target network parameters $\varphi = \theta$

13: **for** $m = 1 \ldots MAX\_STEPS$ **do**

14:     Gather and store h experiences $(s_i, a_i, r_i, s'_i, p_i)$ where $p_i = P$

15:     **for** $b = 1 \ldots B$ **do**

16:         Sample a **prioritized** batch, b, of experiences from the experience replay
            $\hookrightarrow$ memory

17:         **for** $u = 1 \ldots U$ **do**

18:             **for** $i = 1 \ldots N$ **do**

19:                 # Calculate target Q-values for each example

20:                 $y_i = r_i + \delta_{s'_i} \gamma Q^{\pi_\varphi}(s'_i, \max_{a'_i} Q^{\pi_\theta}(s'_i, a'_i))$ where $\delta_{s'_i} = 0$
                    $\hookrightarrow$ if s'_i is terminal, 1 otherwise

21:                 # Calculate the absolute TD error for each example

22:                 $\omega_i = |y_i - Q^{\pi_\theta}(s_i, a_i)|$

23:             **end for**

24:             # Calculate the loss, for example using MSE

25:             $L(\theta) = \frac{1}{N} \sum_i (y_i - Q^{\pi_\theta}(s_i, a_i))^2$

26:             # Update the network's parameters

27:             $\theta = \theta - \alpha \nabla_\theta L(\theta)$

28:             # Calculate the priorities for each example

29:             $p_i = \frac{(|\omega_i| + \varepsilon)^\eta}{\sum_j (|\omega_j| + \varepsilon)^\eta}$

30:             Update the experience replay memory with the new priorities

31:         **end for**

32:     **end for**

33:     Decay τ

34:     **if** $(m \mod F) == 0$ **then**

35:         # Update the target network

36:         $\varphi = \theta$

37:     **end if**

38: **end for**

5.4 Modified DQN Implementation

In this section, we introduce an implementation of DQN that flexibly incorporates a target network and the Double DQN algorithm. Prioritized Experience Replay is implemented by a new `Memory` class, `PrioritizedReplay`, and by adding just a few lines of code to `calc_q_loss`.

The modifications to the DQN algorithm are implemented in the `DQNBase` class which inherits from `VanillaDQN`. Most of the code can be reused but we need to modify `init_nets`, `calc_q_loss`, and `update`.

To make the different DQN variations and the relationship between them as clear as possible, each variant is associated with a separate class even if no additional code is required. DQN with target networks is therefore implemented in the `DQN` class which extends `DQNBase`. Double DQN is implemented in `DoubleDQN` which extends `DQN`.

5.4.1 Network Initialization

It makes sense to briefly look at the `init_nets` method in `DQNBase` (Code 5.1) because it shows how the two networks are handled.

In lines 12–13, the networks are initialized. `self.net` is the training network with parameters θ and `self.target_net` is the target network with parameters φ. Additionally, there are two more class attributes, `self.online_net` and `self.eval_net` (lines 16–17). Depending on the variant of DQN being run, `self.online_net` and `self.eval_net` point to either `self.net` or `self.target_net`. They may also point to different networks, one to `self.net` and the other to `self.target_net`. This approach makes it easy to switch between DQN and Double DQN with target networks by changing which networks are assigned to `self.online_net` and `self.eval_net`. In `DQNBase`, they both point to the target network.

Code 5.1   Modified DQN implementation: initializing networks

```
1  # slm_lab/agent/algorithm/dqn.py
2
3  class DQNBase(VanillaDQN):
4      ...
5
6      @lab_api
7      def init_nets(self, global_nets=None):
8          ...
9          in_dim = self.body.state_dim
10         out_dim = net_util.get_out_dim(self.body)
11         NetClass = getattr(net, self.net_spec['type'])
12         self.net = NetClass(self.net_spec, in_dim, out_dim)
13         self.target_net = NetClass(self.net_spec, in_dim, out_dim)
14         self.net_names = ['net', 'target_net']
15         ...
16         self.online_net = self.target_net
17         self.eval_net = self.target_net
```

5.4.2 Calculating the Q-Loss

`calc_q_loss` is shown in Code 5.2. There are two differences compared to the original DQN implementation—estimating $Q^{\pi}(s', a')$ and updating the batch priorities.

We first calculate $\hat{Q}^{\pi}(s, a)$ for all actions a for each state in the batch (line 9) and select the Q-value-maximizing action (line 15) for each state s.

Then we calculate $\hat{Q}^{\pi}(s', a')$ for all actions a' for each next state s' in the batch. This is done twice using `self.online_net` and `self.eval_net` (lines 11–14). Next, we select the Q-value-maximizing action for each s' using `self.online_net` and store them in `online_actions` (line 16). Then, we select the Q-values that correspond to these actions using `self.eval_net` (line 17). `max_next_q_preds` is the estimate for $\hat{Q}^{\pi}(s', a')$.

$Q_{\text{tar}}^{\pi}(s, a)$ is calculated on line 18. This and the `q_loss` (line 20) calculation are the same as in the original DQN implementation.

To incorporate Prioritized Experience Replay, we optionally calculate the TD error for each experience in the batch (line 23) and use these values to update the priorities (line 24).

Code 5.2   Modified DQN implementation: calculating Q-loss

```
1   # slm_lab/agent/algorithm/dqn.py
2
3   class DQNBase(VanillaDQN):
4       ...
5
6       def calc_q_loss(self, batch):
7           states = batch['states']
8           next_states = batch['next_states']
9           q_preds = self.net(states)
10          with torch.no_grad():
11              # Use online_net to select actions in next state
12              online_next_q_preds = self.online_net(next_states)
13              # Use eval_net to calculate next_q_preds for actions chosen by
                ↪  online_net
14              next_q_preds = self.eval_net(next_states)
15          act_q_preds = q_preds.gather(-1,
                ↪  batch['actions'].long().unsqueeze(-1)).squeeze(-1)
16          online_actions = online_next_q_preds.argmax(dim=-1, keepdim=True)
17          max_next_q_preds = next_q_preds.gather(-1, online_actions).squeeze(-1)
18          max_q_targets = batch['rewards'] + self.gamma * (1 - batch['dones']) *
                ↪  max_next_q_preds
19          ...
20          q_loss = self.net.loss_fn(act_q_preds, max_q_targets)
21
22          if 'Prioritized' in util.get_class_name(self.body.memory):   # PER
23              errors = (max_q_targets -
                ↪  act_q_preds.detach()).abs().cpu().numpy()
24              self.body.memory.update_priorities(errors)
25          return q_loss
```

5.4.3 Updating the Target Network

After each training step, an algorithm's `update` method is called. This is modified to incorporate the target network update shown in Code 5.3.

The implementation is straightforward. If we are using replacement update, then we directly copy `self.net` to `self.target_net` (lines 13–14, 21–22). If we are using a Polyak update, then we calculate a weighted average of each parameter in `self.net` and the current `self.target_net`, then update `self.target_net` with the result (lines 15–16, 24–26).

Code 5.3 Modified DQN implementation: updating the target network

```
1   # slm_lab/agent/algorithm/dqn.py
2
3   class DQNBase(VanillaDQN):
4       ...
5
6       @lab_api
7       def update(self):
8           self.update_nets()
9           return super().update()
10
11      def update_nets(self):
12          if util.frame_mod(self.body.env.clock.frame,
            ↪ self.net.update_frequency, self.body.env.num_envs):
13              if self.net.update_type == 'replace':
14                  net_util.copy(self.net, self.target_net)
15              elif self.net.update_type == 'polyak':
16                  net_util.polyak_update(self.net, self.target_net,
                ↪ self.net.polyak_coef)
17              ...
18
19  # slm_lab/agent/net/net_util.py
20
21  def copy(src_net, tar_net):
22      tar_net.load_state_dict(src_net.state_dict())
23
24  def polyak_update(src_net, tar_net, old_ratio=0.5):
25      for src_param, tar_param in zip(src_net.parameters(),
        ↪ tar_net.parameters()):
26          tar_param.data.copy_(old_ratio * src_param.data + (1.0 - old_ratio) *
            ↪ tar_param.data)
```

5.4.4   DQN with Target Networks

We do not need any additional code to implement DQN with target networks, as shown in Code 5.4.

DQN inherits from DQNBase and, as we saw in Code 5.1, self.target_net is initialized and assigned to self.online_net and self.eval_net. Consequently, in calc_q_loss, self.target_net is the only network that is used to calculate $Q_{\mathrm{tar}}^{\pi}(s, a)$.

Code 5.4   The DQN class

```
1  # slm_lab/agent/algorithm/dqn.py
2
3  class DQN(DQNBase):
4
5      @lab_api
6      def init_nets(self, global_nets=None):
7          super().init_nets(global_nets)
```

5.4.5   Double DQN

DoubleDQN inherits from DQN, as shown in Code 5.5. When the networks are initialized in init_nets, self.net is assigned to self.online_net and self.target_net is assigned to self.eval_net (lines 8–9).

Now, when we calculate $Q_{\mathrm{tar}}^{\pi}(s, a)$, self.net is used to select action a' because self.online_net points to it, and self.target_net estimates the Q-value for (s', a') because self.eval_net points to it.

Code 5.5   The DoubleDQN class

```
1  # slm_lab/agent/algorithm/dqn.py
2
3  class DoubleDQN(DQN):
4
5      @lab_api
6      def init_nets(self, global_nets=None):
7          super().init_nets(global_nets)
8          self.online_net = self.net
9          self.eval_net = self.target_net
```

5.4.6 Prioritized Experienced Replay

Prioritized Experience Replay (PER) changes how experiences are sampled from memory to improve the sample efficiency of DQN. As with the preceding sections on memory classes, this section can be skipped on first reading without loss of understanding of the improvements to DQN. It is sufficient to understand the main ideas behind Prioritized Experience Replay discussed in Section 5.3.

To implement PER, we need a new `Memory` class, `PrioritizedReplay`. Much of the implementation is shared with `Replay` memory class which `PrioritizedReplay` extends. However, we need to add three features—storing priorities, updating priorities, and proportional sampling.

- **Storing priorities:** An experience should contain its priority, so we need to add an additional buffer in a replay memory to keep track of priorities. This can be handled by overriding the `__init__`, `reset`, and `add_experience` functions of the `Replay` memory class.

- **Updating priorities:** Each time an agent is trained, the priority of each experience in a batch may change. We add a new function `update_priorities` which modifies the priorities of experiences stored in memory and keeps track of the indices of the most recently sampled batch so it knows which experiences to update.

- **Proportional sampling:** This is the trickiest part of implementing PER. Experiences need to be sampled in proportion to their priority—but this sampling still has to be fast, even when the memory is very large, so as not to slow down training. Consequently, `sample_idxs` needs overriding and we need a new data structure, a `SumTree`, to store the priorities and achieve efficient sampling even as the memory size increases. Note that `Replay` memory does not have this problem since each index is sampled randomly.

In what follows, we first discuss the new data structure, a `SumTree`, and why it is useful for implementing PER. Then we review the `PrioritizedReplay` memory class and discuss how it implements each of the features required by PER.

Algorithm 5.3 demonstrated that it is straightforward to extract the absolute TD error $Q^{\pi_\theta}(s, a)$ and $Q^{\pi}_{\text{tar}}(s, a)$ for each experience in a batch. Equation 5.8 showed how to translate this measure of error (referred to as $|\omega|$) into a priority for each element.

To calculate the priority of a single experience, we need to keep track of the sum of un-normalized priorities $\sum_j (|\omega_j| + \varepsilon)^\eta$ (the denominator of Equation 5.8), which is calculated using all of the experiences in the memory. Once we have all of the priorities $P(i)$, we can sample from the memory using them.

Consider the following approach to sampling a batch of experiences:

1. Modify Algorithm 5.3 to also keep track of $\sum_j (|\omega_j| + \varepsilon)^\eta$. When updating the priorities, first calculate the change in $\sum_j (|\omega_j| + \varepsilon)^\eta$ so that it can be updated appropriately.

2. Randomly sample a number, x, uniformly from the range 0 to $\sum_j (|\omega_j| + \varepsilon)^\eta$.

3. Iterate through the all the experiences in memory summing all the $|\omega_i| + \varepsilon$ seen so far.

4. When $\sum_i^k (|\omega_i| + \varepsilon) \geq x$, stop. The index, k, of the current $|\omega_k| + \varepsilon$ is the index of the experience to sample from memory.

5. Repeat steps 3–4 until you have a full batch of indices.

6. Construct a batch of experiences with the indices identified in steps 5.

This method will sample experiences from memory in proportion to their priority because x is uniformly distributed from 0 to $\sum_j (|\omega_j| + \varepsilon)^\eta$, and the larger $|\omega_j| + \varepsilon$, the higher proportion of the range of x the experience j will take up, and the more likely it is to be the experience which changes $\sum_i (|\omega_i| + \varepsilon) \leq x$ to $\sum_i (|\omega_i| + \varepsilon) \geq x$.

The problem with this approach is that it is slow because identifying the index k of the experience to be sampled requires iterating sequentially through the entire memory. It has computational complexity $\mathcal{O}(n)$, where n is the current size of the memory. When sampling a batch, this process needs to be repeated N (batch size) times.

Replay memories can be large, with a million elements or more, and batches are sampled very often while an agent is training. A sampling method that iterates through each experience in the memory will slow training down significantly. Training that took hours or days may now take weeks.

As an alternative, we can use a binary tree known as a *sum tree* to store the priorities. This data structure makes it possible to sample an experience with computational complexity $\mathcal{O}(\log_2 n)$ instead of $\mathcal{O}(n)$, as discussed in Box 5.2. This is a significant improvement if memory is large. For example, if the memory contains 1 million experiences, sampling an index will require just 20 steps, since $\log_2(1,000,000) \approx 20$, instead of 1,000,000 steps in the worst-case scenario of iterating through the entire memory.

Box 5.2 Sum Trees

A sum tree is a binary tree in which the leaves store the priorities of experiences and each internal node stores the sum of the values stored by the node's children. Consequently, the root note will store the sum of $(|\omega_j| + \varepsilon)^\eta$. This is exactly the denominator of Equation 5.8.

The structure of a sum tree makes it straightforward to sample experiences in proportion to their priorities. First, sample a number, x, random–uniformly between 0 and $\sum_j (|\omega_j| + \varepsilon)^\eta$; the latter value can be obtained in constant time by querying the value stored in the root node. Then, traverse the tree until you reach a leaf. The decision to choose the left or right child of a node is made as follows. If `x <= node.left_child`, select the left child and set that to the current node; otherwise, set `x = x - node.left_child` and set the right child to the current node. Repeat until you have reached a leaf, then return the index of that leaf.

To build intuition for why this results in proportional sampling, it is helpful to work through an example of just a few elements. Figure 5.1 shows an example for six elements, corresponding to six experiences. The $(|\omega_j| + \varepsilon)^\eta$ values for each element, shown in the leaf nodes at the bottom of the tree, are $(5, 25, 10, 0, 35, 24)$. $\sum_j (|\omega_j| + \varepsilon)^\eta = 99$, as can be seen in the root node at the top of the tree.

If x is sampled random-uniformly between 0 and 99, the values of x for which each element will be selected are shown below each leaf, along with the corresponding percentage of times each element will be sampled. The larger $(|\omega_j| + \varepsilon)^\eta$, the more often element i will be sampled. For example, element 5 with $(|\omega_j| + \varepsilon)^\eta = 35$ will be sampled 35% of the time, whereas element 3 with $(|\omega_j| + \varepsilon)^\eta = 10$ will only be sampled 10% of the time.

Figure 5.1 also shows a traversal of the tree when $x = 37$. At the root node, since $x \le 40$ which is the value of the left child node, we move to the left child. Next, $x > 30$ so we move to the right child with value 10 and set x to $x - 30 = 7$. Finally, we compare 7 with 10, and since $7 \le 10$, we select the left child and have reached a leaf. The index of this leaf is 3, and this is what we select.

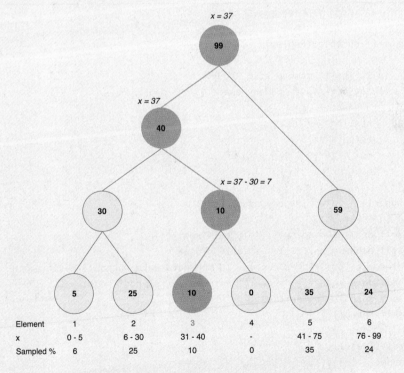

Element	1	2	3	4	5	6
x	0 - 5	6 - 30	31 - 40	-	41 - 75	76 - 99
Sampled %	6	25	10	0	35	24

Figure 5.1   A sum tree containing six elements

> The number of steps required to sample the index of an experience to include in a batch is now just the height of the binary tree, which is $\log_2 n$. For example, if there are 100,000 experiences in the memory, sampling an index takes only 17 steps, since $\log_2(100{,}000) \approx 17$.

Memory Initialization and Reset   __init__ in Code 5.6 calls the parent class init (line 13) which initializes the class variables, including the storage keys. In PrioritizedReplay memory we also need to store the priorities and initialize the sum tree. This is done by redefining the storage keys self.data_keys with an additional "priorities" element (line 18) and then calling self.reset again (line 19).

reset calls the parent class method and additionally initializes the sum tree (line 23).

Code 5.6   Prioritized Experience Replay: initialization and reset

```
1   # slm_lab/agent/memory/prioritized.py
2
3   class PrioritizedReplay(Replay):
4
5       def __init__(self, memory_spec, body):
6           util.set_attr(self, memory_spec, [
7               'alpha',
8               'epsilon',
9               'batch_size',
10              'max_size',
11              'use_cer',
12          ])
13          super().__init__(memory_spec, body)
14
15          self.epsilon = np.full((1,), self.epsilon)
16          self.alpha = np.full((1,), self.alpha)
17          # adds a 'priorities' scalar to the data_keys and call reset again
18          self.data_keys = ['states', 'actions', 'rewards', 'next_states',
             ↪ 'dones', 'priorities']
19          self.reset()
20
21      def reset(self):
22          super().reset()
23          self.tree = SumTree(self.max_size)
```

Storing Priorities In Code 5.7, add_experience first calls the parent class method to add the (state, action, reward, next_state, done) to the memory (line 7).

Next, we need to get the priority of the experience given the absolute TD error error (line 8). One heuristic we use is that new experiences are likely to be informative for an agent, so should have a high probability of being sampled. This is implemented by assigning them a large error of 100,000.

Finally, we add the priority to both the memory and the sum tree (lines 9–10).

Code 5.7   Prioritized Experience Replay: storing priorities

```
# slm_lab/agent/memory/prioritized.py

class PrioritizedReplay(Replay):
    ...

    def add_experience(self, state, action, reward, next_state, done,
    ↪  error=100000):
        super().add_experience(state, action, reward, next_state, done)
        priority = self.get_priority(error)
        self.priorities[self.head] = priority
        self.tree.add(priority, self.head)

    def get_priority(self, error):
        return np.power(error + self.epsilon, self.alpha).squeeze()
```

Updating Priorities Code 5.8 shows how the priorities are updated. This is straightforward once the SumTree is implemented. First, the absolute TD errors are converted to priorities (line 7). Then, the priorities in the main memory structure are updated (lines 9–10) using the indices of the experiences in the batch. Note that self.batch_idxs always stores the indices of the last sampled batch. Finally, the priorities are updated in the SumTree (lines 11–12).

Code 5.8   Prioritized Experience Replay: updating priorities

```
# slm_lab/agent/memory/prioritized.py

class PrioritizedReplay(Replay):
    ...

    def update_priorities(self, errors):
        priorities = self.get_priority(errors)
        assert len(priorities) == self.batch_idxs.size
        for idx, p in zip(self.batch_idxs, priorities):
```

```
10          self.priorities[idx] = p
11      for p, i in zip(priorities, self.tree_idxs):
12          self.tree.update(i, p)
```

Proportional Sampling   `sample_idxs` (Code 5.9) is responsible for identifying the indices of the experiences that should constitute a batch. To select an index, we first sample a number between 0 and the sum of $\sum_j (|\omega_j| + \varepsilon)^\eta$ (line 11). This number is used to select an element from the tree using the procedure described in Box 5.2 (line 12), and this element is associated with an index in the `PrioritizedReplay` memory. Once all the indices have been selected, they are stored in `self.batch_idxs` to use when building a batch of training data (line 13), and in `self.tree_idxs` to use when updating the priorities (line 14).

Note that this implementation of proportional sampling is adapted from Jaromar Janisch's which is available at his blog: https://jaromiru.com/2016/09/27/lets-make-a-dqn-theory/. For the sum tree implementation, see `slm_lab/agent/memory/prioritized.py`.

Code 5.9   Prioritized Experience Replay: proportional sampling

```
1   # slm_lab/agent/memory/prioritized.py
2
3   class PrioritizedReplay(Replay):
4       ...
5
6       def sample_idxs(self, batch_size):
7           batch_idxs = np.zeros(batch_size)
8           tree_idxs = np.zeros(batch_size, dtype=np.int)
9
10          for i in range(batch_size):
11              s = random.uniform(0, self.tree.total())
12              (tree_idx, p, idx) = self.tree.get(s)
13              batch_idxs[i] = idx
14              tree_idxs[i] = tree_idx
15
16          batch_idxs = np.asarray(batch_idxs).astype(int)
17          self.tree_idxs = tree_idxs
18          ...
19          return batch_idxs
```

5.5   Training a DQN Agent to Play Atari Games

At this point, we have all of the elements we need to train DQN agents to play Atari games from image states. However, to achieve good performance, we need to modify the environment states and rewards. These modifications were first introduced in the well-known paper "Human-Level Control through Deep Reinforcement Learning" [89] and have since become standard practice to apply to the Atari environment.

In this section, we first give some brief background on the Atari games as well as the modifications to their states and rewards. Then, we configure a spec file for Double DQN agent with PER to play Atari Pong.

The Atari 2600 was a popular video game console released in 1977. Alongside the original games, a large number of (now classic) arcade games were ported to the console. The games available on the Atari 2600 were often complex and challenging to play; however, the computational demands of the games were low, making them easy to emulate on a modern computer. The console RAM holds just 128 bytes and the game screen is only 160 pixels wide by 210 pixels high. In 2012, Bellemare et al. realized that these conditions make the Atari games an ideal testing ground for reinforcement learning algorithms, and created the Arcade Learning Environment (ALE) which emulates over fifty games [14].

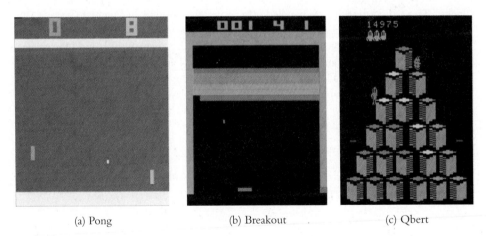

(a) Pong   (b) Breakout   (c) Qbert

Figure 5.2   Example states from three Atari games provided through the OpenAI Gym [18]

SLM Lab uses the Atari games provided through the OpenAI Gym [18]. The state in each Atari game is a low-resolution RGB image of the gameplay window, encoded as a 3D array of size $(210, 160, 3)$. The action space is discrete with few dimensions. Depending on the game, there are 4–18 different actions an agent may take at each time step. For example, the Pong actions in OpenAI Gym are: 0 (no-op), 1 (fire), 2 (up), and 3 (down).

The Atari state space has significantly higher dimensionality than any game we have seen so far. Each state has $210 \times 160 \times 3 = 100{,}800$ dimensions compared with four dimensions for CartPole. The Atari games are also much more complex than CartPole. Episodes last for thousands of time steps and good performance requires sophisticated sequences of actions. The combination of these two factors makes the learning problem for an agent significantly more difficult. To help an agent learn under these conditions, the authors of [88, 141] made the following adjustments to the standard DQN or Double DQN algorithms:

- **Specialized network design to process images:** The Q-function approximator is a convolutional neural network with three hidden convolutional layers and one hidden dense layer.

- **State preprocessing:** This includes image downsizing, grayscaling, frame concatenation, and frame skipping with max pixel values.

- **Reward preprocessing:** At every time step, the reward is transformed to $-1, 0, +1$ based on the sign of the original reward.

- **Environment reset:** Depending on the game, once a game life is lost, the environment is reset, start state randomized, and "FIRE" may be pressed at reset.

The network design is implemented using SLM Lab's `ConvNet` class. The state, reward, and environment modifications are discussed in more detail in Section 10.3, "Atari Tricks." These modifications are handled using a wrapper around an OpenAI Gym environment. The wrapper simply wraps an environment without changing its interface, so it has the advantage of carrying out all of the desired transformations behind the scenes. This makes it possible to train a DQN or a Double DQN agent with these modifications without having to change any code in the implementations we have discussed so far.

The configuration to train a Double DQN agent to play Atari Pong using Prioritized Experience Replay is shown in Code 5.10. The file is also available in SLM Lab at `slm_lab/spec/benchmark/dqn/ddqn_per_pong_spec.json`.

Code 5.10   A Double DQN with PER spec file configured to play Atari Pong

```
1  # slm_lab/spec/benchmark/dqn/ddqn_per_pong.json
2
3  {
4    "ddqn_per_pong": {
5      "agent": [{
6        "name": "DoubleDQN",
7        "algorithm": {
8          "name": "DoubleDQN",
9          "action_pdtype": "Argmax",
10         "action_policy": "epsilon_greedy",
11         "explore_var_spec": {
12           "name": "linear_decay",
```

```
13              "start_val": 1.0,
14              "end_val": 0.01,
15              "start_step": 10000,
16              "end_step": 1000000
17            },
18            "gamma": 0.99,
19            "training_batch_iter": 1,
20            "training_iter": 4,
21            "training_frequency": 4,
22            "training_start_step": 10000
23          },
24          "memory": {
25            "name": "PrioritizedReplay",
26            "alpha": 0.6,
27            "epsilon": 0.0001,
28            "batch_size": 32,
29            "max_size": 200000,
30            "use_cer": false,
31          },
32          "net": {
33            "type": "ConvNet",
34            "conv_hid_layers": [
35              [32, 8, 4, 0, 1],
36              [64, 4, 2, 0, 1],
37              [64, 3, 1, 0, 1]
38            ],
39            "fc_hid_layers": [256],
40            "hid_layers_activation": "relu",
41            "init_fn": null,
42            "batch_norm": false,
43            "clip_grad_val": 10.0,
44            "loss_spec": {
45              "name": "SmoothL1Loss"
46            },
47            "optim_spec": {
48              "name": "Adam",
49              "lr": 2.5e-5,
50            },
51            "lr_scheduler_spec": null,
52            "update_type": "replace",
53            "update_frequency": 1000,
54            "gpu": true
55          }
56        }],
```

```
57      "env": [{
58        "name": "PongNoFrameskip-v4",
59        "frame_op": "concat",
60        "frame_op_len": 4,
61        "reward_scale": "sign",
62        "num_envs": 16,
63        "max_t": null,
64        "max_frame": 4e6
65      }],
66      "body": {
67        "product": "outer",
68        "num": 1
69      },
70      "meta": {
71        "distributed": false,
72        "eval_frequency": 10000,
73        "log_frequency": 10000,
74        "max_session": 4,
75        "max_trial": 1
76      }
77    }
78  }
```

Let's review the main components.

- **Algorithm:** The algorithm is Double DQN (line 8). To use DQN, change line 8 from `"name": "DoubleDQN"` to `"name": "DQN"`. The action policy is ε-greedy (line 10) with linear decay. ε is initialized to 1.0 and annealed to 0.01 between time steps 10,000 and 1,000,000 (lines 12–16).

- **Network architecture:** The network is a convolutional neural network (line 33) with ReLU activations (line 40). The network has three convolutional layers (lines 34–38) followed by one fully connected layer (line 39). Training takes place on a GPU (line 54).

- **Optimizer and loss function:** The optimizer is Adam [68] (lines 47–50) and the loss is the Huber loss, named `SmoothL1Loss` in PyTorch (lines 44–46). It is quadratic for absolute values less than 1 and linear everywhere else, making it less sensitive to outliers.

- **Training frequency:** Training starts after an agent has taken 10,000 steps in total in the environment (line 22) and occurs every four steps from then on (line 21). At each training step, four batches are sampled from the memory (line 20). Each batch has 32 elements (line 28) and is used to make one parameter update to the network (line 19).

- **Memory:** The memory type is `PrioritzedReplay` (line 25) and it has a maximum size of 200,000 experiences (line 29). The prioritization parameter η is set with the variable `alpha` (line 26) and the small constant ε is set with the variable `epsilon` (line 27).

- **Environment:** The environment is the Atari game Pong (line 58). Four frames are concatenated to form a single state (lines 59–60); during training, the rewards for each time step are transformed into their sign -1, 0, or $+1$ (line 61). To speed up training, we use 16 parallel environments (line 62)—this simple technique is the subject of Chapter 8.

- **Training length:** Training continues for 4,000,000 time steps (line 64).

- **Checkpointing:** The agent is evaluated every 10,000 time steps (line 72). The parameters of the network are also checkpointed after each eval.

To train this DQN agent using SLM Lab, run the commands shown in Code 5.11 in a terminal.

Code 5.11 Training a Double DQN agent with PER to play Atari Pong

```
1  conda activate lab
2  python run_lab.py slm_lab/spec/benchmark/dqn/ddqn_per_pong.json ddqn_per_pong
↪    train
```

This will use the spec file to run a training `Trial` with four `Sessions` to obtain an average result. The result is then plotted with an error band. A moving-average version with a window of 100 evaluations is also generated. Both graphs are shown in Figure 5.3. At the beginning of training, an agent will have an average score of -21. Performance improves steadily for two million frames, after which an agent achieves close to the maximum score of 21 on average.

Note that training this agent requires more computational resources than the other agents described so far in this book. The trial should take about one day to complete when running on a GPU.

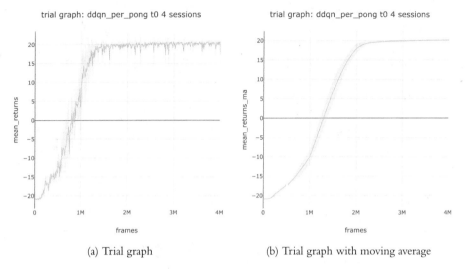

(a) Trial graph   (b) Trial graph with moving average

Figure 5.3   Double DQN + PER trial graphs from SLM Lab averaged over four sessions. The vertical axis shows the total rewards (`mean_return` for evaluation is computed without discount) averaged over eight episodes during checkpoints, and the horizontal axis shows the total training frames. The graph on the right is a moving average with a window of 100 evaluation checkpoints.

5.6   Experimental Results

In this section we will look at the effects of the DQN improvements—namely, target networks, Double DQN, and PER. Starting with DQN with target network (which we will simply call DQN), we will run a grid of trials to study the effect of the improvements. The trials include four combinations: DQN, DQN + PER, Double DQN, and Double DQN + PER. The trials will be run on Atari Pong environment to produce trial graphs which are then combined for comparison.

5.6.1   Experiment: The Effect of Double DQN and PER

First, we have the DQN spec file shown in Code 5.12. This is similar to Code 5.10 apart from using DQN (lines 4–8), disabling PER by using a plain replay memory class (lines 11–16), and increasing the learning rate (line 21). This file can be found in SLM Lab at `slm_lab/spec/benchmark/dqn /dqn_pong_spec.json`.

Code 5.12   A DQN spec file configured to play Atari Pong

```
1   # slm_lab/spec/benchmark/dqn/dqn_pong.json
2
3   {
4       "dqn_pong": {
```

```
5        "agent": [{
6          "name": "DQN",
7          "algorithm": {
8            "name": "DQN",
9            ...
10         },
11         "memory": {
12           "name": "Replay",
13           "batch_size": 32,
14           "max_size": 200000,
15           "use_cer": false
16         },
17         "net": {
18           ...
19           "optim_spec": {
20             "name": "Adam",
21             "lr": 1e-4,
22           },
23         ...
24       }
25  }
```

Second, we have the DQN + PER spec file shown in Code 5.13, also similar to Code 5.10 but modified to use DQN (lines 4–8). This file can be found in SLM Lab at `slm_lab/spec/benchmark/dqn/dqn_per_pong_spec.json`.

Code 5.13   A DQN + PER spec file configured to play Atari Pong

```
1  # slm_lab/spec/benchmark/dqn/dqn_per_pong.json
2
3  {
4    "dqn_per_pong": {
5      "agent": [{
6        "name": "DQN",
7        "algorithm": {
8          "name": "DQN",
9          ...
10     }
11  }
```

Third, we have the Double DQN spec file shown in Code 5.14 with modifications from Code 5.10 to disable PER (lines 11–16) and to use a higher learning rate (line 21). This file can be found in SLM Lab at `slm_lab/spec/benchmark/dqn/ddqn_pong_spec.json`.

Code 5.14   A Double DQN spec file configured to play Atari Pong

```
1   # slm_lab/spec/benchmark/dqn/ddqn_pong.json
2
3   {
4     "ddqn_pong": {
5       "agent": [{
6         "name": "DoubleDQN",
7         "algorithm": {
8           "name": "DoubleDQN",
9           ...
10        },
11        "memory": {
12          "name": "Replay",
13          "batch_size": 32,
14          "max_size": 200000,
15          "use_cer": false,
16        },
17        "net": {
18          ...
19          "optim_spec": {
20            "name": "Adam",
21            "lr": 1e-4,
22          },
23        ...
24      }
25  }
```

Finally, we have the Double DQN + PER spec file shown earlier in Code 5.10, also available in SLM Lab at `slm_lab/spec/benchmark/dqn/ddqn_per_pong_spec.json`. Note that when using PER, we tend to use a lower learning rate. This is because PER selects higher-error transitions more often and leads to larger gradients on average. To compensate for the larger gradients, Schaul et al. [121] found it was helpful to reduce the learning rate by a factor of 4.

The four commands to train these four DQN variants using SLM Lab are shown in Code 5.15. All these trials will each require nearly one day to complete when running on a GPU, though they may be run separately in parallel if there are sufficient computing resources.

Code 5.15   Training four variants of DQN, DQN + PER, Double DQN, and Double DQN + PER to play Atari Pong

```
1   # run DQN
2   conda activate lab
3   python run_lab.py slm_lab/spec/benchmark/dqn/dqn_pong.json dqn_pong train
```

```
4
5   # run DQN + PER
6   conda activate lab
7   python run_lab.py slm_lab/spec/benchmark/dqn/dqn_per_pong.json dqn_per_pong
    ↪   train
8
9   # run Double DQN
10  conda activate lab
11  python run_lab.py slm_lab/spec/benchmark/dqn/ddqn_pong.json ddqn_pong train
12
13  # run Double DQN + PER
14  conda activate lab
15  python run_lab.py slm_lab/spec/benchmark/dqn/ddqn_per_pong.json ddqn_per_pong
    ↪   train
```

Each of the four `Trials` will produce its own graphs using an average from four `Sessions`. For comparison, they are plotted together, using the `viz.plot_multi_trial` utility method in SLM Lab, as a multitrial graph shown in Figure 5.4.

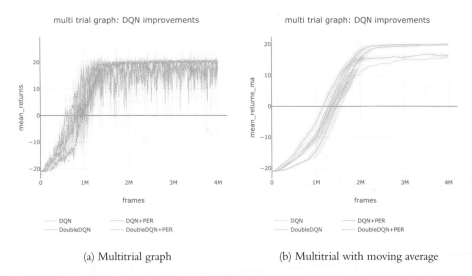

(a) Multitrial graph   (b) Multitrial with moving average

Figure 5.4   These graphs compare the performance of the four variants of DQN improvements using Atari Pong. As expected, Double DQN + PER performs the best, followed by DQN + PER, Double DQN, and DQN.

Figure 5.4 compares the performance of the four variants of DQN improvements using Atari Pong. As expected, when using all the improvements, Double DQN + PER performs the best. This is closely followed by DQN + PER, then Double DQN, and DQN. Overall, using PER yields significant improvement and helps stabilize learning, as seen in the higher, smoother learning returns curve. In comparison, using Double DQN provides a smaller improvement.

5.7   Summary

This chapter discussed three techniques for improving the DQN algorithm, each addressing one of its limitations.

- **Target network:** Using a lagged copy of the original network to calculate $Q_{\text{tar}}^{\pi}(s, a)$ makes the optimization problem easier and helps stabilize training.

- **Double DQN:** Using two different networks to estimate the Q-value of the next state when calculating $Q_{\text{tar}}^{\pi}(s, a)$ reduces DQN's tendency to overestimate Q-values. In practice, the training network θ and the target network φ are used as the two networks.

- **Prioritized Experience Replay:** Not all experiences are equally informative for an agent. Prioritizing experiences that the agent can learn the most from, as measured by the absolute TD error between $\hat{Q}^{\pi}(s, a)$ and $Q_{\text{tar}}^{\pi}(s, a)$, improves the sample efficiency of DQN.

We also discussed a specific implementation of DQN with a target network and PER that is designed to play Atari games. Atari games are the most complex environments we have seen so far; to achieve good performance we needed to modify the states and rewards. The modifications included reducing the state space dimensionality by downsizing, cropping, and converting the images to grayscale, stacking the most recent four states so that an agent can see the recent past when selecting an action, increasing the time elapsed between consecutive frames by only showing the agent every fourth frame, and designing a Q-function network specialized for image processing.

5.8   Further Reading

- "Human-Level Control through Deep Reinforcement Learning," Mnih et al., 2015 [89].

- "Double Q-Learning," van Hasselt, 2010 [140].

- "Deep Reinforcement Learning with Double Q-Learning," van Hasselt et al., 2015 [141].

- "Prioritized Experience Replay," Schaul et al., 2015 [121].

- "Dueling Network Architectures for Deep Reinforcement Learning," Wang et al., 2016 [144].

- "The Arcade Learning Environment: An Evaluation Platform for General Agents," Bellemare et al., 2013 [14].

Part II

Combined Methods

Advantage Actor-Critic (A2C)

In this chapter, we look at Actor-Critic algorithms which elegantly combine the ideas we have seen so far in this book—namely, the policy gradient and a learned value function. In these algorithms, a policy is reinforced with a *learned reinforcing signal* generated using a learned value function. This contrasts with REINFORCE which uses a high-variance Monte Carlo estimate of the return to reinforce the policy.

All Actor-Critic algorithms have two components which are learned jointly—an *actor*, which learns a parameterized policy, and a *critic* which learns a value function to evaluate state-action pairs. The critic provides a reinforcing signal to the actor.

The main motivation behind these algorithms is that a learned reinforcing signal can be more informative for a policy than the rewards available from an environment. For example, it can transform a sparse reward in which the agent only receives +1 upon success into a dense reinforcing signal. Furthermore, learned value functions typically have lower variance than Monte Carlo estimates of the return. This reduces the uncertainty under which a policy learns [11], making the learning process easier. However, training also becomes more complex. Now learning the policy depends on the quality of the value function estimate which is being learned simultaneously. Until the value function is generating reasonable signals for the policy, learning how to select good actions will be challenging.

It is common to learn the *advantage* function $A^\pi(s, a) = Q^\pi(s, a) - V^\pi(s)$ as the reinforcing signals in these methods. The key idea is that it is better to select an action based on how it performs relative to the other actions available in a particular state, instead of using the absolute value of that action as measured by the Q-function. The advantage quantifies how much better or worse an action is than the average available action. Actor-Critic algorithms which learn the advantage function are known as Advantage Actor-Critic (A2C) algorithms.

First, we discuss the actor in Section 6.1. This is brief because it is similar to REINFORCE. Then, in Section 6.2 we introduce the critic and two different methods for estimating the advantage function—n-step returns and Generalized Advantage Estimation [123].

Section 6.3 covers the Actor-Critic algorithm and Section 6.4 contains an example of how it can be implemented. The chapter ends with instructions for training an Actor-Critic agent.

6.1 The Actor

Actors learn parametrized policies π_θ using the policy gradient as shown in Equation 6.1. This is very similar to REINFORCE (Chapter 2) except we now use the advantage A_t^π as a reinforcing signal instead of a Monte Carlo estimate of the return $R_t(\tau)$ (Equation 2.1).

$$\text{Actor-Critic:}\quad \nabla_\theta J(\pi_\theta) = \mathbb{E}_t\big[A_t^\pi \nabla_\theta \log \pi_\theta(a_t \mid s_t)\big] \tag{6.1}$$

$$\text{REINFORCE:}\quad \nabla_\theta J(\pi_\theta) = \mathbb{E}_t\big[R_t(\tau)\nabla_\theta \log \pi_\theta(a_t \mid s_t)\big] \tag{6.2}$$

Next, we look at how to learn the advantage function.

6.2 The Critic

Critics are responsible for learning how to evaluate (s, a) pairs and using this to generate A^π.

In what follows, we first describe the advantage function and why it is a good choice for a reinforcing signal. Then, we present two methods for estimating the advantage function—n-step returns and Generalized Advantage Estimation [123]. Finally, we discuss how they can be learned in practice.

6.2.1 The Advantage Function

Intuitively, the advantage function $A^\pi(s_t, a_t)$ measures the extent to which an action is better or worse than the policy's average action in a particular state. The advantage is defined in Equation 6.3.

$$A^\pi(s_t, a_t) = Q^\pi(s_t, a_t) - V^\pi(s_t) \tag{6.3}$$

It has a number of nice properties. First, $\mathbb{E}_{a \in A}[A^\pi(s_t, a)] = 0$. This implies that if all actions are essentially equivalent, then A^π will be 0 for all actions and the probability of taking these actions will remain unchanged when the policy is trained using A^π. Compare this to a reinforcing signal based on absolute state or state-action values. This signal would have a constant value in the same situation, but it may not be 0. Consequently, it would actively encourage (if positive) or discourage (if negative) the action taken. Since all actions were equivalent, this may not be problematic in practice, although it is unintuitive.

A more problematic example is if the action taken was worse than the average action, but the expected return is still positive. That is, $Q^\pi(s_t, a_t) > 0$, but $A^\pi(s_t, a_t) < 0$. Ideally, the action taken should become less likely since there were better options available. In this case using A^π yields behavior which matches our intuition more closely since it will discourage the action taken. Using Q^π, or even Q^π with a baseline, may encourage the action.

The advantage is also a relative measure. For a particular state s and action a, it considers the value of the state-action pair, $Q^\pi(s, a)$, and evaluates whether a will take the policy to a better or worse place, measured relative to $V^\pi(s)$. The advantage avoids penalizing an action for the policy currently being in a particularly bad state. Conversely, it does not give credit to an action for the policy being in a good state. This is beneficial because a can only affect the future trajectory, but not how a policy arrived in the current state. We should evaluate the action based on how it changes the value in the future.

Let's look at an example. In Equation 6.4, the policy is in a good state with $V^\pi(s) = 100$, whereas in Equation 6.5, it is in a bad state with $V^\pi(s) = -100$. In both cases, action a yields a relative improvement of 10, which is captured by each case having the same advantage. However, this would not be clear if we looked at just $Q^\pi(s, a)$.

$$Q^\pi(s, a) = 110, \quad V^\pi(s) = 100, \quad A^\pi(s, a) = 10 \tag{6.4}$$
$$Q^\pi(s, a) = -90, \quad V^\pi(s) = -100, \quad A^\pi(s, a) = 10 \tag{6.5}$$

Understood this way, the advantage function is able to capture the long-term effects of an action, because it considers all future time steps,[1] while ignoring the effects of all the actions to date. Schulman et al. present a similar interpretation in their paper "Generalized Advantage Estimation" [123].

Having seen why the advantage function $A^\pi(s, a)$ is a good choice of reinforcing signal to use in an Actor-Critic algorithm, let's look at two ways of estimating it.

6.2.1.1 Estimating Advantage: n-Step Returns

To calculate the advantage A^π, we need an estimate for Q^π and V^π. One idea is that we could learn Q^π and V^π separately with different neural networks. However, this has two disadvantages. First, care needs to be taken to ensure the two estimates are consistent. Second, it is less efficient to learn. Instead, we typically learn just V^π and combine it with rewards from a trajectory to estimate Q^π.

Learning V^π is preferred to learning Q^π for two reasons. First, Q^π is a more complex function and may require more samples to learn a good estimate. This can be particularly problematic in the setting where the actor and the critic are trained jointly. Second, it can be more computationally expensive to estimate V^π from Q^π. Estimating $V^\pi(s)$ from $Q^\pi(s, a)$ requires computing the values for all possible actions in state s, then taking the action-probability weighted average to obtain $V^\pi(s)$. Additionally, this is difficult for environments with continuous actions since estimating V^π would require a representative sample of actions from a continuous space.

Let's look at how to estimate Q^π from V^π.

If we assume for a moment that we have a perfect estimate of $V^\pi(s)$, then the Q-function can be rewritten as a mix of the expected rewards for n time steps, followed by $V^\pi(s_{n+1})$ as shown in Equation 6.6. To make this tractable to estimate, we use a single trajectory of rewards $(r_1, \ldots, r_n)$ in place of the expectation, and substitute in $\hat{V}^\pi(s)$ learned by the critic. Shown in Equation 6.7, this is known as n-step forward returns.

---

1. Within the time horizon implicitly given by γ.

$$Q^{\pi}(s_t, a_t) = \mathbb{E}_{\tau \sim \pi}[r_t + \gamma r_{t+1} + \gamma^2 r_{t+2} + \cdots + \gamma^n r_{t+n}] + \gamma^{n+1} V^{\pi}(s_{t+n+1}) \quad (6.6)$$

$$\approx r_t + \gamma r_{t+1} + \gamma^2 r_{t+2} + \cdots + \gamma^n r_{t+n} + \gamma^{n+1} \hat{V}^{\pi}(s_{t+n+1}) \quad (6.7)$$

Equation 6.7 makes the tradeoff between bias and variance of the estimator explicit. The n steps of actual rewards are unbiased but have high variance since they come from only a single trajectory. $\hat{V}^{\pi}(s)$ has lower variance since it reflects an expectation over all of the trajectories seen so far, but is biased because it is calculated using a function approximator. The intuition behind mixing these two types of estimates is that the variance of the actual rewards typically increases the more steps away from t you take. Close to t, the benefits of using an unbiased estimate may outweigh the variance introduced. As n increases, the variance in the estimates will likely start to become problematic, and switching to a lower-variance but biased estimate is better. The number of steps of actual rewards, n, controls the tradeoff between the two.

Combining the n-step estimate for Q^{π} with $\hat{V}^{\pi}(s_t)$, we get an formula for estimating the advantage function, shown in Equation 6.8.

$$
\begin{aligned}
A^{\pi}_{\text{NSTEP}}(s_t, a_t) &= Q^{\pi}(s_t, a_t) - V^{\pi}(s_t) \\
&\approx r_t + \gamma r_{t+1} + \gamma^2 r_{t+2} + \cdots + \gamma^n r_{t+n} \\
&\quad + \gamma^{n+1} \hat{V}^{\pi}(s_{t+n+1}) - \hat{V}^{\pi}(s_t)
\end{aligned}
\quad (6.8)
$$

The number of steps of actual rewards, n, controls the amount of variance in the advantage estimator, and is a hyperparameter that needs to be tuned. Small n results in an estimator with lower variance but higher bias, large n results in an estimator with higher variance but lower bias.

6.2.1.2   Estimating Advantage: Generalized Advantage Estimation (GAE)

Generalized Advantage Estimation (GAE) [123] was proposed by Schulman et al. as an improvement over the n-step returns estimate for the advantage function. It addresses the problem of having to explicitly choose the number of steps of returns, n. The main idea behind GAE is that instead of picking one value of n, we mix multiple values of n. That is, we calculate the advantage using a weighted average of individual advantages calculated with $n = 1, 2, 3, \ldots, k$. The purpose of GAE is to significantly reduce the variance of the estimator while keeping the bias introduced as low as possible.

GAE is defined as an exponentially weighted average of all of the n-step forward return advantages. It is shown in Equation 6.9 and the full derivation for GAE is given in Box 6.1.

$$A^{\pi}_{\text{GAE}}(s_t, a_t) = \sum_{\ell=0}^{\infty} (\gamma \lambda)^{\ell} \delta_{t+\ell},$$
$$\text{where } \delta_t = r_t + \gamma V^{\pi}(s_{t+1}) - V^{\pi}(s_t) \quad (6.9)$$

Intuitively, GAE is taking a weighted average of a number of advantage estimators with different bias and variance. GAE weights the high–bias, low-variance 1-step advantage the most, but also includes contributions from lower-bias, higher-variance estimators using $2, 3, \ldots, n$ steps. The contribution decays at an exponential rate as the number of steps increases. The decay rate is controlled by the coefficient λ. Therefore, the larger λ, the higher the variance.

Box 6.1 Generalized Advantage Estimation Derivation

The derivation of GAE is a little involved, but worth working through to understand how GAE estimates the advantage function. Fortunately, at the end of it we will have a simple expression for GAE that is reasonably straightforward to implement.

$A_t^\pi(n)$ is used to denote the advantage estimator calculated with n-step forward returns. For example, Equation 6.10 shows $A_t^\pi(1)$, $A_t^\pi(2)$, and $A_t^\pi(3)$.

$$
\begin{aligned}
A_t^\pi(1) &= r_t + \gamma V^\pi(s_{t+1}) - V^\pi(s_t) \\
A_t^\pi(2) &= r_t + \gamma r_{t+1} + \gamma^2 V^\pi(s_{t+2}) - V^\pi(s_t) \\
A_t^\pi(3) &= r_t + \gamma r_{t+1} + \gamma^2 r_{t+2} + \gamma^3 V^\pi(s_{t+3}) - V^\pi(s_t)
\end{aligned}
\tag{6.10}
$$

GAE is defined as an exponentially weighted average of all of the n-step forward return advantage estimators.

$$
A_{\text{GAE}}^\pi(s_t, a_t) = (1 - \lambda)(A_t^\pi(1) + \lambda A_t^\pi(2) + \lambda^2 A_t^\pi(3) + \cdots),
$$
$$
where\ \lambda \in [0, 1]
\tag{6.11}
$$

Equation 6.11 is not very easy to work with. Fortunately, Schulman et al. [123] introduce a variable δ_t for simplifying GAE.

$$
\delta_t = r_t + \gamma V^\pi(s_{t+1}) - V^\pi(s_t)
\tag{6.12}
$$

Notice that $r_t + \gamma V^\pi(s_{t+1})$ is the 1-step estimator for $Q^\pi(s_t, a_t)$, so δ_t represents the advantage function for time step t calculated with 1-step forward returns. Let's consider how to represent the n-step advantage function using δ. First, Equation 6.10 can be expanded and rewritten as Equation 6.13. Notice that in Equation 6.13 all of the intermediate $V^\pi(s_{t+1})$ to $V^\pi(s_{t+n-1})$ cancel to leave just $V^\pi(s_t)$ and a term involving $V^\pi(s_{t+n})$ for the last time step, as in Equation 6.10.

$$
\begin{aligned}
A_t^\pi(1) =\ & r_t + \gamma V^\pi(s_{t+1}) - V^\pi(s_t) \\
A_t^\pi(2) =\ & r_t + \gamma V^\pi(s_{t+1}) - V^\pi(s_t) \\
& + \gamma\big(r_{t+1} + \gamma V^\pi(s_{t+2}) - V^\pi(s_{t+1})\big) \\
A_t^\pi(3) =\ & r_t + \gamma V^\pi(s_{t+1}) - V^\pi(s_t) \\
& + \gamma\big(r_{t+1} + \gamma V^\pi(s_{t+2}) - V^\pi(s_{t+1})\big) \\
& + \gamma^2\big(r_{t+2} + \gamma V^\pi(s_{t+3}) - V^\pi(s_{t+2})\big)
\end{aligned}
\tag{6.13}
$$

Writing the advantage function in this form is useful because it shows that it consists of multiple 1-step advantages weighted exponentially by γ as the time step increases. Simplify the terms in Equation 6.13 with δ to obtain Equation 6.14. This shows that the n-step advantage $A^{\pi}(n)$ is the sum of exponentially weighted δs—that is, 1-step advantages.

$$\begin{aligned} A_t^{\pi}(1) &= \delta_t \\ A_t^{\pi}(2) &= \delta_t + \gamma\delta_{t+1} \\ A_t^{\pi}(3) &= \delta_t + \gamma\delta_{t+1} + \gamma^2\delta_{t+2} \end{aligned} \tag{6.14}$$

Having expressed $A^{\pi}(i)$ in terms of δ, we can substitute it into Equation 6.11 and simplify to obtain a simple expression for GAE shown in Equation 6.15.

$$A_{\text{GAE}}^{\pi}(s_t, a_t) = \sum_{\ell=0}^{\infty}(\gamma\lambda)^{\ell}\delta_{t+l} \tag{6.15}$$

Both GAE and the n-step advantage function estimates include the discount factor γ which controls how much an algorithm "cares" about future rewards compared to the current reward. Additionally, they both have a parameter that controls the bias-variance tradeoff: n for the advantage function and λ for GAE. So what have we gained with GAE?

Even though n and λ both control the bias-variance tradeoff, they do so in different ways. n represents a hard choice, since it precisely determines the point at which the high-variance rewards are switched for the V-function estimate. In contrast, λ represents a *soft* choice: smaller values of λ will more heavily weight the V-function estimate, whilst larger values will weight the actual rewards more. However, unless $\lambda = 0^2$ or $\lambda = 1$,[3] using λ still allows higher or lower variance estimates to contribute—hence the *soft* choice.

6.2.2   Learning the Advantage Function

We have seen two ways to estimate the advantage function. Both these methods assume we have access to an estimate for V^{π}, as shown below.

$$A_{\text{NSTEP}}^{\pi}(s_t, a_t) \approx r_t + \gamma r_{t+1} + \cdots + \gamma^n r_{t+n} + \gamma^{n+1}\hat{V}^{\pi}(s_{t+n+1}) - \hat{V}^{\pi}(s_t) \tag{6.16}$$

$$A_{\text{GAE}}^{\pi}(s_t, a_t) \approx \sum_{\ell=0}^{\infty}(\gamma\lambda)^{\ell}\delta_{t+l}, \text{ where } \delta_t = r_t + \gamma\hat{V}^{\pi}(s_{t+1}) - \hat{V}^{\pi}(s_t) \tag{6.17}$$

We learn V^{π} using TD learning in the same way we used it to learn Q^{π} for DQN. In brief, learning proceeds as follows. Parametrize V^{π} with θ, generate V_{tar}^{π} for each of the

---

2. This reduces GAE to the 1-step advantage function estimate—this is the Temporal Difference estimate of returns.
3. In this case, only the actual rewards are used in the estimate—this is the Monte Carlo estimate of returns.

experiences an agent gathers, and minimize the difference between $\hat{V}^{\pi}(s;\theta)$ and V_{tar}^{π} using a regression loss such as MSE. Repeat this process for many steps.

V_{tar}^{π} can be generated using any appropriate estimate. The simplest method is to set $V_{\text{tar}}^{\pi}(s) = r + \hat{V}^{\pi}(s';\theta)$. This naturally generalizes to an n-step estimate, as shown in Equation 6.18.

$$V_{\text{tar}}^{\pi}(s_t) = r_t + \gamma r_{t+1} + \cdots + \gamma^n r_{t+n} + \gamma^{n+1} \hat{V}^{\pi}(s_{t+n+1}) \qquad (6.18)$$

Alternatively, we can use a Monte Carlo estimate for V_{tar}^{π} shown in Equation 6.19.

$$V_{\text{tar}}^{\pi}(s_t) = \sum_{t'=t}^{T} \gamma^{t'-t} r_{t'} \qquad (6.19)$$

Or, we can set

$$V_{\text{tar}}^{\pi}(s_t) = A_{\text{GAE}}^{\pi}(s_t, a_t) + \hat{V}^{\pi}(s_t) \qquad (6.20)$$

Practically, to avoid additional computation, the choice of V_{tar}^{π} is often related to the method used to estimate the advantage. For example, we can use Equation 6.18 when estimating advantages using n-step returns, or Equation 6.20 when estimating advantages using GAE.

It is also possible to use a more advanced optimization procedure when learning $\hat{V}^{\pi}$. For example, in the GAE paper [123], $\hat{V}^{\pi}$ is learned using a trust-region method.

6.3 A2C Algorithm

Here we put the actor and critic together to form the Advantage Actor-Critic (A2C) algorithm, shown in Algorithm 6.1.

Algorithm 6.1 A2C algorithm

1: Set $\beta \geq 0$ # entropy regularization weight
2: Set $\alpha_A \geq 0$ # actor learning rate
3: Set $\alpha_C \geq 0$ # critic learning rate
4: Randomly initialize the actor and critic parameters θ_A, θ_C[4]
5: **for** $episode = 0 \ldots MAX\_EPISODE$ **do**
6:     Gather and store data (s_t, a_t, r_t, s_t') by acting in the environment using
        $\hookrightarrow$ the current policy
7:     **for** $t = 0 \ldots T$ **do**
8:         Calculate predicted V-value $\hat{V}^{\pi}(s_t)$ using the critic network θ_C

---

4. Note that the actor and critic can either be separate networks or a shared network. For more details, see Section 6.5.

9:          Calculate the advantage $\hat{A}^{\pi}(s_t, a_t)$ using the critic network θ_C
10:         Calculate $V_{\mathrm{tar}}^{\pi}(s_t)$ using the critic network θ_C and/or trajectory data
11:         Optionally, calculate entropy H_t of the policy distribution, using
            $\hookrightarrow$ the actor network θ_A. Otherwise, set $\beta = 0$
12:    **end for**
13:    Calculate value loss, for example using MSE:
14:    $L_{\mathrm{val}}(\theta_C) = \frac{1}{T}\sum_{t=0}^{T}(\hat{V}^{\pi}(s_t) - V_{\mathrm{tar}}^{\pi}(s_t))^2$
15:    Calculate policy loss:
16:    $L_{\mathrm{pol}}(\theta_A) = \frac{1}{T}\sum_{t=0}^{T}(-\hat{A}^{\pi}(s_t, a_t)\log \pi_{\theta_A}(a_t \mid s_t) - \beta H_t)$
17:    Update critic parameters, for example using SGD:[5]
18:    $\theta_C = \theta_C + \alpha_C \nabla_{\theta_C} L_{\mathrm{val}}(\theta_C)$
19:    Update actor parameters, for example using SGD:
20:    $\theta_A = \theta_A + \alpha_A \nabla_{\theta_A} L_{\mathrm{pol}}(\theta_A)$
21: **end for**

Each algorithm we have studied so far focused on learning one of two things: how to act (a policy) or how to evaluate actions (a critic). Actor-Critic algorithms learn both together. Aside from that, each element of the training loop should look familiar, since they have been part of the algorithms presented earlier in this book. Let's go through Algorithm 6.1 step by step.

- Lines 1–3: Set the values of important hyperparameters: $\beta, \alpha_A, \alpha_C$. β determines how much entropy regularization to apply (see below for more details). α_A and α_C are the learning rates used when optimizing each of the networks. They can be the same or different. These values vary depending on the RL problem we are trying to solve, and need to be determined empirically.

- Line 4: Randomly initialize the parameters of both networks.

- Line 6: Gather some data using the current policy network θ_A. This algorithm shows episodic training, but this approach also applies to batch training.

- Lines 8–10: For each (s_t, a_t, r_t, s_t') experience in the episode, calculate $\hat{V}^{\pi}(s_t)$, $V_{\mathrm{tar}}^{\pi}(s_t)$, and $\hat{A}^{\pi}(s_t, a_t)$ using the critic network.

- Line 11: For each (s_t, a_t, r_t, s_t') experience in the episode, optionally calculate the entropy of the current policy distribution π_{θ_A} using the actor network. The role of entropy is discussed in detail in Box 6.2.

- Lines 13–14: Calculate the value loss. As with the DQN algorithms, we selected MSE[6] as the measure of distance between $\hat{V}^{\pi}(s_t)$ and $V_{\mathrm{tar}}^{\pi}(s_t)$. However, any other appropriate loss function, such as the Huber loss, could be used.

---

5. Stochastic gradient descent.
6. Mean squared error.

- Lines 15–16: Calculate the policy loss. This has the same form as we saw in the REINFORCE algorithm with the addition of an optional entropy regularization term. Notice that we are minimizing the loss, but we want to maximize the policy gradient, hence the negative sign in front of $\hat{A}^\pi(s_t, a_t) \log \pi_{\theta_A}(a_t \mid s_t)$ as in REINFORCE.

- Lines 17–18: Update the critic parameters using the gradient of the value loss.

- Lines 19–20: Update the actor parameters using the policy gradient.

Box 6.2 Entropy Regularization

The role of entropy regularization is to encourage exploration through diverse actions. This idea was first proposed by Williams and Peng in 1991 [149] and has since become a popular modification to reinforcement learning algorithms which involve policy gradients.

To understand why it encourages exploration, first note that a distribution that is more uniform has higher entropy. The more uniform a policy's action distribution is, the more diverse actions it produces. Conversely, policies which are less uniform and produce similar actions have low entropy.

Let's see why the entropy modification to the policy gradient shown in Equation 6.21 encourages a more uniform policy.

$$L_{\text{pol}}(\theta_A) = \frac{1}{T} \sum_{i=0}^{T} \left(- \hat{A}^\pi(s_t, a_t) \log \pi_{\theta_A}(a_t \mid s_t) - \beta H_t \right) \qquad (6.21)$$

Entropy H and β are always non-negative, so $-\beta H$ is always negative. When a policy is far from uniform, entropy decreases, $-\beta H$ increases and contributes more to the loss, and the policy will be encouraged to become more uniform. Conversely, when a policy is more uniform, entropy increases, $-\beta H$ decreases and contributes less to the loss, and the policy will have little incentive to change through the entropy term.

Modifying the loss in this way expresses a preference for a greater variety of actions, provided that it does not reduce the term $\hat{A}^\pi(s_t, a_t) \log \pi_{\theta_A}(a_t \mid s_t)$ too much. The balance between these two terms of the objective is controlled through the β parameter.

6.4 Implementing A2C

We now have all of the elements needed to implement the Actor-Critic algorithms. The main components are

- Advantage estimation –for example, n–step returns or GAE
- Value loss and policy loss
- The training loop

In what follows, we discuss an implementation of each of these components, ending with the training loop which brings them all together. Since Actor-Critic conceptually extends REINFORCE, it is implemented by inheriting from the `Reinforce` class.

Actor-Critic is also an on-policy algorithm since the actor component learns a policy using the policy gradient. Consequently, we train Actor-Critic algorithms using an on-policy `Memory`, such as `OnPolicyReplay` which trains in an episodic manner, or `OnPolicyBatchReplay` which trains using batches of data. The code that follows applies to either approach.

6.4.1   Advantage Estimation

6.4.1.1   Advantage Estimation with n-Step Returns

The main trick when implementing the n-step Q^π estimate is to notice that we have access to the rewards received in an episode in sequence. We can calculate the discounted sum of n rewards for each element of the batch in parallel by taking advantage of vector arithmetic, as shown in Code 6.1. The approach goes as follows:

1. Initialize a vector `rets` to populate with the Q-value estimates—that is, n-step returns (line 4).

2. For efficiency, the computation is done from the last term to the first. The `future_ret` is a placeholder to accumulate the summed rewards as we work backwards (line 5). It is initialized to `next_v_pred` since the last term in the n-step Q-estimate is $\hat{V}^\pi(s_{t+n+1})$.

3. `not_dones` is a binary variable to handle the episodic boundary and stop the sum from propagating across episodes.

4. Note that the n-step Q-estimate is defined recursively, that is, $Q_{\text{current}} = r_{\text{current}} + \gamma Q_{\text{next}}$. This is mirrored exactly by line 8.

Code 6.1 Actor-Critic implementation: calculate n-step $\hat{Q}^\pi(s, a)$

```
1    # slm_lab/lib/math_util.py
2
3    def calc_nstep_returns(rewards, dones, next_v_pred, gamma, n):
4        rets = torch.zeros_like(rewards)
5        future_ret = next_v_pred
6        not_dones = 1 - dones
7        for t in reversed(range(n)):
8            rets[t] = future_ret = rewards[t] + gamma * future_ret * not_dones[t]
9        return rets
```

Now, the `ActorCritic` class needs a method to compute the advantage estimates and the target V values for computing the policy and value losses, respectively. This is relatively straightforward, as shown in Code 6.2.

One detail about `advs` and `v_targets` is important to highlight. They do not have a gradient, as can be seen in the `torch.no_grad()` and `.detach()` operations in lines 9–11. In policy loss (Equation 6.1), the advantage only acts as a scalar multiplier to the gradient of the policy log probability. As for the value loss from Algorithm 6.1 (lines 13–14), we assume the target V-value is fixed, and the goal is to train the critic to predict V-value that closely matches it.

Code 6.2   Actor-Critic implementation: calculate n-step advantages and V-target values

```
1   # slm_lab/agent/algorithm/actor_critic.py
2
3   class ActorCritic(Reinforce):
4       ...
5
6       def calc_nstep_advs_v_targets(self, batch, v_preds):
7           next_states = batch['next_states'][-1]
8           ...
9           with torch.no_grad():
10              next_v_pred = self.calc_v(next_states, use_cache=False)
11          v_preds = v_preds.detach()  # adv does not accumulate grad
12          ...
13          nstep_rets = math_util.calc_nstep_returns(batch['rewards'],
             ↪  batch['dones'], next_v_pred, self.gamma, self.num_step_returns)
14          advs = nstep_rets - v_preds
15          v_targets = nstep_rets
16          ...
17          return advs, v_targets
```

6.4.1.2 Advantage Estimation with GAE

The implementation of GAE shown in Code 6.3 has a very similar form to that of n-step. It uses the same backward computation, except that we need an extra step to compute the δ term at each time step (line 11).

Code 6.3   Actor-Critic implementation: calculate GAE

```
1   # slm_lab/lib/math_util.py
2
3   def calc_gaes(rewards, dones, v_preds, gamma, lam):
4       T = len(rewards)
```

```
5      assert T + 1 == len(v_preds)  # v_preds includes states and 1 last
       ↪ next_state
6      gaes = torch.zeros_like(rewards)
7      future_gae = torch.tensor(0.0, dtype=rewards.dtype)
8      # to multiply with not_dones to handle episode boundary (last state has no
       ↪ V(s'))
9      not_dones = 1 - dones
10     for t in reversed(range(T)):
11         delta = rewards[t] + gamma * v_preds[t + 1] * not_dones[t] -
           ↪ v_preds[t]
12         gaes[t] = future_gae = delta + gamma * lam * not_dones[t] * future_gae
13     return gaes
```

Likewise, in Code 6.4, the Actor-Critic class method to compute the advantages and target V-values closely follows that of n-step with two important differences. First, calc_gaes (line 14) returns the full advantage estimates, whereas calc_nstep_returns in the n-step case returns Q value estimates. To recover the target V values, we therefore need to add the predicted V-values (line 15). Second, it is good practice to standardize the GAE advantage estimates (line 16).

Code 6.4   Actor-Critic implementation: calculate GAE advantages and V-target values

```
1    # slm_lab/agent/algorithm/actor_critic.py
2
3    class ActorCritic(Reinforce):
4        ...
5
6        def calc_gae_advs_v_targets(self, batch, v_preds):
7            next_states = batch['next_states'][-1]
8            ...
9            with torch.no_grad():
10                next_v_pred = self.calc_v(next_states, use_cache=False)
11            v_preds = v_preds.detach()  # adv does not accumulate grad
12            ...
13            v_preds_all = torch.cat((v_preds, next_v_pred), dim=0)
14            advs = math_util.calc_gaes(batch['rewards'], batch['dones'],
                 ↪ v_preds_all, self.gamma, self.lam)
15            v_targets = advs + v_preds
16            advs = math_util.standardize(advs)  # standardize only for advs, not
                 ↪ v_targets
17            ...
18            return advs, v_targets
```

6.4.2 Calculating Value Loss and Policy Loss

In Code 6.5, the policy loss has the same form as in the REINFORCE implementation. The only difference is that it uses the advantages instead of returns as a reinforcing signal, so we can inherit and reuse the method from REINFORCE (line 7).

The value loss is simply a measure of the error between $\hat{V}^\pi$ (v_preds) and V_{tar}^π (v_targets). We are free to choose any appropriate measure such as MSE by setting the net.loss_spec param in the spec file. This will initialize a loss function self.net_loss_fn used in line 11.

Code 6.5 Actor-Critic implementation: two loss functions

```
1   # slm_lab/agent/algorithm/actor_critic.py
2
3   class ActorCritic(Reinforce):
4       ...
5
6       def calc_policy_loss(self, batch, pdparams, advs):
7           return super().calc_policy_loss(batch, pdparams, advs)
8
9       def calc_val_loss(self, v_preds, v_targets):
10          assert v_preds.shape == v_targets.shape, f'{v_preds.shape} !=
            ↪  {v_targets.shape}'
11          val_loss = self.val_loss_coef * self.net.loss_fn(v_preds, v_targets)
12          return val_loss
```

6.4.3 Actor-Critic Training Loop

The actor and critic can be implemented with either separate networks or a single shared network. This is reflected in the train method in Code 6.6. Lines 10–15 calculate the policy and value losses for training. If the implementation uses a shared network (line 16), the two losses are combined and used to train the network (lines 17–18). If the actor and critic are separate networks, the two losses are used separately to train the relevant networks (lines 20–21). Section 6.5 goes into more details on network architecture.

Code 6.6 Actor-Critic implementation: training method

```
1   # slm_lab/agent/algorithm/actor_critic.py
2
3   class ActorCritic(Reinforce):
4       ...
5
6       def train(self):
7           ...
```

```
8          clock = self.body.env.clock
9          if self.to_train == 1:
10             batch = self.sample()
11             clock.set_batch_size(len(batch))
12             pdparams, v_preds = self.calc_pdparam_v(batch)
13             advs, v_targets = self.calc_advs_v_targets(batch, v_preds)
14             policy_loss = self.calc_policy_loss(batch, pdparams, advs)  # from
            ↪   actor
15             val_loss = self.calc_val_loss(v_preds, v_targets)  # from critic
16             if self.shared:  # shared network
17                 loss = policy_loss + val_loss
18                 self.net.train_step(loss, self.optim, self.lr_scheduler,
                ↪   clock=clock, global_net=self.global_net)
19             else:
20                 self.net.train_step(policy_loss, self.optim,
                ↪   self.lr_scheduler, clock=clock,
                ↪   global_net=self.global_net)
21                 self.critic_net.train_step(val_loss, self.critic_optim,
                ↪   self.critic_lr_scheduler, clock=clock,
                ↪   global_net=self.global_critic_net)
22                 loss = policy_loss + val_loss
23             # reset
24             self.to_train = 0
25             return loss.item()
26         else:
27             return np.nan
```

6.5   Network Architecture

In Actor-Critic algorithms, we learn two parametrized functions—π (actor) and $V^\pi(s)$ (critic). This makes it different from all of the other algorithms we have seen so far which only learned one function. Naturally, there are more factors to consider when designing the neural networks. Should they share any parameters? And if so, how many?

Sharing some parameters has its pros and cons. Conceptually, it is more appealing because learning π and learning $V^\pi(s)$ for the same task are related. Learning $V^\pi(s)$ is concerned with evaluating states effectively, and learning π is concerned with understanding how to take good actions in states. They share the same input. In both cases, good function approximations will involve learning how to represent the state space so that similar states are clustered together. It is therefore likely that both approximations could benefit by sharing the lower-level learning about the state space. Additionally, sharing parameters helps reduce the total number of learnable parameters, so may improve the sample efficiency of the algorithm. This is particularly relevant for Actor-Critic algorithms since the policy is being reinforced by a learned critic. If the actor and critic networks are separate, the actor may not learn anything useful until the critic has become reasonable, and this may take many training steps. However, if they share parameters, the actor can benefit from the state representation being learning by the critic.

The high-level shared network architecture, shown on the right-hand side of Figure 6.1, demonstrates how parameter sharing typically works for Actor-Critic algorithms. The Actor and the Critic share the lower layers of the network. This can be interpreted as learning a common representation of the state space. They also have one or more separate layers at the top of the network. This is because the output space for each network is different—for the actor, it's a probability distribution over actions, and for the critic, it's a single scalar value representing $V^\pi(s)$. However, since both networks also have different tasks, we should also expect that they need a number of specialized parameters to perform well. This could be a single layer on top of the shared body or a number of layers. Furthermore, the actor-specific and critic-specific layers do not have to be the same in number or type.

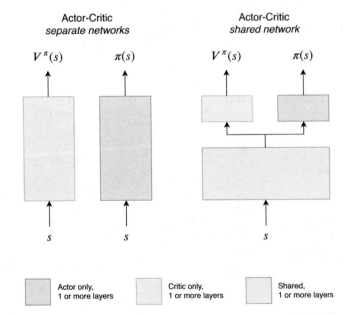

Figure 6.1   Actor-Critic network architectures: shared vs. separate networks

One serious downside of sharing parameters is that it can make learning more unstable. That's because now there are two components to the gradient being backpropagated simultaneously through the network—the policy gradient from the actor and the value function gradient from the critic. The two gradients may have different scales which need to be balanced for the agent to learn well [75]. For example, the log probability component of the policy loss has a range $\in (-\infty, 0]$, and the absolute value of the advantage function may be quite small, particularly if the action resolution[7] is small. This combination of these two factors can result in small absolute values for the policy loss. On the other hand, the scale of the value loss is related to the value of being in a state, which may be very large.

Balancing two potentially different gradient scales is typically implemented by adding a scalar weight to one of the losses to scale it up or down. For example, the value loss in Code 6.5 was scaled with a `self.val_loss_coef` (line 11). However, this becomes another hyperparameter to tune during training.

6.6 Training an A2C Agent

In this section we show how to train an Actor-Critic agent to play Atari Pong using different advantage estimates—first n-step returns, then GAE. Then, we apply A2C with GAE to a continuous-control environment BipedalWalker.

6.6.1 A2C with n-Step Returns on Pong

A spec file which configures an Actor-Critic agent with n-step returns advantage estimate is shown in Code 6.7. The file is available in SLM Lab at `slm_lab/spec/benchmark/a2c /a2c_nstep_pong.json`.

Code 6.7   A2C with n-step returns: spec file

```
1   # slm_lab/spec/benchmark/a2c/a2c_nstep_pong.json
2
3   {
4     "a2c_nstep_pong": {
5       "agent": [{
6         "name": "A2C",
7         "algorithm": {
8           "name": "ActorCritic",
9           "action_pdtype": "default",
10          "action_policy": "default",
11          "explore_var_spec": null,
12          "gamma": 0.99,
13          "lam": null,
14          "num_step_returns": 11,
15          "entropy_coef_spec": {
16            "name": "no_decay",
17            "start_val": 0.01,
```

---

7. Resolution can be interpreted as simulated time elapsed between time steps. High-resolution environments simulate time in a fine-grained manner. This means that the change from one state to the next is small because only a small amount of "time" has passed. Low-resolution environments simulate time more coarsely, leading to larger changes from one state to the next.

```
18        "end_val": 0.01,
19        "start_step": 0,
20        "end_step": 0
21      },
22      "val_loss_coef": 0.5,
23      "training_frequency": 5
24    },
25    "memory": {
26      "name": "OnPolicyBatchReplay"
27    },
28    "net": {
29      "type": "ConvNet",
30      "shared": true,
31      "conv_hid_layers": [
32        [32, 8, 4, 0, 1],
33        [64, 4, 2, 0, 1],
34        [32, 3, 1, 0, 1]
35      ],
36      "fc_hid_layers": [512],
37      "hid_layers_activation": "relu",
38      "init_fn": "orthogonal_",
39      "normalize": true,
40      "batch_norm": false,
41      "clip_grad_val": 0.5,
42      "use_same_optim": false,
43      "loss_spec": {
44        "name": "MSELoss"
45      },
46      "actor_optim_spec": {
47        "name": "RMSprop",
48        "lr": 7e-4,
49        "alpha": 0.99,
50        "eps": 1e-5
51      },
52      "critic_optim_spec": {
53        "name": "RMSprop",
54        "lr": 7e-4,
55        "alpha": 0.99,
56        "eps": 1e-5
57      },
58      "lr_scheduler_spec": null,
59      "gpu": true
60    }
61  }],
```

```
62        "env": [{
63          "name": "PongNoFrameskip-v4",
64          "frame_op": "concat",
65          "frame_op_len": 4,
66          "reward_scale": "sign",
67          "num_envs": 16,
68          "max_t": null,
69          "max_frame": 1e7
70        }],
71        "body": {
72          "product": "outer",
73          "num": 1,
74        },
75        "meta": {
76          "distributed": false,
77          "log_frequency": 10000,
78          "eval_frequency": 10000,
79          "max_session": 4,
80          "max_trial": 1
81        }
82      }
83    }
```

Let's walk through the main components.

- **Algorithm:** The algorithm is Actor-Critic (line 8), the action policy is the default policy (line 10) for discrete action space (categorical distribution). γ is set on line 12. If lam is specified for λ (not null), then GAE is used to estimate the advantages. If num_step_returns is specified instead, then n-step returns is used (lines 13–14). The entropy coefficient and its decay during training is specified in lines 15–21. The value loss coefficient is specified in line 22.

- **Network architecture:** Convolutional neural network with three convolutional layers and one fully connected layer with ReLU activation function (lines 29–37). The actor and critic use a shared network as specified in line 30. The network is trained on a GPU if available (line 59).

- **Optimizer:** The optimizer is RMSprop [50] with a learning rate of 0.0007 (lines 46–51). If separate networks are used instead, it is possible to specify a different optimizer setting for the critic network (lines 52–57) by setting use_same_optim to false (line 42). Since the network is shared in this case, this is not used. There is no learning rate decay (line 58).

- **Training frequency:** Training is batch-wise because we have selected OnPolicyBatchReplay memory (line 26) and the batch size is 5×16. This is controlled by the training_frequency (line 23) and the number of parallel environments (line 67). Parallel environments are discussed in Chapter 8.

- **Environment:** The environment is Atari Pong [14, 18] (line 63).
- **Training length:** Training consists of 10 million time steps (line 69).
- **Evaluation:** The agent is evaluated every 10,000 time steps (line 78).

To train this Actor-Critic agent using SLM Lab, run the commands shown in Code 6.8 in a terminal. The agent should start with the score of -21 and achieve close to the maximum score of 21 on average after 2 million frames.

Code 6.8 A2C with n-step returns: training an agent

```
1  conda activate lab
2  python run_lab.py slm_lab/spec/benchmark/a2c/a2c_nstep_pong.json
↪    a2c_nstep_pong train
```

This will run a training `Trial` with four `Sessions` to obtain an average result. The trial should take about half a day to complete when running on a GPU. The graph and its moving average are shown in Figure 6.2.

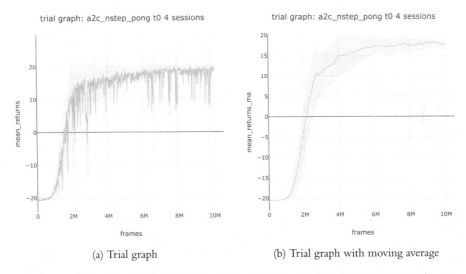

(a) Trial graph   (b) Trial graph with moving average

Figure 6.2 Actor-Critic (with n-step returns) trial graphs from SLM Lab averaged over four sessions. The vertical axis shows the total rewards averaged over eight episodes during checkpoints, and the horizontal axis shows the total training frames. A moving average with a window of 100 evaluation checkpoints is shown on the right.

6.6.2 A2C with GAE on Pong

Next, to switch from n-step returns to GAE, simply modify the spec from Code 6.7 to specify a value for `lam` and set `num_step_returns` to null, as shown in Code 6.9. The file is also available in SLM Lab at `slm_lab/spec/benchmark/a2c/a2c_gae_pong.json`.

Code 6.9   A2C with GAE: spec file

```
1   # slm_lab/spec/benchmark/a2c/a2c_gae_pong.json
2
3   {
4     "a2c_gae_pong": {
5       "agent": [{
6         "name": "A2C",
7         "algorithm": {
8           ...
9           "lam": 0.95,
10          "num_step_returns": null,
11          ...
12    }
13  }
```

Then, run the commands shown in Code 6.10 in a terminal to train an agent.

Code 6.10   A2C with GAE: training an agent

```
1   conda activate lab
2   python run_lab.py slm_lab/spec/benchmark/a2c/a2c_gae_pong.json a2c_gae_pong
    ↪   train
```

Similarly, this will run a training Trial to produce the graphs shown in Figure 6.3.

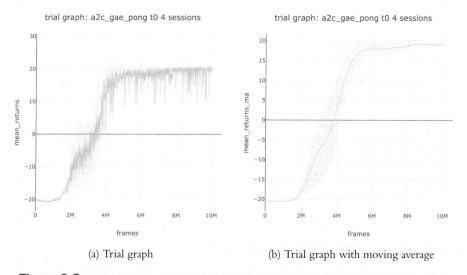

(a) Trial graph   (b) Trial graph with moving average

Figure 6.3   Actor-Critic (with GAE) trial graphs from SLM Lab averaged over four sessions.

6.6.3 A2C with *n*-Step Returns on BipedalWalker

So far, we have been training on discrete environments. Recall that policy-based method can also be applied directly to continuous-control problems. Now we will look at the BipedalWalker environment that was introduced in Section 1.1.

Code 6.11 shows a spec file which configures an A2C with *n*-step returns agent for the BipedalWalker environment. The file is available in SLM Lab at `slm_lab/spec/benchmark/a2c /a2c_nstep_cont.json`. In particular, note the changes in network architecture (lines 29–31) and environment (lines 54–57).

Code 6.11   A2C with *n*-step returns on BipedalWalker: spec file

```
1  # slm_lab/spec/benchmark/a2c/a2c_nstep_cont.json
2
3  {
4    "a2c_nstep_bipedalwalker": {
5      "agent": [{
6        "name": "A2C",
7        "algorithm": {
8          "name": "ActorCritic",
9          "action_pdtype": "default",
10          "action_policy": "default",
11          "explore_var_spec": null,
12          "gamma": 0.99,
13          "lam": null,
14          "num_step_returns": 5,
15          "entropy_coef_spec": {
16            "name": "no_decay",
17            "start_val": 0.01,
18            "end_val": 0.01,
19            "start_step": 0,
20            "end_step": 0
21          },
22          "val_loss_coef": 0.5,
23          "training_frequency": 256
24        },
25        "memory": {
26          "name": "OnPolicyBatchReplay",
27        },
28        "net": {
29          "type": "MLPNet",
30          "shared": false,
31          "hid_layers": [256, 128],
32          "hid_layers_activation": "relu",
33          "init_fn": "orthogonal_",
```

```
34        "normalize": true,
35        "batch_norm": false,
36        "clip_grad_val": 0.5,
37        "use_same_optim": false,
38        "loss_spec": {
39          "name": "MSELoss"
40        },
41        "actor_optim_spec": {
42          "name": "Adam",
43          "lr": 3e-4,
44        },
45        "critic_optim_spec": {
46          "name": "Adam",
47          "lr": 3e-4,
48        },
49        "lr_scheduler_spec": null,
50        "gpu": false
51      }
52    }],
53    "env": [{
54      "name": "BipedalWalker-v2",
55      "num_envs": 32,
56      "max_t": null,
57      "max_frame": 4e6
58    }],
59    "body": {
60      "product": "outer",
61      "num": 1
62    },
63    "meta": {
64      "distributed": false,
65      "log_frequency": 10000,
66      "eval_frequency": 10000,
67      "max_session": 4,
68      "max_trial": 1
69    }
70  }
71 }
```

Run the commands shown in Code 6.12 in a terminal to train an agent.

Code 6.12   A2C with n-step returns on BipedalWalker: training an agent

```
1  conda activate lab
2  python run_lab.py slm_lab/spec/benchmark/a2c/a2c_nstep_cont.json
   ↪  a2c_nstep_bipedalwalker train
```

This will run a training `Trial` to produce the graphs shown in Figure 6.4.

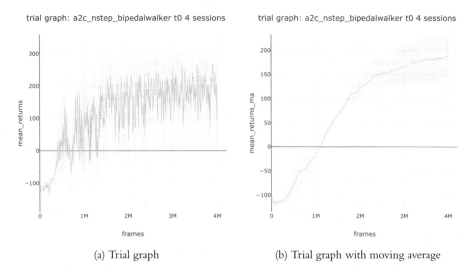

(a) Trial graph   (b) Trial graph with moving average

Figure 6.4   Trial graphs of A2C with n-step returns on BipedalWalker from SLM Lab averaged over four sessions.

BipedalWalker is a challenging continuous environment that is considered solved when the total reward moving average is above 300. In Figure 6.4, our agent did not achieve this within 4 million frames. We will return to this problem in Chapter 7 with a better attempt.

6.7   Experimental Results

In this section we will run two Actor–Critic experiments using SLM Lab. The first experiment will study the effect of the step size when using the n-step returns advantage estimate. The second experiment studies the effect of λ when using GAE. We will use the Atari Breakout game as a more challenging environment.

6.7.1   Experiment: The Effect of n-Step Returns

The step size n controls the bias–variance trade-off in the n-step returns advantage estimate—the larger n, the larger the variance. The step size n is a tunable hyperparameter.

In this experiment, we study the effect of using different values of n for the n-step returns in Actor-Critic by performing a grid search. The experiment spec file is extended from Code 6.7 by adding a search spec for num_step_returns, as shown in Code 6.13.

Note that we now use a different environment, Breakout, which is slightly more challenging than Pong. Lines 4 and 7 specify the change in the environment. Line 19 specifies a grid search over a list of n values num_step_returns. The full spec file is available in SLM Lab at slm_lab/spec/experimental/a2c/a2c_nstep_n_search.json.

Code 6.13   A2C with n-step returns spec file with search spec for different values of n, num_step_returns.

```
1   # slm_lab/spec/experimental/a2c/a2c_nstep_n_search.json
2
3   {
4     "a2c_nstep_breakout": {
5       ...
6       "env": [{
7         "name": "BreakoutNoFrameskip-v4",
8         "frame_op": "concat",
9         "frame_op_len": 4,
10        "reward_scale": "sign",
11        "num_envs": 16,
12        "max_t": null,
13        "max_frame": 1e7
14      }],
15      ...
16      "search": {
17        "agent": [{
18          "algorithm": {
19            "num_step_returns__grid_search": [1, 3, 5, 7, 9, 11]
20          }
21        }]
22      }
23    }
24  }
```

To run the experiment in SLM Lab, use the commands shown in Code 6.14.

Code 6.14   Run an experiment to search over different step sizes n in n-step returns, as defined in the spec file.

```
1  conda activate lab
2  python run_lab.py slm_lab/spec/experimental/a2c/a2c_nstep_n_search.json
   ↪  a2c_nstep_breakout search
```

This will run an `Experiment` which spawns six `Trials`, each with a different value of `num_step_returns` substituted in the original Actor-Critic spec. Each `Trial` runs four `Sessions` to obtain an average. The multitrial graphs are shown in Figure 6.5.

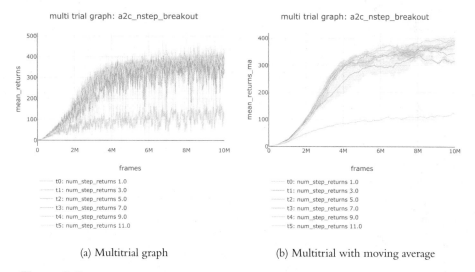

(a) Multitrial graph   (b) Multitrial with moving average

Figure 6.5   The effect of different n-step returns step sizes of Actor-Critic on the Breakout environment. Larger step sizes n perform better.

Figure 6.5 shows the effect of different n-step returns step sizes on Actor-Critic in the Breakout environment. Larger step sizes n perform better, and we can also see that n is not a very sensitive hyperparameter. With $n = 1$, the n-step returns reduce to the Temporal Difference estimate of returns, which yields the worst performance in this experiment.

6.7.2   Experiment: The Effect of λ of GAE

Recall that GAE is an exponentially weighted average of all the n-step returns advantages, and the higher the decay factor λ, the higher the variance of the estimate. The optimal value of λ is a hyperparameter that is tuned for a specific problem.

In this experiment, we look at the effect of using different λ values on GAE in Actor-Critic by performing a grid search. The experiment spec file is extended from Code 6.9 by adding a search spec for `lam`, as shown in Code 6.15.

We will also use Breakout as the environment. Lines 4 and 7 specify the change in the environment. Line 19 specifies a grid search over a list of λ values lam. The full spec file is available in SLM Lab at slm_lab/spec/experimental/a2c/a2c_gae_lam_search.json.

Code 6.15   Actor-Critic spec file with search spec for different values of GAE λ, lam

```
1   # slm_lab/spec/experimental/a2c/a2c_gae_lam_search.json
2
3   {
4     "a2c_gae_breakout": {
5       ...
6       "env": [{
7         "name": "BreakoutNoFrameskip-v4",
8         "frame_op": "concat",
9         "frame_op_len": 4,
10        "reward_scale": "sign",
11        "num_envs": 16,
12        "max_t": null,
13        "max_frame": 1e7
14      }],
15      ...
16      "search": {
17        "agent": [{
18          "algorithm": {
19            "lam__grid_search": [0.50, 0.70, 0.90, 0.95, 0.97, 0.99]
20          }
21        }]
22      }
23    }
24  }
```

To run the experiment in SLM Lab, use the commands shown in Code 6.16.

Code 6.16   Run an experiment to search over different values of GAE λ as defined in the spec file.

```
1   conda activate lab
2   python run_lab.py slm_lab/spec/experimental/a2c/a2c_gae_lam_search.json
    ↪   a2c_gae_breakout search
```

This will run an Experiment which spawns six Trials, each with a different value of lam substituted in the original Actor-Critic spec. Each Trial runs four Sessions to obtain an average. The multitrial graphs are shown in Figure 6.6.

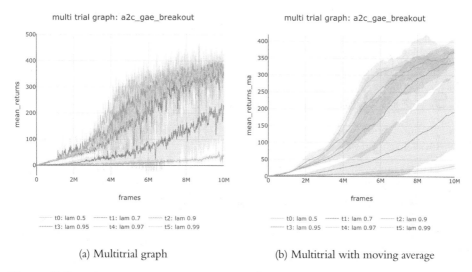

(a) Multitrial graph   (b) Multitrial with moving average

Figure 6.6   The effect of different values of GAE λ on Actor-Critic in the Breakout environment. $\lambda = 0.97$ performs best, followed closely by 0.90 and 0.99.

As we can see in Figure 6.6, $\lambda = 0.97$ performs best with an episodic score of near 400, followed closely by $\lambda = 0.90$ and 0.99. This experiment also demonstrates that λ is not a very sensitive hyperparameter. Performance is impacted only slightly when λ is deviates from the optimal value. For instance, $\lambda = 0.70$ still produces good result, but $\lambda = 0.50$ yields poor performance.

6.8   Summary

This chapter introduced Actor-Critic algorithms. We saw that these algorithms have two components, an actor and a critic. The actor learns a policy π and the critic learns the value function V^π. The learned $\hat{V}^\pi$ is used in combination with actual rewards to generate a reinforcing signal for the policy. The reinforcing signal is often the advantage function.

Actor-Critic algorithms combine ideas from policy-based and value-based methods that were introduced in earlier chapters. Optimizing the actor is similar to REINFORCE but with a learned reinforcing signal instead of a Monte-Carlo estimate generated from the current trajectory of rewards. Optimizing the critic is similar to DQN in that it uses the bootstrapped temporal difference learning technique.

This chapter discussed two ways to estimate the advantage function—n-step returns and GAE. Each method allows users to control the amount of bias and variance in the advantage by choosing how much to weight the actual trajectory of rewards compared to the value function estimate $\hat{V}^\pi$. The n-step advantage estimate has a hard cutoff controlled by n, whereas GAE has a soft cutoff controlled by the parameter λ.

The chapter ended with a discussion of two approaches to designing neural network architectures for Actor-Critic algorithms—either by sharing parameters or by keeping the Actor and Critic networks entirely separate.

6.9   Further Reading

- "Neuronlike Adaptive Elements That Can Solve Difficult Learning Control Problems," Barto et al., 1983 [11].

- "High Dimensional Continuous Control with Generalized Advantage Estimation," Schulman et al., 2015 [123].

- "Trust Region Policy Optimization," Schulman et al., 2015 [122].

6.10   History

Most of the fundamental concepts underlying modern Actor-Critic algorithms were outlined in 1983 in Sutton, Barto, and Anderson's paper "Neuronlike Adaptive Elements That Can Solve Difficult Learning Control Problems" [11]. This paper introduced the idea of jointly learning two interacting modules: a policy unit or actor, referred to in this paper as an "Associative Search Element" or ASE, and a critic, named an "Adaptive Critic Element" or ACE. The algorithm was motivated by neuroscience which is a field that has often inspired deep learning research. For example, CNNs were originally inspired by the human visual cortex [43, 71]. Sutton et al. argue that modeling a structure as complex as a neuron at the level of a logic-gate-like unit is inadequate. They proposed the ASE/ACE as an initial exploration into systems that consist of a network of complex learned sub-units. Their hope was that shifting from simple to complex primitive units would help solve significantly more complex problems.

It is likely that the name ACE was inspired by Widrow et al. [146] who ten years earlier, in 1973, used the phrase "learning with a critic" to distinguish RL from supervised learning (SL) which can be thought of as "learning with a teacher" [11].[8] However, applying a learned critic to improve the reinforcing signal given to another part of the system was novel. Sutton et al. explain the ACE's purpose very clearly:

> It [the ACE] adaptively develops an evaluation function that is more informative than the one directly available from the learning system's environment. This reduces the uncertainty under which the ASE will learn [11].[9]

---

8. In SL, a "teacher" gives you the correct answer for each datapoint, whereas in RL, an agent only gets "critiqued" via the reward function. The "critique" is analogous to being told that what you just did was good, bad, or OK. You are not told "what you should have done was X."

9. If you wish to learn more about this, the original paper is really worth reading. It is clearly written and contains a good explanation of the credit assignment problem in RL and the difference between reinforcement learning and supervised learning.

Credit assignment and sparse reward signals are two of the most important challenges in RL. The ACE tackles the problem of credit assignment in RL by using the critic to transform a potentially sparse reward into a more informative, dense reinforcing signal. A significant amount of research since this paper has been focused on developing better critics.

The advantage function was first mentioned in 1983 by Baird [9]. However, it was in 1999 that Sutton et al. [133] defined the advantage as $A^\pi(s, a) = Q^\pi(s, a) - V^\pi(s)$.

There was a surge of interest in Actor-Critic algorithms after the publication of the Asynchronous Advantage Actor-Critic (A3C) [87] algorithm by Mnih et al. in 2016. This paper introduced a simple scalable method for parallelizing the training of reinforcement learning algorithms using asynchronous gradient ascent. We will look at this in Chapter 8.

7

Proximal Policy Optimization (PPO)

One challenge when training agents with policy gradient algorithms is that they are susceptible to *performance collapse* in which an agent suddenly starts to perform badly. This scenario can be hard to recover from because an agent will start to generate poor trajectories which are then used to further train the policy. We have also seen that on-policy algorithms are sample-inefficient because they cannot reuse data.

Proximal Policy Optimization (PPO) by Schulman et al. [124] is a class of optimization algorithms that addresses these two issues. The main idea behind PPO is to introduce a *surrogate objective* which avoids performance collapse by guaranteeing monotonic policy improvement. This objective also has the benefit of reusing off-policy data in the training process.

PPO can be used to extend REINFORCE or Actor-Critic by replacing the original objective $J(\pi_\theta)$ with the modified PPO objective. This modification leads to more stable and more sample-efficient training.

In this chapter we first discuss the problem of performance collapse in Section 7.1.1. Then, we see how this can be addressed with the Monotonic Improvement Theory in Section 7.1.2. We apply the theory to modify the policy gradient objective into a surrogate objective.

After introducing the theoretical foundations, we discuss the PPO algorithm in Section 7.2. We then show how PPO is implemented in SLM Lab as an extension of the Actor-Critic algorithm in Section 7.4.

7.1 Surrogate Objective

In this section, we introduce the surrogate objective for the PPO algorithm. First, we motivate this by discussing the problem of performance collapse. Then we see how the original policy gradient objective can be modified to avoid this problem.

7.1.1 Performance Collapse

In our discussions of policy gradient algorithms, we have seen that a policy π_θ is optimized by changing the policy parameters θ using the policy gradient $\nabla_\theta J(\pi_\theta)$. This is an indirect approach because we are searching for the optimal policy in a policy space which we do not have direct control over. To understand why, we first need to look at the distinction between a policy space and a parameter space.

During the optimization process, we search over a sequence of policies $\pi_1, \pi_2, \pi_3, \ldots, \pi_n$ within the set of all policies. This is known as the *policy space*[1] Π.

$$\Pi = \{\pi_i\} \tag{7.1}$$

With the policy parametrized as π_θ, we can also conveniently express the parameter space for θ. Each unique θ parametrizes an instance of the policy. The *parameter space* is Θ.

$$\Theta = \{\theta \in \mathbb{R}^m, \text{ where } m \text{ is the number of parameters}\} \tag{7.2}$$

Although the objective $J(\pi_\theta)$ is computed using trajectories produced by a policy in the policy space, $\pi_\theta \in \Pi$, the search for the optimal policy actually occurs in the parameter space by finding the right parameters, $\theta \in \Theta$. That is, our control is in Θ, but the result is in Π. In practice, we control the step size of parameter updates using a learning rate α, as shown in Equation 7.3.

$$\Delta\theta = \alpha \nabla_\theta J(\pi_\theta) \tag{7.3}$$

Unfortunately, the policy space and the parameter space do not always map congruently, and the distances in both spaces don't necessarily correspond. Take two pairs of parameters, say (θ_1, θ_2) and (θ_2, θ_3), and suppose they have the same distance in the parameter space, that is, $d_\theta(\theta_1, \theta_2) = d_\theta(\theta_2, \theta_3)$. However, their mapped policies $(\pi_{\theta_1}, \pi_{\theta_2})$ and $(\pi_{\theta_2}, \pi_{\theta_3})$ do not necessarily have the same distance. That is to say,

$$d_\theta(\theta_1, \theta_2) = d_\theta(\theta_2, \theta_3) \not\Leftrightarrow d_\pi(\pi_{\theta_1}, \pi_{\theta_2}) = d_\pi(\pi_{\theta_2}, \pi_{\theta_3}) \tag{7.4}$$

This presents a potential problem because the ideal step size α for a parameter update becomes difficult to determine. It is not clear beforehand how small or large a step in the policy space Π it is going to map to. If α is too small, it will require many iterations and training will take a long time. Alternatively, the policy may also get stuck in some local maxima. If α is too large, the corresponding step in policy space will overshoot the neighborhood of good policies and cause a performance collapse. When this happens, the new policy, which is much worse, will be used to generate bad trajectory data for the next

---

1. Note that there can be infinitely many policies in the policy space.

update and ruin future policy iterations. Because of this, a performance collapse can be very difficult to recover from. Figure 7.1 shows an example of a brief performance collapse.

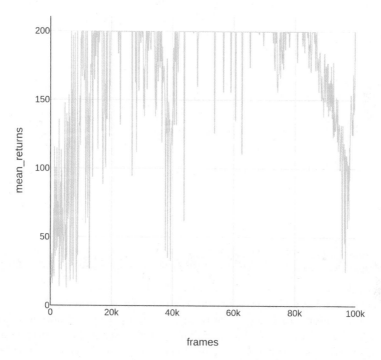

session graph: reinforce_cartpole t0 s13

Figure 7.1   Example graph from SLM Lab showing performance collapse in REINFORCE on CartPole. Notice that the return (no-discount, i.e. total episodic reward) reaches its maximum of 200 then collapses after 80k frames.

In general, a constant step size does not avoid these issues. In gradient ascent $\theta \leftarrow \theta + \alpha \nabla_\theta J(\pi_\theta)$, the learning rate α is usually fixed or decayed, with only the direction $\nabla_\theta J(\pi_\theta)$ varying. However, since the mapping is nonisometric, a constant step size may still map to varying distances in Π.

The optimal choice for α will vary depending on where the current policy π_θ is in the policy space Π, and how the current parameter θ maps to the neighborhood of π_θ in Π from its own neighborhood in Θ. Ideally, an algorithm should adaptively vary the parameter step size based on these factors.

To derive an adaptive step size based on how a particular update in parameter space will affect policy space, we first need way to measure the difference in performance between two policies.

7.1.2 Modifying the Objective

In this section, we introduce the *relative policy performance identity* which measures the difference in performance between two policies. We then show how this can be used to modify the policy gradient objective so as to guarantee monotonic performance improvement during optimization.

Intuitively, since the problem is with the step size, we can try to introduce a constraint that bounds it to a safe size to prevent performance collapse. By imposing the right constraint, we can derive what is known as the *Monotonic Improvement Theory*.[2]

First, let a policy π be given, and let its next iteration (after a parameter update) be π'. We can define a *relative policy performance identity* as the difference in the objectives between them, shown in Equation 7.5. Note that the advantage $A^\pi(s_t, a_t)$ is always computed from the older policy π.

$$J(\pi') - J(\pi) = \mathbb{E}_{\tau \sim \pi'}\left[\sum_{t=0}^{T} \gamma^t A^\pi(s_t, a_t) \right] \tag{7.5}$$

Box 7.1   Relative Policy Performance Identity Derivation

Here we derive the relative policy performance identity shown in Equation 7.5.

First, we rewrite the advantage in the form suitable for our derivation. This is shown in Equation 7.6. The Q-term is expanded into the expectation of the first reward and the expected V-value over all possible next states. The expectation is necessary to account for stochastic environment transitions which do not depend on any particular policy.

$$\begin{aligned} A^\pi(s_t, a_t) &= Q^\pi(s_t, a_t) - V^\pi(s_t) \\ &= \mathbb{E}_{s_{t+1}, r_t \sim p(s_{t+1}, r_t \mid s_t, a_t)}[r_t + \gamma V^\pi(s_{t+1})] - V^\pi(s_t) \end{aligned} \tag{7.6}$$

This will be used in the transformation on the right-hand side of Equation 7.5 as follows.

---

2. The derivations in this section are adapted and expanded from the wonderful Berkeley lecture *CS 294: Deep Reinforcement Learning, Fall 2017* taught by Sergey Levine. Some of the more advanced proofs will be omitted as they are beyond the scope of this book, but curious readers may find them in original lecture notes by Joshua Achiam from "Lecture 13: Advanced Policy Gradient Methods" [78]. This book and the notes use mostly similar notations, so it will be easy to read and compare both. Additionally, a recorded lecture which covers the notes in greater detail is also available on YouTube under the title *CS294-112 10/11/17* at https://youtu.be/ycCtmp4hcUs.

$$\mathbb{E}_{\tau\sim\pi'}\left[\sum_{t\geq 0}\gamma^t A^\pi(s_t, a_t)\right] \tag{7.7}$$

$$= \mathbb{E}_{\tau\sim\pi'}\left[\sum_{t\geq 0}\gamma^t\left(\mathbb{E}_{s_{t+1},r_t\sim p(s_{t+1},r_t\,|\,s_t,a_t)}\left[r_t + \gamma V^\pi(s_{t+1})\right] - V^\pi(s_t)\right)\right] \tag{7.8}$$

$$= \mathbb{E}_{\tau\sim\pi'}\left[\sum_{t\geq 0}\gamma^t\left(r_t + \gamma V^\pi(s_{t+1}) - V^\pi(s_t)\right)\right] \tag{7.9}$$

$$= \mathbb{E}_{\tau\sim\pi'}\left[\sum_{t\geq 0}\gamma^t r_t + \sum_{t\geq 0}\gamma^{t+1} V^\pi(s_{t+1}) - \sum_{t\geq 0}\gamma^t V^\pi(s_t)\right] \tag{7.10}$$

$$= \mathbb{E}_{\tau\sim\pi'}\left[\sum_{t\geq 0}\gamma^t r_t\right] + \mathbb{E}_{\tau\sim\pi'}\left[\sum_{t\geq 0}\gamma^{t+1} V^\pi(s_{t+1}) - \sum_{t\geq 0}\gamma^t V^\pi(s_t)\right] \tag{7.11}$$

$$= J(\pi') + \mathbb{E}_{\tau\sim\pi'}\left[\sum_{t\geq 1}\gamma^t V^\pi(s_t) - \sum_{t\geq 0}\gamma^t V^\pi(s_t)\right] \tag{7.12}$$

$$= J(\pi') - \mathbb{E}_{\tau\sim\pi'}[V^\pi(s_0)] \tag{7.13}$$

$$= J(\pi') - \mathbb{E}_{\tau\sim\pi'}[J(\pi)] \tag{7.14}$$

$$= J(\pi') - J(\pi) \tag{7.15}$$

First, let's restate 7.5, then substitute the definition of the advantage from Equation 7.6 to obtain 7.8. For the next step, notice that the outer expectation $\mathbb{E}_{\tau\sim\pi'}$ in fact contains expected actions from the policy ($\mathbb{E}_{a_t\sim\pi'}$) and expected states and rewards from the transition function ($\mathbb{E}_{s_{t+1},r_t\sim p(s_{t+1},r_t\,|\,s_t,a_t)}$). Consequently, we can absorb the inner expectation into the outer expectation due to overlapping terms to yield 7.9.

Next, distribute the summation sign in 7.10. By linearity of expectation, isolate the first term in 7.11, which is simply the new objective $J(\pi')$. This gives us 7.12. Now, make an index shift for the first summation inside the expectation by replacing index $t+1$ with index t that starts at 1. Now, both summations look identical except for the index, so they cancel out to leave only the term for $t = 0$, which is $V^\pi(s_0)$ in 7.13. The value function at the initial state is simply the objective $J(\pi)$, since $V^\pi(s_0) = \mathbb{E}_{\tau\sim\pi}[\sum_{t\geq 0}\gamma^t r_t] = J(\pi)$. This gives us 7.14. Finally, the objective of policy π is independent of the new policy π', so we drop the expectation to obtain $J(\pi') - J(\pi)$.

The relative policy performance identity $J(\pi') - J(\pi)$ serves as a metric to measure policy improvements. If the difference is positive, the newer policy π' is better than π. During a policy iteration, we should ideally choose a new policy π' such that this difference is maximized. Therefore, maximizing objective $J(\pi')$ is equivalent to maximizing this identity, and they can both be done by gradient ascent.

$$\max_{\pi'} J(\pi') \iff \max_{\pi'} \left(J(\pi') - J(\pi) \right) \tag{7.16}$$

Framing the objective this way also means that every policy iteration should ensure a non-negative (monotonic) improvement—that is, $J(\pi') - J(\pi) \geq 0$—since in the worst case we can simply let $\pi' = \pi$ to get no improvement. With this, there will be no performance collapses throughout the training, which is the property we are looking for.

However, there is a limitation that won't let us use this identity as an objective function. Note that in the expression $\mathbb{E}_{\tau \sim \pi'}\left[\sum_{t \geq 0} A^\pi(s_t, a_t) \right]$, the expectation requires trajectories to be sampled from the new policy π' for an update, but π' is not available until after the update. To remedy this paradox, we need to find a way to alter it to use the old policy π that is available.

To this end, we can assume that successive policies π, π' are relatively close (this can be measured by low KL divergence), so that the state distributions from them are similar.

Then, Equation 7.5 can be approximated by using trajectories from the old policy, $\tau \sim \pi$, adjusted with *importance sampling* weights[3] $\frac{\pi'(a_t \mid s_t)}{\pi(a_t \mid s_t)}$. This adjusts the returns generated using π by the ratio of action probabilities between the two successive policies π, π'. The rewards associated with actions that are more likely under the new policy π' will be upweighted, and rewards associated with relatively less likely actions under π' will be downweighted. This approximation is shown in Equation 7.17.

$$\begin{aligned} J(\pi') - J(\pi) &= \mathbb{E}_{\tau \sim \pi'}\left[\sum_{t \geq 0} A^\pi(s_t, a_t) \right] \\ &\approx \mathbb{E}_{\tau \sim \pi}\left[\sum_{t \geq 0} A^\pi(s_t, a_t) \frac{\pi'(a_t \mid s_t)}{\pi(a_t \mid s_t)} \right] = J_\pi^{\mathrm{CPI}}(\pi') \end{aligned} \tag{7.17}$$

The new objective on the right-hand side of Equation 7.17, $J_\pi^{\mathrm{CPI}}(\pi')$, is called a *surrogate objective* because it contains a ratio of the new and old policies, π' and π. The superscript CPI stands for "conservative policy iteration."

Now that we have a new objective, to use it for a policy gradient algorithm we need to check if *optimization under this objective is still performing policy gradient ascent*. Fortunately, we can show that the gradient of the surrogate objective is equal to the policy gradient, as stated in Equation 7.18. The derivation is shown in Box 7.2.

$$\nabla_\theta J_{\theta_{\mathrm{old}}}^{\mathrm{CPI}}(\theta)|_{\theta_{\mathrm{old}}} = \nabla_\theta J(\pi_\theta)|_{\theta_{\mathrm{old}}} \tag{7.18}$$

---

3. Importance sampling is a method used to estimate an unknown distribution while using only data sampled from a known distribution. The full derivation of Equation 7.5 is beyond the scope of this book, but can be found in "Lecture 13: Advanced Policy Gradient Methods" [78].

Box 7.2   Surrogate Policy Gradient Derivation

Here, we will show that gradient of the surrogate objective is equal to the policy gradient, as stated in Equation 7.18.

We start by taking the gradient of $J_\pi^{\mathrm{CPI}}(\pi')$. To do so, write the variable θ explicitly. In particular, write the new policy π' as a variable π_θ, and the old policy π as a constant $\pi_{\theta_{\mathrm{old}}}$ at which we evaluate the gradient notated $|_{\theta_{\mathrm{old}}}$ (this is necessary because of the explicit dependence of $J_\pi^{\mathrm{CPI}}(\pi')$ on π, which cannot be dropped).

$$\nabla_\theta J_{\theta_{\mathrm{old}}}^{\mathrm{CPI}}(\theta)|_{\theta_{\mathrm{old}}} = \nabla_\theta \mathbb{E}_{\tau \sim \pi_{\theta_{\mathrm{old}}}} \left[\sum_{t \geq 0} A^{\pi_{\theta_{\mathrm{old}}}}(s_t, a_t) \frac{\pi_\theta(a_t \mid s_t)}{\pi_{\theta_{\mathrm{old}}}(a_t \mid s_t)} \right]|_{\theta_{\mathrm{old}}} \tag{7.19}$$

$$= \mathbb{E}_{\tau \sim \pi_{\theta_{\mathrm{old}}}} \left[\sum_{t \geq 0} A^{\pi_{\theta_{\mathrm{old}}}}(s_t, a_t) \frac{\nabla_\theta \pi_\theta(a_t \mid s_t)|_{\theta_{\mathrm{old}}}}{\pi_{\theta_{\mathrm{old}}}(a_t \mid s_t)} \right] \tag{7.20}$$

$$= \mathbb{E}_{\tau \sim \pi_{\theta_{\mathrm{old}}}} \left[\sum_{t \geq 0} A^{\pi_{\theta_{\mathrm{old}}}}(s_t, a_t) \frac{\nabla_\theta \pi_\theta(a_t \mid s_t)|_{\theta_{\mathrm{old}}}}{\pi_\theta(a_t \mid s_t)|_{\theta_{\mathrm{old}}}} \right] \tag{7.21}$$

$$= \mathbb{E}_{\tau \sim \pi_{\theta_{\mathrm{old}}}} \left[\sum_{t \geq 0} A^{\pi_{\theta_{\mathrm{old}}}}(s_t, a_t) \nabla_\theta \log \pi_\theta(a_t \mid s_t)|_{\theta_{\mathrm{old}}} \right] \tag{7.22}$$

$$= \nabla_\theta J(\pi_\theta)|_{\theta_{\mathrm{old}}} \tag{7.23}$$

First, evaluate the gradient at the old policy on the surrogate objective from Equation 7.17. Since only the upper fraction term contains variable θ, we can bring in the gradient and evaluation term to give 7.20. Now, note that the lower fraction term $\pi_{\theta_{\mathrm{old}}}(a_t \mid s_t)$ is the same as writing π_θ evaluated at $\theta = \theta_{\mathrm{old}}$, we can do so and get 7.21. Finally, recall the log-derivative trick $\nabla_\theta \log p(x|\theta) = \frac{\nabla_\theta p(x|\theta)}{p(x|\theta)}$ from Equation 2.14 that we used to derive the policy gradient. With this, we can rewrite the fraction and obtain 7.22. This is just the policy gradient $\nabla_\theta J(\pi_\theta)$. Hence, we have Equation 7.24.

$$\nabla_\theta J_{\theta_{\mathrm{old}}}^{\mathrm{CPI}}(\theta)|_{\theta_{\mathrm{old}}} = \nabla_\theta J(\pi_\theta)|_{\theta_{\mathrm{old}}} \tag{7.24}$$

Equation 7.24 says that the gradient of surrogate objective is equal to the policy gradient. This gives the assurance that optimization under surrogate objective is still performing policy gradient ascent. It is also useful because policy improvement can now be measured directly, and maximizing it means maximizing policy improvement. Additionally, now we know that in Equation 7.17 $J_\pi^{\mathrm{CPI}}(\pi')$ is a linear approximation to $J(\pi') - J(\pi)$, since their first-order derivatives (gradients) are equal.

Before $J_\pi^{\mathrm{CPI}}(\pi')$ can stand in as the new objective for a policy gradient algorithm, there is one final requirement to satisfy. $J_\pi^{\mathrm{CPI}}(\pi')$ is only an approximation for $J(\pi') - J(\pi)$, so it will contain some error. However, we want to guarantee when we use

$J_\pi^{\text{CPI}}(\pi') \approx J(\pi') - J(\pi)$ that $J(\pi') - J(\pi) \geq 0$. We therefore need to understand the error introduced by the approximation.

If successive policies π, π' are sufficiently close as measured by their KL divergence, then one can write a *relative policy performance bound*.[4] To do so, express the absolute error by taking the difference between the new objective $J(\pi')$ and its estimated improvement $J(\pi) + J_\pi^{\text{CPI}}(\pi')$. Then, the error can be bounded in terms of the KL divergence between π and π'.

$$\left| \left(J(\pi') - J(\pi) \right) - J_\pi^{\text{CPI}}(\pi') \right| \leq C \sqrt{\mathbb{E}_t \left[KL\left(\pi'(a_t \,|\, s_t) \,||\, \pi(a_t \,|\, s_t) \right) \right]} \qquad (7.25)$$

C is a constant that needs to be chosen, and KL is the KL divergence.[5] Equation 7.25 shows that if successive policies π, π' are close in their distributions, so that KL divergence on the right-hand side is low, then the error term on the left-hand side is low.[6] With low error, $J_\pi^{\text{CPI}}(\pi')$ is a good approximation for $J(\pi') - J(\pi)$.

Using this, it is quite straightforward to derive the result we are after, namely $J(\pi') - J(\pi) \geq 0$. This is called the *monotonic improvement theory* [78], because it guarantees at least a positive or zero improvement at every policy iteration, but never deterioration. To obtain this, first expand Equation 7.25 and consider its lower bound in Equation 7.26.

$$J(\pi') - J(\pi) \geq J_\pi^{\text{CPI}}(\pi') - C \sqrt{\mathbb{E}_t \left[KL\left(\pi'(a_t \,|\, s_t) \,||\, \pi(a_t \,|\, s_t) \right) \right]} \qquad (7.26)$$

Now, let's look at the worst-case scenario during a step in policy iteration. Consider all the choices for the new policy π', which also includes the old policy π (parameter update size is 0). If there is no candidate which performs better, simply set $\pi' = \pi$ and do not perform an update during this iteration. When that is the case, Equation 7.17 tells us that $J_\pi^{\text{CPI}}(\pi) = \mathbb{E}_{\tau \sim \pi}[\sum_{t \geq 0} A^\pi(s_t, a_t) \frac{\pi(a_t|s_t)}{\pi(a_t|s_t)}] = 0$, since a policy has no expected advantage over itself. KL divergence $KL(\pi \,||\, \pi) = 0$ by identity.

In order to accept a change in a policy, Equation 7.26 says that the estimated policy improvement $J_\pi^{\text{CPI}}(\pi')$ has to be greater than the maximum error $C \sqrt{\mathbb{E}_t[KL(\pi'(a_t \,|\, s_t) \,||\, \pi(a_t \,|\, s_t))]}$.

If we add the error bound as a penalty in our optimization problem, we can guarantee monotonic policy improvement. Our optimization problem now becomes the following:

$$\underset{\pi'}{\text{argmax}} \left(J_\pi^{\text{CPI}}(\pi') - C \sqrt{\mathbb{E}_t \left[KL\left(\pi'(a_t \,|\, s_t) \,||\, \pi(a_t \,|\, s_t) \right) \right]} \right)$$
$$\Rightarrow J(\pi') - J(\pi) \geq 0 \qquad (7.27)$$

---

4. This was introduced in the paper "Constrained Policy Optimization" by Achiam et al. in 2017 [2].
5. The KL divergence between two distributions $p(x)$, $q(x)$ with random variable $x \in X$ is defined as $KL(p(x) \,||\, q(x)) = \sum_{x \in X} p(x) \log \frac{p(x)}{q(x)}$ for discrete distributions, or $KL(p(x) \,||\, q(x)) = \int_{-\infty}^{\infty} p(x) \log \frac{p(x)}{q(x)} dx$ for continuous distributions.
6. The full derivation can be found in "Lecture 13: Advanced Policy Gradient Methods" [78].

This result satisfies our final requirement. It allows us to avoid performance collapse that may occur when using the original objective $J(\pi)$. One key distinction to note is that a monotonic improvement does not guarantee convergence to an optimal policy π^*. For instance, policy optimization can still get stuck at a local maximum in which every policy iteration produces no improvement—that is, $J(\pi') - J(\pi) = 0$. Guaranteeing convergence remains a difficult open problem.

The final step is to consider how to implement the optimization problem from Equation 7.27 in practice. One idea is to directly constrain the expectation of KL as shown in Equation 7.28.

$$\mathbb{E}_t\big[KL\big(\pi'(a_t \mid s_t) \,\|\, \pi(a_t \mid s_t)\big)\big] \leq \delta \qquad (7.28)$$

δ limits how large KL divergence can be, so it effectively restricts how far a new policy π' can diverge away from the old policy π. Only candidates in a close neighborhood around π in the policy space will be considered. This neighborhood is called a *trust region*, and Equation 7.28 is called a *trust region constraint*. Note that δ is a hyperparameter that needs to be tuned.

The constraint term $\mathbb{E}_t[KL(\pi'(a_t \mid s_t) \,\|\, \pi(a_t \mid s_t))]$ is written as an expectation over a single time step t, so it is helpful to write the objective $J_\pi^{\mathrm{CPI}}(\pi')$ in this way as well, as shown in Equation 7.29. Additionally, since we will be maximizing the objective with respect to θ, let's also express the policies in terms of θ as shown in Equation 7.30. The new policy is written as $\pi' = \pi_\theta$, whereas the older policy with fixed parameters is written as $\pi = \pi_{\theta_{\mathrm{old}}}$. The advantage computed from the old policy is also written concisely as $A^\pi(s_t, a_t) = A_t^{\pi_{\theta_{\mathrm{old}}}}$.

$$J_\pi^{\mathrm{CPI}}(\pi') = \mathbb{E}_t\left[\frac{\pi'(a_t \mid s_t)}{\pi(a_t \mid s_t)} A^\pi(s_t, a_t)\right] \qquad (7.29)$$

$$J^{\mathrm{CPI}}(\theta) = \mathbb{E}_t\left[\frac{\pi_\theta(a_t \mid s_t)}{\pi_{\theta_{\mathrm{old}}}(a_t \mid s_t)} A_t^{\pi_{\theta_{\mathrm{old}}}}\right] \qquad (7.30)$$

Putting the constraint and surrogate objective together, the trust region policy optimization problem is shown in Equation 7.31.

$$\max_\theta \mathbb{E}_t\left[\frac{\pi_\theta(a_t \mid s_t)}{\pi_{\theta_{\mathrm{old}}}(a_t \mid s_t)} A_t^{\pi_{\theta_{\mathrm{old}}}}\right]$$
$$\textit{subject to } \mathbb{E}_t\big[KL\big(\pi_\theta(a_t \mid s_t) \,\|\, \pi_{\theta_{\mathrm{old}}}(a_t \mid s_t)\big)\big] \leq \delta \qquad (7.31)$$

To sum up, $J_\pi^{\mathrm{CPI}}(\pi')$ is a linear approximation to $J(\pi') - J(\pi)$ since its gradient is equal to the policy gradient. It also guarantees monotonic improvement to within an error bound. To ensure improvement while accounting for this potential error, we impose a trust region constraint to limit the difference between the new and the old policies. Provided changes in the policy stay within the trust region, we can avoid performance collapse.

A number of algorithms have been proposed to solve this trust region optimization problem. Some of these include *Natural Policy Gradient* (NPG) [63, 112, 113], *Trust Region Policy Optimization* (TRPO) [122], and *Constrained Policy Optimization* (CPO) [2]. The theories behind them are fairly complex, and the algorithms are difficult to implement. Their gradients can be expensive to compute, and it is difficult to choose a good value for δ. These algorithms are beyond the scope of this book, but their drawbacks serve to motivate our next algorithm: Proximal Policy Optimization.

7.2   Proximal Policy Optimization (PPO)

The "Proximal Policy Optimization Algorithms" (PPO) paper [124] was published by Schulman et al. in 2017. PPO is easy to implement, computationally inexpensive, and we do not have to choose δ. For these reasons, it has become one of the most popular policy gradient algorithms.

PPO is a family of algorithms that solve the trust-region constrained policy optimization problem with simple and effective heuristics. Two variants exist. The first is based on an adaptive KL penalty, and the second is based on a clipped objective. This section will present both of these variants.

Before we do that, let's simplify the surrogate objective $J^{\text{CPI}}(\theta)$ by writing $r_t(\theta) = \frac{\pi_\theta(a_t|s_t)}{\pi_{\theta_{\text{old}}}(a_t|s_t)}$ as shown in Equation 7.32. The advantage $A_t^{\pi_{\theta_{\text{old}}}}$ is also written as A_t for brevity, since we know advantages are always calculated using the older policy $\pi_{\theta_{\text{old}}}$.

$$J^{\text{CPI}}(\theta) = \mathbb{E}_t\left[\frac{\pi_\theta(a_t \mid s_t)}{\pi_{\theta_{\text{old}}}(a_t \mid s_t)} A_t^{\pi_{\theta_{\text{old}}}}\right] = \mathbb{E}_t[r_t(\theta)A_t] \qquad (7.32)$$

The first variant of PPO is called *PPO with adaptive KL penalty*, with the objective shown in Equation 7.33. It turns the KL constraint $\mathbb{E}_t[KL(\pi_\theta(a_t \mid s_t) \| \pi_{\theta_{\text{old}}}(a_t \mid s_t))] \leq \delta$ into an adaptive KL penalty which is subtracted from the importance-weighted advantage. The expectation of the result is the new objective to be maximized.

$$J^{\text{KLPEN}}(\theta) = \max_\theta \mathbb{E}_t\left[r_t(\theta)A_t - \beta KL\big(\pi_\theta(a_t \mid s_t) \| \pi_{\theta_{\text{old}}}(a_t \mid s_t)\big)\right] \qquad (7.33)$$

Equation 7.33 is known as a *KL-penalized surrogate objective*. β is an adaptive coefficient which controls the size of the KL penalty. It serves the same purpose as Equation 7.31 in controlling the trust region of optimization. The larger β, the more the difference between π_θ and $\pi_{\theta_{\text{old}}}$. The smaller β, the higher the tolerance between the two policies.

One challenge of using a constant coefficient is that different problems have different characteristics, so it is hard to find one value which will work everywhere. Even on a single problem, the loss landscape changes as policy iterates, so a β that worked earlier may not work later—it needs to adapt to these changes.

To tackle this problem, the PPO paper proposes a heuristic-based update rule for β that allows it to adapt over time. β is updated after every policy update and the new value is used in the next iteration. The update rule for β is shown in Algorithm 7.1. It can be used as a subroutine in the PPO algorithm which will be presented later in this section.

Algorithm 7.1 Adaptive KL penalty coefficient

1: Set a target value δ_{tar} for the expectation of KL
2: Initialize β to a random value
3: Use multiple epochs of minibatch SGD, optimize (maximize) the KL-penalized
   $\hookrightarrow$ surrogate objective: $J^{\text{KLPEN}}(\theta) = \mathbb{E}_t[r_t(\theta)A_t - \beta KL(\pi_\theta(a_t \mid s_t) \| \pi_{\theta_{\text{old}}}(a_t \mid s_t))]$
4: Compute $\delta = \mathbb{E}_t[KL(\pi_\theta(a_t \mid s_t) \| \pi_{\theta_{\text{old}}}(a_t \mid s_t))]$:
5: **if** $\delta < \delta_{\text{tar}}/1.5$ **then**
6:     $\beta \leftarrow \beta/2$
7: **else if** $\delta > \delta_{\text{tar}} \times 1.5$ **then**
8:     $\beta \leftarrow \beta \times 2$
9: **else**
10:     pass
11: **end if**

At the end of each iteration, we estimate δ and compare it to the desired target δ_{tar}. If δ is less than δ_{tar} by some margin, we decrease the KL penalty by reducing β. However, if δ is greater than δ_{tar} by some margin, we increase the KL penalty by increasing β. The specific values used to determine the margins and the update rules for β are chosen empirically. The authors selected 1.5 and 2 respectively, but also found that the algorithm is not very sensitive to these values.

It was also observed that KL divergence occasionally departs far away from its target value δ_{tar}, but β adjusts quickly. Good values for δ_{tar} also need to be determined empirically.

This approach has the benefit of being simple to implement. However, it doesn't solve the problem of choosing a target δ. Furthermore, it can be computationally expensive because of the need to calculate the *KL*.

PPO with clipped surrogate objective remedies this by doing away with the KL constraint and using a simpler modification to the surrogate objective from Equation 7.30, shown in Equation 7.34.

$$J^{\text{CLIP}}(\theta) = \mathbb{E}_t\left[\min\left(r_t(\theta)A_t, \text{clip}(r_t(\theta), 1-\varepsilon, 1+\varepsilon)A_t\right)\right] \qquad (7.34)$$

Equation 7.34 is known as *clipped surrogate objective*. ε is a value which defines the clipping neighborhood $|r_t(\theta) - 1| \le \varepsilon$. It is a hyperparameter to be tuned, and can be decayed during training. The first term within $\min(\cdot)$ is simply the surrogate objective J^{CPI}. The second term $\text{clip}(r_t(\theta), 1-\varepsilon, 1+\varepsilon)A_t$ bounds the value of J^{CPI} to be between $(1-\varepsilon)A_t$ and $(1+\varepsilon)A_t$. When $r_t(\theta)$ is within the interval $[1-\varepsilon, 1+\varepsilon]$, both terms inside $\min(\cdot)$ are equal.

This objective prevents parameter updates which could cause large and risky changes to the policy π_θ. To quantify large policy changes, we use the probability ratio $r_t(\theta)$. When a new policy is equal to the old policy, $r_t(\theta) = r_t(\theta_{\text{old}}) = \frac{\pi_{\theta_{\text{old}}}(a_t|s_t)}{\pi_{\theta_{\text{old}}}(a_t|s_t)} = 1$. If a new policy deviates from the old policy, $r_t(\theta)$ deviates away from 1.

The idea is to limit $r_t(\theta)$ to an ε-neighborhood $[1 - \varepsilon, 1 + \varepsilon]$. Normally, maximizing the surrogate objective J^{CPI} without a constraint could encourage large policy updates. This is because one mechanism by which performance on the objective can be improved is through large changes to $r_t(\theta)$. By clipping the objective, we remove the incentive for large policy updates that would cause $r_t(\theta)$ to deviate outside of the neighborhood. To see why this is the case, consider when $r_t(\theta)A_t$ would assume large positive values, which is either $A_t > 0$, $r_t(\theta) > 0$ or $A_t < 0$, $r_t(\theta) < 0$.

When $A_t > 0$, $r_t(\theta) > 0$, if $r_t(\theta)$ becomes much larger than 1, the upper clip term $1 - \varepsilon$ applies to upper-bound $r_t(\theta) \leq 1 + \varepsilon$, hence $J^{\text{CLIP}} \leq (1 + \varepsilon)A_t$. On the other hand, when $A_t < 0$, $r_t(\theta) < 0$, if $r_t(\theta)$ becomes much smaller than 1, the lower clip term $1 - \varepsilon$ applies to again upper-bound $J^{\text{CLIP}} \leq (1 - \varepsilon)A_t$. When taking the minimum in Equation 7.34, J^{CLIP} is always upper-bounded in either of the two ways. Additionally, taking the minimum also implies that J^{CLIP} is a pessimistic lower bound of the original surrogate objective J^{CPI}. This way, the effect of $r_t(\theta)$ is ignored when it tries to make the objective better by more than εA_t, but is always considered when it makes the objective worse.

Since objective J^{CLIP} is upper-bounded, there is no incentive for large policy updates that deviate $r_t(\theta)$ outside of the neighborhood $[1 - \varepsilon, 1 + \varepsilon]$. Hence, policy updates are safe.

Additionally, since this objective assumes samples are generated from $\pi_{\theta_{\text{old}}}$—that is, the objective does not depend on the current policy π_θ except through the importance weights—we are also justified to reuse a sampled trajectory multiple times to perform parameter updates. This increases the sample efficiency of the algorithm. Notice that the objective depends on $\pi_{\theta_{\text{old}}}$ which is updated after each training step. This means that PPO is an on-policy algorithm, so the old trajectory must be discarded after a training step.

The clipped objective J^{CLIP} is cheap to compute, very easy to understand, and its implementation requires only a few trivial modifications to the original surrogate objective J^{CPI}.

The most costly computations are the probability ratio $r_t(\theta)$ and advantage A_t. However, these are the minimal calculations needed by any algorithms optimizing the surrogate objective. The other calculations are clipping and minimizing, which are essentially constant-time.

In the PPO paper, the clipped surrogate objective variant outperformed the KL-penalized objective variant. Since it is both simpler and performs better, the clipped variant of PPO is preferred.

This concludes this chapter's discussions on constraints to the policy gradient. We started with the policy gradient objective $J(\theta) = \mathbb{E}_t[A_t \log \pi_\theta(a_t \mid s_t)]$ used in REINFORCE and Actor-Critic. We then introduced a surrogate objective $J^{\text{CPI}}(\theta)$ with the promise of monotonic improvements, which holds if we constrain the difference between successive policies. PPO presented two ways to constrain the surrogate objective—using a KL penalty or a clipping heuristic, giving us J^{KLPEN} and J^{CLIP}, respectively. Let's gather all these policy gradient objectives together and compare them.

$$J(\theta) = \mathbb{E}_t[A_t^{\pi_\theta} \log \pi_\theta(a_t \mid s_t)] \qquad \textit{original objective} \quad (7.35)$$

$$J^{\mathrm{CPI}}(\theta) = \mathbb{E}_t[r_t(\theta)A_t^{\pi_{\theta_{\mathrm{old}}}}] \qquad \textit{surrogate objective} \quad (7.36)$$

$$J^{\mathrm{CPI}}(\theta) \textit{ subject to } \mathbb{E}_t[KL(\pi_\theta \mid\mid \pi_{\theta_{\mathrm{old}}})] \leq \delta \qquad \textit{constrained surrogate objective} \quad (7.37)$$

$$J^{\mathrm{KLPEN}}(\theta) = \mathbb{E}_t[r_t(\theta)A_t^{\pi_{\theta_{\mathrm{old}}}} - \beta KL(\pi_\theta \mid\mid \pi_{\theta_{\mathrm{old}}})] \qquad \textit{PPO with KL penalty} \quad (7.38)$$

$$J^{\mathrm{CLIP}}(\theta)$$

$$= \mathbb{E}_t\left[\min\left(r_t(\theta)A_t^{\pi_{\theta_{\mathrm{old}}}}, \mathrm{clip}(r_t(\theta), 1-\varepsilon, 1+\varepsilon)A_t^{\pi_{\theta_{\mathrm{old}}}}\right)\right] \quad \textit{PPO with clipping} \quad (7.39)$$

For clarity, we fully express the equations in terms of θ to show which policies are variable and which of them are used to compute the advantages. Notice that only the original objective uses the current policy π_θ to compute the advantage $A_t^{\pi_\theta}$, while the rest of them use the older policy to compute the advantage $A_t^{\pi_{\theta_{\mathrm{old}}}}$.

7.3 PPO Algorithm

Since PPO is a policy gradient method with a modified objective, it is compatible with both of the policy gradient algorithms we have learned, REINFORCE and Actor-Critic. Algorithm 7.2 shows PPO with a clipped objective implemented as an extension of the Actor-Critic from Chapter 6.

Algorithm 7.2   PPO with clipping, extending Actor-Critic

1: Set $\beta \geq 0$, entropy regularization weight
2: Set $\varepsilon \geq 0$, the clipping variable
3: Set K, the number of epochs
4: Set N, the number of actors
5: Set T, the time horizon
6: Set $M \leq NT$, the minibatch size
7: Set $\alpha_A \geq 0$, actor learning rate
8: Set $\alpha_C \geq 0$, critic learning rate
9: Randomly initialize the actor and critic parameters θ_A, θ_C
10: Initialize the "old" actor network $\theta_{A_{\mathrm{old}}}$
11: **for** $i = 1, 2, \ldots$ **do**
12:     Set $\theta_{A_{\mathrm{old}}} = \theta_A$
13:     **for** *actor* $= 1, 2, \ldots, N$ **do**
14:         Run policy $\theta_{A_{\mathrm{old}}}$ in environment for T time steps and collect the trajectories
15:         Compute advantages $A_1, \ldots, A_T$ using $\theta_{A_{\mathrm{old}}}$
16:         Calculate $V_{\mathrm{tar},1}^\pi, \ldots, V_{\mathrm{tar},T}^\pi$ using the critic network θ_C and/or trajectory data
17:     **end for**
18:     Let *batch* with size NT consist of the collected trajectories, advantages,
     ↪   and target V-values
19:     **for** *epoch* $= 1, 2, \ldots, K$ **do**

20:         **for** minibatch m in *batch* **do**
21:              The following are computed over the whole minibatch m
22:              Calculate $r_m(\theta_A)$
23:              Calculate $J_m^{\text{CLIP}}(\theta_A)$ using the advantages A_m from the minibatch
                 $\hookrightarrow$ and $r_m(\theta_A)$
24:              Calculate entropies H_m using using the actor network θ_A
25:              Calculate policy loss:
26:              $L_{\text{pol}}(\theta_A) = J_m^{\text{CLIP}}(\theta_A) - \beta H_m$
27:
28:              Calculate predicted V-value $\hat{V}^\pi(s_m)$ using the critic network θ_C
29:              Calculate value loss using the V-targets from the minibatch:
30:              $L_{\text{val}}(\theta_C) = MSE(\hat{V}^\pi(s_m), V_{\text{tar}}^\pi(s_m))$
31:
32:              Update actor parameters, for example using SGD:
33:              $\theta_A = \theta_A + \alpha_A \nabla_{\theta_A} L_{\text{pol}}(\theta_A)$
34:              Update critic parameters, for example using SGD:
35:              $\theta_C = \theta_C + \alpha_C \nabla_{\theta_C} L_{\text{val}}(\theta_C)$
36:         **end for**
37:     **end for**
38: **end for**

Let's walk through the algorithm.

- Lines 1–8: Set all the hyperparameter values.

- Line 9: Initialize the actor and critic networks.

- Line 10: Initialize an old actor network to act as $\pi_{\theta_{\text{old}}}$ for calculating the probability ratio $r_t(\theta)$.

- Lines 12–18: Update the old actor network to the main actor network. Gather trajectory data using the old actor network, and compute the advantages and V-targets. Then store the trajectories along with the advantages and V-targets in a batch to be sampled later. Note that this version of Actor-Critic uses multiple parallel actors. This will be discussed as a parallelization method in Chapter 8.

- Line 19: Loop over the entire batch for K epochs.

- Lines 20–21: Sample minibatches of size M from the batch. The calculations in this block utilize every element in the minibatch.

- Lines 22–23: Calculate the clipped surrogate objective.

- Line 24: Calculate the policy entropy for the actions in the minibatch.

- Lines 25–26: Calculate the policy loss.

- Lines 28–30: Calculate the value loss. Note that the V-target values are computed once in the batch and reused.

- Lines 32–33: Update the actor parameters using the gradient of the policy loss.
- Lines 34–35: Update the critic parameters using the gradient of the value loss.

7.4 Implementing PPO

We have seen how PPO can be used to extend the Actor-Critic algorithm. In this section, we will see how this is implemented in SLM Lab.

Naturally, PPO can extend the `ActorCritic` class and reuse most of its methods. The PPO modification involves only changing the objective function and the training loop—these are the two methods we need to override. Furthermore, the objective modification concerns just the policy loss; the method for calculating the value loss remains the same.

7.4.1 Calculating the PPO Policy Loss

In Code 7.1, the policy loss overrides its parent method from `ActorCritic` to calculate the PPO policy loss using the clipped surrogate objective.

The action log probabilities are calculated from both the current and old actor networks (lines 14–18). These are used to calculate the probability ratio $r_t(\theta)$ (line 20). Note that we use the exponent of their differences to convert log probabilities to probability ratio.

The clipped surrogate objective is calculated piece-wise and combined in lines 21 to 24. The remainder of the policy loss calculation has the same form as the parent method.

Code 7.1 PPO implementation: calculating the PPO policy loss

```
1   # slm_lab/agent/algorithm/ppo.py
2
3   class PPO(ActorCritic):
4       ...
5
6       def calc_policy_loss(self, batch, pdparams, advs):
7           clip_eps = self.body.clip_eps
8           action_pd = policy_util.init_action_pd(self.body.ActionPD, pdparams)
9           states = batch['states']
10          actions = batch['actions']
11          ...
12
13          # L^CLIP
14          log_probs = action_pd.log_prob(actions)
15          with torch.no_grad():
16              old_pdparams = self.calc_pdparam(states, net=self.old_net)
17              old_action_pd = policy_util.init_action_pd(self.body.ActionPD,
                ↪  old_pdparams)
```

```
18              old_log_probs = old_action_pd.log_prob(actions)
19          assert log_probs.shape == old_log_probs.shape
20          ratios = torch.exp(log_probs - old_log_probs)
21          sur_1 = ratios * advs
22          sur_2 = torch.clamp(ratios, 1.0 - clip_eps, 1.0 + clip_eps) * advs
23          # flip sign because need to maximize
24          clip_loss = -torch.min(sur_1, sur_2).mean()
25
26          # H entropy regularization
27          entropy = action_pd.entropy().mean()
28          self.body.mean_entropy = entropy  # update logging variable
29          ent_penalty = -self.body.entropy_coef * entropy
30
31          policy_loss = clip_loss + ent_penalty
32          return policy_loss
```

7.4.2 PPO Training Loop

Code 7.2 shows the PPO training loop. First, the old actor network is updated from the main actor network (line 10). A batch of collected trajectories is sampled from the memory (line 11). The advantages and target V-values are calculated and cached to be used in the minibatches for efficiency (lines 12–15). The version here is an optimization to compute the advantages and target V-values in batch, as opposed to computing them at every time step as per Algorithm 7.2.

To reuse data for training, we iterate through the all of the data multiple times (line 18). For each epoch, we split the data into minibatches for training (lines 19–20). The rest of the training logic is the same as the ActorCritic class. This involves calculating the policy and value losses and using them to train the actor and critic networks.

Code 7.2   PPO implementation: training method

```
1   # slm_lab/agent/algorithm/ppo.py
2
3   class PPO(ActorCritic):
4       ...
5
6       def train(self):
7           ...
8           clock = self.body.env.clock
9           if self.to_train == 1:
10              net_util.copy(self.net, self.old_net)  # update old net
11              batch = self.sample()
12              clock.set_batch_size(len(batch))
```

```
13          _pdparams, v_preds = self.calc_pdparam_v(batch)
14          advs, v_targets = self.calc_advs_v_targets(batch, v_preds)
15          batch['advs'], batch['v_targets'] = advs, v_targets
16          ...
17          total_loss = torch.tensor(0.0)
18          for _ in range(self.training_epoch):
19              minibatches = util.split_minibatch(batch, self.minibatch_size)
20              for minibatch in minibatches:
21                  ...
22                  advs, v_targets = minibatch['advs'],
                    ↪  minibatch['v_targets']
23                  pdparams, v_preds = self.calc_pdparam_v(minibatch)
24                  policy_loss = self.calc_policy_loss(minibatch, pdparams,
                    ↪  advs)  # from actor
25                  val_loss = self.calc_val_loss(v_preds, v_targets)  # from
                    ↪  critic
26                  if self.shared:  # shared network
27                      loss = policy_loss + val_loss
28                      self.net.train_step(loss, self.optim,
                        ↪  self.lr_scheduler, clock=clock,
                        ↪  global_net=self.global_net)
29                  else:
30                      self.net.train_step(policy_loss, self.optim,
                        ↪  self.lr_scheduler, clock=clock,
                        ↪  global_net=self.global_net)
31                      self.critic_net.train_step(val_loss,
                        ↪  self.critic_optim, self.critic_lr_scheduler,
                        ↪  clock=clock, global_net=self.global_critic_net)
32                      loss = policy_loss + val_loss
33                  total_loss += loss
34          loss = total_loss / self.training_epoch / len(minibatches)
35          # reset
36          self.to_train = 0
37          return loss.item()
38      else:
39          return np.nan
```

7.5   Training a PPO Agent

In this section we will train PPO to play Atari Pong and BipedalWalker.

7.5.1   PPO on Pong

Code 7.3 shows a spec file which configures a PPO agent to play Atari Pong. The file is also available in SLM Lab at slm_lab/spec/benchmark/ppo/ppo_pong.json.

Code 7.3   PPO: spec file

```
1   # slm_lab/spec/benchmark/ppo/ppo_pong.json
2
3   {
4     "ppo_pong": {
5       "agent": [{
6         "name": "PPO",
7         "algorithm": {
8           "name": "PPO",
9           "action_pdtype": "default",
10          "action_policy": "default",
11          "explore_var_spec": null,
12          "gamma": 0.99,
13          "lam": 0.70,
14          "clip_eps_spec": {
15            "name": "no_decay",
16            "start_val": 0.10,
17            "end_val": 0.10,
18            "start_step": 0,
19            "end_step": 0
20          },
21          "entropy_coef_spec": {
22            "name": "no_decay",
23            "start_val": 0.01,
24            "end_val": 0.01,
25            "start_step": 0,
26            "end_step": 0
27          },
28          "val_loss_coef": 0.5,
29          "time_horizon": 128,
30          "minibatch_size": 256,
31          "training_epoch": 4
32        },
33        "memory": {
34          "name": "OnPolicyBatchReplay",
```

```
35          },
36          "net": {
37            "type": "ConvNet",
38            "shared": true,
39            "conv_hid_layers": [
40              [32, 8, 4, 0, 1],
41              [64, 4, 2, 0, 1],
42              [32, 3, 1, 0, 1]
43            ],
44            "fc_hid_layers": [512],
45            "hid_layers_activation": "relu",
46            "init_fn": "orthogonal_",
47            "normalize": true,
48            "batch_norm": false,
49            "clip_grad_val": 0.5,
50            "use_same_optim": false,
51            "loss_spec": {
52              "name": "MSELoss"
53            },
54            "actor_optim_spec": {
55              "name": "Adam",
56              "lr": 2.5e-4,
57            },
58            "critic_optim_spec": {
59              "name": "Adam",
60              "lr": 2.5e-4,
61            },
62            "lr_scheduler_spec": {
63              "name": "LinearToZero",
64              "frame": 1e7
65            },
66            "gpu": true
67          }
68        }],
69        "env": [{
70          "name": "PongNoFrameskip-v4",
71          "frame_op": "concat",
72          "frame_op_len": 4,
73          "reward_scale": "sign",
74          "num_envs": 16,
75          "max_t": null,
76          "max_frame": 1e7
77        }],
78        "body": {
```

```
79        "product": "outer",
80        "num": 1
81      },
82      "meta": {
83        "distributed": false,
84        "log_frequency": 10000,
85        "eval_frequency": 10000,
86        "max_session": 4,
87        "max_trial": 1,
88      }
89    }
90  }
```

Let's walk through the main components.

- **Algorithm:** The algorithm is PPO (line 8), the action policy is the default policy (line 10) for discrete action space (categorical distribution). γ is set on line 12. We use GAE to estimate advantages, with `lam` for λ set in line 13. The clipping hyperparameter ε and its decay are specified in lines 14–20, and the entropy coefficient is specified in lines 21–27. The value loss coefficient is set in line 28.

- **Network architecture:** Convolutional neural network with three convolutional layers and one fully connected layer with ReLU activation function (lines 37–45). The actor and critic use a shared network as specified in line 38. The network is trained on a GPU if available (line 66).

- **Optimizer:** The optimizer is Adam [68] with a learning rate of 0.00025 (lines 54–57). The learning rate is decayed to 0 over 10 million frames (lines 62–65).

- **Training frequency:** Training is batch-wise as required by the algorithm, so we use `OnPolicyBatchReplay` memory (line 34). The number of epochs is 4 (line 31), and the minibatch size is 256 (line 30). The time horizon T is set in line 29, and the number of actors is set in line 74 as `num_envs`.

- **Environment:** The environment is Atari Pong [14, 18] (line 70).

- **Training length:** Training consists of 10 million time steps (line 76).

- **Evaluation:** The agent is evaluated every 10,000 time steps (line 85).

To train this PPO agent using SLM Lab, run the commands shown in Code 7.4 in a terminal. The agent should start with the score of −21 and achieve close to the maximum score of 21 on average.

Code 7.4   PPO: spec file

```
1  conda activate lab
2  python run_lab.py slm_lab/spec/benchmark/ppo/ppo_pong.json ppo_pong train
```

This will run a training Trial with four Sessions to obtain an average result. The trial should take about half a day to complete when running on a GPU. The graph and its moving average are shown in Figure 7.2.

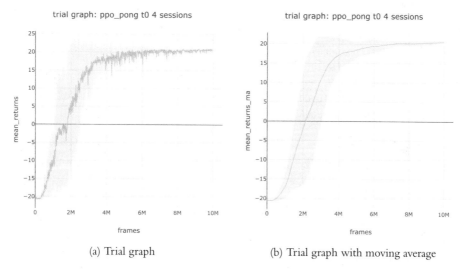

(a) Trial graph (b) Trial graph with moving average

Figure 7.2 PPO trial graphs from SLM Lab averaged over four sessions. The vertical axis shows the total rewards averaged over eight episodes during checkpoints, and the horizontal axis shows the total training frames. Compared to Actor-Critic from Chapter 6, PPO learns and obtains the top score much faster.

7.5.2 PPO on BipedalWalker

As a policy-based method, PPO can also be applied to continuous-control problems. Code 7.5 shows a spec file which configures a PPO agent for the BipedalWalker environment. The file is available in SLM Lab at slm_lab/spec/benchmark/ppo /ppo_cont.json. In particular, note the different network architecture (lines 37–39) and environment (lines 62–65).

Code 7.5 PPO on BipedalWalker: spec file

```
1  # slm_lab/spec/benchmark/ppo/ppo_cont.json
2
3  {
4    "ppo_bipedalwalker": {
5      "agent": [{
6        "name": "PPO",
7        "algorithm": {
```

```
8          "name": "PPO",
9          "action_pdtype": "default",
10         "action_policy": "default",
11         "explore_var_spec": null,
12         "gamma": 0.99,
13         "lam": 0.95,
14         "clip_eps_spec": {
15           "name": "no_decay",
16           "start_val": 0.20,
17           "end_val": 0.0,
18           "start_step": 10000,
19           "end_step": 1000000
20         },
21         "entropy_coef_spec": {
22           "name": "no_decay",
23           "start_val": 0.01,
24           "end_val": 0.01,
25           "start_step": 0,
26           "end_step": 0
27         },
28         "val_loss_coef": 0.5,
29         "time_horizon": 512,
30         "minibatch_size": 4096,
31         "training_epoch": 15
32       },
33       "memory": {
34         "name": "OnPolicyBatchReplay",
35       },
36       "net": {
37         "type": "MLPNet",
38         "shared": false,
39         "hid_layers": [256, 128],
40         "hid_layers_activation": "relu",
41         "init_fn": "orthogonal_",
42         "normalize": true,
43         "batch_norm": false,
44         "clip_grad_val": 0.5,
45         "use_same_optim": true,
46         "loss_spec": {
47           "name": "MSELoss"
48         },
49         "actor_optim_spec": {
50           "name": "Adam",
51           "lr": 3e-4,
```

```
52          },
53          "critic_optim_spec": {
54            "name": "Adam",
55            "lr": 3e-4,
56          },
57          "lr_scheduler_spec": null,
58          "gpu": false
59        }
60      }],
61      "env": [{
62        "name": "BipedalWalker-v2",
63        "num_envs": 32,
64        "max_t": null,
65        "max_frame": 4e6
66      }],
67      "body": {
68        "product": "outer",
69        "num": 1
70      },
71      "meta": {
72        "distributed": false,
73        "log_frequency": 10000,
74        "eval_frequency": 10000,
75        "max_session": 4,
76        "max_trial": 1
77      }
78    }
79  }
```

Run the commands in Code 7.6 in a terminal to train an agent.

Code 7.6   PPO on BipedalWalker: training an agent

```
1  conda activate lab
2  python run_lab.py slm_lab/spec/benchmark/ppo/ppo_cont.json ppo_bipedalwalker
   ↪  train
```

This will run a training Trial to produce the graphs in Figure 7.3.

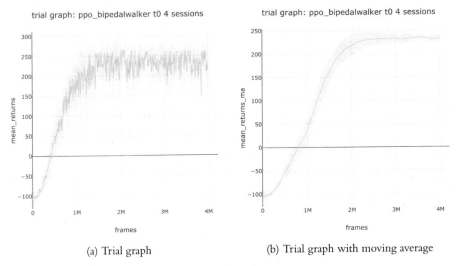

(a) Trial graph   (b) Trial graph with moving average

Figure 7.3   PPO on BipedalWalker from SLM Lab averaged over four sessions. This trial yields performance closer to the solution score of 300.

7.6 Experimental Results

In this section we will run an experiment using SLM Lab to study the effect of GAE's λ variable in PPO. We will use the Atari Breakout game as a more challenging environment.

7.6.1 Experiment: The Effect of λ of GAE

Since PPO is implemented as an extension of Actor-Critic which uses GAE, we will run the same experiment from Section 6.7.2 to study the effect of different λ values in PPO by performing a grid search. The experiment spec file is extended from Code 7.3 by adding a search spec for `lam` shown in Code 7.7. Lines 4 and 7 specify the change in environment, and line 19 specifies a grid search over a list of λ values `lam`. The full spec file is available in SLM Lab at `slm_lab/spec/experimental/ppo/ppo_lam_search.json`.

Code 7.7   PPO spec file with search spec for different values of GAE λ `lam`

```
1   # slm_lab/spec/experimental/ppo/ppo_lam_search.json
2
3   {
4     "ppo_breakout": {
5       ...
6       "env": [{
```

```
 7        "name": "BreakoutNoFrameskip-v4",
 8        "frame_op": "concat",
 9        "frame_op_len": 4,
10        "reward_scale": "sign",
11        "num_envs": 16,
12        "max_t": null,
13        "max_frame": 1e7
14      }],
15      ...
16      "search": {
17        "agent": [{
18          "algorithm": {
19            "lam__grid_search": [0.50, 0.70, 0.90, 0.95, 0.97, 0.99]
20          }
21        }]
22      }
23    }
24  }
```

To run the experiment in SLM Lab, use the commands shown in Code 7.8.

Code 7.8   Run an experiment to search over different values of GAE λ as defined in the spec file.

```
1  conda activate lab
2  python run_lab.py slm_lab/spec/experimental/ppo/ppo_lam_search.json
   ↪  ppo_breakout search
```

This will run an `Experiment` which spawns six `Trials`, each with a different value of `lam` substituted in the original PPO spec. Each `Trial` runs four `Sessions`. The multitrial graphs are shown in Figure 7.4.

Figure 7.4 shows the effect of different values of GAE λ in PPO on the Breakout environment. $\lambda = 0.70$ performs the best with an episodic score of above 400, followed closely by $\lambda = 0.50$. Higher λ values close to 0.90 do not perform as well. Compared to the same experiment on the same problem for Actor-Critic in Section 6.7.2, the optimal λ value for PPO (0.70) is significantly different from that of Actor-Critic (0.90), while PPO obtains a better performance than Actor-Critic as expected. Again, this experiment also demonstrates that λ is not a very sensitive hyperparameter in PPO.

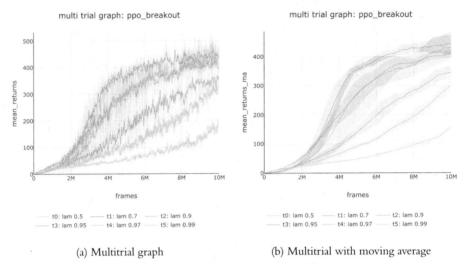

(a) Multitrial graph

(b) Multitrial with moving average

Figure 7.4   The effect of different values of GAE λ in PPO on the Breakout environment. $\lambda = 0.70$ performs the best, while λ values closer to 0.90 do not perform as well.

7.6.2   Experiment: The Effect of Clipping Variable ε

The clipping variable ε defines the clipping neighborhood $|r_t(\theta) - 1| \le \varepsilon$ for the clipped surrogate objective in Equation 7.34.

In this experiment, we look at the effect of ε values by performing a grid search. The experiment spec file is extended from Code 7.3 by adding a search spec for `clip_eps` shown in Code 7.9. We also use a more challenging environment, Atari Qbert. Lines 4 and 7 specify the change in environment, and line 19 specifies a grid search over a list of ε values `clip_eps`. The full spec file is available in SLM Lab at `slm_lab/spec/experimental/ppo/ppo_eps_search.json`.

Code 7.9   PPO spec file with search spec for different clipping ε values `clip_eps`

```
1   # slm_lab/spec/experimental/ppo/ppo_eps_search.json
2
3   {
4     "ppo_qbert": {
5       ...
6       "env": [{
7         "name": "QbertNoFrameskip-v4",
8         "frame_op": "concat",
9         "frame_op_len": 4,
10        "reward_scale": "sign",
11        "num_envs": 16,
12        "max_t": null,
```

```
13        "max_frame": 1e7
14      }],
15      ...
16      "search": {
17        "agent": [{
18          "clip_eps_spec": {
19            "start_val__grid_search": [0.1, 0.2, 0.3, 0.4]
20          }
21        }]
22      }
23    }
24  }
```

To run the experiment in SLM Lab, use the commands shown in Code 7.10.

Code 7.10   Run an experiment to search over different clipping ε values as defined in the spec file.

```
1  conda activate lab
2  python run_lab.py slm_lab/spec/experimental/ppo/ppo_eps_search.json ppo_qbert
   ↪   search
```

This will run an Experiment consisting of four Trials each with four Sessions. The multitrial graphs are shown in Figure 7.5.

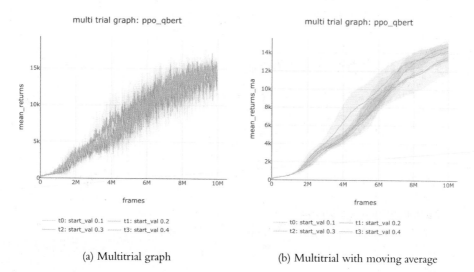

(a) Multitrial graph   (b) Multitrial with moving average

Figure 7.5   The effect of different clipping ε values of PPO on the Qbert environment. Overall, the algorithm is not very sensitive to this hyperparameter.

Figure 7.5 shows the effect of different clipping ε values of PPO on the Qbert environment. $\varepsilon = 0.20$ performs the best. Overall, the algorithm is not very sensitive to this hyperparameter as shown by the close performance of different ε values.

7.7 Summary

In this chapter, we looked at the problem of performance collapse in policy gradient methods caused by the fact that we are searching for policies by indirectly controlling parameters in the parameter space. This can lead to unstable changes in the policy during training.

To remedy this problem, we modify the policy gradient objective to yield a surrogate objective so that changes in the parameter space will guarantee monotonic policy improvement. This is known as the Monotonic Improvement Theory. In practice, the surrogate objective can only be approximated, thereby introducing some error. The error can be bounded, and we turn this error bound into a constraint for the objective so that we can guarantee policy improvements in practice as well as in theory.

We saw that the PPO algorithm is a simple and effective approach to solving this constrained optimization problem. There are two variants—PPO with KL penalty and PPO with clipping. Of these, clipping is the simplest, cheapest to compute, and the most performant.

The three policy gradient algorithms we looked at in this book are natural extensions of each other. Starting with the simplest algorithm, REINFORCE, we extended this into the Actor-Critic, which improves the reinforcing signal given to the policy. Finally, we showed that PPO can be used to extend the Actor-Critic by modifying its policy loss, which improves the stability and sample efficiency of training.

7.8 Further Reading

- "Oct 11: Advanced Policy Gradients, Lecture 13," *CS 294: Deep Reinforcement Learning, Fall 2017*, Levine [78].
- "A Natural Policy Gradient," Kakade, 2002 [63].
- "Trust Region Policy Optimization," Schulman et al., 2015 [122].
- "Benchmarking Deep Reinforcement Learning for Continuous Control," Duan et al., 2016 [35].
- "Constrained Policy Optimization," Achiam et al., 2017 [2].
- "Proximal Policy Optimization," Schulman et al., 2017 [124].
- "Policy Gradient Methods: Tutorial and New Frontiers," Microsoft Research, 2017 [86].

- "Proximal Policy Optimization," OpenAI Blog, 2017 [106].
- "More on Dota 2," OpenAI Blog, 2017 [102].
- "OpenAI Five Benchmark: Results," OpenAI Blog, 2018 [105].
- "OpenAI Five," OpenAI Blog, 2018 [104].
- "Learning Dexterity," OpenAI Blog, 2018 [101].

8

Parallelization Methods

One common theme in our discussions of the deep RL algorithms introduced in this book is that they are sample-inefficient. For nontrivial problems, millions of experiences are typically required before an agent learns to perform well. It may take days or weeks to generate sufficiently many experiences if data gathering is done sequentially by a single agent running in a single process.

Another theme arising from our discussion of the DQN algorithm is the importance of diverse and decorrelated training data to stabilize and accelerate learning. The use of experience replay helps achieve this, but it depends on DQN being an off-policy algorithm. Consequently, this approach is not available to policy gradient algorithms, at least not in a straightforward way.[1] However, these algorithms also benefit substantially from training with diverse data.

In this chapter, we discuss parallelization methods that can be applied to all deep RL algorithms. These can both substantially reduce the wall-clock training time and help generate more diverse training data for on-policy algorithms.

The key idea is to parallelize the agent and environment by creating multiple identical instances to gather trajectories independently of each other. Since an agent is parametrized by a network, we create multiple identical worker networks and a global network. The workers gather trajectories continuously, and the global network is periodically updated using worker data before pushing changes back to the workers.

There are two main categories of parallelization—synchronous and asynchronous. We first discuss synchronous parallelization in Section 8.1 and then asynchronous in Section 8.2.

---

1. It is possible to train on-policy algorithms with off-policy data using importance sampling which corrects for the difference in action probabilities between policies. However, the importance weight can vary wildly, either exploding or shrinking towards zero. For this reason, it is difficult to make off-policy correction work well in practice.

8.1 Synchronous Parallelization

When parallelization is synchronous (blocking), the global network waits to receive a set of updates from all the workers before updating its parameters. Correspondingly, after sending updates, the workers wait for the global network to update and push the new parameters, so that all workers have the same updated parameters. This is shown in Algorithm 8.1.

Algorithm 8.1   Synchronous parallelization, global gradient calculation

---

1: Set learning rate α
2: Initialize the global network θ_G
3: Initialize N worker networks $\theta_{W,1}, \theta_{W,2}, \ldots, \theta_{W,N}$
4: **for** each worker **do synchronously**
5:      Pull parameters from the global network and set $\theta_{W,i} \leftarrow \theta_G$
6:      Collect trajectories
7:      Push trajectories for the global network to use
8:      Wait until the global network has updated
9: **end for**
10: Wait for all worker trajectories
11: Compute gradient ∇_{θ_G} using all trajectories
12: Update the global network $\theta_G \leftarrow \theta_G + \alpha \nabla_{\theta_G}$

In this variant of parallelism, the workers are used to collect trajectories which are sent to the global network. The global network is responsible for using the trajectories to calculate gradients and perform parameter updates. Importantly, all these happen with a synchronization barrier—that's what makes it synchronous.

With parallelism, every worker gets to experience a different instance of an environment, which will unfold and branch out to different scenarios due to randomness in the policy and the environment. To ensure this, the workers and environment instances need to be initialized with different random seeds. As parallelization trajectories unfold, workers may end up in different phases of the environment—some near the beginning time steps, some near the end. Parallelization adds diversity to the training data for the global network because it is trained on multiple scenarios and phases of the environment. Overall, this helps stabilize the policy (represented by the global network) and makes it more robust to noise and variations.

The interleaving of experiences from multiple workers also helps decorrelate the data because at any time step, the global network receives a collection of experiences from different phases of the environment. For example, if an environment consists of multiple game levels, the global network will likely train on a few of them simultaneously. Workers will end up exploring different scenarios already due to randomness, but additionally we may let them use different exploration policies to further increase data diversity. One way to do this is to use different annealing schedules for the ε-greedy policy in Q-learning from Chapter 4.

In SLM Lab, synchronous parallelization is implemented using OpenAI's vector environment wrapper [99]. This creates multiple instances of an environment on different CPU processes, which communicate with the main process where the agent is located. The agent then acts on these environments in batch, effectively acting as multiple workers. This takes advantage of the fact that in synchronous parallelization, all the workers are guaranteed to have the same copy of the global network. The vector environment wrapper is quite extensive and its details are beyond the scope of this book; the source code can be found at `slm_lab/env/vec_env.py` in SLM Lab.

It is simple to use synchronous parallelization in SLM Lab by specifying the `num_envs` desired in a spec file. This applies to any algorithm; we have been using it for trials and experiments in this book. An example is shown in line 74 of Code 7.3 in the PPO spec file.

8.2 Asynchronous Parallelization

If parallelization is asynchronous (nonblocking), the global network updates its parameters whenever it receives data from any worker. Likewise, each worker periodically updates itself from the global network. This means that workers may have slightly different sets of parameters. This is shown in Algorithm 8.2.

Asynchronous parallelization was first applied to deep RL in the paper "Asynchronous Methods for Deep Reinforcement Learning" by Mnih et al. [87], also known as the "A3C paper." It played a critical role in popularizing Actor-Critic methods by making them competitive with value-based methods such as DQN. Not only did they achieve state-of-the-art performance on the Atari games, using an Asynchronous Advantage Actor-Critic (A3C) algorithm, but also demonstrated how deep RL algorithms could be trained faster and on CPUs, which are significantly cheaper than GPUs. A3C is simply an asynchronous version of the Advantage Actor-Critic algorithms from Chapter 6.

Algorithm 8.2   Asynchronous parallelization, worker gradient calculation

---

1: Set learning rate α
2: Initialize the global network θ_G
3: Initialize N worker networks $\theta_{W,1}, \theta_{W,2}, \ldots, \theta_{W,N}$
4: **for** each worker **do asynchronously**
5:     Pull parameters from the global network and set $\theta_{W,i} \leftarrow \theta_G$
6:     Collect trajectories
7:     Compute gradient $\nabla_{\theta_{W,i}}$
8:     Push $\nabla_{\theta_{W,i}}$ to the global network
9: **end for**
10: On receiving a worker gradient, update the global network $\theta_G \leftarrow \theta_G + \alpha \nabla_{\theta_{W,i}}$

In this example, in addition to collecting trajectories, workers also calculate their own gradients using their own data. The gradients are sent asynchronously to the global network whenever they become available. Similarly, the global network updates its own parameters immediately on receiving a gradient. Unlike the synchronous case, this variant does not have a synchronization barrier.

There are many ways to implement asynchronous training. The main design choices include:

1. **Lagged vs. not lagged:** Workers have to periodically update their networks to the global network parameters. This can be done at different frequencies. If the update is instantaneous, then the worker parameters are always equal to the global parameters. One way to do this is by sharing the network in the computer memory. However, this means that all the workers need access to the same shared memory, so they need to be running on the same machine. If the update occurs infrequently, the worker ends up with, on average, a lagged copy of the global parameters. A lagged network helps ensure each worker stays on-policy because it guarantees that the policy does not change when generating trajectories and computing gradients.

2. **Local vs. global gradient calculation:** The gradient calculation can either be done locally by the workers or globally using the global network. On-policy training requires local gradient calculation to stay on-policy, since the global network is constantly changing; off-policy algorithms do not have this restriction. A further practical consideration is the cost of data transfer between workers and the global network. Sending trajectory data between processes is typically more costly than sending gradients.

3. **Locked vs. lock-free:** A global network can be locked during a parameter update to ensure that the parameters are updated sequentially. Simultaneous updates may overwrite parts of one another. This is usually considered problematic, so in most cases the global network is locked. This adds to the training time as simultaneous updates need to be resolved sequentially. However, for certain problems, lock-free global network can be used to save time. This is the inspiration behind the Hogwild! algorithm discussed in Section 8.2.1.

8.2.1 Hogwild!

In SLM Lab, asynchronous parallelization is implemented using the Hogwild! algorithm,[2] which is a *lock-free* stochastic gradient descent parallelization method [93]. In Hogwild!, the global network is not locked during parameter updates. The implementation also uses a shared global network without lag and local gradient calculation.

Before going through the code, it is worth spending some time understanding why the Hogwild! algorithm works.

The problem with lock-free parallel parameter updates is overwriting, which leads to destructive conflicts. However, this effect is minimized if we assume that the optimization problem is sparse—that is, for a given function parametrized by a neural network,

---

2. Hogwild is an aptly chosen name for the algorithm, as it implies wildness and lack of restraint.

parameter updates will typically modify only a small subset of them. When this is the case, they rarely interfere with each other and overwriting is uncommon. With this *sparsity assumption*, the parameters modified in multiple simultaneous updates are probabilistically nonoverlapping. Consequently, lock-free parallelism becomes a viable strategy. It trades a small number of conflicts for a gain in training speed.

To see how sparsity is exploited to parallelize an otherwise sequential set of parameter updates, we can compare both schemes. Let θ_i be the network parameter at iteration i. A sequential update can be written as follows.

$$\theta_1 \xrightarrow{u_{1\to 2}} \theta_2 \xrightarrow{u_{2\to 3}} \theta_3 \cdots \xrightarrow{u_{n-1\to n}} \theta_n \tag{8.1}$$

$u_{i\to i+1}$ is an update such that $\theta_{i+1} = \theta_i + u_{i\to i+1}$. Now, the sparsity assumption implies that a small collection of w updates $u_{j\to j+1}, \ldots, u_{j+w-1\to j+w}$ have so few overlapping components that the sequential updates can be compressed into a parallel update generated by w workers independently to yield $u_{j\to j+1}, \ldots, u_{j\to j+w}$. Given w updates in sequence and in parallel, shown below,

$$\theta_j \xrightarrow{u_{j\to j+1}} \theta_{j+1} \xrightarrow{u_{j+1\to j+2}} \theta_{j+2} \cdots \xrightarrow{u_{j+w-1\to j+w}} \theta_{j+w} \qquad \text{(sequential)}$$

$$\theta_j \xrightarrow{u_{j\to j+1}} \theta_{\|j+1} \xrightarrow{u_{j\to j+2}} \theta_{\|j+2} \cdots \xrightarrow{u_{j\to j+w}} \theta_{\|j+w} \qquad \text{(parallel)}$$

the w-th iterations obtained from both are precisely or approximately equal, $\theta_{j+w} \simeq \theta_{\|j+w}$. Hence, parallelization with w workers can provide a fast and close approximation to the sequential case. Since we are solving the same optimization problem in either case, they should produce almost or precisely the same results.

When applying Hogwild!, beware that the more workers you have, the higher the chance of parameter update conflicts. Sparsity only holds true relative to the number of parallel operations. If conflicts become too frequent, the assumption breaks down.

How reasonable is the sparsity assumption when applied to deep RL? Unfortunately, this is not well understood. Still, this was the approach taken by Mnih et al. in the A3C paper. The success of this approach suggests a few possible explanations. First, it may be that the parameter updates were often sparse for the problems it was applied to. Second, there may be some additional training benefit to the noise introduced by the conflicting updates. Third, simultaneous parameter updates may be occurring rarely, for example because there were few workers with staggered update schedules. Or, fourth, research into neural network pruning [30, 41, 90] suggests that there are many unimportant or redundant neural network parameters during training. If conflicts occur on these parameters, the overall performance is unlikely to be affected. The results may also be explained by a combination of these factors. The effectiveness of Hogwild! in deep RL remains an interesting open problem.

Code 8.1 shows a minimal implementation of Hogwild! applied to a typical neural network training workflow. The crucial logic is when the network is created and put into a shared memory before being passed to workers for updates. Such a simple implementation is possible thanks to PyTorch's first-class integration with multiprocessing.

Code 8.1   A minimal Hogwild! example

```
1   # Minimal hogwild example
2   import torch
3   import torch.multiprocessing as mp
4
5   # example pytorch net, optimizer, and loss function
6   net = Net()
7   optimizer = torch.optim.SGD(net.parameters(), lr=0.001)
8   loss_fn = torch.nn.F.smooth_l1_loss
9
10  def train(net):
11      # construct data_loader, optimizer, loss_fn
12      net.train()
13      for x, y_target in data_loader:
14          optimizer.zero_grad()  # flush any old accumulated gradient
15          # autograd begins accumulating gradients below
16          y_pred = net(x)  # forward pass
17          loss = loss_fn(y_pred, y_target)  # compute loss
18          loss.backward()  # backpropagate
19          optimizer.step()  # update network weights
20
21  def hogwild(net, num_cpus):
22      net.share_memory()  # this makes all workers share the same memory
23      workers = []
24      for _rank in range(num_cpus):
25          w = mp.Process(target=train, args=(net, ))
26          w.start()
27          workers.append(w)
28      for w in workers:
29          w.join()
30
31  if __name__ == '__main__':
32      net = Net()
33      hogwild(net, num_cpus=4)
```

8.3 Training an A3C Agent

When the Actor-Critic algorithm using any advantage function is parallelized using an asynchronous method, it is known as A3C [87]. In SLM Lab, any implemented algorithms can be parallelized simply by adding a flag in the spec file. An example is shown in Code 8.2, which is modified from the Actor-Critic spec from Chapter 6. The full file is available in SLM Lab at `slm_lab/spec/benchmark/a3c/a3c_nstep_pong.json`.

Code 8.2 A3C spec file to play Atari Pong

```
1   # slm_lab/spec/benchmark/a3c/a3c_nstep_pong.json
2
3   {
4     "a3c_nstep_pong": {
5       "agent": [{
6         "name": "A3C",
7         "algorithm": {
8           "name": "ActorCritic",
9           "action_pdtype": "default",
10          "action_policy": "default",
11          "explore_var_spec": null,
12          "gamma": 0.99,
13          "lam": null,
14          "num_step_returns": 5,
15          "entropy_coef_spec": {
16            "name": "no_decay",
17            "start_val": 0.01,
18            "end_val": 0.01,
19            "start_step": 0,
20            "end_step": 0
21          },
22          "val_loss_coef": 0.5,
23          "training_frequency": 5
24        },
25        "memory": {
26          "name": "OnPolicyBatchReplay",
27        },
28        "net": {
29          "type": "ConvNet",
30          "shared": true,
31          "conv_hid_layers": [
32            [32, 8, 4, 0, 1],
33            [64, 4, 2, 0, 1],
34            [32, 3, 1, 0, 1]
35          ],
36          "fc_hid_layers": [512],
37          "hid_layers_activation": "relu",
38          "init_fn": "orthogonal_",
39          "normalize": true,
40          "batch_norm": false,
41          "clip_grad_val": 0.5,
42          "use_same_optim": false,
```

```
43        "loss_spec": {
44          "name": "MSELoss"
45        },
46        "actor_optim_spec": {
47          "name": "GlobalAdam",
48          "lr": 1e-4
49        },
50        "critic_optim_spec": {
51          "name": "GlobalAdam",
52          "lr": 1e-4
53        },
54        "lr_scheduler_spec": null,
55        "gpu": false
56      }
57    }],
58    "env": [{
59      "name": "PongNoFrameskip-v4",
60      "frame_op": "concat",
61      "frame_op_len": 4,
62      "reward_scale": "sign",
63      "num_envs": 8,
64      "max_t": null,
65      "max_frame": 1e7
66    }],
67    "body": {
68      "product": "outer",
69      "num": 1
70    },
71    "meta": {
72      "distributed": "synced",
73      "log_frequency": 10000,
74      "eval_frequency": 10000,
75      "max_session": 16,
76      "max_trial": 1,
77    }
78  }
79 }
```

Code 8.2 sets the meta spec "distributed": "synced" (line 72) and sets the number of workers, max_session, to 16 (line 75). The optimizer is changed to variant GlobalAdam (line 47) that is more suitable for Hogwild!. We also change the number of environments num_envs to 8 (line 63). Note that if the number of environments is greater than 1, the algorithm becomes a hybrid of synchronous (vector environments) and asynchronous (Hogwild!) methods, and there will be num_envs × max_session workers. Conceptually, this can be thought of as a hierarchy of Hogwild! workers, each spawning a number of synchronous workers.

To train this A3C agent with n-step returns using SLM Lab, run the commands shown in Code 8.3 in a terminal.

Code 8.3   A3C: training an agent

```
1  conda activate lab
2  python run_lab.py slm_lab/spec/benchmark/a3c/a3c_nstep_pong.json
   ↪  a3c_nstep_pong train
```

As usual, this will run a training Trial to produce the graphs shown in Figure 8.1. However, note that now the sessions take on the role of asynchronous workers. The trial should take only a few hours to complete when running on CPUs, although it will require a machine with at least 16 CPUs.

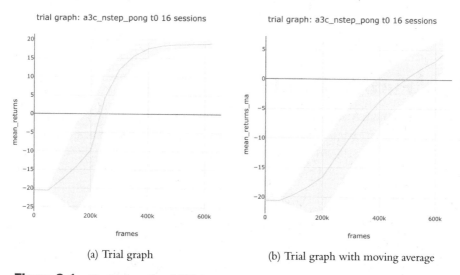

(a) Trial graph   (b) Trial graph with moving average

Figure 8.1   The trial graphs of A3C (n-step returns) with 16 workers. Since sessions take on the role of workers, the horizontal axis measures the number of frames experienced by individual worker. Therefore, the total number of frames experienced collectively is equal to the sum of the individual frames which will add to 10 million total frames.

8.4 Summary

In this chapter, we discussed two widely applicable parallelization methods—synchronous and asynchronous. We showed that they can be implemented using, respectively, vector environments or the Hogwild! algorithm.

The two benefits of parallelization are faster training and more diverse data. The second benefit plays a crucial role in stabilizing and improving the training of policy gradient algorithms. In fact, it often makes the difference between success and failure.

When determining which of the parallelization methods to apply, it helps to consider the factors of the ease of implementation, compute cost, and scale.

Synchronous methods (e.g., vector environments) are often straightforward and easier to implement than asynchronous methods, particularly if only data gathering is parallelized. Data generation is usually cheaper, so they require fewer resources for the same number of frames and so better scale up to a moderate number of workers—for example, less than 100. However, the synchronization barrier becomes a bottleneck when applied at a larger scale. In this case, asynchronous methods will likely be significantly faster.

It is not always necessary to parallelize. As a general rule, try to understand if a problem is simple enough to be solved without parallelization before investing time and resources into implementing it. Also, the need to parallelize depends on the algorithm used. Off-policy algorithms, such as DQN, can often achieve strong performance without parallelization since the experience replay already provides diverse training data. Even if training takes a very long time, agents can still learn. This is often not the case for on-policy algorithms such as Actor-Critic, which need to be parallelized so they can learn from diverse data.

8.5   Further Reading

- "Asynchronous Methods for Deep Reinforcement Learning," Mnih et al., 2016 [87].
- "HOGWILD!: A Lock-Free Approach to Parallelizing Stochastic Gradient Descent," Niu et al., 2011 [93].

9

Algorithm Summary

There are three defining characteristics of the algorithms we have introduced in this book. First, is an algorithm on-policy or off-policy? Second, what types of action spaces can it be applied to? And third, what functions does it learn?

REINFORCE, SARSA, A2C, and PPO are all on-policy algorithms, whereas DQN and Double DQN + PER are off-policy. SARSA, DQN, and Double DQN + PER are value-based algorithms that learn to approximate the Q^π function. Consequently, they are only applicable to environments with discrete action spaces.

REINFORCE is a pure policy-based algorithm and so only learns a policy π. A2C and PPO are hybrid methods which learn a policy π and the V^π function. REINFORCE, A2C, and PPO can all be applied to environments with either discrete or continuous action spaces. The characteristics of the algorithms are summarized in Table 9.1.

Table 9.1 Summary of algorithms in this book and their characteristics

Algorithm	on/off-policy	environment		functions learned		
		discrete	continuous	V^π	Q^π	policy π
REINFORCE	on-policy	✓	✓			✓
SARSA	on-policy	✓			✓	
DQN	off-policy	✓			✓	
Double DQN + PER	off-policy	✓			✓	
A2C	on-policy	✓	✓	✓		✓
PPO	on-policy	✓	✓	✓		✓

The algorithms we have discussed form two families, as depicted in Figure 9.1. Each family has an ancestor algorithm from which the others extend. The first family is the value-based algorithms—SARSA, DQN, and Double DQN + PER. SARSA is the ancestor of this family. DQN can be thought of as an extension of SARSA with better sample efficiency because it is off-policy. PER and Double DQN are extensions of DQN which improve on the sample efficiency and stability of the original DQN algorithm.

The second family consists of the policy-based and combined algorithms—
REINFORCE, A2C, and PPO. REINFORCE is the ancestor of this family. A2C extends
REINFORCE by replacing the Monte Carlo estimate of the return with a learned value
function. PPO extends A2C by modifying the objective to avoid performance collapse and
improve sample efficiency.

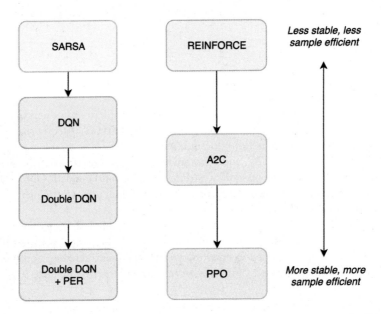

Figure 9.1   All the algorithms in this book are extensions of SARSA and REINFORCE.

Of all the algorithms we have discussed, the best-performing ones are Double DQN +
PER and PPO. They are typically the most stable and sample-efficient algorithms in their
respective families. They are therefore good first algorithms to try when working on a new
problem.

There are two important factors to consider when deciding whether to use Double
DQN + PER or PPO—the environment action space and the cost of generating
trajectories. A PPO agent can be trained on environments with any type of action space,
whereas Double DQN + PER is limited to discrete actions. However, Double DQN +
PER can be trained by reusing off-policy data generated by any means. This is
advantageous when data is expensive or time-consuming to gather—for example if the
data must be gathered from the real world. In contrast, PPO is on-policy, so it can only
train on data generated from its own policy.

Part III

Practical Details

10

Getting Deep RL to Work

A deep RL system consists of an agent interacting with an environment. Agents further consist of components which include a memory, policy, neural networks, and algorithmic functions. Individually, each of these components can be quite complex, and they also have to integrate and operate together to produce a working deep RL algorithm. As a result, a code base that implements multiple deep RL algorithms starts to enter the realm of large software systems with substantial amounts of code. This complexity leads to interdependencies and constraints and leaves more room for bugs to creep in. Consequently, the software can be fragile and difficult to get working.

This chapter is filled with some practical tips for debugging implementations of deep RL algorithms. In Section 10.1, we introduce some useful engineering practices to help manage code complexity. Then, we discuss a number of general debugging practices in Section 10.2, as well as some specific tricks that help when training agents on the Atari environments (Section 10.3). The chapter ends with a *Deep RL Almanac* (Section 10.4) that lists good hyperparameter values for the main algorithms and environments that we have discussed in this book and provides some information on approximate run time and computational resource requirements.

10.1 Software Engineering Practices

At the highest level, there is the matter of theoretical correctness vs. implementation correctness. When designing a new RL algorithm or component, it needs to be proven theoretically correct before implementation. This is especially relevant when conducting research. Similarly, when trying to solve a new environment, one needs to first ensure that the problem is indeed solvable by RL before applying any algorithms. This is especially relevant for applications. If everything is theoretically correct and the problem at hand is solvable, then the failure of a RL algorithm can be attributed to implementation errors. We then need to debug the code.

Debugging involves identifying the errors in a piece of code and fixing them. Often, the most time-consuming process is searching for the errors and understanding why they are there in the first place. Once an error is understood, implementing a fix can be straightforward and fast.

Deep RL algorithms can fail for many different reasons. Also, RL development cycles are resource- and time-intensive, which makes the debugging process harder. To efficiently debug RL code, one must use a systematic approach to identify errors in order to narrow down the potential candidates quickly. Fortunately, the field of software engineering is used to such problems, with many established best practices we can borrow from—in particular, unit tests, code quality, and git workflow.

10.1.1   Unit Tests

Unit testing is a universal requirement for good software engineering, and the reason is simple—*any untested code is risky code*. A reliable software system must be built on top of a rigorous foundation: the core components which serve as the basis for other code must be thoroughly tested and verified to be correct. If the foundation is unreliable, the unresolved errors will propagate and affect even more components as the software system grows. Progress will become slower because we will have to spend more time debugging and less time developing.

Unit tests provide a guarantee that the tested components work as intended. Once a piece of code is properly tested, we can trust it and develop using it with more confidence. When unit tests are applied systematically to a code base, they help eliminate many of the things that can go wrong, thereby narrowing down the list of error candidates when debugging.

Test coverage is a useful metric used by software engineers to measure what percentage of a code base is covered by unit tests. This is calculated by a static analysis tool which measures the total number of lines of code or logical paths, and checks how many lines are covered when all the unit tests are run. This ratio is converted into the percentage test coverage. Any modern unit testing tools automatically calculate and report this metric. In SLM Lab, it is done by `PyTest` whenever unit tests are run.

It may be tempting to achieve 100% test coverage, but doing so can be counterproductive. Perfect test coverage may be desirable for industrial software running in a production environment, but makes little sense for research that needs to move at a rapid pace. Writing unit tests takes time and effort, and overdoing it may compete with the main priority of development and research. To achieve a balanced middle ground, it should be reserved for the most important code. The author of the code should be able to judge what is important enough to test—but, as a rule-of-thumb, code that is widely used, complicated, error-prone, or crucial should be tested.

Unit tests essentially assert facts about how a piece of code runs. However, we have to define the domain of behavior to test. For example, when testing a function, a test defines the input along with the expected result which is compared to the computed output. A few aspects of a function are commonly tested: the function needs to run correctly and without crashing for a range of inputs, common and edge cases should be tested, and data shapes and types should be checked. If the function implements a formula, test it empirically—calculate some example numerical results by hand and compare them with the function outputs to verify the correctness of an implementation. When a new bug is fixed, a test should be added to prevent reoccurrence of the bug.

To illustrate these points, Code 10.1 shows an example test which runs a DQN algorithm on the Atari Pong environment end-to-end. The test initializes the agent and environment and runs the full training loop for a small number of steps. Despite its simplicity, this serves as a broad and complete check to ensure everything can run without crashing. It also ensures that important assertions throughout the algorithm pass, such as the loss computation and network update. Broad, basic tests such as `test_atari` are particularly useful as a code base grows because they help check that new features do not break the core functionality of old ones.

Code 10.1   End-to-end test of the DQN algorithm in the Atari Pong environment

```
1   # slm_lab/test/spec/test_spec.py
2
3   from flaky import flaky
4   from slm_lab.experiment.control import Trial
5   from slm_lab.spec import spec_util
6   import pytest
7
8   # helper method to run all tests in test_spec
9   def run_trial_test(spec_file, spec_name=False):
10      spec = spec_util.get(spec_file, spec_name)
11      spec = spec_util.override_test_spec(spec)
12      spec_util.tick(spec, 'trial')
13      trial = Trial(spec)
14      trial_metrics = trial.run()
15      assert isinstance(trial_metrics, dict)
16
17  ...
18
19  @flaky
20  @pytest.mark.parametrize('spec_file,spec_name', [
21      ('benchmark/dqn/dqn_pong.json', 'dqn_pong'),
22      ('benchmark/a2c/a2c_gae_pong.json', 'a2c_gae_pong'),
23  ])
24  def test_atari(spec_file, spec_name):
25      run_trial_test(spec_file, spec_name)
```

Code 10.2 shows two empirical tests. `test_calc_gaes` tests the Generalized Advantage Estimation (GAE) implementation from Chapter 6, and `test_linear_decay` tests a function which linearly decays a variable. This is used frequently in SLM Lab, for example to decay the exploration variables ε or τ. Empirical tests such as these are particularly important for functions that are complex or tricky to implement—they bring us peace of mind that the function is producing the expected outputs.

Code 10.2   Example empirical tests. Results for some mathematical formulas are manually calculated and compared with function outputs.

```
1   # slm_lab/test/lib/test_math_util.py
2
3   from slm_lab.lib import math_util
4   import numpy as np
5   import pytest
6   import torch
7
8   def test_calc_gaes():
9       rewards = torch.tensor([1., 0., 1., 1., 0., 1., 1., 1.])
10      dones = torch.tensor([0., 0., 1., 1., 0., 0., 0., 0.])
11      v_preds = torch.tensor([1.1, 0.1, 1.1, 1.1, 0.1, 1.1, 1.1, 1.1, 1.1])
12      assert len(v_preds) == len(rewards) + 1  # includes last state
13      gamma = 0.99
14      lam = 0.95
15      gaes = math_util.calc_gaes(rewards, dones, v_preds, gamma, lam)
16      res = torch.tensor([0.84070045, 0.89495, -0.1, -0.1, 3.616724, 2.7939649,
        ↪   1.9191545, 0.989])
17      # use allclose instead of equal to account for atol
18      assert torch.allclose(gaes, res)
19
20  @pytest.mark.parametrize('start_val, end_val, start_step, end_step, step,
    ↪   correct', [
21      (0.1, 0.0, 0, 100, 0, 0.1),
22      (0.1, 0.0, 0, 100, 50, 0.05),
23      (0.1, 0.0, 0, 100, 100, 0.0),
24      (0.1, 0.0, 0, 100, 150, 0.0),
25      (0.1, 0.0, 100, 200, 50, 0.1),
26      (0.1, 0.0, 100, 200, 100, 0.1),
27      (0.1, 0.0, 100, 200, 150, 0.05),
28      (0.1, 0.0, 100, 200, 200, 0.0),
29      (0.1, 0.0, 100, 200, 250, 0.0),
30  ])
31  def test_linear_decay(start_val, end_val, start_step, end_step, step,
    ↪   correct):
32      assert math_util.linear_decay(start_val, end_val, start_step, end_step,
        ↪   step) == correct
```

To decide what tests to write, it helps to organize them according to the structure and components of the software. This is one reason to invest some time in better software design. For instance, organizing all the methods into a single structureless script may get things done in a hackish-and-fast way, but is bad practice if our code is meant to be used

more than once, let alone in a long-term production system. Good software should
be modularized into sensible components that can be developed, used, and tested
independently. Throughout this book we have discussed how an agent can be organized
into components such as a memory class, algorithm, and neural network. SLM Lab follows
this component design, and unit tests are written for each component. When tests are
organized to match the design of a piece of software, we can easily keep track of what has
been tested and, correspondingly, of what works. This significantly improves the efficiency
of debugging because it provides a mental map of untested weak spots that are potential
error candidates.

Code 10.3 shows an example component test for a convolutional network that is
developed and tested as an independent module. It checks for network-specific elements
such as architecture, data shapes, and model update to ensure the implementation is
working as intended.

Code 10.3 Example component test for a convolutional network. Features specific to the
network are developed and tested in an independent module.

```
1   # slm_lab/test/net/test_conv.py
2
3   from copy import deepcopy
4   from slm_lab.env.base import Clock
5   from slm_lab.agent.net import net_util
6   from slm_lab.agent.net.conv import ConvNet
7   import torch
8   import torch.nn as nn
9
10  net_spec = {
11      "type": "ConvNet",
12      "shared": True,
13      "conv_hid_layers": [
14          [32, 8, 4, 0, 1],
15          [64, 4, 2, 0, 1],
16          [64, 3, 1, 0, 1]
17      ],
18      "fc_hid_layers": [512],
19      "hid_layers_activation": "relu",
20      "init_fn": "xavier_uniform_",
21      "batch_norm": False,
22      "clip_grad_val": 1.0,
23      "loss_spec": {
24          "name": "SmoothL1Loss"
25      },
26      "optim_spec": {
27          "name": "Adam",
28          "lr": 0.02
```

```
29         },
30         "lr_scheduler_spec": {
31             "name": "StepLR",
32             "step_size": 30,
33             "gamma": 0.1
34         },
35         "gpu": True
36     }
37     in_dim = (4, 84, 84)
38     out_dim = 3
39     batch_size = 16
40     net = ConvNet(net_spec, in_dim, out_dim)
41     # init net optimizer and its lr scheduler
42     optim = net_util.get_optim(net, net.optim_spec)
43     lr_scheduler = net_util.get_lr_scheduler(optim, net.lr_scheduler_spec)
44     x = torch.rand((batch_size,) + in_dim)
45
46     def test_init():
47         net = ConvNet(net_spec, in_dim, out_dim)
48         assert isinstance(net, nn.Module)
49         assert hasattr(net, 'conv_model')
50         assert hasattr(net, 'fc_model')
51         assert hasattr(net, 'model_tail')
52         assert not hasattr(net, 'model_tails')
53
54     def test_forward():
55         y = net.forward(x)
56         assert y.shape == (batch_size, out_dim)
57
58     def test_train_step():
59         y = torch.rand((batch_size, out_dim))
60         clock = Clock(100, 1)
61         loss = net.loss_fn(net.forward(x), y)
62         net.train_step(loss, optim, lr_scheduler, clock=clock)
63         assert loss != 0.0
64
65     def test_no_fc():
66         no_fc_net_spec = deepcopy(net_spec)
67         no_fc_net_spec['fc_hid_layers'] = []
68         net = ConvNet(no_fc_net_spec, in_dim, out_dim)
69         assert isinstance(net, nn.Module)
70         assert hasattr(net, 'conv_model')
71         assert not hasattr(net, 'fc_model')
72         assert hasattr(net, 'model_tail')
```

```
73        assert not hasattr(net, 'model_tails')
74
75        y = net.forward(x)
76        assert y.shape == (batch_size, out_dim)
77
78    def test_multitails():
79        net = ConvNet(net_spec, in_dim, [3, 4])
80        assert isinstance(net, nn.Module)
81        assert hasattr(net, 'conv_model')
82        assert hasattr(net, 'fc_model')
83        assert not hasattr(net, 'model_tail')
84        assert hasattr(net, 'model_tails')
85        assert len(net.model_tails) == 2
86
87        y = net.forward(x)
88        assert len(y) == 2
89        assert y[0].shape == (batch_size, 3)
90        assert y[1].shape == (batch_size, 4)
```

Given their importance, unit tests should be written frequently, so they need to be easy to write. Tests do not have to be complicated. In fact, the simpler they are, the better. Good tests should be short and clear while covering all the important aspects of the functions they test. They should also be fast and stable, since tests are often used as a qualifier for accepting newly developed code, thus affecting the speed of development cycle. A function can be trusted through unit tests that give evidence of how it works that can be understood easily and quickly. With trust and reliability, further development and research can proceed more smoothly.

10.1.2 Code Quality

Unit tests are necessary but not sufficient for good software engineering. It also requires good code quality. Code does not just convey instructions for a computer—it also communicates ideas to programmers. Good code is easy to understand and work with—this applies to any collaborators as well as the original code authors. If we cannot understand a piece of code written by ourselves three months from now, it is bad code with poor maintainability.

Standard practice in software engineering to ensure code quality is to adopt a style guide and do code reviews. A *style guide* for a programming language is a set of best practices and conventions for writing code in it. It includes guidelines from general syntax formatting and naming conventions to specific dos and don'ts for writing safe and performant code. Style guides are usually established by a large community of programmers in order to share common conventions. It not only makes code more understandable in a collaborative setting, but also increases the overall quality of the code.

Style guides are constantly evolving to match the growth of the programming languages as well as the requirements of their communities. They are usually maintained as crowd-sourced documents on Github with open source licenses. SLM Lab uses the *Google Python Style Guide* (`https://github.com/google/styleguide`) as its primary style guide, and additionally the *Python Style Guide* (`https://github.com/kengz/python`) by Wah Loon Keng.

To help programmers write better code, modern style guides are also converted into programs called *linters*, which work with text editors to help enforce the guidelines by providing visual aids and autoformatting. The same programs are also used for automated code reviews—which brings us to our next topic.

Code reviews help ensure the quality of code added to a software repository. Usually this involves one or more people checking newly committed code for logical correctness and adherence to a style guide. Major code-hosting platforms such as Github support code review. Every new chunk of code is first reviewed through what is known as a *pull request* before it gets accepted. This code review workflow is now a standard software development practice.

In the last few years, automated code review has also proliferated, with companies like Code Climate [27] and Codacy [26] providing free and paid cloud services to perform code quality checks. Typically these tools perform static code analysis checking for a number of elements, such as adherence to a style guide, security issues, code complexity, and test coverage. These tools are used as gatekeepers to ensure that only code that passes code review can be accepted and merged into a repository. Any identified issues contribute to what is known as *technical debt*. Like monetary debt, technical debt needs to be paid—either now or later. It also grows with interest—as a software project expands, unresolved bad code creeps into more places wherever it gets used. To ensure the long-term health of a project, it is important to keep technical debt under check.

10.1.3 Git Workflow

Git is a modern version control tool for source code. Its core idea is simple—every addition and deletion of code should be committed to a code base in a traceable way. This means it is versioned with a message describing what was done in that commit. When a code change breaks software, it is easy to quickly revert to a previous version. Additionally, the differences between commits can also be used for debugging. This can be shown using the `git diff` command or by looking at a Github pull request page. If software suddenly fails in a new commit, it is likely due to the recent code changes. The Git workflow is simply to commit code changes incrementally, with clear messages, and then review the commits before accepting them into the main code base.

Given how fragile and involved deep RL software is, using a Git workflow can be tremendously helpful. It has been an indispensable aid in the development of SLM Lab. It is useful not just for functional code, but also for algorithm hyperparameters. Figure 10.1 shows an example Git diff view in which a Double DQN agent spec file is tuned by changing its gradient clipping norm, neural network optimizer, and network update type. If the resultant agent performs better or worse, we know why.

```
14 ▪▪▪▪  slm_lab/spec/experimental/ddqn_breakout.json                    Copy path   View file  🖥  ∨

⁑   @@ -38,21 +38,17 @@
38          "hid_layers_activation": "relu",        38          "hid_layers_activation": "relu",
39          "init_fn": null,                        39          "init_fn": null,
40          "batch_norm": false,                    40          "batch_norm": false,
41  -       "clip_grad_val": 1.0,                    41  +       "clip_grad_val": 10.0,
42          "loss_spec": {                          42          "loss_spec": {
43            "name": "SmoothL1Loss"                43            "name": "SmoothL1Loss"
44          },                                      44          },
45          "optim_spec": {                         45          "optim_spec": {
46  -         "name": "RMSprop",                     46  +         "name": "Adam",
47  -         "lr": 2.5e-4,                          47  +         "lr": 1e-4,
48  -         "alpha": 0.95,
49  -         "eps": 1e-1,
50  -         "momentum": 0.95
51          },                                      48          },
52          "lr_scheduler_spec": null,              49          "lr_scheduler_spec": null,
53  -       "update_type": "polyak",                50  +       "update_type": "replace",
54  -       "update_frequency": 10,                 51  +       "update_frequency": 1000,
55  -       "polyak_coef": 0.992,
56          "gpu": true                             52          "gpu": true
57        }                                         53        }
58      }],                                         54      }],
⁑
```

Figure 10.1   A screenshot of an SLM Lab pull request Git diff view showing the before/after code changes side by side.

The Git workflow helps SLM Lab experiments to be reproducible. In SLM Lab, any result can be reproduced by simply supplying the Git SHA. This is used to check out the exact version of the code that was used to run an experiment and to rerun it precisely as it was written. Without the Git workflow, we would have to resort to manual code changes, which can quickly get complicated given how many moving parts there are in deep RL.

The main activity for manual code review involves reviewing the Git diff just like the one shown in Figure 10.1. A pull request accumulates multiple relevant commits for a new feature or a bug fix and summarizes the changes clearly on a page for reviewers and authors to inspect and discuss. This is how software gets developed incrementally. Git workflow together with unit tests and style guides form the cornerstone of modern software engineering.

Unit tests, style guides, and code reviews help us manage complex software projects. They facilitate building large and complex software, and help keep it running correctly as it grows. Given the complexity of deep RL algorithms, it is reasonable to adopt these practices, just as SLM Lab did. To learn about the specifics of applying them to deep RL, look at some example pull requests from the SLM Lab Github repository. Figure 10.2 shows an example in which a pull request runs unit tests and code quality checks automatically. Until a pull request passes these checks, the code changes cannot be merged.

Good software engineering is necessary for building complex software in a manageable way. What's described in this section are just a few pointers for those starting to think about this topic—which is a large and deep field in its own right. Unfortunately, it is not a subject taught in computer science courses. Good engineering can only be learned through observation and experience. Luckily, given the abundance of good open

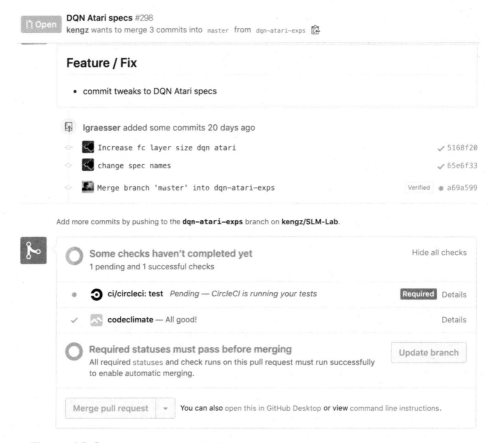

Figure 10.2   A screenshot of an SLM Lab pull request, which runs unit tests on a remote server, and automated code quality checks using Code Climate

source projects and communities, it can be learned through hands-on involvement in those projects. With an open and caring attitude towards code, it is not a difficult skill to achieve. With this as foundation, we will look at some guidelines for getting deep RL to work.

10.2   Debugging Tips

In this section, we'll look at some debugging tips that may come in useful when trying to get an RL algorithm to work. Due to its complexity and novelty, debugging in deep RL is still more of an art than a science. It requires significant hands-on experience with the quirks of deep learning software, numerical computation, and hardware. Most importantly, just like any challenging project, it takes a great deal of *persistence* to get things to work.

The primary goal of debugging is to identify the root cause of a failure. The process is essentially problem isolation where we systematically check various suspects to find the error. It is important to be methodical. We should have a prioritized list of hypotheses and suspects, then test them one by one, if possible in isolation. Each unsuccessful test eliminates another candidate and refines the next hypothesis. Hopefully, this will quickly lead us to the root cause.

In what follows we use the design of SLM Lab to outline a general RL debugging checklist.

10.2.1 Signs of Life

To know if a deep RL algorithm is working or not, we need to check for some basic signs of life. The simplest indicator is the *total reward* and its running average. A working algorithm should obtain rewards higher than a random agent. If it is anything equal or lower, the algorithm is not working. Additionally, for a task in which success correlates with the number of time steps, check the *episode length*. If a task relies on quick completion, shorter episodes are better; if a task involves multiple stages, longer episodes are better.

Additionally, if the *learning rate* or *exploration variable* is decayed over time, we should also read the printout to check if the decay is done properly. For instance, if the ε variable of an ε-greedy policy does not decay due to some bug, the algorithm will always perform random actions. These variables are logged periodically when a session is run in SLM Lab, as shown in a log snippet in Code 10.4.

Code 10.4 Example of diagnostic variables logged by SLM Lab when a session is running

```
1  [2019-07-07 20:42:55,791 PID:103674 INFO __init__.py log_summary] Trial 0
   ↪    session 0 dqn_pong_t0_s0 [eval_df] epi: 0  t: 0  wall_t: 48059  opt_step:
   ↪    4.775e+06  frame: 3.83e+06  fps: 79.6937  total_reward: 9.25
   ↪    total_reward_ma: 14.795  loss: 0.00120682  lr: 0.0001  explore_var: 0.01
   ↪    entropy_coef: nan  entropy: nan  grad_norm: nan
2  [2019-07-07 20:44:51,651 PID:103674 INFO __init__.py log_summary] Trial 0
   ↪    session 0 dqn_pong_t0_s0 [train_df] epi: 0  t: 3.84e+06  wall_t: 48178
   ↪    opt_step: 4.7875e+06  frame: 3.84e+06  fps: 79.7044  total_reward: 18.125
   ↪    total_reward_ma: 18.3331  loss: 0.000601919  lr: 0.0001  explore_var: 0.01
   ↪    entropy_coef: nan  entropy: nan  grad_norm: nan
```

10.2.2 Policy Gradient Diagnoses

For policy gradient methods, there are also variables specific to a policy that can be monitored. These are the quantities that can be computed from the action probability distribution, such as its entropy. Usually, a policy is random at the beginning of training, so the entropy of the action probability distribution should be close to the theoretical maximum; the specific value will vary according to the size and type of the action space. If the action *entropy* does not decrease, this means the policy remains random and no learning is taking place. If it decreases too quickly, an agent may also not be learning properly because this indicates that an agent has stopped exploring the action space and is selecting actions with very high probability. As a rule of thumb, if an agent usually takes 1 million time steps to learn a good policy, but if the action probability entropy drops rapidly over the first 1,000 steps, then it is highly unlikely that the agent has learned a good policy.

Action *probability* or log-probability is closely related to the entropy of the action probability distribution. It shows the probability of a chosen action. At the start of training, action probabilities should be close to uniformly random. As an agent learns a better policy, a chosen action should be more deliberate and hence have higher probability on average.

Another useful indicator is the *KL divergence* (KL), which measures the "size" of a policy update. If KL is small, this implies that the change in the policy between updates is also small and suggests that learning is slow or nonexistent. On the other hand, if KL suddenly becomes very large, this indicates that a large policy update just took place which could cause a performance collapse as we discussed in Chapter 7. Some of these variables are also logged in SLM Lab, as shown in Code 10.4.

10.2.3   Data Diagnoses

Ensuring the correctness of data is crucial, especially when the information exchanged between an agent and an environment passes through many transformations. Each step is a potential source of error. *Manual debugging* of data is often very useful. The state, action, and reward can be traced at different transformation steps and checked. For states and rewards, the raw data comes out of the environment, gets preprocessed, stored by agent, and is then used in training. For actions, data is produced by a neural network, gets composed and potentially preprocessed, then is passed back to the environment. At each step, the values of these variables can be printed out and checked manually. After looking at them long enough, we will start developing intuitions about the raw data, which helps select useful debugging information and identify when something looks wrong.

For an image state, besides printing out the numbers, it should also be *rendered* and looked at. It is useful to render both the raw image from the environment and the preprocessed image seen by an algorithm. When they are compared side by side, we are better able to identify any subtle bugs in the preprocessing steps that may result in missing or erroneous information presented to the algorithm. Stepping through the images or video as an environment runs also helps us see how an agent is performing the task. This can reveal much more information than just looking at the pixel numbers or logs. A method from SLM Lab for rendering a preprocessed image is shown in Code 10.5. This is used to generate the downsized and grayscaled image, shown in Figure 10.3 below the original RGB image from the environment for comparison. In this mode, the process is paused for a user to do visual inspection and continues after any key is pressed.

Code 10.5   A method to render preprocessed images for debugging in SLM Lab. When called on a preprocessed image state, this will render what an agent sees and compare it with what the environment produces.

```
1   # slm_lab/lib/util.py
2
3   import cv2
4
5   def debug_image(im):
6       '''
7       Use this method to render image the agent sees
8       waits for a key press before continuing
9       '''
10      cv2.imshow('image', im.transpose())
11      cv2.waitKey(0)
```

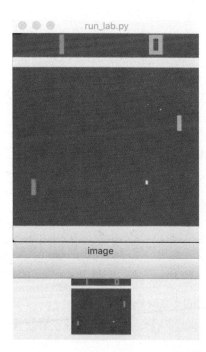

Figure 10.3   Example of image debugging for Atari Pong in SLM Lab. The raw colored image is rendered on top, while the preprocessed image (downsized and grayscaled) is rendered below it for comparison. Frames can be stepped through by pressing any key.

10.2.4   Preprocessor

States and rewards from an environment are usually preprocessed before getting stored in an agent's memory or used for training. To complement the manual data inspection, we need to check the functions which produce the data. If preprocessed data looks wrong, then the *preprocessor* implements some transformations incorrectly. Perhaps the output data shape or orientation is wrong, or erroneous typecasting reduces all data to 0. One minor detail when handling image data is the difference in *image channel ordering conventions*. Most computer vision libraries, as a historical design legacy, put the image channels last, so the image shape is (width, height, channel). PyTorch's convention reverses it for efficiency, and its image shape is (channel, height, width). Images produced by an environment in OpenAI Gym use the older convention, so this needs to be handled properly before getting passed into a PyTorch convolutional network.

10.2.5   Memory

Agent memory acts as a data storage. First, we check that the data has the correct shape and type. We also need to ensure that the ordering of data is correct. This is especially crucial when generating sequential data for a recurrent network. For on-policy memory, it is vital to ensure that the memory is cleared properly after every training step. When sampling data for training, also check that the methods used for generating random indices and getting data are correct. More advanced memory structures, such as Prioritized Experience Replay, have their own sampling algorithms and data structures which need to be tested separately.

10.2.6   Algorithmic Functions

If data is generated and stored correctly, then we need to debug the primary algorithmic functions that consume it. RL functions such as the Bellman equation or Generalized Advantage Estimation (GAE) can be quite complicated, so implementation bugs are likely. *Empirical unit tests*, such as the examples shown in Code 10.2, should be done by comparing the implementation's output with manually computed values. Sometimes, the error may be due to an array indexing issue, numerical bug, a missed corner case, or a simple typecasting mistake. We should also print and *manually inspect* the inputs and outputs of the advantage function, the *V*- or *Q*-value functions, and the computed losses. Check the range of these values, how they change over time, and whether they look strange. Often, these computations are closely tied to the neural networks.

10.2.7   Neural Networks

When a RL algorithm fails to learn, a reasonable place to look is the neural network, since this is where learning occurs. The easiest thing to check is the network *architecture*. The input and output dimensions need to be correct. The hidden layers should be of the right kind with an appropriate size. Activation functions must also be applied correctly. Any squeezing functions, such as a tanh or sigmoid, will restrict the range of values, so output layers typically do not have an activation function. One exception is policy networks which output action probabilities—these may have activation functions applied to the output layer. Deep RL algorithms are also known to be sensitive to network parameter initializations, since this affects the initial learning conditions.

The *value ranges* of input and output data should also be checked. Neural networks are quite sensitive to inputs with different scales, so it is common practice to normalize or standardize network inputs per dimension. During training, we want to avoid an *exploding loss* where the loss suddenly becomes very large. If a network suddenly outputs a NaN value, this likely means that some network parameters have become infinite due to large updates from an excessively large loss and a correspondingly large parameter update. The loss computation should be fixed. Also, a good rule of thumb is to always apply *gradient clipping* with a norm of 0.5 or 1.0 as this helps to avoid large parameter updates.

Next, ensure that the training steps are actually updating the *network parameters*. If the parameters do not change after multiple training steps with a nonzero loss, check the *computation graph*. A common cause is a detached graph—somewhere along the chain of computations from input to output, gradient propagation is accidentally dropped, so backpropagation cannot be applied completely to all the relevant operations. Modern deep learning frameworks have built-in checks to flag a detached computation graph and to indicate whether gradients can be calculated properly. SLM Lab implements a decorator method for training steps which automatically checks for network parameter updates in development mode. This is shown in Code 10.6.

Code 10.6   SLM Lab implements a decorator method that can be used with a training step method. It automatically checks for network parameter updates in development mode, and throws an error if the check fails.

```
1   # slm_lab/agent/net/net_util.py
2
3   from functools import partial, wraps
4   from slm_lab.lib import logger, optimizer, util
5   import os
6   import pydash as ps
7   import torch
8   import torch.nn as nn
9
10  logger = logger.get_logger(__name__)
11
12  def to_check_train_step():
13      '''Condition for running assert_trained'''
14      return os.environ.get('PY_ENV') == 'test' or util.get_lab_mode() == 'dev'
15
16  def dev_check_train_step(fn):
17      '''
18      Decorator to check if net.train_step actually updates the network weights
    ↪   properly
```

```
19          Triggers only if to_check_train_step is True (dev/test mode)
20          @example
21
22          @net_util.dev_check_train_step
23          def train_step(self, ...):
24              ...
25          '''
26          @wraps(fn)
27          def check_fn(*args, **kwargs):
28              if not to_check_train_step():
29                  return fn(*args, **kwargs)
30
31              net = args[0]  # first arg self
32              # get pre-update parameters to compare
33              pre_params = [param.clone() for param in net.parameters()]
34
35              # run train_step, get loss
36              loss = fn(*args, **kwargs)
37              assert not torch.isnan(loss).any(), loss
38
39              # get post-update parameters to compare
40              post_params = [param.clone() for param in net.parameters()]
41              if loss == 0.0:
42                  # if loss is 0, there should be no updates
43                  for p_name, param in net.named_parameters():
44                      assert param.grad.norm() == 0
45              else:
46                  # check parameter updates
47                  try:
48                      assert not all(torch.equal(w1, w2) for w1, w2 in
                         ↪  zip(pre_params, post_params)), f'Model parameter is not
                         ↪  updated in train_step(), check if your tensor is detached
                         ↪  from graph. Loss: {loss:g}'
49                      logger.info(f'Model parameter is updated in train_step().
                         ↪  Loss: {loss: g}')
50                  except Exception as e:
51                      logger.error(e)
52                      if os.environ.get('PY_ENV') == 'test':
53                          # raise error if in unit test
54                          raise(e)
55
56                  # check grad norms
57                  min_norm, max_norm = 0.0, 1e5
58                  for p_name, param in net.named_parameters():
```

```
59              try:
60                  grad_norm = param.grad.norm()
61                  assert min_norm < grad_norm < max_norm, f'Gradient norm
                    ↪ for {p_name} is {grad_norm:g}, fails the extreme value
                    ↪ check {min_norm} < grad_norm < {max_norm}. Loss:
                    ↪ {loss:g}. Check your network and loss computation.'
62              except Exception as e:
63                  logger.warning(e)
64          logger.info(f'Gradient norms passed value check.')
65      logger.debug('Passed network parameter update check.')
66      # store grad norms for debugging
67      net.store_grad_norms()
68      return loss
69  return check_fn
```

If a loss function is computed as a contribution from multiple individual losses, then each of them must be checked to ensure they each produce the correct training behavior and network updates. To check an *individual loss*, simply disable the other losses and run some training steps. For example, a shared-network Actor-Critic algorithm has a loss that is a sum of a policy loss and a value loss. To check the policy loss, simply remove the value loss and run training to verify that the network gets updated from the policy loss. Then, do the same to check the value loss by disabling the policy loss.

10.2.8 Algorithm Simplification

Deep RL algorithms often have many components—trying to make all of them work at the same time is difficult. When faced with a complex problem, a tried and tested method is *simplification*—starting with just the bare essentials before adding more features. We have seen that various deep RL algorithms are extensions and modifications of simpler algorithms, as shown in the RL family tree in Figure 9.1 of Chapter 9. For example, PPO improves on A2C by changing the policy loss, and A2C, in turn, modifies REINFORCE. We can use our understanding of the relationships among algorithms to our advantage. If an implementation of PPO does not work, we can disable the PPO loss to turn it into A2C, and focus on getting that to work first. Then, we can reenable the extension and debug the full algorithm.

This method works the other way as well—by building from the ground up. For example, we can first implement REINFORCE. When it works, we can extend it to implement A2C. When that works, we can extend A2C to implement PPO. This fits naturally within the programming framework of class inheritance, in which a more complex class extends from a simpler parent class. This approach also allows components to be reused, which means less new code to debug.

10.2.9 Problem Simplification

When implementing and debugging an algorithm, it is often beneficial to first test it on simpler problems, such as CartPole. Simpler problems usually require less hyperparameter tuning and are less computationally intensive to solve. For example, training an agent to play CartPole can run on a modest CPU in tens of minutes, whereas training an agent to play an Atari game may need GPUs and hours or days to run. By focusing on a simple problem first, each test iteration becomes much quicker, and we can speed up our debugging and development workflow.

However, even when things work for simpler problems, they do not necessarily translate directly to harder problems. There may still be some bugs left in the code. Harder problems may also require modification. For example, CartPole uses a small state with four elements and needs a multilayer perceptron network to solve, but an Atari game has an image state and needs a convolutional network combined with some image preprocessing and environment modifications. These new components still need to be debugged and tested—but most of the core components will have already been tested, thus making debugging much easier.

10.2.10 Hyperparameters

Although deep RL can be very sensitive to hyperparameters, tuning them is often a small part of debugging if we are implementing an existing algorithm. We can often refer to working hyperparameters from research papers or other implementations and check that our agent achieves comparable performance with them. Once all the major bugs are fixed, we can spend time to fine-tune the hyperparameters trying to get the best result. For reference, Section 10.4 contains details of successful hyperparameter values for the different algorithms and environments discussed in this book.

10.2.11 Lab Workflow

Deep RL is still very much an empirical science, so it is natural to adopt a scientific workflow. This means establishing some hypotheses, identifying the variables, and running experiments to obtain results. Each experiment may take days or weeks to complete, so it is important to be strategic about which experiments to run. Think about which ones should be prioritized, which experiments can be parallelized, and which are the most promising. To keep track of all the experiments, keep a lab notebook to record and report the results. This can be done in SLM Lab by committing the code used for an experiment and recording the Git SHA together with the experiment results in an informative report. All of the reports are submitted as Github pull requests and made available along with the data needed to reproduce the results. An example of an SLM Lab report is shown in Figure 10.4.

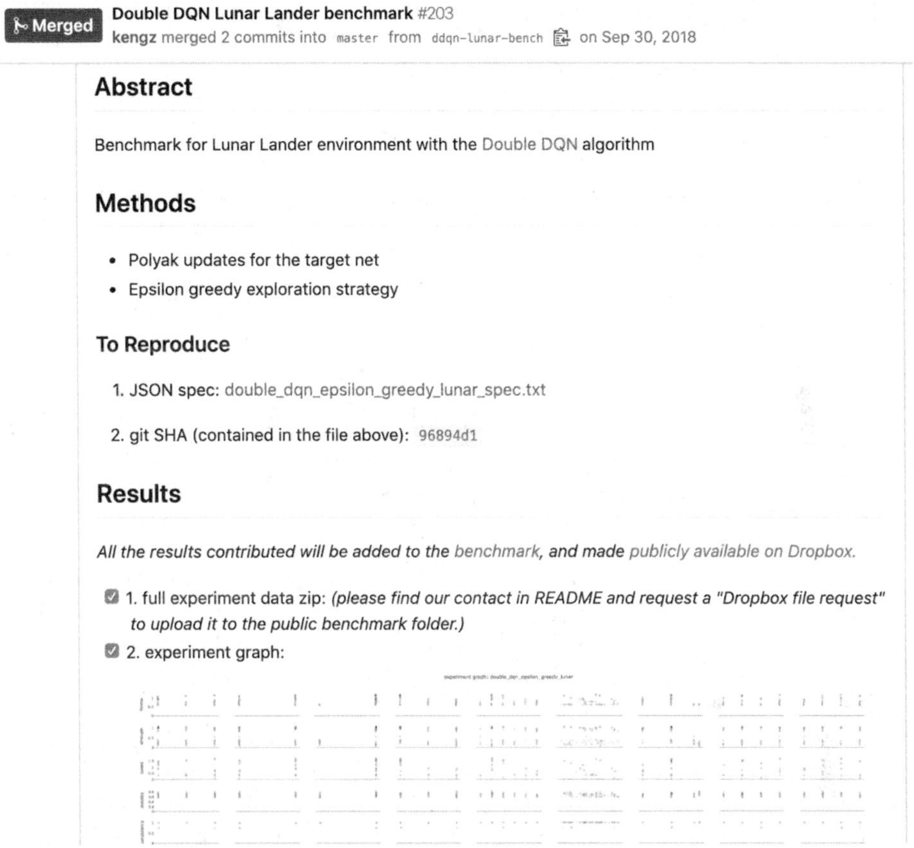

Merged **Double DQN Lunar Lander benchmark** #203
kengz merged 2 commits into `master` from `ddqn-lunar-bench` 🗐 on Sep 30, 2018

Abstract

Benchmark for Lunar Lander environment with the Double DQN algorithm

Methods

- Polyak updates for the target net
- Epsilon greedy exploration strategy

To Reproduce

1. JSON spec: double_dqn_epsilon_greedy_lunar_spec.txt

2. git SHA (contained in the file above): 96894d1

Results

All the results contributed will be added to the benchmark, and made publicly available on Dropbox.

☑ 1. full experiment data zip: *(please find our contact in README and request a "Dropbox file request" to upload it to the public benchmark folder.)*

☑ 2. experiment graph:

Figure 10.4   A screenshot of an SLM Lab pull request with an experiment report, which includes the method writeup, Git SHA, spec file, graphs, and other data for reproducibility

The tips presented in this section are not exhaustive; bugs can arise in various ways. However, they do provide a good selection of entry points to start debugging, while the rest requires hands-on experience to learn from. We should also not shy away from referring to existing implementations written by other people, since they may reveal insights we would otherwise miss—just remember to be a good open source citizen and credit other people's work properly.

Good debugging requires thoughtful hypothesizing and problem isolation, which is made easier with good engineering practices. Many problems require a deep dive into the code, and it is not uncommon to spend weeks or months getting a RL algorithm working. A crucial human component is a positive attitude and great persistence—with faith and grit, things will eventually work, and when they do, the reward is large.

10.3 Atari Tricks

In this section we will look at some specific tricks to achieve good performance on the Atari environments. We'll first discuss the different versions of the environments available through OpenAI Gym, and then look at the environment preprocessing steps that have become standard practice.

The Atari environments offered in OpenAI Gym come in many variations. For example, there are six versions of the Pong environment:

1. `Pong-v4`

2. `PongDeterministic-v4`

3. `PongNoFrameskip-v4`

4. `Pong-ram-v4`

5. `Pong-ramDeterministic-v4`

6. `Pong-ramNoFrameskip-v4`

Each version differs in terms of internal implementation, but the underlying game is still the same. For example, *NoFrameskip* implies that raw frames are returned from the environment, so users needs to implement their own frame skipping mechanism. A *ram* environment returns the game RAM data as state, instead of an image. Most research literature uses the environment with *NoFrameskip*, or *PongNoFrameskip-v4* for the Pong environment.

When the *NoFrameskip* version is used, most of the data preprocessing is implemented and controlled by users. It is often written as environment wrappers. OpenAI's Baselines [99] Github repository remains a leading reference for specific environment wrappers. SLM Lab also adapted many of these under the `wrapper` module at `slm_lab/env/wrapper.py`, as shown in Code 10.7. Each of these wrappers serves to address some specific quirks of the Atari environments which we discuss in this short section.

Code 10.7   SLM Lab adapts the environment preprocessing wrappers from OpenAI Baselines. These methods are used to create Atari environments with the *NoFrameskip* suffix for training and evaluation. Most of the code snippets are excluded here, but can be referenced in the source file on SLM Lab.

```
1  # slm_lab/env/wrapper.py
2
3  ...
4
5  def wrap_atari(env):
6      '''Apply a common set of wrappers for Atari games'''
7      assert 'NoFrameskip' in env.spec.id
8      env = NoopResetEnv(env, noop_max=30)
9      env = MaxAndSkipEnv(env, skip=4)
10     return env
```

```
11
12    def wrap_deepmind(env, episode_life=True, stack_len=None):
13        '''Wrap Atari environment DeepMind-style'''
14        if episode_life:
15            env = EpisodicLifeEnv(env)
16        if 'FIRE' in env.unwrapped.get_action_meanings():
17            env = FireResetEnv(env)
18        env = PreprocessImage(env)
19        if stack_len is not None:  # use concat for image (1, 84, 84)
20            env = FrameStack(env, 'concat', stack_len)
21        return env
22
23    def make_gym_env(name, seed=None, frame_op=None, frame_op_len=None,
   ↪    reward_scale=None, normalize_state=False):
24        '''General method to create any Gym env; auto wraps Atari'''
25        env = gym.make(name)
26        if seed is not None:
27            env.seed(seed)
28        if 'NoFrameskip' in env.spec.id:  # Atari
29            env = wrap_atari(env)
30            # no reward clipping to allow monitoring; Atari memory clips it
31            episode_life = not util.in_eval_lab_modes()
32            env = wrap_deepmind(env, episode_life, frame_op_len)
33        elif len(env.observation_space.shape) == 3:  # image-state env
34            env = PreprocessImage(env)
35            if normalize_state:
36                env = NormalizeStateEnv(env)
37            if frame_op_len is not None:  # use concat for image (1, 84, 84)
38                env = FrameStack(env, 'concat', frame_op_len)
39        else:  # vector-state env
40            if normalize_state:
41                env = NormalizeStateEnv(env)
42            if frame_op is not None:
43                env = FrameStack(env, frame_op, frame_op_len)
44        if reward_scale is not None:
45            env = ScaleRewardEnv(env, reward_scale)
46        return env
```

1. NoopResetEnv: When an Atari game resets, the initial state passed to an agent is actually a random frame from the first 30 in the raw environment. The helps prevent an agent from memorizing the environment.

2. `FireResetEnv`: Some games require an agent to press "FIRE" during reset. For example, Breakout requires the player to launch the ball at the start. This wrapper does it once at reset, so that "FIRE" is not an agent action during the game.

3. `EpisodicLifeEnv`: Many Atari games have multiple lives before the game is over. In general, it helps an agent to learn better when every life is treated as equally precious. This wrapper breaks up each life into a new episode.

4. `MaxAndSkipEnv`: The difference between two consecutive states is too small for agents to learn good policies. To increase the difference between consecutive states, agents are constrained to choose an action every four time steps,[1] and the selected action is repeated in the intermediate frames, which are skipped in this wrapper. What agents perceive to be s_t and s_{t+1} are actually s_t and s_{t+4}. Additionally, this wrapper also selects the maximum-valued pixel from the corresponding pixels in all the skipped frames. A separate maximum is taken for each pixel in the state. In some games, some objects are only rendered in even frames and others in odd frames. Depending on the frame skip rate, this could lead to objects being entirely omitted from the state. Using the maximum pixel from the skipped frames resolves this potential problem.

5. `ScaleRewardEnv`: This scales the time step reward. The most common scaling factor for the Atari games is to clip the reward to -1, 0, or 1 by taking the sign of its original value which helps standardize the scale of the reward between games.

6. `PreprocessImage`: This is an image preprocessing wrapper specific to the image convention of PyTorch (color channel first). It grayscales and downsizes the image, then swaps the axes to be consistent with PyTorch's convention of channel-first.

7. `FrameStack`: For most agents, each network input frame is formed by stacking four consecutive game images. This wrapper implements an efficient frame-stacking method which only resolves the data into a stacked image during training. The motivation behind frame-stacking is that some useful information about the game state is not available in a single image. Recall the discussion in Box 1.1 from Chapter 1 about the difference between MDPs and POMDPs. The Atari games are not perfect MDPs, so the game state cannot be inferred from a single observed state—the image. For example, an agent cannot infer the speed or direction in which game objects are moving from a single image. However, knowing these values is important when deciding how to act, and may make the difference between a good score and losing the game. To remedy this issue, the previous four image states are stacked before being passed to the agent. An agent can use four-image frames in combination to infer important properties such as object motion. The dimension of the states passed to an agent then becomes $(84, 84, 4)$.

---

1. In Space Invaders, this is changed to acting every three steps so that the lasers are visible.

Additionally, for algorithms such as Actor-Critic and PPO, a vectorized environment is used. This is a wrapped environment consisting of a vector of multiple parallel game instances running on separate CPUs. Parallelization allows for much faster and diverse sampling of experiences to improve training. This is also part of SLM Lab's environment wrappers under the `slm_lab.env.vec_wrapper` module.

10.4 Deep RL Almanac

In this section, we provide a set of hyperparameters for the algorithms and environments discussed in this book. It can be time-consuming to find a good starting point for tuning the hyperparameters of an algorithm. This section is intended as a simple reference to help with tuning.

We list hyperparameters by algorithm family for a number of environments. These tables show which hyperparameters tend to vary more when the environment changes. When tackling a new problem, the more sensitive (widely varying) hyperparameters are a good place to start.

Finally, we briefly compare the performance of different algorithms on a few environments.

A larger set of algorithm hyperparameters and performance comparisons is available in the SLM Lab repository at `https://github.com/kengz/SLM-Lab/blob/master/BENCHMARK.md`.

10.4.1 Hyperparameter Tables

This section contains three hyperparameter tables organized by the main types of algorithms. The columns shows some examples of environments the algorithm can be applied to (discrete or continuous control) in the order of increasing complexity from left to right. Note that it is conventional for an algorithm to use the same hyperparameters for all the Atari games. REINFORCE and SARSA are excluded because they are not as frequently used in practice.

The hyperparameters are shown for a specific algorithm, but most values are applicable to its variants. Table 10.1 shows the hyperparameters for Double DQN + PER, but they can also be applied to DQN, DQN + PER, and Double DQN with one exception—the learning rate should be lowered when using PER (see Section 5.6.1).

Table 10.1   Hyperparameters for Double DQN + PER across environments

Hyperparameters \ Env	LunarLander	Atari
algorithm.gamma	0.99	0.99
algorithm.action_policy	ε-greedy	ε-greedy
algorithm.explore_var_spec.start_val	1.0	1.0
algorithm.explore_var_spec.end_val	0.01	0.01
algorithm.explore_var_spec.start_step	0	10,000
algorithm.explore_var_spec.end_step	50,000	1,000,000
algorithm.training_batch_iter	1	1
algorithm.training_iter	1	4
algorithm.training_frequency	1	4
algorithm.training_start_step	32	10,000
memory.max_size	50,000	200,000
m memory.alpha	0.6	0.6
memory.epsilon	0.0001	0.0001
memory.batch_size	32	32
net.clip_grad_val	10	10
net.loss_spec.name	SmoothL1Loss	SmoothL1Loss
net.optim_spec.name	Adam	Adam
net.optim_spec.lr	0.00025	0.000025
net.lr_scheduler_spec.name	None	None
net.lr_scheduler_spec.frame	—	—
net.update_type	replace	replace
net.update_frequency	100	1,000
net.gpu	False	True
env.num_envs	1	16
env.max_frame	300,000	10,000,000

Table 10.2 shows the hyperparameters for A2C with GAE. The same set of values can be applied to A2C with n-step returns except for replacing the GAE-specific `algorithm.lam` with `algorithm.num_step_returns` for n-step returns.

Table 10.2 Hyperparameters for A2C (GAE) across environments

Hyperparameters \ Env	LunarLander	BipedalWalker	Atari
algorithm.gamma	0.99	0.99	0.99
algorithm.lam	0.95	0.95	0.95
algorithm.entropy_coef_spec.start_val	0.01	0.01	0.01
algorithm.entropy_coef_spec.end_val	0.01	0.01	0.01
algorithm.entropy_coef_spec.start_step	0	0	0
algorithm.entropy_coef_spec.end_step	0	0	0
algorithm.val_loss_coef	1.0	0.5	0.5
algorithm.training_frequency	128	256	32
net.shared	False	False	True
net.clip_grad_val	0.5	0.5	0.5
net.init_fn	orthogonal_	orthogonal_	orthogonal_
net.normalize	False	False	True
net.loss_spec.name	MSELoss	MSELoss	MSELoss
net.optim_spec.name	Adam	Adam	RMSprop
net.optim_spec.lr	0.002	0.0003	0.0007
net.lr_scheduler_spec.name	None	None	None
net.lr_scheduler_spec.frame	—	—	—
net.gpu	False	False	True
env.num_envs	8	32	16
env.max_frame	300,000	4,000,000	10,000,000

Finally, Table 10.3 shows the hyperparameters for PPO. These hyperparameters are available as SLM Lab `spec` files in the `slm_lab/spec/benchmark/` folder, which also contain many other tuned `spec` files. They can be run directly using the SLM Lab commands outlined in Section 11.3.1.

Table 10.3   Hyperparameters for PPO across environments

Hyperparameters \ Env	LunarLander	BipedalWalker	Atari
algorithm.gamma	0.99	0.99	0.99
algorithm.lam	0.95	0.95	0.70
algorithm.clip_eps_spec.start_val	0.2	0.2	0.1
algorithm.clip_eps_spec.end_val	0	0	0.1
algorithm.clip_eps_spec.start_step	10,000	10,000	0
algorithm.clip_eps_spec.end_step	300,000	1,000,000	0
algorithm.entropy_coef_spec.start_val	0.01	0.01	0.01
algorithm.entropy_coef_spec.end_val	0.01	0.01	0.01
algorithm.entropy_coef_spec.start_step	0	0	0
algorithm.entropy_coef_spec.end_step	0	0	0
algorithm.val_loss_coef	1.0	0.5	0.5
algorithm.time_horizon	128	512	128
algorithm.minibatch_size	256	4096	256
algorithm.training_epoch	10	15	4
net.shared	False	False	True
net.clip_grad_val	0.5	0.5	0.5
net.init_fn	orthogonal_	orthogonal_	orthogonal_
net.normalize	False	False	True
net.loss_spec.name	MSELoss	MSELoss	MSELoss
net.optim_spec.name	Adam	Adam	Adam
net.optim_spec.lr	0.0005	0.0003	0.00025
net.lr_scheduler_spec.name	None	None	LinearToZero
net.lr_scheduler_spec.frame	—	—	10,000,000
net.gpu	False	False	True
env.num_envs	8	32	16
env.max_frame	300,000	4,000,000	10,000,000

10.4.2   Algorithm Performance Comparison

This section compares the performance of different algorithms on a number of environments. The environments are listed in the order of increasing complexity.

The results in Table 10.4 and the graphs shown in this section give an indication of the relative performance of different algorithms. However, the results can vary significantly depending on the hyperparameters.

It is possible to further fine-tune the hyperparameters. This may change the relative ranking among the algorithms if they have similar performance. However, if the performance gap is large, it is unlikely that further tuning will change the ranking.

Note that there is no one best algorithm across all the environments. PPO, on the whole, performs the best, but for some particular environments other algorithms can perform better.

Table 10.4 The final `mean_returns_ma`. This is the 100-checkpoint moving average for the total rewards, averaged across four sessions in a trial. These are obtained using the hyperparameters shown in Section 10.4.1.

Env \ Algorithm	DQN	Double DQN+PER	A2C(n-step)	A2C(GAE)	PPO
LunarLander	192.4	**232.9**	68.2	25.2	214.2
BipedalWalker	—	—	187.0	15.7	**231.5**
Pong	16.3	20.5	18.6	19.2	**20.6**
Breakout	86.9	178.8	394.1	372.6	**445.4**
Qbert	2913.2	10863.3	**13590.4**	12498.1	13379.2

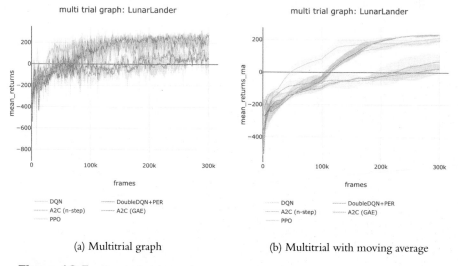

(a) Multitrial graph   (b) Multitrial with moving average

Figure 10.5 Comparing the performance of algorithms on the LunarLander environment

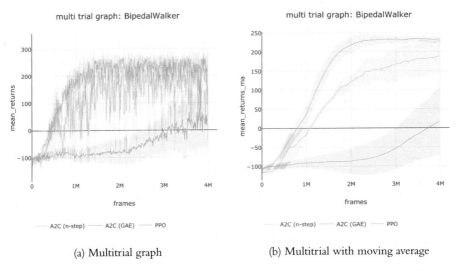

(a) Multitrial graph   (b) Multitrial with moving average

Figure 10.6   Comparing the performance of algorithms on the BipedalWalker environment

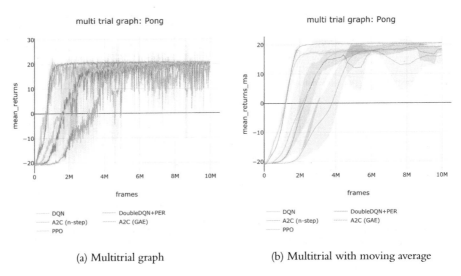

(a) Multitrial graph   (b) Multitrial with moving average

Figure 10.7   Comparing the performance of algorithms on the Atari Pong environment

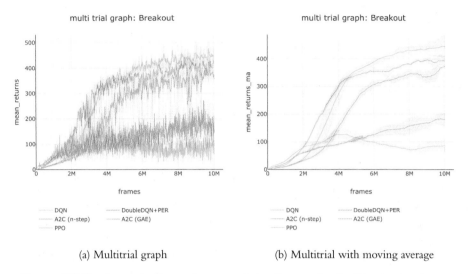

(a) Multitrial graph   (b) Multitrial with moving average

Figure 10.8 Comparing the performance of algorithms on the Atari Breakout environment

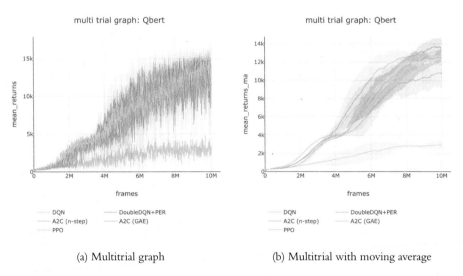

(a) Multitrial graph   (b) Multitrial with moving average

Figure 10.9 Comparing the performance of algorithms on the Atari Qbert environment

10.5   Summary

Getting a deep RL algorithm to work can be a challenging endeavor. In this chapter, we discussed some good engineering practices to help lay the groundwork and make implementation and debugging more manageable. They include unit tests, style guides, automated code review, and a Git workflow.

We then moved on to some practical debugging tips. These include checking for signs of life, inspecting the data manually, and checking the agent components such as the preprocessor, memory, neural network, and algorithm. General tips also include simplifying the problem and adopting a scientific workflow. We briefly discussed the specific tricks used to successfully train agents to play Atari games. Finally, we listed sets of good hyperparameters for the main algorithms and environments discussed in this book. We hope this will be a useful guide for someone working on these problems for the first time.

The ideas discussed in this chapter are not exhaustive; there are many other scenarios and bugs we may encounter. However, these tips provide a good starting place for debugging. Other techniques require more hands-on experience to learn. Given the multitude of potential bugs, it is not uncommon to spend weeks or months trying to get an implementation working. Deep RL is not easy, but the reward of getting something hard to work is also very motivating. Most importantly, it takes a positive attitude and great persistence to see things through.

11

SLM Lab

We have used SLM Lab to run trials and experiments through this book. This chapter is intended as a reference for its main features and commands.

The chapter begins with a summary of the algorithms implemented in SLM Lab. Then we discuss the spec file in more detail, including the syntax for configuring hyperparameter search. Next, we introduce the experiment framework consisting of Session, Trial, and Experiment, as well as the main lab commands. The chapter ends with a walkthrough of the graphs and data automatically generated when using SLM Lab.

In this chapter, we assume that SLM Lab has been installed by following the instructions in the Preface. The source code is available on Github at `https://github.com/kengz/SLM-Lab`. Since new algorithms and features are frequently added to the library, we use the dedicated `book` branch for this book.

11.1 Algorithms Implemented in SLM Lab

SLM Lab implements the algorithms we have seen in this book, which are

- REINFORCE [148]
- SARSA [118]
- DQN [88]
- Double DQN [141], Prioritized Experience Replay [121]
- Advantage Actor-Critic (A2C)
- PPO [124]
- Asynchronous Advantage Actor-Critic (A3C) [87]

Features and algorithms are often being added and SLM Lab is under active development. Here are a few examples of extensions to the core algorithms that have been added to it recently.

- Combined Experience Replay (CER) [153]: This is a simple modification to experience replay which always appends the most recent experience to a batch of training data. The authors of CER showed that this reduced the sensitivity of the agent to the size of the replay buffer, reducing the need to spend as much time tuning its size.

- Dueling DQN [144]: This algorithm uses a modification to the typical structure of the neural network used to approximate the Q-function in DQN. In DQN, the network typically outputs the Q-values directly. Dueling DQN decomposes this estimation into two parts—estimating the state-value function V^π and the state-action advantage function A^π. These estimations are combined within the network module to produce an estimate for Q-values, so that the final form of the network output is the same as in DQN. Training then proceeds in exactly the same way as the DQN algorithm or its variants. Dueling DQN is based on the idea that in some states, action selection is not very important and does not significantly affect outcomes, whereas in others it is of critical importance. Consequently, it helps to separate the estimation of a state's value from the advantage of actions. When the Dueling DQN algorithm was published, it achieved state of the art results on the Atari games.

- Soft Actor-Critic (SAC) [47]: This algorithm is an Actor-Critic algorithm specifically designed to be sample-efficient and stable. It is more sample-efficient than A2C and PPO because the algorithm is off-policy so it can reuse data stored in an experience replay memory. It also uses the maximum-entropy RL framework, adding an entropy term to the objective function. By maximizing both the entropy and the return, an agent learns to achieve high rewards while acting as randomly as possible. This makes SAC less fragile and therefore training is more stable.

SLM Lab breaks the implementation of all algorithms into three components organized into three corresponding classes.

- `Algorithm`: Handles interaction with the environment, implements an action policy, computes the algorithm-specific loss functions, and runs the training step. The `Algorithm` class also controls the other components and their interactions.

- `Net`: Stores the neural networks which serve as the function approximators for the algorithm.

- `Memory`: Provides the necessary data storage and retrieval for training.

Organized in this way, implementations can benefit from class inheritance. Furthermore, each component implements a standardized API through which the different elements interact and integrate. Inheritance and a standardized API make it easier to implement and test a new component. To illustrate this, let's discuss an example, Prioritized Experience Replay (PER).

PER, introduced in Chapter 5, changes the sampling distribution from a replay memory. To briefly recap, in the standard DQN algorithm, experiences are sampled random-uniformly from the replay memory whereas in PER experiences are sampled according to a probability distribution generated from the priority of each experience. Experiences need a priority which is typically based on the absolute TD error. The priorities of the relevant experiences therefore need to be updated each time an agent is trained. Other than this, the experience replay memory and the training procedure is the same as in the DQN algorithm. In SLM Lab, this is implemented through the `PrioritizedReplay` memory class which inherits from `Replay` so only requires around 100 lines of new code. The source code can be found in SLM Lab at `slm_lab/agent /memory/prioritized.py`.

With this design, once a component is ready, it can immediately apply to all relevant algorithms. For example, Double DQN can automatically use PER because it inherits from DQN. Similarly, Dueling DQN can also make use of it because Dueling DQN is implemented independently through a modification to a `Net` class which interacts with the PER memory through the standardized API.

SLM Lab is designed to maximally reuse components—this brings additional benefits of shorter code and larger unit test coverage. The key idea is that we can trust the well-established components and focus only on those under research and development. It is also easier to isolate the effects of different elements because the components are designed to be easily switched on or off, or swapped with another component, all by using a spec file. This is helpful when debugging, but also when evaluating new ideas, since it is straightforward to establish a baseline.

11.2 Spec File

In this section we will look at how to write a `spec` file in SLM Lab.

In SLM Lab, all of the configurable hyperparameters for an algorithm are specified in a spec file. This design choice is intended to make deep RL experiments more reproducible. Implemented code is typically version-controlled and trackable with a Git SHA—but running an experiment also requires specifying hyperparameters that are not tracked as part of the code. These missing or hidden hyperparameters have contributed to the reproducibility problem in deep RL because there is not a standard practice to track them each time an experiment is run. To address this issue, SLM Lab exposes all of the hyperparameters in a single spec file and automatically saves it along with the Git SHA and random seed used as part of the output data generated for every run.

Code 11.1 shows an example snippet of a saved `spec` from a run. The Git SHA (line 22) allows us to recover the version of code used to run the `spec`, and the random seed (line 23) makes it possible to reemulate processes that are stochastic in an agent and an environment.

Code 11.1 An example spec file saved in a session along with the Git SHA and the random seed used

```
1  {
2    "agent": [
3      {
4        "name": "A2C",
5          ...
6      }
7    ],
```

```
8      ...
9      "meta": {
10       "distributed": false,
11       "log_frequency": 10000,
12       "eval_frequency": 10000,
13       "max_session": 4,
14       "max_trial": 1,
15       "experiment": 0,
16       "trial": 0,
17       "session": 0,
18       "cuda_offset": 0,
19       "experiment_ts": "2019_07_08_073946",
20       "prepath": "data/a2c_nstep_pong_2019_07_08_073946/a2c_nstep_pong_t0_s0",
21       "ckpt": null,
22       "git_sha": "8687422539022c56ae41600296747180ee54c912",
23       "random_seed": 1562571588,
24       "eval_model_prepath": null,
25       "graph_prepath":
         ↪    "data/a2c_nstep_pong_2019_07_08_073946/graph/a2c_nstep_pong_t0_s0",
26       "info_prepath":
         ↪    "data/a2c_nstep_pong_2019_07_08_073946/info/a2c_nstep_pong_t0_s0",
27       "log_prepath":
         ↪    "data/a2c_nstep_pong_2019_07_08_073946/log/a2c_nstep_pong_t0_s0",
28       "model_prepath":
         ↪    "data/a2c_nstep_pong_2019_07_08_073946/model/a2c_nstep_pong_t0_s0"
29     },
30     "name": "a2c_nstep_pong"
31   }
```

Designed this way, any experiment run in SLM Lab can be rerun using a spec file that contains all the hyperparameters and the Git SHA of the code version used to runthe experiment. The spec file has all of the necessary information to *fully reproduce an RL experiment*. This is done by simply checking out the code at the Git SHA and running the saved spec. We have used spec files throughout this book to run trials and experiments; now, let's look at a spec file in more detail.

A spec file is used by SLM Lab to construct an agent and an environment. Its format is standardized to follow the lab's modular component design. The different components of a spec file are:

1. **agent:** The format is a list, to allow for multiple agents. However, for our purposes we can assume that there is only one agent. Each element in the list is an agent spec which contains the specs for its components:

   a. **algorithm:** The main parameters specific to the algorithm, such as the policy type, algorithm coefficients, rate decays, and training schedules.

b. **memory:** Specifies which memory to use as appropriate to the algorithm along with any specific memory hyperparameters such as the batch size and the memory size.

c. **net:** The type of neural network, its hidden layer architecture, activations, gradient clipping, loss function, optimizer, rate decays, update method, and CUDA usage.

2. **env:** The format is also a list to accommodate multienvironments, but for now we can assume only one environment. This specifies which environment to use, an optional maximum time step per episode, and the total time steps (frames) in a Session. It also specifies the state and reward preprocessing methods and the number of environments in a vector environment (Chapter 8).

3. **body:** Specifies how multiagent connects to multienvironments. This can be ignored for our single-agent single-environment use case—simply use the default values.

4. **meta:** The high-level configuration of how the lab is run. It gives the number of Trials and Sessions to run, the evaluation and logging frequency, and a toggle to activate asynchronous training (Chapter 8).

5. **search:** The hyperparameters to search over, and the methods used to sample them. Any variables in the spec file can be searched over, including environment variables, although it is typical to search over a subset of the agent variables.

11.2.1 Search Spec Syntax

The syntax to specify a hyperparameter to search over is `"{key}__{space_type}": {v}`. The {key} is the name of the hyperparameter specified in the rest of the spec file. {v} typically specifies the range to search within, as in random search. However, to allow for more flexible search strategies, v may also be a list of choices, or the mean and standard deviation of a probability distribution. There are four distributions to choose from in SLM Lab, two each for discrete and continuous variables, and the interpretation of v depends on the space_type, which defines the method for sampling values.

- Discrete variables space_type
    - choice: str/int/float. v = list of choices
    - randint: int. v = [low, high)
- Continuous variables space_type
    - uniform: float. v = [low, high)
    - normal: float. v = [mean, stdev)

Additionally, grid_search is also available as a space_type to iterate through a list of choices completely instead of sampling them randomly as above. We have seen it used in all the algorithm chapters in this book.

Let's look at an example search spec that can be used to run an experiment in SLM Lab. In this experiment, we train a DQN agent with a target network to play CartPole and search over three hyperparameters—the discount rate γ, the number of batches to sample from memory at each training step, and the replacement update frequency of the target network. The spec is fully enumerated in Code 11.2. Each line is annotated with a brief description of the hyperparameter.

Code 11.2   DQN CartPole search spec

```
1   # slm_lab/spec/experimental/dqn/dqn_cartpole_search.json
2
3   {
4     "dqn_cartpole": {
5       "agent": [{
6         "name": "DQN",
7         "algorithm": {
8           "name": "DQN",                 # class name of the algorithm to run
9           "action_pdtype": "Argmax",          # action policy distribution
10          "action_policy": "epsilon_greedy",  # action sampling method
11          "explore_var_spec": {
12            "name": "linear_decay",   # how to decay the exploration variable
13            "start_val": 1.0,         # initial exploration variable value
14            "end_val": 0.1,           # minimum exploration variable value
15            "start_step": 0,          # time step to start decay
16            "end_step": 1000,         # time step to end decay
17          },
18          "gamma": 0.99,              # discount rate
19          "training_batch_iter": 8,   # parameter updates per batch
20          "training_iter": 4,         # batches per training step
21          "training_frequency": 4,    # how often to train the agent
22          "training_start_step": 32   # time step to start training
23        },
24        "memory": {
25          "name": "Replay",           # class name of the memory
26          "batch_size": 32,           # batch size sampled from memory
27          "max_size": 10000,          # max. experiences to store
28          "use_cer": false    # whether to use combined experience replay
29        },
30        "net": {
31          "type": "MLPNet",           # class name of the network
32          "hid_layers": [64],         # size of the hidden layers
33          "hid_layers_activation": "selu",    # hidden layers activation fn
34          "clip_grad_val": 0.5,       # maximum norm of the gradient
35          "loss_spec": {              # loss specification
36            "name": "MSELoss"
37          },
```

```
38        "optim_spec": {           # optimizer specification
39          "name": "Adam",
40          "lr": 0.01
41        },
42        "lr_scheduler_spec": null, # learning rate scheduler spec
43        "update_type": "polyak",   # method for updating the target net
44        "update_frequency": 32,    # how often to update the target net
45        "polyak_coef": 0.1,        # weight of net params used in update
46        "gpu": false               # whether to train using a GPU
47      }
48    }],
49    "env": [{
50      "name": "CartPole-v0",       # name of the environment
51      "max_t": null,               # max time steps per episode
52      "max_frame": 50000           # max time steps per Session
53    }],
54    "body": {
55      "product": "outer",
56      "num": 1
57    },
58    "meta": {
59      "distributed": false,    # whether to use async parallelization
60      "eval_frequency": 1000,      # how often to evaluate the agent
61      "max_session": 4,            # number of sessions to run
62      "max_trial": 32              # number of trials to run
63    },
64    "search": {
65      "agent": [{
66        "algorithm": {
67          "gamma__uniform": [0.50, 1.0],
68          "training_iter__randint": [1, 10]
69        },
70        "net": {
71          "optim_spec": {
72            "lr__choice": [0.0001, 0.001, 0.01, 0.1]
73          }
74        }
75      }]
76    }
77  }
78 }
```

In Code 11.2, the three variables to search over are specified in lines 64–76. We search over one continuous variable gamma with values sampled using a random uniform distribution. A discrete variable `training_iter` is searched with values sampled uniformly from integers $\in [0, 10]$. The learning rate `lr` is sampled randomly from a list of choices $[0.0001, 0.001, 0.01, 0.1]$. This illustrates some of the different sampling methods that can be used in hyperparameter search in SLM Lab.

The other important variable when running an experiment is `max_trial` (line 62). This specifies how many sets of hyperparameter values will be generated and used to run trials. In this example, with `max_trial = 32`, there will be 32 random combinations of values for `gamma`, `training_iter`, and `lr` and these are used to replace their default values in the complete `spec` file. This produces 32 spec files containing distinct sets of hyperparameters used to run the trials. Each trial will run four `Sessions` (line 61).

Now that we know how to write a spec file, let's look at how to run an experiment using SLM Lab.

11.3 Running SLM Lab

Running a deep RL experiment typically involves testing different sets of hyperparameters. Deep RL results are known to have high variance even for the same set of hyperparameters, so a good practice is to perform multiple runs using different random seeds and average the results.

The experiment framework in SLM Lab incorporates this practice and is organized hierarchically into three components.

1. **Session:** A session, at the lowest level of the SLM Lab experiment framework, runs the RL control loop. It initializes the agent and the environment using a specific set

   of hyperparameters and a given random seed, and trains the agent. When a session finishes, it saves the trained agent, `spec` file, data, and graphs into a data folder for analysis.

2. **Trial:** A trial runs multiple sessions using the same set of hyperparameters and different random seeds, then averages the session results and plots trial graphs.

3. **Experiment:** An experiment, at the highest level of SLM Lab's experiment framework, generates different sets of hyperparameters and runs a trial for each one. It can be thought of as a study—for example, "What values of gamma and learning rate provide the fastest, most stable solution, if the other variables are held constant?" When an experiment completes, it compares the trials by plotting multitrial graphs.

11.3.1 SLM Lab Commands

Let's look at the main commands in SLM Lab. They follow a basic pattern `python run_lab.py {spec_file} {spec_name} {lab_mode}`. There are four core commands with different use cases.

1. `python run_lab.py slm_lab/spec/benchmark/a2c/a2c_nstep_pong.json a2c_nstep_pong dev`: Development mode. This differs from `train` mode described below in that it is limited to a single `Session`, renders the environment, checks network parameter updates, and uses a verbose debugging log.

2. `python run_lab.py slm_lab/spec/benchmark/a2c/a2c_nstep_pong.json a2c_nstep_pong train`: Train an agent using the given spec by spawning a `Trial`.

3. `python run_lab.py slm_lab/spec/benchmark/a2c/a2c_nstep_pong.json a2c_nstep_pong search`: Run an experiment with a hyperparameter search by spawning an `Experiment`.

4. `python run_lab.py data/a2c_nstep_pong_2018_06_16_214527 /a2c_nstep_pong_spec.json a2c_nstep_pong enjoy@a2c_nstep_pong_t1_s0`: Load a saved agent from the SLM Lab `data/` folder of a completed trial or experiment. The lab mode `enjoy@a2c_nstep_pong_t1_s0` specifies the trial-session of a model file.

11.4 Analyzing Experiment Results

After an experiment completes, it will output data automatically into a folder located at `SLM-Lab/data/`. This section focuses on how to use that data to gain insights into the experiment. Experiment data mirrors the session-trial-experiment hierarchy discussed in Section 11.3. We give an overview of the data generated by SLM Lab along with some examples.

11.4.1 Overview of the Experiment Data

Experiments generate data which is automatically saved to the `data/{experiment_id}` folder. The `{experiment_id}` is the concatenation of the `spec` name and a timestamp generated when the experiment starts.

Each session generates a plot of the learning curve and its moving average, the saved agent model parameters, a CSV file containing the session data, and session-level metrics. The session data includes rewards, loss, learning rate, exploration variable value, and more. Figure 11.1 shows an example of the session graphs of an Actor-Critic experiment from Section 6.7.1.

Each trial generates a plot of the session-averaged learning curves with an error band of ± 1 standard deviation. A moving average version of the plot is also included. It also produces trial-level metrics. Figure 11.2 shows an example of the trial graphs.

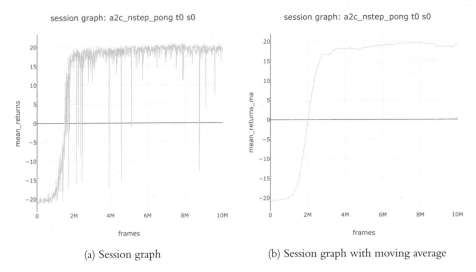

(a) Session graph   (b) Session graph with moving average

Figure 11.1   An example of the session graphs. The vertical axis shows the total rewards averaged over eight episodes during checkpoints, and the horizontal axis shows the total training frames. The moving average with a window of 100 evaluation checkpoints is shown on the right.

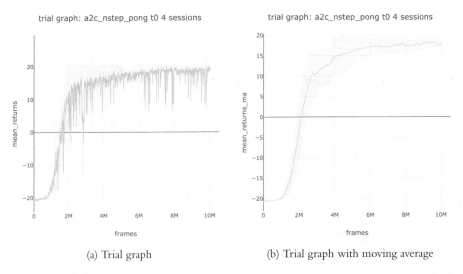

(a) Trial graph   (b) Trial graph with moving average

Figure 11.2   An example of the trial graphs averaged from session data. The vertical axis shows the total rewards averaged over eight episodes during checkpoints, and the horizontal axis shows the total training frames. The moving average with a window of 100 evaluation checkpoints is shown on the right.

An experiment generates a multitrial graph which compares all the trials. It also includes a moving average version. Additionally, it produces an experiment_df CSV file which summarizes the variables and the results from the experiment, sorted from the best-performing to worst-performing trial. It is intended to clearly show the hyperparameter value ranges and combinations from the most successful to the least. Figure 11.3 shows an example of the multitrial graphs.

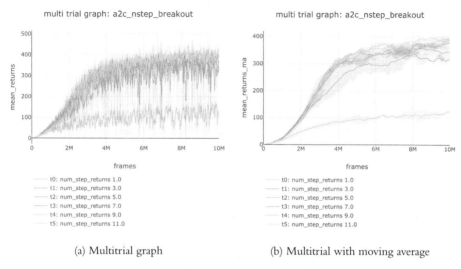

(a) Multitrial graph   (b) Multitrial with moving average

Figure 11.3   An example of the multitrial graphs

11.5 Summary

This chapter took a closer look at the companion library, SLM Lab. We discussed the algorithms it implements and the spec files which are used to configure them. We also introduced the main lab commands.

We then looked at the experiment framework consisting of Session, Trial, and Experiment. They each produce graphs and data useful for analyzing algorithm performance.

SLM Lab is in active development with new algorithms and features added frequently to the latest version. To use this, check out the main master branch on the Github repository at https://github.com/kengz/SLM-Lab.

Network Architectures

Neural networks are a component of every algorithm we have discussed in this book. However, up to this point, we have never discussed in detail the design of these networks, nor their functionality that is useful when combining neural networks with RL. The purpose of this chapter is to take a closer look at neural network design and training in the context of deep RL.

The chapter begins with a brief introduction to the different neural network families and the types of data they are specialized to process. Then we discuss how to select an appropriate network based on two characteristics of an environment—how *observable* it is and what the nature of the state space is. To characterize the observability of an environment, we discuss the difference between Markov decision processes (MDPs) and partially observable Markov decision processes (POMDPs) and introduce three different types of POMDPs.

The remainder of the chapter discusses SLM Lab's `Net` API which is designed to encapsulate the common functionality for training neural networks in the context of deep RL. We review some desirable properties for the `Net` API and, using examples from SLM Lab, show how these properties can be implemented.

12.1 Types of Neural Networks

Neural networks can be organized into families. Each network family has particular characteristics and each is good at different tasks and for processing different types of input data. There are three main categories—multilayer perceptrons (MLPs), convolutional neural networks (CNNs), and recurrent neural networks (RNNs). These network types can also be combined to produce hybrids—for example, a CNN-RNN.

Each family is characterized by the types of layers a network contains and the way the flow of computation through the network is organized. These families can also be interpreted as incorporating different prior knowledge about their inputs and exploiting this knowledge to better learn from data with certain characteristics. What follows in this section is a very brief overview of the characteristics of the main network families. Readers familiar with neural networks can skip this section entirely or just briefly look at Figure 12.4. For readers wishing to learn more, we recommend two excellent books,

Neural Networks and Deep Learning by Michael Nielsen [92] and *Deep Learning* by Ian Goodfellow, Yoshua Bengio, and Aaron Courville [45], both of which were freely available online at the time of writing.

12.1.1   Multilayer Perceptrons (MLPs)

Multilayer perceptrons (MLPs) are the simplest and most general type of neural network. They consist only of *fully connected layers* (also known as *dense layers*). In a fully connected layer, every output from the previous layer is connected to every node in the current layer by a distinct weight. Nonlinear activation functions are typically applied to the outputs of each dense layer. These nonlinear activation functions give neural networks their expressivity, making it possible for them to approximate highly complex nonlinear functions.

MLPs are general-purpose, and inputs to these networks are organized as a single vector with n elements. MLPs assume very little about the nature of their inputs. For example, they don't encode any information about how different dimensions of the input relate to each other. This is both a strength and a limitation. It makes it possible for MLPs to take a global view of their inputs. They can respond to global structure and patterns by learning features which are a combination of all of the input elements.

However, MLP's may also ignore structure in the data they are trained on. Consider the two images, Figures 12.1a and 12.1b. Figure 12.1a is a picture of a mountainous landscape. Figure 12.1b looks like random noise. The pixel values in Figure 12.1a exhibit very strong 2D spatial correlation. In most cases, a strong indicator of the value of a particular pixel is the values of the neighboring pixels. In contrast, a pixel value in Figure 12.1b does not correlate strongly with its neighboring pixels. Any realistic image is much more like Figure 12.1a than 12.1b, exhibiting a high degree of local correlation in the pixel values.

(a) Mountain   (b) Random image

Figure 12.1   Image of a mountain vs. a random image

The 2D structure of an image is not readily available to a MLP because each image will be flattened into a long 1D list of numbers before being passed as input to the network. Before training, the order of the pixel values could be randomly permuted and the representation of the image in 1D would be equivalent. In contrast, consider what would happen if the pixels of a 2D image were randomly permuted. This is what Figure 12.1b is—Figure 12.1a after the pixels have been randomly permuted. In 2D space, Figures 12.1a and 12.1b are clearly not the same and it is impossible to determine just from looking at Figure 12.1b what the pixels represent. The meaning of these pixels more readily emerges from the pixel values combined with how they are ordered in 2D space.

Converting a 2D image to 1D is an example of a meta state information loss discussed in more detail in Section 14.4. Images are inherently two-dimensional as each pixel is related to other pixels in 2D space. When images are converted to a 1D representation, the problem becomes harder. The network has to do some work to reconstruct the 2D relationships between pixels because this information is not apparent in the way the input is represented.

Another characteristic of MLPs is that the number of parameters tends to grow very quickly. For example, consider an MLP which takes an input $\in \mathbb{R}^{784}$, has two hidden layers, with 1024 and 512 nodes respectively, and an output layer of 10 nodes. The function the MLP computes is shown in Equation 12.1. The activation function in this network is a sigmoid: $\sigma(x) = \frac{1}{1+e^{-x}}$.

$$f_{\text{MLP}}(x) = \sigma\big(W_2 \, \sigma(W_1 x + b_1) + b_2\big) \tag{12.1}$$

There are two weight matrices, W_1 and W_2, and two bias vectors, b_1 and b_2. W_1 has $1024 \times 784 = 802{,}816$ elements, W_2 has $512 \times 1024 = 524{,}288$ elements, and the two bias vectors, b_1 and b_2, have 1024 and 512 elements, respectively. There will be $802{,}816 + 524{,}288 + 1024 + 512 = 1{,}328{,}640$ parameters in the network. By contemporary standards, this is a small network but it already has many parameters that need to be learned. This can be problematic because the number of examples needed to learn good values for each of the parameters increases with the total number of parameters in a network. When a large number of learnable parameters is combined with the sample inefficiency of current deep RL algorithms, an agent may take a very long time to train. Consequently, MLPs tend to be well suited to environments with two characteristics: their state space is low-dimensional and learning features requires all of the elements of a state.

Finally, MLPs are stateless. This means they do not remember anything about the history of inputs that came before the current one. Inputs to MLPs are not ordered and each input is processed independently of all other inputs.

12.1.2 Convolutional Neural Networks (CNNs)

Convolutional neural networks (CNNs) excel at learning from images. CNNs are specifically designed to exploit the spatial structure of image data because they contain one or more convolutional layers each consisting of a number of convolution kernels. Convolution kernels are applied repeatedly to subsets of their input to produce an output. We say that a kernel is *convolved* with its input and this is known as a *convolution* operation. For example, a kernel might be convolved with a 2D image to produce a 2D output. In this case, a single application of a kernel would correspond to it being applied to a small patch of an image consisting of just a few pixels, for instance 3×3 or 5×5 pixels; this operation produces a scalar output.

This scalar output can be interpreted as signaling the presence or absence of a particular feature in the local region of the input to which it was applied. Consequently, a kernel can be thought of as a local feature detector because it produces an output based on a spatially contiguous subset of the input features. The kernel (feature detector) is applied locally across the entire image to produce a *feature map* that describes all of the places that a particular feature occurs in that image.

A single convolutional layer typically consists of a number of kernels (8–256 is common), each of which may learn to detect a different feature. For example, one kernel may learn to detect vertical straight edges, another horizontal straight edges, and a third a curved edge. When layers are composed, subsequent layers can learn increasingly complex features using the outputs from the feature detectors in the layer below. For example, a feature in a higher-level network layer may learn to detect the paddle in a game of Atari Pong, and another may learn to detect the ball.

One advantage of structuring layers in this way is that a kernel can detect the presence of a feature regardless of where it appears in the image. This is beneficial because the position of useful features in an image may vary. For example, the positions of the player's and opponent's paddles, as well as the ball, vary in a game of Atari Pong. Applying a "paddle detector" kernel to an image will produce a 2D map with the locations of all of the paddles in the image.

Using convolutions, a network learns "for free" that a particular configuration of values represents the same feature in different parts of an image. Convolutional layers are also more efficient than fully connected layers in terms of the number of parameters. One kernel can be used to identify the same feature anywhere in an image—we don't have to learn a separate kernel to detect that feature in many different locations. As a result, applied to inputs with the same number of elements, convolutional layers typically have significantly fewer parameters than fully connected layers. This is a consequence of applying a single kernel repeatedly to many subsections of an input.

A disadvantage of convolutional layers is that they are local—they only process a subset of the input space at a time and ignore the global structure of the image. However, global structure is often important. Consider again the game of Atari Pong. Good performance requires using the locations of the ball and paddles to decide how to act. Location is only defined relative to the whole input space.

This limitation of convolutions is often mitigated by increasing the receptive field of the kernels in higher layers.[1] This means the effective area of the input space that a kernel processes is increased—such kernels can "see" more of the input space. The larger the receptive field of a kernel, the more global its perspective. An alternative approach is to add a small MLP to the top of a CNN to get the best of both worlds. Going back to the Atari Pong example, the output of the CNN would produce 2D maps containing the locations of the ball and paddles; these maps are passed as input to an MLP which combines all of the information and produces an action.

Like MLPs, CNNs are also stateless. However, unlike MLPs, CNNs are ideally suited to learning from images because they assume that their inputs have spatial structure.

---

1. For example, through pooling operations, dilated convolutions, strided convolutions, or larger kernels.

Furthermore, the use of kernels is an effective way to reduce the number of parameters in a network when the number of elements in the input is large—and digital representations of images typically have thousands or millions of elements each. In fact, CNNs are so much better at learning from images than the other network families that a general rule of thumb is: if the state provided by the environment is an image, include some convolutional layers in the network.

12.1.3 Recurrent Neural Networks (RNNs)

Recurrent neural networks (RNNs) are specialized to learn from sequential data. A single datapoint for an RNN consists of a sequence of elements where each element is a vector. Unlike MLPs and CNNs, RNNs assume that the order in which elements are received has meaning. Sentences are one example of the type of data that RNNs are good at processing. Each element of the sequence is a word, and the order of these words affects the overall meaning of the sentence. However, a datapoint could also be a sequence of states—for example, an ordered sequence of states experienced by an agent.

The distinguishing feature of RNNs is that they are stateful, which means they remember previous elements they have seen. When processing element x_i in a sequence, an RNN remembers the $x_0, x_1, \ldots, x_{i-1}$ elements that have come before it. This is achieved with specialized recurrent layers that have a hidden state. The hidden state is a learned representation of the elements in the sequence that the network has seen so far, and it is updated each time the network receives a new element. An RNN's memory lasts for the length of the sequence. At the beginning of a new sequence, the hidden state of an RNN is reset. Long Short-Term Memory (LSTM) [52] and Gated Recurrent Units (GRUs) [21] are the most common layers with this characteristic.

A mechanism for remembering the past is useful when the information provided by the environment at time step t doesn't fully capture everything that would be useful to know at the current point in time. Consider a maze environment in which gold coins are spawned in the same position and can be picked up by an agent to get positive reward. Suppose further that the gold coins reappear after being picked up by an agent once a fixed amount of time has elapsed. Even if an agent can *see* where all of the currently existing coins are in the maze, it will only be capable of predicting when specific coins will reappear if it remembers how long ago it picked them up. It is easy to imagine that under time constraints, maximizing the score will involve keeping track of which coins it has picked up and when. For this task, an agent requires a memory. This is the main advantage that RNNs provide over CNNs or MLPs.

Fortunately, one does not have to choose a single network type exclusively. Instead, it is very common to create hybrid networks which contain multiple subnetworks, each of which might belong to a different family. For example, we could design a network with a state processing module which is an MLP or CNN that outputs a representation of the raw state,[2] and a temporal processing module which is an RNN. At each time step, the raw state is passed through the state processing module, and the output is passed as

---

2. This representation will typically have fewer elements than the original state.

input to the RNN. The RNN then uses this information to produce the final output of the overall network. A network containing both CNN and RNN subnetworks is called a CNN-RNN. Since MLPs are so commonly used as additional small subnetworks, they are typically dropped from the name.

To sum up, RNNs are best suited to problems where data is represented as ordered sequences. In the context of deep RL, they are typically used when an agent needs to remember what happened over a long time horizon in order to make good decisions.

12.2   Guidelines for Choosing a Network Family

Having introduced the different types of neural networks, we can ask: given a particular environment, what type of network should an agent use? In this section, we discuss guidelines for choosing a network family based on the characteristics of the environment.

All deep RL environments can be interpreted as generating sequential data. We saw that RNNs are specialized to handle this type of input. So why not always use an RNN or a CNN-RNN in deep RL? To answer this question, we need to discuss the difference between MDPs and partially observable MDPs (or POMDPs).

12.2.1   MDPs vs. POMDPs

Chapter 1 introduced the formal definition of an MDP which we briefly recap here. An MDP is a mathematical framework which models sequential decision making. At the core of an MDP is the transition function which models how the state s_t transitions into the next state s_{t+1}. The MDP transition function is shown in Equation 12.2.

$$s_{t+1} \sim P(s_{t+1} \mid s_t, a_t) \tag{12.2}$$

The transition function has the Markov property—the transition to s_{t+1} is fully determined by the current state and action, (s_t, a_t). There may have been many earlier states experienced by the agent in the episode, $s_0, s_1, \ldots, s_{t-1}$, but these do not convey any additional information about the state the environment will transition to.

The concept of state appears in two places. First, we have the state that is produced by an environment and observed by an agent. This is called the observed state s_t. Second, there is the state that is used by transition function. This is the environment's internal state s_t^{int}.

If an environment is an MDP, then it is described as *fully observable*, and $s_t = s_t^{\text{int}}$. For example, the CartPole and LunarLander problems are both fully observable environments. The CartPole environment provides four pieces of information at each time step: the cart's position along the linear axis, the cart velocity, the pole angle and the pole velocity at the tip. Given an action—left or right—this information is sufficient to determine the next state of the environment.

However, the internal state of the environment may be hidden from the agent—that is, $s_t \neq s_t^{\text{int}}$. These types of environments are known as *partially observable* MDPs (POMDPs). POMDPs have the same transition function as MDPs. However, POMDPs do not provide the internal state s_t^{int} of the environment to an agent; instead, they provide the observed state s_t. This means that an agent no longer knows the internal state s_t^{int} and must infer it from some or all of the observed states $(s_t, s_{t-1}, \ldots, s_1, s_0)$.

Internal states fully describe the system that we care about. For example, in Atari Pong the internal state s_t^{int} of the environment will include the position and velocity of the paddles and ball. Observed states s_t typically consist of the raw data provided by the sensors of a system—for example, the game image. When playing the game, we use the image to infer the environment's internal state.

Let's consider a modified version of the CartPole environment. Suppose the environment only provides two pieces of information at each time step—the cart's position along the linear axis and the pole angle.[3] This is the observed state s_t because it is the information the agent has access to. However, the environment still keeps track of the cart and pole velocity in addition the the cart position and pole angle. This is the environment's internal state since it fully describes the cartpole.

It was not necessary to make the distinction between observed and internal states until now because we were only considering MDPs. The internal state *is* what the agent observes in an MDP. However, in POMDPs, we need a way to distinguish between the observed state and the internal state of the environment.

POMDPs can be split into three categories:

- Fully observable given partial history
- Fully observable given full history
- Never fully observable

Fully Observable Given Partial History   In these environments, the internal state s_t^{int} can be inferred from the last few observed states, $(s_t, s_{t-1}, \ldots, s_{t-k})$, where k is small, for example 2–4. Most Atari games are generally considered to have this characteristic [65]. As an example, consider the observed state in the Atari game of Breakout. Figure 12.2 shows the agent's paddle, the position of the ball, the unbroken bricks, the number of lives the agent has left, and the score. This is almost sufficient to identify which internal state the game is in—except for one crucial piece of information: the direction in which the ball is moving. This can be inferred from s_t and s_{t-1} by taking the difference between them to obtain the direction of movement. Once we know which way the ball is moving, it is possible to determine which state the game is in[4] and predict what would happen next. If it was relevant to infer the acceleration as well as the speed of the ball, we could use the previous three observed states to estimate these values.

---

3. This is the modification suggested in "Recurrent Policy Gradients" by Wierstra et al.[147]

4. In Atari Breakout, the ball moves at constant speed, so we can ignore higher-order information such as acceleration.

Figure 12.2 Atari Breakout

We have already seen in Chapter 5 that for Atari games, it is common practice to select every fourth frame and stack four of the skipped frames together. An agent can use the differences between stacked frames in a single input to infer useful motion-based information about the game objects.

Fully Observable Given Full History   In these environments, it is always possible to determine the internal state of a game by tracking the history of all the observed states. For example, the T-maze proposed by Bram Bakker in "Reinforcement Learning with Long Short-Term Memory" [10] has this property. Figure 12.3 shows the environment which consists of a long corridor with a T-junction at the end. An agent always starts in the same state at the bottom of the T. The agent only observes its immediate surroundings and has four available actions at each time step—moving up, down, left, or right. The objective is to move to a goal state which is always positioned at one end of the T.

At the start state of the game, the agent observes at which end of the T the goal is located. In each episode, the position of the goal state changes to either end of the T. Upon reaching the junction, an agent can choose to go left or right. If it moves to the goal state, the game ends with a reward of 4. If it moves to the wrong end of the T, the game ends with a reward of −1. Provided the agent can remember what it observed in the start state, it is always possible to behave optimally. Hence, this environment is fully observable given the full history of observed states.

Figure 12.3 T-Maze [10]

Let's look at another example from DMLab-30 [12] which is an open source library by DeepMind. Many of its environments are specifically designed to test an agent's memory, so they fall into this category of POMDPs. `natlab_varying_map_regrowth` is a mushroom foraging task in which an agent must collect mushrooms within a naturalistic environment. The observed state is an RGBD[5] image generated based on an agent's current viewpoint. The mushrooms regrow in the same location after about a minute, so it is advantageous for an agent to remember which mushrooms it has collected and how long ago it happened. This environment is interesting because the number of observed states an agent needs in order to infer the internal state of the game varies depending on the time step and the actions the agent takes. For this reason, it is helpful to use the entire history of observed states so that the agent never misses important information.

Never Fully Observable In these environments, the internal state s_t^{int} cannot be inferred even when we have the entire history of observed states $(s_0, s_1, \ldots, s_{t-1}, s_t)$. Poker is a game with this characteristic: even if you remember all of the cards dealt so far, you are not aware of the cards the other players hold.

Or, consider a navigation task in which an agent is placed in a large room containing a number of balls of different colors. The location of each ball is randomly generated at the start of every episode, and there is always exactly one red ball in the room. An agent is equipped with an ego-centric grayscale camera to perceive the environment, so the camera images are the observed states. Suppose the agent's task is to navigate to the red ball. The task is unambiguous, but without colored images the agent is unable to perceive the color of the balls—so it never has enough information to solve the task.

12.2.2 Choosing Networks for Environments

Given a new environment, how can one tell whether it is an MDP or one of the three types of POMDPs? A good approach is to take some time to understand the environment. Consider how a human would solve the task—try playing the environment yourself if possible. Based on the information contained in a single observed state, could we decide on a good action at each time step? If the answer is yes, the environment is likely an MDP. If not, then how many observed states do we need to remember in order to perform well? Is it a few states or the entire history? Then the environment is likely a fully observable POMDP given partial history or full history, respectively. Finally, consider if there is any crucial information missing from the history of observed states. If so, the environment may be a POMDP that is never fully observable. How does this affect potential performance? Is it still possible to achieve a reasonably good solution or is the task unsolvable? If reasonable performance is still achievable despite the missing information, deep RL may still be applicable.

We have characterized environments according to their *observability*—the extent to which the internal state of an environment can be inferred from the observed states. This

---

5. RGB plus Depth.

approach can be combined with information about the environment state space to yield some clues about which neural network architectures will be most suitable for an agent.

The most important characteristic of a neural network in relation to an environment's observability is whether it is *stateful* or not—that is, does a network have the capacity to remember the history of observed states?

MLPs and CNNs are stateless, so they are best suited to environments which are MDPs because it is not necessary to remember any history. They can also perform well when applied to POMDPs that are fully observable given partial history. However, in this case it will be necessary to transform the observed states so that the input to the network contains information about the previous k time steps. This way we can provide MLPs and CNNs with sufficient information in a single input to infer the environment's state.

RNNs are stateful, so they are best suited to POMDPs that are fully observable given full history because the task requires remembering a potentially long sequence of observed states. RNNs may also perform well on POMDPs that are never fully observable, but there is no guarantee that an agent will perform well—there may simply be too much missing information.

How does the state space affect the choice of network? Section 12.1 described how CNNs are the best suited of the three network families to learning from image data. Consequently, if the observed states are images, as in the Atari games, then it is usually best to use a CNN. Otherwise, an MLP will likely be sufficient. If the observed state is a mix of image and nonimage data, consider having multiple subnetworks, MLPs and CNNs, to process data of different types, then combine their outputs.

If the environment is fully observable given full history or never fully observable, then it is important to have an RNN subnetwork. Try a hybrid network that uses a CNN or MLP to process the observed state before passing data to an RNN subnetwork.

Figure 12.4 sums up this discussion of network architectures and environments. It shows some common variations of networks for each of the three different families, MLP, CNN, and RNN, as well as the hybrid CNN-RNN. Solid boxes show the required subnetworks while dashed boxes show optional subnetworks. It also describes the characteristics of the network inputs, some example environments, and some algorithms that achieved state-of-the-art performance using their respective network types.

CartPole, LunarLander, and BipedalWalker are some of the environments we have discussed in this book. Humanoid and Ant are two more challenging continuous-control environments available through OpenAI Gym. All of these environments are MDPs that provide a low-dimensional observed state to an agent. Thus, they are best solved using MLPs. At the time of writing, the Twin Delayed Deep Deterministic Policy Gradient (TD3) [42] and Soft Actor-Critic (SAC) [47] algorithms achieved the best known results on the Humanoid and Ant environments using only MLPs.

We have often discussed the Atari games throughout this book. These environments are mostly POMDPs that are fully observable given partial history. The observed state is an RGB image, so CNNs are best suited to these problems. The strongest results over the past few years for these environments include a CNN component—for example, DQN [88], Double DQN [141], Dueling DQN [144], and ApeX [54].

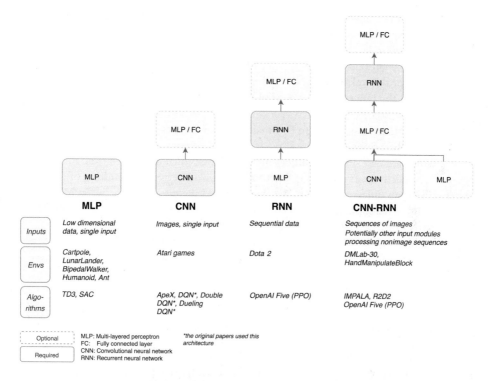

Figure 12.4   Neural network families

Dota 2 is a complex multiplayer game that requires strategies over a long time horizon. It can be characterized as a POMDP that is fully observable given full history. The OpenAI Five [104] PPO agents used nonimage observed states derived from the game API. The state contains about 20,000 elements and includes a game map and unit information. A suitable network type for this state is MLP. Since the game requires long-term strategies, an agent needs to remember the history of the observed states. The MLP output is then passed into an LSTM network of 1024 units. For more details, see the model architecture linked under the "Model Structure" section in the OpenAI Five blogpost [104]. Combined with some serious engineering effort and computing power, they managed to defeat the world's top players in 2019 [107].

DMLab-30 environments have image-based observed states. The best architectures are those combining CNN and RNN modules so that the networks can process images well and keep track of the history of observed states. IMPALA [37] and R2D2 [65] are two of the best-performing algorithms on these environments; both make use of CNN-RNN hybrid networks.

Finally, HandManipulateBlock is another environment provided by OpenAI. The objective is to change the orientation of a block placed in a robotic hand. It is a complex continuous-control environment with a robot that has 24 degrees of freedom. The observed state is a combination of three images of the hand and the block and a vector describing the robot fingertip positions [98]. To diversify the training data, OpenAI randomizes some of the environment's internal parameters, such as the weight of the block, at every episode. Solving the task therefore requires an agent to infer the internal parameters of the episode using a sequence of observed states passed to an RNN. The network used for this task had a CNN and an MLP to process and combine observed state; the sequence of the processed states is passed to an RNN.

Summary   Neural networks can be organized into families according to the type of data they learn best from. There are three main types of networks—MLPs, CNNs, and RNNs, which are best suited for processing low-dimensional unordered data, images, and sequences, respectively. It is also possible to create hybrid networks consisting of multiple subnetworks from different families. We also discussed the distinction between MDPs and POMDPs. RL environments differ according to the (observed) state space and whether they are MDPs or POMDPs. We saw that this information can be used to choose a network architecture best suited to solving a particular environment.

Now, let's shift focus and look at the practical side of neural network design for deep RL.

12.3 The Net API

Deep RL algorithms use neural networks. Even though the function that a network approximates differs depending on the algorithm, their network training workflows share many common routines, such as calculating the loss and updating the parameters. Therefore, it is helpful to use a standardized Net API for all the neural networks used by different algorithms. Modularized network components also make algorithm implementations easier to read and debug by using less code.

A Net API for deep RL has the following requirements:

1. **Input and output layer shape inference:** The shape of the input and output layers changes depending on the combination of environment and algorithm. These can be inferred automatically, so users do not need to specify the input and output dimensions manually every time. This feature saves time and makes code less error-prone.

2. **Automatic network construction:** Network architecture is an important factor in algorithm performance and varies by environment. Since it is common to try many different network architectures in deep RL, it is better to specify network architectures through a configuration file instead of code changes. This requires a method to take a configuration and automatically construct the corresponding neural network.

3. **Training step:** All neural networks need a training step, which involves computing the loss, calculating the gradient, and updating the network parameters. It is useful to standardize these steps in a single function so they can be reused for each algorithm.

4. **Exposure of underlying methods:** The API, as a wrapper on top of a neural network library, should also expose its most commonly used methods, such as activation functions, optimizers, learning rate decay, and model checkpointing.

The `Net` is a base class which implements a number of common methods shown in Code 12.1, also available in SLM Lab at `slm_lab/agent/net/base.py`. This base class is extended by the `MLPNet, ConvNet, RecurrentNet` classes tailored to different network types.

Code 12.1   The Net base class defining the API methods

```
1   # slm_lab/agent/net/base.py
2
3   class Net(ABC):
4       '''Abstract Net class to define the API methods'''
5
6       def __init__(self, net_spec, in_dim, out_dim):
7           '''
8           @param {dict} net_spec is the spec for the net
9           @param {int|list} in_dim is the input dimension(s) for the network.
    ↪   Usually use in_dim=body.state_dim
10          @param {int|list} out_dim is the output dimension(s) for the network.
    ↪   Usually use out_dim=body.action_dim
11          '''
12          ...
13
14      @abstractmethod
15      def forward(self):
16          '''The forward step for a specific network architecture'''
17          ...
18
19      @net_util.dev_check_train_step
20      def train_step(self, loss, optim, lr_scheduler, clock, global_net=None):
21          '''Makes one network parameter update'''
22          ...
23
24      def store_grad_norms(self):
25          '''Stores the gradient norms for debugging.'''
26          ...
```

The `Net` class is also supported by a set of utility functions which aid with automatic network construction and exposing the useful methods of the underlying neural network library. Let's take a look at each of the API requirements in detail.

12.3.1   Input and Output Layer Shape Inference

To appropriately construct a network, it is necessary to infer the shape of the input and output layers. The input layer shape is given by the environment's state space. For example, if the environment states are vectors with 16 elements, the input layer should have 16 nodes. Alternatively, if the observed states are 84×84 grayscale images, the input layer should be defined as a $(84, 84)$ matrix. Additionally, CNNs should also include the number of channels, and RNNs need to know the sequence length.

The shape of the output layer is determined by the environment's action space and the algorithm used to train an agent. Based on the deep RL algorithms discussed in this book, there are three variants of network output to consider. An agent may learn the Q-function, a policy, or both a policy and the V-function. The outputs of a network will therefore represent, respectively, Q-values, action probabilities, or action probabilities and V-values.

Inferring the output shape is more complex than the input, so SLM Lab includes some helper methods for doing this, shown in Code 12.2. These methods are located at `slm_lab/agent/net/net_util.py` in the library.

First, the `get_policy_out_dim` method (lines 3–19) infers the output shape when a network learns a policy.

- The shape of the environment's action space is stored in an agent's `body.action_dim` attribute (line 5).

- Discrete cases are handled on lines 6–12: when there are multiple actions (lines 7–9) or when there is a single action (lines 10–12).

- Continuous cases are handled on lines 13–18: when there are multiple actions (lines 17–18) or when there is a single action (lines 15–16).

Next, the `get_out_dim` method (lines 21–31) infers the output shape for a network from the algorithm. If an algorithm learns a V-function (uses a Critic), we add an extra output layer with one output unit (lines 24–28). Otherwise, the output shape is simply the policy output shape (lines 29–30).

A Q-function can be seen as an instance of a discrete `Argmax` policy (probability = 1 for the maximum Q-value), so we can use the policy output shape to infer the output dimension when an algorithm learns a Q-network.

Code 12.2   Helper method to infer network output layer shape

```
1   # slm_lab/agent/net/net_util.py
2
3   def get_policy_out_dim(body):
4       '''Helper method to construct the policy network out_dim for a body
        ↪   according to is_discrete, action_type'''
5       action_dim = body.action_dim
6       if body.is_discrete:
7           if body.action_type == 'multi_discrete':
8               assert ps.is_list(action_dim), action_dim
9               policy_out_dim = action_dim
```

```
10          else:
11              assert ps.is_integer(action_dim), action_dim
12              policy_out_dim = action_dim
13      else:
14          assert ps.is_integer(action_dim), action_dim
15          if action_dim == 1:  # single action, use [loc, scale]
16              policy_out_dim = 2
17          else:  # multiaction, use [locs], [scales]
18              policy_out_dim = [action_dim, action_dim]
19      return policy_out_dim
20
21  def get_out_dim(body, add_critic=False):
22      '''Construct the NetClass out_dim for a body according to is_discrete,
        ↪ action_type, and whether to add a critic unit'''
23      policy_out_dim = get_policy_out_dim(body)
24      if add_critic:
25          if ps.is_list(policy_out_dim):
26              out_dim = policy_out_dim + [1]
27          else:
28              out_dim = [policy_out_dim, 1]
29      else:
30          out_dim = policy_out_dim
31      return out_dim
```

The get_out_dim method is used to construct neural networks inside algorithm classes. Code 12.3 shows an example from Reinforce. When the network is constructed in the method init_nets (lines 7–13), the output dimension is inferred using the get_out_dim method (line 10).

Code 12.3   Network construction in the Reinforce class

```
1   # slm_lab/agent/algorithm/reinforce.py
2
3   class Reinforce(Algorithm):
4       ...
5
6       @lab_api
7       def init_nets(self, global_nets=None):
8           ...
9           in_dim = self.body.state_dim
10          out_dim = net_util.get_out_dim(self.body)
11          NetClass = getattr(net, self.net_spec['type'])
12          self.net = NetClass(self.net_spec, in_dim, out_dim)
13          ...
```

A chosen `Net` class (`MLPNet`, `ConvNet`, or `RecurrentNet`) is initialized using the net spec and the inferred input and output dimensions (lines 11–12). Let's now look at how the `Net` class constructs an instance of a neural network using these inputs.

12.3.2 Automatic Network Construction

A `Net` class is able to build a neural network from a given net `spec`. Code 12.4 shows two example net `specs`, one for a MLP (lines 2–20) and one for a CNN (lines 21–44). The MLP has a hidden layer of 64 units (lines 7–8), SeLU activation function (line 9), gradient norm clipping to 0.5 (line 10), the loss function (lines 11–13), optimizer (lines 14–17), and a learning rate decay scheduler (line 18). The CNN has three convolutional hidden layers (lines 26–31) and one fully connected layer (line 32); the rest of its `spec` has standard components similar to the MLP (lines 33–43).

Code 12.4   An example net spec for building a Net

```
1   {
2     "reinforce_cartpole": {
3       "agent": [{
4         "name": "Reinforce",
5         ...
6         "net": {
7           "type": "MLPNet",
8           "hid_layers": [64],
9           "hid_layers_activation": "selu",
10          "clip_grad_val": 0.5,
11          "loss_spec": {
12            "name": "MSELoss"
13          },
14          "optim_spec": {
15            "name": "Adam",
16            "lr": 0.002
17          },
18          "lr_scheduler_spec": null
19        }
20     ...
21     "dqn_pong": {
22       "agent": [{
23         "name": "DQN",
24         ...
25         "net": {
26           "type": "ConvNet",
27           "conv_hid_layers": [
28             [32, 8, 4, 0, 1],
29             [64, 4, 2, 0, 1],
```

```
30          [64, 3, 1, 0, 1]
31        ],
32        "fc_hid_layers": [256],
33        "hid_layers_activation": "relu",
34        "clip_grad_val": 10.0,
35        "loss_spec": {
36          "name": "SmoothL1Loss"
37        },
38        "optim_spec": {
39          "name": "Adam",
40          "lr": 1e-4,
41        },
42        "lr_scheduler_spec": null,
43        ...
44  }
```

Internally, a `Net` class uses another helper function to build its network layers using PyTorch's `Sequential` container class. The `MLPNet` class uses the `build_fc_model` method (Code 12.5) to build fully connected layers, and the `ConvNet` additionally uses the `build_conv_layers` method (Code 12.6) to build convolutional layers.

The `build_fc_model` method takes a list of layer dimension `dims`, which is specified in the net `spec` as `hid_layers` for an MLP or `fc_hid_layers` for a CNN. It iterates through the dimensions to construct fully connected `nn.Linear` layers (line 10) with added activation functions (lines 11–12). These layers then get collected into a `Sequential` container to form a full neural network (line 13).

Code 12.5 Automatic network construction: building fully connected layers

```
1   # slm_lab/agent/net/net_util.py
2
3   def build_fc_model(dims, activation):
4       '''Build a full-connected model by interleaving nn.Linear and
        ↪ activation_fn'''
5       assert len(dims) >= 2, 'dims need to at least contain input, output'
6       # shift dims and make pairs of (in, out) dims per layer
7       dim_pairs = list(zip(dims[:-1], dims[1:]))
8       layers = []
9       for in_d, out_d in dim_pairs:
10          layers.append(nn.Linear(in_d, out_d))
11          if activation is not None:
12              layers.append(get_activation_fn(activation))
13      model = nn.Sequential(*layers)
14      return model
```

The `build_conv_layers` method is defined inside the `ConvNet` class specifically to build convolutional layers in a similar manner, although it has extra details specific to convolutional networks.

Code 12.6 Automatic network construction: building convolutional layers

```
1   '# slm_lab/agent/net/conv.py
2
3   class ConvNet(Net, nn.Module):
4       ...
5
6       def build_conv_layers(self, conv_hid_layers):
7           '''
8           Builds all of the convolutional layers in the network and stores in a
            ↪ Sequential model
9           '''
10          conv_layers = []
11          in_d = self.in_dim[0]  # input channel
12          for i, hid_layer in enumerate(conv_hid_layers):
13              hid_layer = [tuple(e) if ps.is_list(e) else e for e in hid_layer]
                ↪ # guard list-to-tuple
14              # hid_layer = out_d, kernel, stride, padding, dilation
15              conv_layers.append(nn.Conv2d(in_d, *hid_layer))
16              if self.hid_layers_activation is not None:
17                  conv_layers.append(net_util.get_activation_fn(
                    ↪ self.hid_layers_activation))
18              # Don't include batch norm in the first layer
19              if self.batch_norm and i != 0:
20                  conv_layers.append(nn.BatchNorm2d(in_d))
21              in_d = hid_layer[0]  # update to out_d
22          conv_model = nn.Sequential(*conv_layers)
23          return conv_model
```

The source code for automatically building different types of neural networks is located in SLM Lab under `slm_lab/agent/net/`. It may be useful to read the code to gain a detailed understanding of the `Net` classes, but this is not necessary.

12.3.3 Training Step

The Net base class implements a standardized train_step method used by all the subclasses to make a network parameter update. This follows a standard deep learning training logic as shown in Code 12.7. The main steps are:

1. Update the learning rate using the learning rate scheduler and the clock (line 8).

2. Clear any existing gradients (line 9).

3. An algorithm will compute its loss before passing it into this method. Call loss.backward() to calculate the gradient using backpropagation (line 10).

4. Optionally clip the gradient (lines 11–12). This prevents overly large parameter updates.

5. Update the network parameters using the optimizer (line 15).

6. If training asynchronously, a global_net will be passed into this method to push local gradients to the global network (lines 13–14). After the network update, copy the latest global network parameters to the local network (lines 16–17).

7. A @net_util.dev_check_training_step function decorator is used to check if the network parameters are updated. This is only active in development mode, and is discussed in more detail in Section 10.2.

Code 12.7 Standardized method to make a network parameter update

```
1   # slm_lab/agent/net/base.py
2
3   class Net(ABC):
4       ...
5
6       @net_util.dev_check_train_step
7       def train_step(self, loss, optim, lr_scheduler, clock, global_net=None):
8           lr_scheduler.step(epoch=ps.get(clock, 'frame'))
9           optim.zero_grad()
10          loss.backward()
11          if self.clip_grad_val is not None:
12              nn.utils.clip_grad_norm_(self.parameters(), self.clip_grad_val)
13          if global_net is not None:
14              net_util.push_global_grads(self, global_net)
15          optim.step()
16          if global_net is not None:
17              net_util.copy(global_net, self)
18          clock.tick('opt_step')
19          return loss
```

12.3.4 **Exposure of Underlying Methods**

Code 12.8 shows a number of examples of how useful PyTorch features can be exposed in SLM Lab with minimal code.

get_activation_fn (lines 3–6) and get_optim (lines 22–27) show how the components in a net spec are used to retrieve and initialize the relevant PyTorch classes to be used by the Net classes.

get_lr_scheduler (lines 8–20) is a simple wrapper around PyTorch's LRSchedulerClass. It can also use custom schedulers defined in SLM Lab.

save (lines 29–31) and load (lines 33–36) are simple methods to save and load network parameters at checkpoints.

Code 12.8   Exposing common PyTorch functionality

```
1   # slm_lab/agent/net/net_util.py
2
3   def get_activation_fn(activation):
4       '''Helper to generate activation function layers for net'''
5       ActivationClass = getattr(nn, get_nn_name(activation))
6       return ActivationClass()
7
8   def get_lr_scheduler(optim, lr_scheduler_spec):
9       '''Helper to parse lr_scheduler param and construct PyTorch
        ↪   optim.lr_scheduler'''
10      if ps.is_empty(lr_scheduler_spec):
11          lr_scheduler = NoOpLRScheduler(optim)
12      elif lr_scheduler_spec['name'] == 'LinearToZero':
13          LRSchedulerClass = getattr(torch.optim.lr_scheduler, 'LambdaLR')
14          frame = float(lr_scheduler_spec['frame'])
15          lr_scheduler = LRSchedulerClass(optim, lr_lambda=lambda x: 1 - x /
            ↪   frame)
16      else:
17          LRSchedulerClass = getattr(torch.optim.lr_scheduler,
            ↪   lr_scheduler_spec['name'])
18          lr_scheduler_spec = ps.omit(lr_scheduler_spec, 'name')
19          lr_scheduler = LRSchedulerClass(optim, **lr_scheduler_spec)
20      return lr_scheduler
21
22  def get_optim(net, optim_spec):
23      '''Helper to parse optim param and construct optim for net'''
24      OptimClass = getattr(torch.optim, optim_spec['name'])
25      optim_spec = ps.omit(optim_spec, 'name')
26      optim = OptimClass(net.parameters(), **optim_spec)
27      return optim
28
```

```
29   def save(net, model_path):
30       '''Save model weights to path'''
31       torch.save(net.state_dict(), util.smart_path(model_path))
32
33   def load(net, model_path):
34       '''Save model weights from a path into a net module'''
35       device = None if torch.cuda.is_available() else 'cpu'
36       net.load_state_dict(torch.load(util.smart_path(model_path),
         ↪    map_location=device))
```

12.4 Summary

This chapter focused on the design and implementation of neural networks for deep RL. We gave a brief overview of the three main network families, MLPs, CNNs, and RNNs, and discussed some guidelines for selecting an appropriate network family based on an environment's characteristics.

An important characteristic is whether an environment is an MDP or a POMDP. A POMDP can be one of three types—fully observable given partial history, fully observable given full history, and never fully observable.

MLPs and CNNs are well suited to solving MDPs and POMDPs that are fully observable given partial history. RNNs and RNN-CNNs are well suited to solving POMDPs that are fully observable given full history. RNNs may also improve performance in POMDPs that are never fully observable, but this is not guaranteed.

There are a set of frequently used methods that are standardized as part of the Net API for reusability. They make algorithm implementation simpler. These include input and output layer shape inference, automatic network construction, and a standardized training step.

12.5 Further Reading

- General
  - *Neural Networks and Deep Learning*, Nielsen, 2015 [92].
  - *Deep Learning*, Goodfellow et al., 2016 [45].
- CNNs
  - "Generalization and Network Design Strategies," LeCun, 1989 [71].
  - "Neural Networks and Neuroscience-Inspired Computer Vision," Cox and Dean, 2014 [28].

- RNNs
    - "The Unreasonable Effectiveness of Recurrent Neural Networks," Karpathy, 2015 [66].
    - "Natural Language Understanding with Distributed Representation," Cho, 2015, pp. 11–53 [20].
    - "Reinforcement Learning with Long Short-Term Memory," Bakker, 2002 [10].
    - "OpenAI Five," OpenAI Blog, 2018 [104].

13

Hardware

Deep RL owes part of its success to the arrival of powerful hardware. To implement or use deep RL algorithms, one inevitably needs to understand some basic details about a computer. These algorithms also require a significant amount of data, memory, and computational resources. When training agents it is useful to be able to estimate an algorithm's memory and computing requirements and to manage data efficiently.

This chapter is intended to build intuition for the types of data encountered in deep RL, their sizes, and how to optimize them. We first briefly describe how hardware components such as CPU, RAM, and GPU work and interact. Then, in Section 13.2 we give an overview of data types. Section 13.3 discusses the common types of data in deep RL and provides some guidelines for managing them. The chapter ends with some reference hardware requirements to run different types of deep RL experiments.

This information is useful for in-depth debugging and for managing or choosing hardware for deep RL.

13.1 Computer

Computers are ubiquitous these days. They are in our phones, laptops, desktops, and in the cloud (remote servers). We have come a long way since Ada Lovelace wrote the first algorithm and Alan Turing envisioned the general-purpose computer, the Turing machine. The first computers were massive mechanical devices made with actual moving parts, with programs being fed in as punch cards, and computer bugs were, well, real bugs.[1] Today, the computer is electronic, small, fast, and very different in appearance from its ancestors. Most people use it without wondering how it works—this is a privilege of living in the computing age.

Even as it evolves, a computer is still an implementation of a Turing machine, and this means certain elements of its design are unchanging. A computer consists of a processor and a random-access memory, which correspond to the head and tape of a Turing machine. The architecture of a modern computer is much more complicated than that,

---

1. A fun fact on the origin of the term "computer bug": it literally referred to a bug that got inside an early mechanical computer and caused it to malfunction. People had to open up the computer to clean it out.

mostly to handle practical issues such as data storage, data transfer, and read/write speed. At the end of the day, a computer still processes information, and the processor and memory are always present.

Let's look at the processor first. Today, it comes packed with a number of processing cores known as central processing units (CPUs)—for example, dual-core or quad-core. Each core can be hyperthreaded, allowing it to run more than one thread simultaneously. This is why processor packaging may say, for example, "2 cores 4 threads," implying that it contains two cores, with two threads each.

Let's look at this example in more detail. A computer with two cores and four threads may show the number of threads as the number of CPUs, even though the number of cores is lower. This is because with the four threads, it can run four processes at 100% process utilization each. However, if needed, we can choose to run only two processes without hyperthreading and maximize the two cores. This is how a CPU may show 200% process utilization. The maximum percentage depends on how many threads there are in a single core.

Depending on the mode, the cores may reorganize and act as if there are more CPUs. For this reason, the true cores are known as physical CPUs, while the organized threads are known as logical CPUs. This can be checked using a terminal command `lscpu` on Linux, or `system_profiler SPHardwareDataType` on MacOS. Code 13.1 shows a Linux server with 32 logical CPUs, which is in fact 16 physical CPUs with 2 threads per core.

Code 13.1 Example output of the command `lscpu` to show the CPU information on a Linux server. This machine has 16 physical cores and 32 logical cores, and the CPU speed is 2.30GHz.

```
1   # On Linux, run `lscpu` to show the CPU info
2   $ lscpu
3   Architecture:          x86_64
4   CPU op-mode(s):        32-bit, 64-bit
5   Byte Order:            Little Endian
6   CPU(s):                32
7   On-line CPU(s) list:   0-31
8   Thread(s) per core:    2
9   Core(s) per socket:    16
10  Socket(s):             1
11  NUMA node(s):          1
12  Vendor ID:             GenuineIntel
13  CPU family:            6
14  Model:                 79
15  Model name:            Intel(R) Xeon(R) CPU E5-2686 v4 @ 2.30GHz
16  Stepping:              1
17  CPU MHz:               2699.625
18  CPU max MHz:           3000.0000
19  CPU min MHz:           1200.0000
20  BogoMIPS:              4600.18
21  Hypervisor vendor:     Xen
```

```
22  Virtualization type:    full
23  L1d cache:              32K
24  L1i cache:              32K
25  L2 cache:               256K
26  L3 cache:               46080K
27  NUMA node0 CPU(s):      0-31
28  ...
```

This implies that we can choose to run more processes more slowly by maximizing the threads, or run fewer processes faster by maximizing the cores. The former mode is great for hyperparameter search where a lot of parallel sessions are run, while the latter is helpful for running a few specific training sessions faster. The limitation is that a single process cannot utilize more than one physical core, so we get no benefit from running fewer processes than the number of physical cores.

A CPU has an internal clock which ticks once every operation, and the clock speed measures the speed of the processor. This is apparent in the model name in Code 13.1 (line 15) as the frequency of 2.30GHz, meaning 2.3 billion clock cycles per second. The true clock speed at a given time may vary depending on multiple factors such as the CPU temperature for safe operation (electronics are still made of physical parts which may overheat).

A CPU can be overclocked to make it run even faster. This can be enabled in the BIOS during booting, but before doing this people usually protect their CPUs with some serious liquid cooling. For deep RL this is not necessary, and it's not doable when using servers remotely—but if you own a personal desktop, it is an option.

Now, let's look at the computer memory. There are multiple types of memory in a computer, organized hierarchically from the closest to the CPU to the furthest. Memory closer to the CPU has a lower transfer latency, therefore data access is faster. On the other hand, it also tends to be smaller because a large amount of memory won't fit into a small CPU. To make up for this, the most frequently accessed chunks of data are put into memory that's closer to the CPU, while the larger but less frequently accessed data is placed further away.

Right inside the CPU are the registers that hold the instructions and data being processed—this is the smallest and the fastest memory. Next is the cache which keeps data that will be reused frequently to prevent duplicate computation. The different cache memories, all slower than registers, are also shown in Code 13.1 (lines 23–26).

Next, we have the Random Access Memory (RAM). This is where data is loaded and placed into during a program's runtime to be processed by the CPUs. RAM is what we refer to when we say "loading data into memory" or "a process is out of memory." A computer motherboard usually fits four or more RAM slots, so if we replace four 4GB cards with four 16GB cards, the memory is upgraded from 16GB to 64GB.

When running a program, one typically cares about the CPU and RAM utilizations. CPU usage has been described above. When reading RAM usage, there are two numbers displayed—VIRT (virtual memory) and RES (resident memory). An example screenshot of a system dashboard generated with Glances [44] is shown in Figure 13.1; in the list of

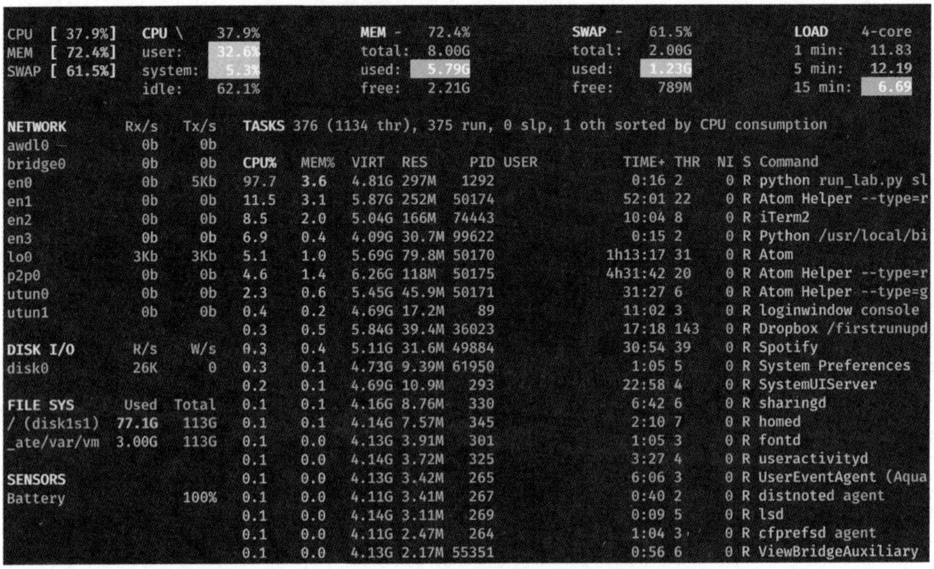

```
CPU  [ 37.9%]   CPU \    37.9%          MEM -    72.4%        SWAP -    61.5%              LOAD    4-core
MEM  [ 72.4%]   user:    32.6%          total:   8.00G        total:   2.00G              1 min:   11.83
SWAP [ 61.5%]   system:  5.3%           used:    5.79G        used:    1.23G              5 min:   12.19
                idle:    62.1%          free:    2.21G        free:    789M              15 min:   6.69

NETWORK    Rx/s   Tx/s    TASKS 376 (1134 thr), 375 run, 0 slp, 1 oth sorted by CPU consumption
awdl0      0b     0b
bridge0    0b     0b     CPU%   MEM%   VIRT   RES    PID USER        TIME+   THR  NI S Command
en0        0b     5Kb    97.7   3.6    4.81G  297M   1292             0:16 2      0 R python run_lab.py sl
en1        0b     0b     11.5   3.1    5.87G  252M   50174           52:01 22     0 R Atom Helper --type=r
en2        0b     0b     8.5    2.0    5.04G  166M   74443           10:04 8      0 R iTerm2
en3        0b     0b     6.9    0.4    4.09G  30.7M  99622            0:15 2      0 R Python /usr/local/bi
lo0        3Kb    3Kb    5.1    1.0    5.69G  79.8M  50170         1h13:17 31     0 R Atom
p2p0       0b     0b     4.6    1.4    6.26G  118M   50175         4h31:42 20     0 R Atom Helper --type=r
utun0      0b     0b     2.3    0.6    5.45G  45.9M  50171          31:27 6      0 R Atom Helper --type=g
utun1      0b     0b     0.4    0.2    4.69G  17.2M  89             11:02 3      0 R loginwindow console
                        0.3    0.5    5.84G  39.4M  36023          17:18 143    0 R Dropbox /firstrunupd
DISK I/O   R/s    W/s    0.3    0.4    5.11G  31.6M  49884          30:54 39     0 R Spotify
disk0      26K    0      0.3    0.1    4.73G  9.39M  61950           1:05 5      0 R System Preferences
                        0.2    0.1    4.69G  10.9M  293            22:58 4      0 R SystemUIServer
FILE SYS   Used   Total  0.1    0.1    4.16G  8.76M  330             6:42 6      0 R sharingd
/ (disk1s1) 77.1G 113G   0.1    0.1    4.14G  7.57M  345             2:10 7      0 R homed
_ate/var/vm 3.00G 113G   0.1    0.0    4.13G  3.91M  301             1:05 3      0 R fontd
                        0.1    0.0    4.14G  3.72M  325             3:27 4      0 R useractivityd
                        0.1    0.0    4.13G  3.42M  265             6:06 3      0 R UserEventAgent (Aqua
SENSORS                 0.1    0.0    4.11G  3.41M  267             0:40 2      0 R distnoted agent
Battery            100%  0.1    0.0    4.14G  3.11M  269             0:09 5      0 R lsd
                        0.1    0.0    4.11G  2.47M  264             1:04 3      0 R cfprefsd agent
                        0.1    0.0    4.13G  2.17M  55351           0:56 6      0 R ViewBridgeAuxiliary
```

Figure 13.1   A screenshot of a system dashboard generated using the monitoring tool Glances [44]. This shows crucial stats such as CPU load, memory usage, I/O, and processes.

processes, the main columns display CPU usage %, memory (RAM) usage %, VIRT, and RES.

A quick glance at the top of the figure shows that the total RAM (MEM total) of this computer is 8.00GB. Looking at the first row of the table of tasks, we can see a process running at 97.7% CPU utilization.

The actual amount of RAM occupied by a process is shown as the resident memory RES—it is quite small, which is also reflected honestly in the MEM %. For example, the top process uses 3.6% of the RAM, which corresponds to 297M resident memory of the total 8GB available.

However, the virtual memory consumption far exceeds that—with the VIRT column summing to over 40GBs. The virtual RAM is in fact simply an estimate of the amount of memory a program might claim. For example, declaring a large empty array in a Python runtime will add to the virtual memory estimate, but no memory will be occupied until the array starts getting filled with actual data.

The size of the virtual memory is not a problem as long as the resident memory does not exceed the actual amount of RAM available—otherwise we risk running out of memory and crashing the computer.

Register, cache, and RAM are fast runtime memories used for computation, but they are nonpersistent. When a computer is rebooted, these memories usually get cleared. For storing information more permanently, a computer uses a hard drive or a portable storage device such as a memory stick. Depending on hardware, a drive can store a large amount of information with decent read/write speed—this is shown on the left side of Figure 13.1 under DISK I/O and FILE SYS. Nevertheless, this kind of memory is still significantly slower than nonpersistent memories. As memory gets further away from the processor, its read/write speed decreases but its storage capacity expands. This rule of thumb is useful when deciding how to manage data during a training session.

A CPU, coupled with its random-access memory, is a general-purpose device. Without a CPU, a computer ceases to be a computer. Computing power has been increasing exponentially, following Moore's law. However, our computing demands seem to always accelerate even more rapidly because bigger computers open up new frontiers of problems to tackle. The rise of deep learning is a great example—symbiotically, it even helps drive the hardware industry.

Although CPUs are general-purpose and quite powerful, they cannot always keep up with our computing demands. Fortunately, some of the things we compute very frequently consist of particular types of operations. For this, one can design specialized hardware that computes these operations very efficiently by giving up the computational generality of a CPU.

One such example is matrix operations. Since matrices can encode and compute data transformations, they are the foundation of image rendering. Camera movement, mesh construction, lighting, shadow casting, and ray tracing are all typical computer graphics functions used in any rendering engine, and they are all matrix operations. A video that renders at a high frame rate needs to compute a lot of these—which motivated the development of the graphics processing unit (GPU).

The video game industry was the first to make use of GPUs. The precursor to the GPU was the graphics processor inside arcade machines. These developed with the growth of personal computers and video games, and in 1999 Nvidia invented the GPU [95]. In parallel, creative studios such as Pixar and Adobe also helped lay the foundation for the computer graphics industry by creating and spreading the software and algorithms for GPUs. Gamers, graphics designers, and animators became the primary consumers of GPUs.

Convolutional networks which process images also involve many matrix operations. Therefore, it was only a matter of time until deep learning researchers started adopting GPUs as well. When this finally happened, the field of deep learning rapidly accelerated.

A GPU computes expensive matrix computations, freeing up the CPUs to perform other tasks. A GPU performs computations in parallel and is highly efficient at what it does because it is so specialized. Compared to a CPU, a GPU has many more processing cores, and it has an analogous memory architecture—registers, caches, and RAM, though its RAM is typically smaller. To send data to a GPU for processing, it first needs to be loaded into the GPU RAM. Code 13.2 shows an example of moving a PyTorch tensor created on a CPU into the GPU RAM.

Code 13.2 An example of creating a PyTorch tensor on a CPU and then moving it into the GPU RAM

```
1  # example code to move a tensor created on CPU into GPU (RAM)
2  import torch
3
4  # specify device only if available
```

```
5   device = 'cuda:0' if torch.cuda.is_available() else 'cpu'
6
7   # tensor is created on CPU first
8   v = torch.ones((64, 64, 1), dtype=torch.float32)
9   # moving to GPU
10  v = v.to(device)
```

With GPUs, computations that are slow on CPUs get accelerated dramatically. This opened up new possibilities in deep learning—researchers started training larger and deeper networks with more and more data. This drove state-of-the-art results in many areas, including computer vision, natural language processing, and speech recognition. GPUs have helped fuel the rapid developments in deep learning and related fields, including deep RL.

Despite their efficacy, GPUs are still optimized for graphics processing, not neural network computations. For industrial applications, even GPUs have limitations. This motivated the development of another type of specialized processor. In 2016, Google announced its tensor processing unit (TPU) to meet this need. This helped to deliver "an order of magnitude better-optimized performance" for deep learning applications [58]. In fact, DeepMind's deep RL algorithm AlphaGo was powered by TPUs.

In this section on computer hardware, we discussed the basic makeup of a computer—processor and memory. A CPU is a general-purpose processor, but it is limited in the amount of data it can process at once. A GPU has many cores which specialize in parallel computation. A TPU specializes in tensor computation for neural networks. Regardless of its specialization, every processor needs a properly designed memory architecture, including registers, caches, and RAM.

13.2   Data Types

To compute efficiently, we need to understand a problem's space and time complexities. For any data-intense applications such as deep RL, it helps to understand some of the important details and processes that are involved at all levels, from software to hardware. So far, we have seen how a computer is organized; now, let's build some intuition for data that is commonly encountered in deep RL.

A bit is the smallest unit used to measure the size of information. Modern data is extremely large, so a bigger scale is needed. For historical reasons, 8 bits is 1 byte, or 8b = 1B. From there, a metric prefix is used. 1,000 bytes is 1 kilobyte (kB), 1,000,000 bytes is 1 megabyte (MB), and so on.

Information encoding is general, so any data can be encoded as digital bits. Data, if it is not already numerical, gets converted into numbers before being represented as raw bits in hardware. An image gets converted into pixel values, sound into frequencies and amplitudes, categorical data into one-hot encodings, words into vectors, and so on. A prerequisite to making data representable by a computer is to make it numerical. Numbers then get converted into bits on the hardware level.

By design, the smallest memory chunk commonly used to encode numbers is 1 byte, or 8 bits. Using the power rule, we know that a bit string of length 8 has the capacity to represent $2^8 = 256$ distinct messages, so 1 byte can represent 256 distinct numbers. A numerical library such as numpy [143] uses this to implement integers of different ranges, namely unsigned 8-bit integers uint8: $[0, 255]$ and signed 8-bit integers int8: $[-128, 127]$.

Bytes are suitable for storing data with small numerical ranges, such as the pixel values in a grayscale image (0–255), as a byte occupies minimum space in the memory. A single uint8 number is 8 bits = 1 byte in size, so for an image grayscaled and downsized to 84×84 pixels, there are only 7,096 numbers to store—that is, 7096B $\approx$ 7kB. A million of these in the replay memory will take 7kB $\times$ 1,000,000 = 7GB which fits in most modern computers' RAM.

Obviously, such a small range is insufficient for most computational purposes. By doubling the size of bit string, we can implement a 16-bit integer with a far larger range, int16: $[-32768, 32768]$. Moreover, since a 16-bit string is sufficiently long, it can also be used to implement floating-point numbers known as "floats," which are numbers with decimals. This yields the 16-bit float float16. The implementation of floats, which we will not discuss here, is quite different from integers; despite this difference, both 16-bit integers and floats use bit strings of the same size of 16 bits = 2 bytes.

The same bit-doubling scheme can be repeated to implement integers and floats of 32 bits and 64 bits, which occupy 4 and 8 bytes respectively, and yield int32, float32, int64, float64. However, every doubling of the number of bits will halve the compute speed, since there are twice as many elements in the bit string to perform binary operations on. More bits is not always better, as it comes with the cost of larger size and slower computation.

Integers can be implemented as int8, int16, int32, int64 with a range of values centered at 0. Unsigned integers can be implemented as uint8, uint16, uint32, uint64 by shifting the range of values to start from 0. The differences between integers with different numbers of bits are the size, computing speed, and the range of values they can represent.

When a signed integer int is assigned a value beyond its range, it will overflow with undefined behavior and break the arithmetic. An unsigned integer uint never overflows—instead, it silently calculates using the modulus, for example np.uint8(257) = np.uint8(1). This behavior may be desirable for some specific applications—but in general, beware of this when downcasting unsigned integer-valued data. If extreme values need to be capped, clip them first before downcasting. These are shown in Code 13.3.

Code 13.3 A simple script showing size comparison and optimization methods for different data types

```
1  import numpy as np
2
3  # beware of range overflow when downcasting
4  np.array([0, 255, 256, 257], dtype=np.uint8)
5  # => array([  0, 255,   0,   1], dtype=uint8)
6
7  # if max value is 255, first clip then downcast
```

```
8    np.clip(np.array([0, 255, 256, 257], dtype=np.int16), 0, 255).astype(np.uint8)
9    # => array([  0, 255, 255, 255], dtype=uint8)
```

Floating-point numbers can be implemented starting from 16 bits as float16, float32, or float64. The differences are the size, computing speed, and the precision of decimals they can represent—more bits have higher precision. This is why float16 is known as half-precision, float32 as single-precision, and float64 as double-precision (or just "double"). There is no implementation of 8-bit floats because the low precision is unreliable for most applications. Half precision can be computed twice as fast as single precision and is sufficient for computations that do not need to be accurate to as many decimal places. It is also ideal for storage, as most raw data does not use that many decimal places. For most computations, single precision suffices, and it is the most common type used by many programs, including deep learning. Double precision is mostly reserved for serious scientific computing such as physics equations that need to be accurate to many significant digits. Byte size, speed, range, precision, and overflow behavior are some of the things to consider when choosing the appropriate type to represent floating-point values.

13.3   Optimizing Data Types in RL

So far we have gained some understanding of how numerical data manifests in hardware, along with the considerations of size, compute speed, range, and precision. Code 13.4 contains some examples of these data types in numpy and their sizes in memory. Let's now look at how they relate to the data we commonly encounter in deep learning and deep RL.

Code 13.4   A simple script showing the various data types and their sizes

```
1    import numpy as np
2
3    # Basic data types and sizes
4
5    # data is encoded as bits in the machine
6    # and so data size is determined by the number of bits
7    # e.g., np.int16 and np.float16 are both 2 bytes, although float is
     ↪   represented differently than int
8
9    # 8-bit unsigned integer, range: [0, 255]
10   # size: 8 bits = 1 byte
11   # useful for storing images or low-range states
12   np.uint8(1).nbytes
13
14   # 16-bit int, range: [-32768, 32768]
15   # size: 16 bits = 2 bytes
16   np.int16(1).nbytes
```

```
17
18   # 32-bit int, 4 bytes
19   np.int32(1).nbytes
20
21   # 64-bit int, 8 bytes
22   np.int64(1).nbytes
23
24   # half-precision float, 2 bytes
25   # may be less precise for computation, but ok for most data storage
26   np.float16(1).nbytes
27
28   # single-precision float, 4 bytes
29   # used by default most computations
30   np.float32(1).nbytes
31
32   # double-precision float, 8 bytes
33   # mostly reserved for high-precision computations
34   np.float64(1).nbytes
```

By default in most libraries, a neural network initializes and computes using float32. This means that all of its input data needs to be cast to float32. However, float32 is not always ideal for data storage because of its large byte size (32b = 4B). Suppose a frame of RL data is 10kB, and we need to store 1 million frames in a replay memory. The total size is 10GB, which will not fit into a typical RAM during runtime. It is therefore common to downcast the data and store it in half-precision float16.

Most of the data we need to store in deep RL consists of the state, action, reward, and a boolean "done" signal indicating the end of an episode. Additionally, there are auxiliary variables necessary for specific algorithms or for debugging, such as the V- and Q-values, log probabilities, and entropies. Typically, these values are either small integers or low-precision floats, so uint8, int8, or float16 are suitable options for storage.

Let's take a million frames as a standard amount of data to be stored in a replay memory. Except for states, many of these variables are scalars. For each scalar variable, storing a million values requires a million elements. When using uint8, it will take $1,000,000 \times 1B = 1MB$, whereas float16 will take $1,000,000 \times 2B = 2MB$. The difference of 1MB in size is quite insignificant for modern computers, so it is common to use float16 for all of them to eliminate the risks of accidentally dropping the decimals or restricting the value range.

However, a lot of memory optimization effort goes into states because they usually constitute most of the data generated in deep RL. If a state is a relatively small tensor, for example a vector of length 4 in CartPole, we can use float16. It is only when each state is large—such as an image—that we need to optimize. These days, images generated from cameras or game engines typically have high resolution that can run above 1920×1080 pixels, and such an image may be several MB in size. Suppose a state is a small RGB image of 256×256 pixels with `float32` values. Then one image state is $(256 \times 256 \times 3) \times 4B$ = 786432B $\approx$ 786kB, and loading a million of these into RAM will require 786GB. This is beyond the capacity of even large servers.

By grayscaling the image, three color channels are reduced to one, so the size shrinks to 262GB, but this is still too big. By downsampling from 256×256 to 84×84 pixels, the size is reduced by roughly 9 times to $\approx$ 28GB. This compression will lose some information, and the downsampled pixel values will depend on the compression algorithm. Note also that the original RGB values are integers with range 0–255, but grayscaling converts them to a single `float32` pixel value with range 0.0–255.0. Most tasks do not require high-precision pixel values, so they can be converted back to `uint8`, which reduces the size further by 4 times.

In the final form, a grayscaled image of 84×84 pixels with `uint8` values occupies just $84 \times 84 \times 1B$ = 7096B. A million of these take up $\approx$ 7GB, which easily fits into the RAM of most modern computers. The data sizes of all these optimization stages are compared in Code 13.5.

Code 13.5   The sizes at different stages of optimizing data for storage in a replay memory

```
1   import numpy as np
2
3   # Handy data sizes for debugging RAM usage
4
5   # replay memory with 1 million uint8 data = 1MB
6   np.ones((1000000, 1), dtype=np.uint8).nbytes
7
8   # replay memory with 1 million float16 data = 2MB
9   np.ones((1000000, 1), dtype=np.float16).nbytes
10
11  # a downsized greyscale image with uint8 range ~ 7kB
12  np.ones((84, 84, 1), dtype=np.uint8).nbytes
13
14  # replay memory with a million images ~ 7GB
15  np.ones((1000000, 84, 84, 1), dtype=np.uint8).nbytes
16
17  # a raw small image is ~ 262kB, 37 times larger than above
18  # a million of these would be 262GB, too large for standard computers
19  np.ones((256, 256, 1), dtype=np.float32).nbytes
```

When running an actual RL algorithm, the memory consumption of the process can be larger than contributions from the state, action, reward, and "done" data alone. In value-based algorithms, the replay memory also needs to store the next state when adding the tuple (s, a, r, s'). When preprocessing states from an Atari game, four frames are concatenated together. These considerations may increase the memory footprint by a few times, although the amount of raw states needed in theory does not change.

To ensure efficient memory management, it is worth extra effort to ensure that only the minimal required amount of data is stored. The general strategy is to keep soft variable references to the raw data and only resolve them when needed for computation. For example, we can concatenate frames from the raw states to produce a larger preprocessed state right before passing them into a network.

Besides data, another significant source of memory consumption is the neural network itself. A feedforward network of two layers can take up to 100MB in RAM, whereas a convolutional network can take up to 2GB. A `Tensor` object also takes up some RAM when accumulating gradients for autograd, although it is usually a few MBs in size depending on the batch size. All these have to be accounted for as well when running a training session.

Having discussed efficient information storage in CPU RAM and GPU RAM, we now consider how to move the data from storage into computation in a neural network.

Since data transfer has latency imposed by hardware, one needs to follow a strategy when creating and moving data. When transferring data, less is better, so it helps to optimize storage as we discussed above. The goal is to ensure that data transfer is not a bottleneck in the training process—such as when the CPU/GPU is idle waiting for data transfer, or when most of the processing time is spent on moving or copying data.

The part of a computer's memory that is closest to the processors and that we typically have programmatic control over is the RAM. As long as we load data efficiently into RAM, the major transfer bottleneck has already been eliminated.

Before being passed into a neural network, data needs to be converted into a `Tensor` object to support various differential operations such as autograd. If the data is already loaded as `numpy` data in the CPU RAM, PyTorch simply refers to this same `numpy` data to construct the `Tensor` without extra copying, making it extremely efficient and easy to work with. An example of this `numpy-to-Tensor` operation is shown in Code 13.6. From there, it passes directly from the CPU RAM into CPUs for computation.

Code 13.6   PyTorch uses numpy data in the CPU RAM to directly construct a Tensor.

```
1   import numpy as np
2   import torch
3
4   # Storage-to-compute tips
5
6   # Often, raw data comes in high precision format such as float64
7   # but this is not so useful for learning (e.g., a high-def game image)
8   # for storage, use a low-precision int/float
9   # to reduce RAM usage by up to x8 (e.g., float64 to uint8)
10
11  # for float data, downcasting to float16 is ok for storage
12  state = np.ones((4), dtype=np.float16)
```

```
13
14   # for storing an image into replay memory and fitting into RAM
15   # use an optimized format by downsizing and downcasting
16   im = np.ones((84, 84, 1), dtype=np.uint8)
17
18   # just right before feeding into a neural network for compute
19   # cast into a consumable format, usually float32
20   im_tensor = torch.from_numpy(im.astype(np.float32))
```

If we wish to use a GPU to compute, the tensors need to be transferred from CPU RAM into GPU RAM. This takes extra time to copy and construct data in the new location. For large networks, this transfer overhead is compensated by the computational speedup from a GPU. However, for smaller networks (e.g., a single hidden layer with less than 1000 units), a GPU does not provide a significant speedup over a CPU, so training will potentially be slower overall due to the transfer overhead. Therefore, a rule of thumb is to not utilize a GPU for small networks.

Since most of the neural networks in deep RL are relatively small, often GPUs are not fully utilized. The other bottleneck can arise from the environment if the data generation process is slow. Recall that GPUs were originally created for gaming, so most game engines can be accelerated with a GPU. Other physics engines or environments may also come with this option. Therefore, it is possible to utilize GPU to speed up environment data generation as well.

Another potential bottleneck arises when parallelizing algorithm training using multiple processes. When we use multiple distributed nodes on multiple machines, communication between the machines can be slow. If it is possible to run the training on a single larger machine, this is preferable because it eliminates the communication bottleneck.

Additionally, within a single machine, the fastest way for multiple parallel workers to share data is by sharing RAM. This eliminates data transfer between processes. PyTorch's native integration with Python's multiprocessing module does precisely this by calling a network's `share_memory()` to share a global network's parameters with all the worker processes, as shown in Code 8.1 of Chapter 8.

An extreme scenario is when the data size is so large that it cannot fit in the RAM but can only be stored in the persistent memory. Disk read/write is extremely slow compared to moving data within RAM, so one needs an intelligent strategy to deal with this. For instance, we can schedule the loading of a chunk of data required by computation before it is needed, so the processors do not have to wait. Once a data chunk is no longer needed, remove it to free up the RAM for the next chunk.

To sum up, the factors we care about when it comes to hardware include where to compute (CPU or GPU), where to put the data (RAM), how much data can fit into RAM, and how to avoid the data generation and transfer bottlenecks.

13.4 Choosing Hardware

With the practical information presented so far, we can use our intuition about data to give some reference hardware requirements for deep RL.

All the nonimage-based environments discussed in this book can run on a laptop. Only the image-based environments such as the Atari games benefit from a GPU. For these, we recommend one GPU and at least four CPUs. This can run a single Atari `Trial` consisting of four `Sessions`.

For desktops, a reference spec is GTX 1080 GPU, four CPUs above 3.0GHz, and 32GB RAM. Tim Dettmers has an excellent guide for building desktops for deep learning available at `https://timdettmers.com/2018/12/16/deep-learning-hardware-guide` [33]. A different option is to rent a remote server in the cloud. A good place to start is an instance of a server with a GPU and four CPUs.

However, for more extensive experimentation, more computing power is desirable. For desktops, this generally means increasing the number of CPUs. In the cloud, one option is to rent a server with 32 CPUs and 8 GPUs. Alternatively, consider a server with 64 CPUs and no GPU. In Chapter 8 we saw that some algorithms such as A2C can be parallelized with many CPUs to compensate for the lack of GPUs.

13.5 Summary

In deep RL, it is helpful to be able to estimate the memory and computing requirements of an algorithm. In this chapter, we built some intuitions for the size of basic data types encountered in RL, such as vector and image states. We also highlighted some ways in which the memory requirements of an algorithm can increase.

We also briefly looked at the different types of processors—CPUs and GPUs. GPUs are most commonly used to speed up training on image-based environments.

The tips introduced in this chapter are intended to help optimize memory consumption in deep RL algorithms in order to use computational resources more efficiently.

Part IV

Environment Design

14

States

Solving a new problem using deep RL involves creating an environment. We will therefore now shift our focus from algorithms to the components of environment design—which are the states, actions, rewards, and the transition function. When designing an environment, we first model the problem and then decide what information, and how, our environment should present to its users.

It is essential that an RL environment provides sufficient information to an algorithm so that it can solve a problem. This is one crucial role of states, which are the subject of this chapter.

First, we will give some examples of states both in the real world and in RL environments. In the sections that follow, we consider the following questions which are important when designing a state:

1. **Completeness:** Does the state representation include sufficient information from the world to solve the problem?
2. **Complexity:** How effective is the representation, and how computationally expensive it is?
3. **Information loss:** Does a representation lose any information—for example, when grayscaling or downsampling an image?

In the final section, we look at some commonly used state-preprocessing techniques.

14.1 Examples of States

A state is information that describes an environment. It can also be referred to as an "observable"—that is, a set of quantities that can be measured.[1] States are more than just numbers representing a game or simulator running on a computer. In the same spirit, an environment is more than just a computer simulation for an RL problem; environments include real-world systems. Let's look at some example states.

---

1. This definition of an observable is widely used in physics and plays a foundational role in many theories, including quantum mechanics.

What we see, hear, and touch are all states of the environment that surrounds us. It is information that we can "measure" with our perceptions via sensory organs such as eyes, ears, and skin. Apart from the raw sensory information, states can also include abstract information, such as the velocity of a moving object.

There is also information that we can detect indirectly, using tools—for example, magnetic fields, infrared light, ultrasound, and more recently gravitational waves.[2] Animals, with perceptions different to ours, sense their surroundings differently. For instance, dogs are red-green colorblind, but they can smell much better than humans.

All of these examples are states—information about an environment *measured* through different instruments of perception, whether biological or mechanical. The same environment may yield different information depending on the context and what gets measured—that is, information may change according to one's perspective. This is one crucial idea to bear in mind, and it should be a guiding principle for designing information-processing systems—not just in RL but in everyday things as well.

Real-world environments contain a lot of complex information. Fortunately, there are ways to manage this complexity, which is the subject of this chapter. For now, let's look at some simple examples. Video games, such as the classic Atari games (Figure 14.1), have states that are observable via vision and sound—game graphics on a screen and sound from a speaker. Robots, either physical or simulated, have higher-level states such as their joint angles, speed, and torque. States in RL tend to get simplified to exclude irrelevant background noise and side effects and to focus only on information the designer deems relevant. For instance, a robotic simulation may not account for friction, drag, thermal expansion, etc.

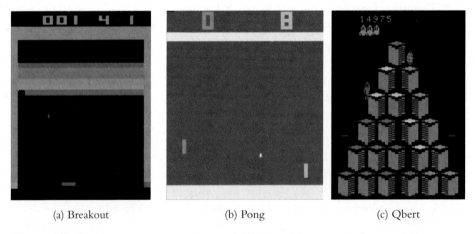

(a) Breakout   (b) Pong   (c) Qbert

Figure 14.1   Examples of Atari games with RGB colored images (rank-3 tensors) for states. These are available as part of OpenAI Gym's [18] offerings of the Arcade Learning Environment (ALE) [14].

---

2. In September 14, 2015, LIGO (operated by Caltech and MIT) detected gravitational waves for the first time [80]. This was truly a remarkable milestone in humanity's scientific achievements.

It is crucial to distinguish states from actions and rewards. A state is information about an environment—even when no action is taken or reward assigned. An action is an effect imposed on the environment by an entity which is not the environment—that is, an agent. A reward is a form of metainformation about a transition of states caused by an imposed action.

We can represent a state with any suitable data structure—for example, a scalar, a vector, or a generic tensor.[3] If not originally numerical, we can always encode it as such. For instance, in natural language, words or characters can be represented numerically using word embeddings. We can also biject[4] information to a list of integers. For example, the 88 keys of a piano can be uniquely labeled with the integers $[1, 2, \ldots, 88]$. A state can also have discrete or continuous values, or a mixture of both. For example, a kettle may indicate that it is on (discrete state) and provide its current temperature (continuous state). It is up to the designer to represent information in a suitable way for an algorithm to use.

A state s is an element of a state space $\mathcal{S}$, which fully defines all the values that the state of an environment can have. A state can have more than one element (dimension), and each element may be of any cardinality[5] (discrete or continuous). However, it is convenient to represent state using tensors with a single data type (int or float) because most computing libraries, such as numpy, PyTorch, or TensorFlow, expect this.

States can come in any ranks and shapes:[6]

- Scalar (rank-0 tensor): temperature
- Vector (rank-1 tensor): [position, velocity, angle, angular velocity]
- Matrix (rank-2 tensor): grayscale pixels from an Atari game
- Data cube (rank-3 tensor): RGB color pixels from an Atari game (see examples in Figure 14.1)

A state can also be a combination of tensors. For instance, a robotic simulator may provide the visual field of the robot as an RGB image (rank-3 tensor) and its joint angles as a separate vector. Having differently shaped tensors as inputs also requires a different neural network architecture to accommodate them; in this case, we consider the separate tensors to be substates which together form the overall state.

Having described what states are in general, let's now look at the workflow for designing a state, shown in Figure 14.2. The process begins by deciding what information to include about the world and in what form. For example, the electromagnetic spectrum can be represented in many different ways using lidar or radar data, RGB images, depth maps, thermal images, etc. The information that is ultimately selected can be described as the *raw state*.

---

3. A tensor is a generalized information cube of N dimensions. A scalar (single number) is a rank-0 tensor; a vector (list of numbers) is rank-1; a matrix (table of numbers) is rank-2; a cube is rank-3, and so on.

4. Bijection is a mathematical term for a one-to-one and onto mapping of two sets of elements—that is, sets with mutual one-to-one correspondence. In our applications, we usually biject a set to a list of integers starting from 0.

5. Cardinality is a measure of the "size" of a set, and is also used to distinguish between discrete and continuous sets.

6. More terminology: "rank," loosely speaking, is the number of dimensions of a tensor, whereas "shape" comprises the sizes of its dimensions. For example, a vector with ten elements has shape (10); a matrix of 2×4 has shape $(2, 4)$.

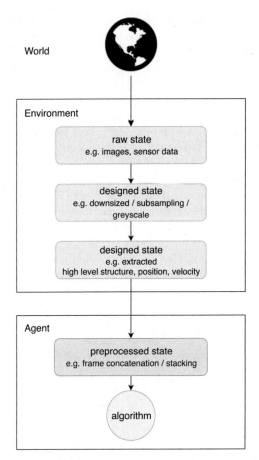

World

Environment

raw state
e.g. images, sensor data

designed state
e.g. downsized / subsampling /
greyscale

designed state
e.g. extracted
high level structure, position, velocity

Agent

preprocessed state
e.g. frame concatenation / stacking

algorithm

Figure 14.2   Information flow from the world to an algorithm

We can use our knowledge about a problem to design a simpler state by more directly presenting the information we consider useful—for example, by downsizing and grayscaling images. This can be described as a *designed state* of an environment.

An agent can take the raw state or designed state from an environment and further preprocess it for its own use. For example, a series of grayscale images can be stacked together to form a single input. This is known as a *preprocessed state*.

Let's take the Atari Pong game from Figure 14.1 as a case study. It is a two-dimensional ping pong game. There are two paddles and one ball, with the paddle on the left controlled by the game, and the paddle on the right controlled by the player. The player that gets the ball past their opponent's paddle earns a point, and the game terminates after 21 rounds. To win a game, an agent needs to be able to sense the ball and both paddles.

In Pong, the *raw state* is the RGB colored image from the computer screen at a particular time step, which contains the complete unfiltered information about the game. If the agent uses this raw state, it would have to learn to identify which patterns in the pixels represent the ball and the paddles and to infer their movements through pixels. Only then can it begin to devise a winning strategy—or at least that's what a human would do.

However, we as humans already know that the useful information includes positions and velocities of those objects. We can use this knowledge to create a *designed state*. One candidate is a vector of numbers representing the positions and velocities of both paddles and the ball.[7] This state contains significantly less information to process than the *raw state*—but it contains things that are far more direct and easier for an algorithm to learn.

Let's look at another example: the CartPole environment from OpenAI Gym in Figure 14.3. Both the raw image and the designed state are available, as shown in Code 14.1. The designed state is the one returned directly from the environment API methods `env.reset` (line 15) and `env.step` (line 37). The RGB raw image state can be obtained using the `env.render(mode='rgb_array')` function (line 21).

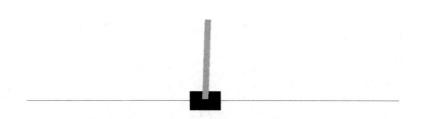

Figure 14.3   `CartPole-v0` is the simplest environment in OpenAI Gym. The objective is to balance the pole for 200 time steps by controlling the left-right motion of the cart.

If we replace the usual state with the RGB raw image state, any algorithm would have a much harder time solving the otherwise simple problem. This is because now there is much more work to be done by the agent—it has to figure out what collection of pixels to pay attention to, work out how to identify the cart and pole objects in an image, infer the movement of objects from the changes in pixel patterns between frames, etc. From all the pixel values, an agent has to filter out the noise, extract useful signals, form high-level concepts, then recover the information similar to that provided by the designed vector state of positions and velocities. Only then can it use these relevant features to inform its policy for solving the problem.

---

7. This designed state is a hypothetical example; the game environment actually only offers the raw image state.

Code 14.1   Example code to obtain the raw and designed state of the `CartPole-v0`
environment

```
1   # snippet to explore the CartPole environment
2   import gym
3
4   # initialize an environment anc check its state space, action space
5   env = gym.make('CartPole-v0')
6   print(env.observation_space)
7   # => Box(4,)
8   print(env.action_space)
9   # => Discrete(2)
10  # the natural maximum time step T to terminate environment
11  print(env.spec.max_episode_steps)
12  # => 200
13
14  # reset the environment and check its states
15  state = env.reset()
16  # example state: [position, velocity, angle, angular velocity]
17  print(state)
18  # => [0.04160531 0.00446476 0.02865677 0.00944443]
19
20  # get the image tensor from render by specifying mode='rgb_array'
21  im_state = env.render(mode='rgb_array')
22
23  # the 3D tensor that is the RGB image
24  print(im_state)
25  # => [[[255 255 255]
26  # [255 255 255]
27  # [255 255 255]
28  # ...
29
30  # the shape of the image tensor (height, width, channel)
31  print(im_state.shape)
32  # => (800, 1200, 3)
33
34  done = False
35  while not done:
36      rand_action = env.action_space.sample()  # random action
37      state, reward, done, _info = env.step(rand_action)
38      print(state)  # check how the state changes
39      im_state = env.render(mode='rgb_array')
```

A raw state should contain all the information that could be relevant to the
problem—but it is typically much harder to learn from. It often has a lot of redundancy

and background noise, so there is the unavoidable processing cost of extracting and contextualizing this information into a useful form. Raw and complete information gives more freedom but there is a heavier burden of extracting and interpreting useful signals from it.

A designed state typically contains extracted signals that are more useful for learning. One risk is that it can miss crucial information—we discuss this in more detail in Section 14.4. Environments may offer both raw and designed states. Which to use depends on the purpose—harder raw states can be used to challenge and test the limits of an algorithm, easier designed states can be used if the goal is to solve a problem.

Research environments tend to have simpler states that can be computed quickly. This is partly due to the fact that model-free deep RL methods require a lot of samples to train, so anything more complex would make learning intractable. Until there is a massive improvement in sample efficiency, this remains a bottleneck. Classical control and robotic environments from OpenAI Gym [18] and MuJoCo [136] have relatively low-dimensional designed states including positions, velocities, and joint angles. Even the image-based Atari game environments produce images that have low but sufficient resolution to solve the problems.

Modern video games are often quite complex and realistic. They mimic the real world very closely, thanks to sophisticated game engines. For these games, the states may correspond to the real-world modes of perception—such as the point-of-view camera vision and surround sound from a desktop computer game. VR headsets have high-fidelity stereoscopic (3D) vision, and their consoles provide touch or vibration feedback. Arcade shooter games with motion seats even simulate physical movements.[8]

It is still uncommon in AI research to utilize these types of complex sensory information. There are several reasons for that: data storage and computation requirements are massive, and the development of environment platforms is still in its early days. Fortunately, more realistic RL environments started to emerge in the past few years by building on top of powerful game engines. To name a few, Unity ML-Agents [59] includes a number of toy environments built on the Unity game engine; Deepdrive 2.0 [115] (built on Unreal Engine) provides a realistic driving simulation; Holodeck [46] (built on Unreal Engine) provides high-fidelity simulation of virtual worlds. These open up a whole new playground for even more challenging tasks in RL.

The complexity of the state space correlates with the complexity of a problem, although the effective problem complexity also depends on how well the states are designed. State design can make the difference between an RL environment that is solvable and one that is not.

Common objects which we interact with serve as great references for state design. Many of these convey information visually—vision being the most powerful of all human senses. Temperature and mass are measured with graded scales; status of an electrical appliance is shown by its light indicators; pressure and vehicle speed are displayed by gauges; games are tracked on scoreboards. There are also nonvisual channels, such as the

---

8. It is worth visiting an arcade center to experience some of the richest and most novel sensory experiences (and a lot of fun).

sound from a car horn or vibrations from a silenced phone. These are examples of how information about a system can be measured and represented. In the information age, we are so used to measuring things—ideas for state design are all around us.

A good environment design accelerates research and applications. It also needs to be thoroughly tested so that users can avoid tinkering with and fixing issues unrelated to their work. Providing a set of standard and robust environments was one of the main motivations for creating OpenAI Gym which contains a large set of environments with carefully designed states, actions, and rewards. Good design coupled with ease of use and permissive license has helped OpenAI Gym contribute to advancing the field by providing a testbed for researchers; since its inception, it has become one of the de facto standard environments in deep RL.

Despite its importance, there are few formal or comprehensive guidelines on state design for deep RL. However, acquiring sufficient skills in state design—or at least an understanding of it—is complementary to having core knowledge of RL algorithms. Without it, you cannot solve new problems.

14.2   State Completeness

Let's talk about raw state design. The most important question is whether the raw state contains sufficient information about the problem.

As a general rule, think about what information a person needs to know in order to solve the problem. Then, consider if this information is available from the world. If we have complete information, then the problem is *fully observable*; for example, chess can be represented completely by the positions of all the pieces on the board. A problem with incomplete information is only *partially observable*; poker is an example since a player cannot observe other players' cards.

A state which contains complete information is ideal, but may not always be possible to have. This may be due to theoretical or practical restrictions. Sometimes a state is fully observable in theory but not in practice due to noise, imperfect conditions, or other unaccounted factors. For example, in real-world robotics scenarios, signals take time to travel from a computer to the motors, so high-precision control needs to account for these effects.

When a state is partially observable, the effects of incomplete information can vary widely. An agent may be able to compensate for noise and latency in the environment if they are not too large. On the other hand, online video games that require split-second decisions to win become impossible to play when latency is too high.

Next, there are some secondary considerations when designing a raw state.

1. What are the data types? Are they discrete or continuous? Will they be dense or sparse? This determines the suitable format for data representation.

2. What is the cardinality of the state space? Will the states be computationally cheap to produce? Depending on this, we may or may not be able to obtain the amount of data required for training.

3. How much data is required to solve a problem? One rule of thumb is to estimate how much data a human would need to solve the problem, then multiply it by a number between 1,000 to 100,000. This is only a rough estimation; the true number will depend on the nature of the problem, the state design, and the efficiency of the algorithm used. For example, a human can take 10 to 100 episodes to learn how to play an Atari game well, but an algorithm typically requires over 10 million frames (roughly 10,000 episodes) to play on the same level.

Answering these questions requires domain expertise and a good understanding of the problem at hand—especially if it has never been solved before. One lens through which to evaluate these options is the complexity of the resulting state.

14.3 State Complexity

States are represented with a data structure—and, as always in data structure design, we need to consider its computational complexity. This complexity can manifest in two forms: *tractability* and *effectiveness of feature representation*. What follows is a number of guidelines for designing efficient state representations. These guidelines apply to both raw states and designed states.

Tractability[9] relates directly to the cardinality of the state space. How large is every sample of data? How many samples are required to get a good representation of the entire problem and to solve it? Recall that a frame refers to all the data produced over a time step. We have seen that RL algorithms typically require millions of frames to perform well on the Atari games. A typical frame of downsized and grayscaled image is 7kB, so 10 million frames will contain 10 million × 7kB, which is 7GB in total. Depending on how many frames an agent stores at once, memory (RAM) consumption can be high. In contrast, consider a modern game with high-resolution images, each 1MB in size. Processing 10 millions frames is equivalent to computing through 10TB worth of data. This is why it is a good idea to downsample images.[10]

An environment model that faithfully reproduces the problem (e.g., uses the highest-quality game images) may generate so much raw data that computation becomes intractable in practice. Therefore, the raw state often has to be compressed and distilled into features that are properly designed to represent what is relevant about a problem. Feature engineering is an extremely critical part of solving a problem, especially when the problem is new. Not all features are created equal, so we need to consider their effectiveness.

Given that there are multiple potential feature representations, ask what happens when the same algorithm runs on them. Will the storage size be too massive? Will computation be so costly that a solution becomes impractical? What is the computation cost for extracting features from the raw state? What we are looking for is the minimum sufficient

---

9. In computer science, a tractable problem is one that can be solved in polynomial time.
10. Preprocessing techniques are discussed in Section 14.5; calculations to determine memory consumption were discussed in Chapter 13.

feature representation that makes computation tractable and does not generate too much data to process.

A good first strategy is to compress raw information. Complexity scales with the size of data—the more bits the algorithm has to compute, the more space and time it will take. Image-based games are good examples: encoding a game in full resolution retains all of the original information—but to effectively play the game, we often do not need high-resolution images that are costly to produce and process.

If a convolutional network is used to process an input image, the number of pixels will cascade down the layers and more computation will be required to process them. A smarter way is to compress the image using any standard techniques. This will downsize it into a reasonable smaller size—say, 84×84 pixels—with a proportional speedup in computation time. Even with the powerful hardware available today, downsizing can make the practical difference between a model that can or cannot fit in memory—and, consequently, between a training session that takes days and one that takes months.

Complexity also grows with the number of dimensions because of the combinatorial explosion that comes with every additional dimension. Even where dimensions represent fundamentally different types of information, they can still be reduced with some clever design. Consider video games again. Instead of using the full 3-channel RGB colors, we can grayscale the image into a single channel. However, this is only applicable if color is of little importance; if *The Matrix* movie were in black and white, Neo would have had a hard time telling the red pill from the blue pill. Converting an image to grayscale reduces it from a 3D pixel volume (with the color channels) to a 2D grayscale pixel matrix (no color channels), and complexity is reduced by a cube root. That is why, besides downsizing, the states of Atari games are usually preprocessed from colored to grayscaled images.

Another strategy for compressing information is feature engineering. Recall the distinction between *raw state* and *designed state*. Feature engineering is the process of transforming the former into the latter—that is, going from low-level raw information to higher-level representations. This is of course limited by what information is available in the raw state. Take CartPole for example. Instead of using an image, the environment can be succinctly represented with only four numbers—the x-position and x-velocity of the cart, and the angle and the angular velocity of the pole. This state is also much more relevant, because the algorithm does not need to perform extra work to understand the concept of positions and velocities from raw images.

A state designer can choose to manually encode useful information. Depending on the choice, the new encoding can either make the problem easier or harder. Let's suppose we do not use the image state of Atari Pong for learning. Then, what useful high-level information can be extracted from the raw image such that it forms a succinct representation of the game, analogous to the CartPole example in the last paragraph? We can guess that such a designed state will include positions, velocities, and accelerations[11] of the ball, the agent's paddle, and the opponent's paddle. If we leave out the information about the opponent's paddle, we make the game harder to beat since the agent will not be able to anticipate or exploit its opponent. On the contrary, if we include the velocities of

---

11. Acceleration is necessary because the longer the ball remains in play, the faster its speed.

the ball and both paddles, the problem becomes easier as the agent will not need to learn to estimate velocities by taking the difference between positions over time.

Feature engineering achieves two things: cardinality of the state is drastically lowered, and its complexity is greatly reduced. By hand-picking only the useful features, irrelevant information from the raw state is excluded, and we are left with a designed state that is more compact with fewer dimensions. Moreover, the designed state could also include information that can only be derived, but not directly observed, from the raw data. The velocity of objects is a good example. When these features are presented directly in a designed state, an agent does not have to learn to extract them from the raw state. Essentially, most of the work in understanding the problem has already been done for the agent. Given a designed state, an agent only needs to utilize it and focus directly on solving the main problem.

One disadvantage of feature engineering is that it relies on humans who use their knowledge about the problem to identify the relevant information from raw data to design an effective and appropriate feature representation. Compared to the raw data, this process inevitably encodes more human-based priors because we utilize our knowledge and heuristics to select what we think is useful. Certainly an agent which learns from such a state is not really doing it "from scratch"—but if solving a problem is our main concern, this is not something we need to worry about. Feature engineering results in designed states with more context built from a human perspective, and it makes them more interpretable—although some might argue that, for the exact same reason, such states are less general or more likely to include human biases.

Although desirable, feature engineering is not always possible or practical. For instance, if the task is to recognize images or navigate visually, it would be impractical to craft states to account for all the relevant features in images, not to mention that it may defeat the purpose. However, sometimes it is extremely difficult, but worth the effort, to do so. Vastly complex games, such as Dota 2,[12] are an example where it requires monumental effort to design states, but using raw game images makes for a much more challenging problem to solve.

To play Dota 2, OpenAI designed a massive game state that consists of a staggering 20,000 elements derived from the game API. The state contains basic map-related information such as terrain and spawn timing. For a number of creeps or hero units, the state also contains a set of information related to each such as attack, health, position, abilities, and items. This massive state is separately processed, then combined before being passed into an LSTM network of 1024 units. For more details, see the model architecture linked under the "Model Structure" section in the OpenAI Five blogpost [104]. Combined with some serious engineering effort and computing power, they managed to defeat the world's top players in 2019 [107].

Overall, state feature engineering is doable and encouraged, especially when the important elements of a game are known and can be described quite straightforwardly.

---

12. Dota 2 is a popular eSports game. It consists of two teams of five players each, picking heroes from a pool of over 100 characters to fight and take over the enemy's throne. With a large map and a mind-boggling number of combinations of characters and skills, it is an extremely complex game.

There may be problems with which obvious elements to include in the designed state. In games, we are generally interested in things that change or move. In robotics, we are interested in the positions, angles, forces, and torques. In the stock market, useful trading indicators include market volume, price changes, moving averages, etc.

There are no hard and fast rules for designing effective states from raw data. However, it is always useful to spend time understanding the problem so that domain knowledge and context can be incorporated into the state. For practical applications, this is often particularly worthwhile.

State design is fundamentally about compressing information and removing noise, so any standard methods for doing this are worth exploring. In general, think about the following:

1. **Obvious information:** Something that is immediately obvious as relevant to a human, such as positions of the paddle, ball, and bricks in Breakout—simply because those are the game objects.

2. **Counterfactual:** If x is missing and a problem cannot be solved, then x must be included. If object velocity is not available in CartPole, we cannot anticipate where the relevant object is moving to, so it is essential to predicting the movement of objects—which means velocity cannot be missing.

3. **Invariance** (borrowed from physics): What is something that remains constant or invariant under transformations, that is, exhibits symmetry? For instance, CartPole is invariant to horizontal translations (as long as it does not veer off the screen), so the absolute x-position of the cart does not matter and can be excluded. However, the pole falling is not invariant to vertical flipping, because gravity acts in one direction only and this fact is reflected in the angular position and velocity.

4. **Changes** (borrowed from physics): Usually we are interested in something that changes. Has the position of the ball changed? Has the price increased or decreased? Has the robotic arm moved? These changes might be relevant. However, other things that change—background noise—may be irrelevant. For instance, a self-driving car does not need to notice tree leaves moving in the wind. It is tempting to think that an agent should only care about the changes its actions can produce. However, there are also purely observational changes that are useful, such as traffic lights which we cannot control but must obey. Overall, the key idea here is: include in the state *relevant* things that change and are useful to the goal. Conversely, if a feature cannot be controlled by an agent and does not contribute towards achieving the objective, it can be excluded.

5. **Time-dependent variables:** Many, but not all, changes happen in time instead of space. However, information from a single frame (time step) cannot indicate any changes in time. If we expect x to change over time, we should include $\frac{dx}{dt}$ in the state. For example, position changes do matter for CartPole, therefore velocity is crucial.

6. **Cause and effect:** If the goal or task is the effect of other causes (it usually is), then all the elements in the causal chain must be included.

7. **Established statistics or quantities**: In stock trading, the common wisdom in technical analysis is to look at quantities such as volume and moving averages. It is more useful to include such well-established data points than to invent one's own using the raw price point data from the stock exchange. Essentially, do not reinvent the wheel.

Finally, it is often useful to borrow techniques from domains with related or similar data types and problems. For images, make use of the downsizing, grayscaling, convolutional and pooling techniques from computer vision, which have helped to advance deep RL—for example, all state-of-the-art results on the Atari games make use of a convolutional neural network. If the data is sparse, look to natural language processing (NLP) and use word embeddings. For sequential data, look to NLP again and use recurrent networks. Do not shy away from borrowing techniques from a wide variety of domains—such as game theory and good old-fashioned AI (GOFAI) for games, classical mechanics for robotics, classic control for control systems, and so on.

14.4 State Information Loss

State design begins with the set of available information in a raw state. Then, various compression methods can be applied to obtain the desired final set of information in the form of a designed state. When compressing information, some of it may be lost—otherwise, the process is called lossless compression.

In this section, we look at a common pitfall when designing a state from raw states—the possibility that *crucial* information is lost. It is the responsibility of the designer to ensure that this does not happen. We look at multiple case studies, including image grayscaling, discretization, hash conflicts, and metainformation loss that arises from an inappropriate representation.

14.4.1 Image Grayscaling

When downsizing images, designers need to check with their eyes that the images do not become too blurry—too low-resolution—to be useful. Furthermore, in video games some elements are color-coded to make it easier for humans to play. When compressing a game image from RGB colors to grayscale, make sure that crucial elements do not disappear when decolorized. This may happen when there is a hashing overlap from mapping a larger set of numbers (3D tensor, RGB with three channels) into a smaller set (2D tensor, grayscale image), so different colors may end up with brightness values that are nearly identical.

Figure 14.4 shows an example of information loss from grayscaling. OpenAI trained an agent to play Atari Seaquest [103] where the player controls a submarine whose mission is to rescue divers while shooting enemy sharks and other submarines to gain rewards. Preprocessed images mapped green and blue to very close grayscale values, making them indistinguishable. This mistake caused the enemy sharks to blend into the background and become invisible to the agent (Algorithm View in Figure 14.4). The loss of this crucial piece of information negatively affected performance. Luckily, there are many grayscale schemes, so this issue can be avoided by choosing an appropriate scheme that does not cause the shark to disappear, as shown in the Corrected View in Figure 14.4. No grayscale scheme is completely foolproof, so we need to always manually check our preprocessed images.

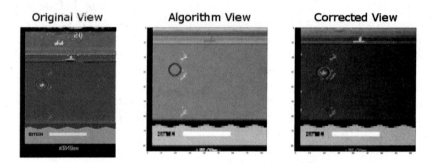

Figure 14.4   Grayscaling can cause crucial game elements to disappear, hence it is good practice to always check the preprocessed images when debugging.
Image from OpenAI Baselines: DQN [103].

14.4.2   Discretization

Another common cause of information loss occurs when discretizing continuous values—that is, mapping a range of continuous or infinite discrete values into a set of finite discrete values. For example, take a task which involves reading an analog watch. An efficient feature design is to discretize the circumference of the watch. Depending on whether we want to read the hour or the minute hand, we need to use different discretization schemes. If the task is to only read the hour, then discretizing the angle into 12 parts makes sense, since there are only 12 hour values on a watch. If we wish to read the minutes, then this will not be sufficient. Depending on the accuracy required, the watch needs to be discretized by intervals of 30, 10, or 1 minute, but anything lower becomes illegible to the human eye. As a matter of fact, the tick marks on a watch are one discretization scheme that helps us read the time with a permissible degree of accuracy. It also influences how we say the time: someone who is wearing a watch with only 30-minute tick marks, when asked the time, will likely respond in the same discretization scheme—whether it is 10:27, 10:28, or 10:29, this person will probably say, "Ten thirty." This example shows that discretization causes information loss (which should not be surprising).

14.4.3 Hash Conflict

The previous two examples are instances of what is known as a *hash conflict*. This occurs when a larger data set is compressed into a smaller set that does not have enough power to represent all of its distinct elements. Therefore, collisions arise when different elements of the original set get mapped to the same value in the smaller set.

Information compression may cause hash conflicts—but they are not always problematic. If we look at the Atari Seaquest example, all grayscaling schemes cause hash conflicts, but only some of them will cause the issue of the disappearing sharks in Figure 14.4. Unfortunately, there is no easy way to determine which hash conflicts are detrimental because it is problem-dependent. We need to rely on manually inspecting samples of the data.

In our everyday lives, we also experience hash conflicts. Humans use colors to convey semantics, such as red for danger and green for safety; the familiar three red-yellow-green bulbs are used for traffic lights worldwide. Even though we have the technology to use a single bulb that changes its color to any of these three, and even though this may make sense economically or technologically, driving would become extremely dangerous for people who are colorblind—they will have a hard time telling whether the light is red or green. This is why traffic lights still use three separate monochromatic bulbs.

14.4.4 Metainformation Loss

Some information provides higher-level knowledge about the data we are dealing with. This is metainformation—information about information. Let's look at some examples.

Chess is played on a two-dimensional board, and players have no trouble moving the pieces during the game. Some really advanced players can play mentally by memorizing the positions of the pieces and calling out moves such as "bishop from A2 to D5." This is harder than using a board because a player has to construct a mental image of these positions on an imaginary board, but this is still doable.

In chess, the coordinates are in two dimensions—an alphabet letter for the horizontal position, and a number for the vertical position. For a challenge, let's switch to a 1-dimensional coordinate by mapping the 2D coordinates to the set of 64 digits—say, $A1 \mapsto 1, B1 \mapsto 2, \ldots, A2 \mapsto 9, B2 \mapsto 10, \ldots, H8 \mapsto 64$. The move "bishop from A2 to D5" now becomes "bishop from 9 to 36."

Imagine playing chess with this 1D system. It is significantly harder because we would have to convert the numbers $9, 36$ back to $A2, D5$ so we can visualize the piece positions on the 2D board. This is assuming we have played chess before. To take it further, imagine introducing chess to a new player without ever showing them any 2D boards—just by describing all the rules using this new 1D coordinate. Furthermore, we never tell them that this is a 2D game, so they do not have the context about the spatial nature of the game. No doubt the new player will be very confused.

Is this compression lossless? All 2D coordinates are mapped to 64 distinct numbers—there are no hash conflicts. So why does the game become so much harder? A quantitative check would not tell us that anything is wrong, but a qualitative check reveals the problem. When we turn the 2D coordinates into 1D, we rid them of their dimensional information—we ignore the fact that the game is designed for two dimensions and that the pieces move in two-dimensional space, so the rules are sensibly devised for 2D. For example, the concept of checkmate which depends on 2D positioning will become very bizarre in 1D.

The same thing happened in the earlier days of digit recognition from images (for example, using the MNIST [73] dataset) before 2D convolutional networks were used. An image would be sliced into strips and then joined adjacently to a vector. This is then passed as an input to an MLP. It is not surprising that the network had a hard time recognizing digits, given that all it got was the 1D version of the image, not knowing that the image was supposed to be 2D. This problem was fixed when 2D convolutions, designed to process 2D data, began to be used. Figure 14.5 shows an image of a digit "8" taken from the MNIST [73] dataset. When flattened into a 1D vector, it looks like Figure 14.6 (only shown partially due to its length), which is much harder to identify as an "8".

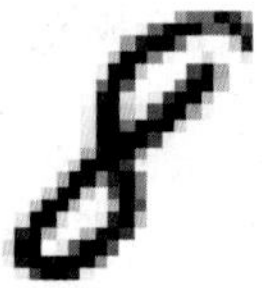

Figure 14.5   An image of the digit "8" from MNIST. This natural two-dimensional representation can be identified easily.

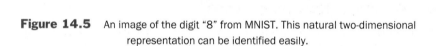

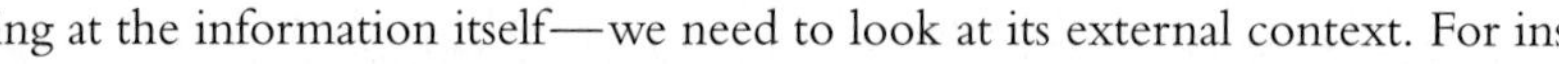

Figure 14.6   What Figure 14.5 looks like when flattened into a 1-dimensional vector by concatenating all the rows together (only shown partially due to its length). This is very difficult to identify as an "8".

This scenario is an example of *metainformation loss*. Such loss is not immediately clear by looking at the information itself—we need to look at its external context. For instance, the collection of 64 numbers in chess does not tell us anything about the data being two-dimensional: that context has to be supplied externally. Such metainformation does not happen just in *space*, but also in *time*.

Consider a frame from the CartPole environment in Figure 14.7a at $t = 1$. Assume that we only have access to the image but not the designed state. Looking at this frame alone, can we tell what is going to happen at $t = 2, 3, \ldots$? It is impossible. Without access to the state, we do not know the cart or pole's velocity. The pole could be standing still, falling leftward, or falling rightward. Only when we look at all the other frames at later time steps in Figure 14.7 do we know that the pole is falling to the left. This illustrates the missing high-level information about *how the information itself changes over time*. A way to restore this information is to collect consecutive frames together and observe them.

In Figure 14.7, we can observe the sequence of changes because the snapshots are taken at reasonable intervals. Our ability to perceive these changes is determined by the frame rate. High-quality games have a frame rate of over 60 frames a second, so the video looks smoother for players. However, with a high frame rate, the changes between consecutive frames are also smaller. When choosing the frame rate for training, we need to ensure that the changes are detectable. What qualifies as "detectable" depends on the perceiver. Humans are less sensitive to changes than machines, so if an object on a screen moves by 1 pixel, humans are likely to miss it. On the other hand, changes will accumulate over time and become more detectable. A common strategy is therefore to accentuate consecutive changes by skipping frames—that is, sampling once every k number of frames. For games with a frame rate of 60, a good frame skipping frequency is $k = 4$. This technique can make learning easier for an agent; it also reduces the total amount of data that needs to be stored.

If we were now told that the frames in Figure 14.7 are being played in reverse, we would conclude that the pole is not actually falling leftward but is recovering and falling rightward. The metainformation about *the direction of ordering* of the data needs to be given. One way to preserve this metainformation is to use a recurrent neural network; the other is to pass the sequence of frames in a consistent manner to an MLP or CNN.

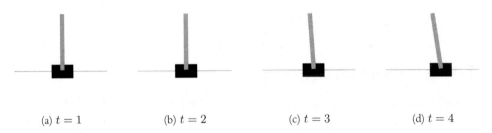

(a) $t = 1$ (b) $t = 2$ (c) $t = 3$ (d) $t = 4$

Figure 14.7   Four consecutive frames of the CartPole environment

Our final example is Chinese text. Chinese characters are written in a grid, and a sentence is made from a sequence of characters. Sometimes a sentence is meant to be read left-right-top-bottom, sometimes top-bottom-left-right, and sometimes top-bottom-right-left. Additionally, a book could be read left-to-right or right-to-left, although it is usually consistent with the sentences' direction of flow. If we try to train a neural network on a 2D grid of Chinese characters without knowing which direction it is supposed to be read, all it will see is some garbled up, disjointed sequence of characters—the story in the book will be lost.

These examples demonstrate how information can be lost in both direct and subtle manners. We can encounter this kind of loss in unexpected places. We can call all such kind of loss "information blindness"—similar to "colorblindness" but in other dimensions and forms of information, including metainformation and exterior context.

To summarize, when compressing data, check for information loss using the methods discussed in this section:

1. **Accidental exclusion** (basic): Check that no critical information is accidentally left out.

2. **Hash conflict** (quantitative): Check that, when mapping a larger set to smaller space, no elements that must remain distinguishable are merged.

3. **Information blindness** (qualitative): Check that, from a human perspective, no subtle, qualitative, or meta information is lost.

As a general rule of thumb, it is always a good thing to simply debug the compressed information manually. If a human cannot use the compressed image or states to play the game or solve the problem, do not be surprised if an algorithm fails too. This principle does not just apply to games but to all problems in general. If the state is an image, render and look at it. If it is a sound, listen to it. If it is some abstract tensors, print them out and inspect the values. Take some examples and try to act based on them. The bottom line is that everything about the environment needs to make sense to a human. We may discover that the problem does not lie with the algorithm, but rather in the designed state providing insufficient information.

The transformation of raw states into designed states can be implemented as a state preprocessor module. It can either be applied within the environment, or by the agent transforming the state produced by the environment. Where to apply it depends on what we have control over; for example, if the environment is given to us by a third party, it makes sense to implement the preprocessor within an agent.

14.5   Preprocessing

In this section we look at common preprocessing implementations. We also take a more detailed look at frame skipping. This section can be omitted on first reading without loss of understanding of what follows.

A preprocessor is a function that transforms data before it gets used. Preprocessing is not unique to deep RL; it is widely used in machine learning. Generally, data preprocessing is done for multiple reasons, including:

1. **Cleanup:** In natural language processing, nonstandard characters are removed from a sentence.

2. **Numerical representation:** In natural language processing, we cannot directly perform computations on alphabetic characters. They have to be encoded as numbers, such as a $0, 1, 2, \ldots$, or as continuous word embeddings that can be fed into a neural network.

3. **Standardization:** It is common to standardize input data so that each feature has a similar range and mean. Networks may pay more or less attention to features depending on their relative scales. Scales can often be arbitrary (e.g., length can be measured in millimeters or meters), and these arbitrary choices should not affect learning. Standardization helps prevent this by subtracting the mean and dividing by the standard deviation for each feature.

4. **Exploration:** Often, it is not clear what the best data representation is for a particular problem. Part of the experimentation workflow involves trying a variety of preprocessing methods, such as embedding, encoding, grayscaling, downsampling, and frame concatenation.

14.5.1 Standardization

To standardize a dataset, first compute the overall mean and standard deviation, then subtract the mean and divide by the standard deviation for every data point. Now, the overall distribution will center at mean 0 and have a standard deviation of 1. This is shown in Equation 14.1, with implementation in Code 14.2 (lines 2–6).

Another closely related method is data normalization, which serves to rescale the value range of *each feature* in a dataset to between 0 and 1. Given a dataset, for each feature, find the minimum, maximum, and the range of values, then for every data point, subtract the minimum and divide by the range. This is shown in Equation 14.2, with implementation in Code 14.2 (lines 8–15).

$$x_{\text{std}} = \frac{x - \overline{x}}{\sigma} \tag{14.1}$$

$$x_{\text{norm}} = \frac{x - x_{\min}}{x_{\max} - x_{\min}} \tag{14.2}$$

Code 14.2   Method to standardize a tensor

```
# source: slm_lab/agent/algorithm/math_util.py
def standardize(v):
    '''Method to standardize a rank-1 np array'''
    assert len(v) > 1, 'Cannot standardize vector of size 1'
    v_std = (v - v.mean()) / (v.std() + 1e-08)
    return v_std


def normalize(v):
    '''Method to normalize a rank-1 np array'''
    v_min = v.min()
    v_max = v.max()
    v_range = v_max - v_min
    v_range += 1e-08  # division guard
    v_norm = (v - v_min) / v_range
    return v_norm
```

Methods in Code 14.2 work only for offline data. In RL, data is generated online—that is, produced gradually over time via agent interactions with an environment. Therefore, we need an online standardization method for states. An implementation of online standardization can be found in SLM Lab at `slm_lab/env/wrapper.py`.

These are effective and commonly used techniques. However, it is important to first sense-check that no crucial information will be lost in the process. Let's illustrate this with an example.

Consider an environment with a large domain and fixed features at specific locations, such as the map in Dota 2. The terrain and crucial game objects are fixed at certain locations. Suppose during training an agent only sees standardized location coordinates. Since the map is large, chances are the agent will only manage to explore a small part of it. This means its standardized data will only represent that specific small patch of the map. If the agent is placed in an unexplored area, the range or standard deviation of the data will suddenly change. This may result in an anomalous data point with extreme values after standardization; even more problematically, it may shift the values that the previously seen states map to, thereby changing their meaning. If standardization or normalization helps, but global information is also needed, we can supply both raw and processed data to the agent. In OpenAI Five's agent architecture, absolute position on the map is used as one of the inputs [104].

To summarize, standardization and normalization are extremely useful methods for cleaning up datasets. They can be beneficial for training, but should be applied with care. Information about relative changes is transformed and retained, but absolute global information may be lost. When considering these methods, it helps to have a deep understanding of the dataset and the information required for the task.

14.5.2   Image Preprocessing

A colored digital image typically comes in three color channels, abbreviated RGB for Red, Green, Blue. This decomposes an image into three two-dimensional slices, where each value in a slice represents intensity (brightness). Each slice is therefore the intensity of the image in one of the color channels. When the 2D slices are stacked together, they form a 3D tensor. Each pixel will be rendered as the combination of its intensities in all three base color channels. On a modern LCD screen, every physical pixel is actually three tiny red, green, and blue light diodes crammed closely together; from far away, we see colorful images without ever noticing these diodes.

Having colored channels means having three sets of values for an image, which require three times as much storage compared to a monochromatic image. We can map each color pixel's three values to a single scalar, using a weighted sum. This is called *grayscaling*, and the resultant image is a 2D tensor that consumes three times less memory storage than the original. The color weights need to be chosen carefully so as not to cause a color hashing conflict. Fortunately, standard computer vision libraries have built-in methods with robust coefficients for grayscaling.

Even after grayscaling, a modern digital image still has a high resolution. This translates to a lot of pixels per image—usually more than necessary for learning purposes. We need to downsize the image to reduce the number of values in the tensor, so that there are fewer elements to store and compute. This is called *downsampling* or "resizing." The problem with downsampling is that it blurs an image and loses some information. There are many downsampling algorithms that blur images in different ways.

Sometimes, only a part of an image is useful. The irrelevant parts, usually the border, can be discarded to further reduce the number of pixels. This is typically done with image *cropping*. For some Atari games, the top or bottom part displays game scores; these do not directly relate to the game state so they can be cropped off, although it is harmless to keep them in.

Finally, the pixel intensity of an image is an integer with 256 distinct values in the range 0–255. It is a common practice to perform *image normalization* by typecasting it into a float tensor, then dividing it, element-wise, by the range 255.0. The final image tensor will thus have values in the range 0.0–1.0.

All these image preprocessing methods can be combined. For efficiency, apply them in the following order: grayscaling, downsampling, cropping, and image normalization. Code 14.3 shows the implementations for these image preprocessing methods, along with some combinations, in SLM Lab.

Code 14.3 Image preprocessing methods in SLM Lab

```
1   # source: slm_lab/lib/util.py
2   import cv2
3   import numpy as np
4
5   def to_opencv_image(im):
6       '''Convert to OpenCV image shape h,w,c'''
7       shape = im.shape
8       if len(shape) == 3 and shape[0] < shape[-1]:
9           return im.transpose(1, 2, 0)
10      else:
11          return im
12
13  def to_pytorch_image(im):
14      '''Convert to PyTorch image shape c,h,w'''
15      shape = im.shape
16      if len(shape) == 3 and shape[-1] < shape[0]:
17          return im.transpose(2, 0, 1)
18      else:
19          return im
20
21  def crop_image(im):
22      '''Crop away the unused top-bottom game borders of Atari'''
23      return im[18:102, :]
24
25  def grayscale_image(im):
26      return cv2.cvtColor(im, cv2.COLOR_RGB2GRAY)
27
28  def resize_image(im, w_h):
```

```
29      return cv2.resize(im, w_h, interpolation=cv2.INTER_AREA)
30
31  def normalize_image(im):
32      '''Normalizing image by dividing max value 255'''
33      return np.divide(im, 255.0)
34
35  def preprocess_image(im):
36      '''
37      Image preprocessing using OpenAI Baselines method: grayscale, resize
38      This resize uses stretching instead of cropping
39      '''
40      im = to_opencv_image(im)
41      im = grayscale_image(im)
42      im = resize_image(im, (84, 84))
43      im = np.expand_dims(im, 0)
44      return im
```

14.5.3 Temporal Preprocessing

Temporal preprocessing is used to restore or accentuate multistep temporal information that is otherwise impossible or difficult to notice from a single frame.

Two effective temporal preprocessing methods are *frame concatenation* and *frame stacking*. These are used to include multistep information, such as the motion of objects in Atari Pong and the temporal ordering of sequential changes.

Concatenation and stacking can be used with any nonrecurrent networks. Suppose state s_k is a state that is input to a network without any concatenation/stacking. Collect a total of c frames, where c is the concatenation/stack length, and combine them into a single tensor using concatenation (e.g., np.concatenate) or stacking (e.g., np.stack [143]).

The preprocessed state is then passed as input to a network. Note that since the new input has a different shape, the network's input layer needs to be modified accordingly to handle it. With training, the network will learn to view the slots in the preprocessed input as representing temporal ordering—that is, the first frame preceding the second, and so on.

The difference between the two methods is the shape of the resulting output. Concatenation retains the tensor rank but extends the length in the combined dimension. For example, concatenating four vectors produces a vector with four times the length of the original. Concatenation is usually done for nonimage states, so they can be easily be fed into a plain multilayer perceptron network with appropriately extended input layer.

In contrast, stacking increases the tensor rank by 1 but retains the shape of the underlying tensors. It is equivalent to organizing a sequence of states into a list. For instance, stacking four grayscale images (2D tensors) produces a 3D tensor. This is similar to an image with four channels, only now the channels correspond not to RGB colors but to temporal positions. Stacking is usually done for grayscaled image states, and the preprocessed 3D tensor is fed to a convolutional network as an image with four channels.

State concatenation and stacking can also be combined with other preprocessing methods. For example, we can first preprocess images using methods from Code 14.3, then stack them together. This is commonly done for the Atari environments.

Frame skipping is a temporal preprocessing method that changes the effective frame rate. For example, a frame skip of 4 will only render one of every four frames in a video and discard the rest. It is a form of downsampling for temporal data.

Frame skipping is most commonly done for video games. A video is shown on a screen by rapidly rendering a series of images in succession. This rendering frequency is called a frame rate, such as 60 frames per second (FPS) for modern video games. When the frame rate is higher than a human's visual response time (roughly 10 FPS), we stop seeing a sequence of static images and perceive a continuous motion video. A high frame rate is needed to make a video smooth, which translates to a lot of images in a short amount of time. This is why movie files are typically huge.

If we lay out all the images that make up a video, there will be a lot of them—more than is needed for an agent to learn a good policy. Most of the images will contain changes that are too small to be meaningful—which is good for making a video smooth, but unhelpful for learning. A learning agent needs to perceive meaningful differences between frames. What's worse, processing all the images would be very computationally expensive and wasteful.

Frame skipping addresses the problem of redundancy in a high-FPS video by skipping most of the images. Given a frame skip frequency of 4 for example, we will only render every fourth frame and discard all the images in between. This will also speed up the environment considerably because it consumes less computing resources for rendering. This has become common practice for the Atari games, ever since it was proposed in the original DQN paper [89], to create an effective frame rate of 15 FPS. The same method can be applied to other videos as well, although the frame skipping frequency needs to be chosen appropriately for each environment.

Generalizing, frame skipping is not limited to videos; it can also be applied to any form of temporal data with an equivalent notion of frame rate. Examples include the stock market signals, audio data, object vibrations, and so on. Reducing the sampling rate is essentially a temporal downsampling method.

Although effective, frame skipping is not without its issues. Video games usually have blinking elements such as character animation in classic Mario, or the bricks in Atari Breakout. If the frame skip frequency unfortunately matches the blink rate of these elements, they will not animate properly—or, worse, they will not show at all if we only get the frames when these blinking elements turn dark. We can thus lose some crucial information.

One workaround is to take the consecutive frames between skips and select the maximum value (maximum brightness) per pixel. This adds extra computing cost to process the originally skipped data, so it may slow things down. Furthermore, it assumes that we are interested in the bright elements, but some games use a negative color scheme, so the crucial game elements are dark instead. In this case, we would need to select the minimum pixel values.

A simpler solution for the problem caused by regular frame skipping is to do it stochastically. To illustrate, let's look at a stochastic frame skip of 4. To do this, we produce and cache the next four frames, then randomly select one of them to render and discard the rest. The downside of this method is that it introduces stochasticity with random frame lags—which may be fine for many problems, but not all. If an environment requires a frame-perfect strategy to solve, this preprocessing method will jeopardize it. Frame-perfect strategies do actually exists in competitive gaming; simply look up the world record in Super Mario Bros speedrun to see how the best human record holders play by acting at precise frames to achieve specific tasks.

Overall, there is no one ideal frame skipping method generally applicable to all problems. Every environment and dataset has its own quirks; we must first understand the data before choosing a suitable frame skipping method.

Frame skipping can also be applied to actions. When playing a game, humans tend to observe multiple frames before making an action. This makes sense because we need enough information before making a deliberate decision. Every game has its own ideal effective action rate to play—shooting games require fast reflexes, while strategy games require slower and longer planning. This is commonly measured as actions-per-minute (APM), with the assumption that the frame rate is constant (e.g., 60Hz). For our discussion, a more reliable measure is the inverse frames-per-action (FPA), obtained by dividing the frame rate by APM. Every game has its typical distribution of FPA, with a fast-paced game having a lower FPA and a slow-pace game having a higher FPA. Normally, since we act once every multiple frames, FPA should be larger than 1.

When implementing frame skipping for actions, there is one detail to handle. Suppose an environment has its underlying *true frame rate*, while state frame skipping produces a lower *effective frame rate*. During frame skips, states are perceived at the effective frame rate, and actions are also applied at the same rate. Relative to the true frames, FPA is equivalent to the frame skip frequency. Under the hood, the environment steps at the true frame rate, so every true frame expects a corresponding action, so FPA under the hood is always equal to 1. Therefore, when skipping frames, the logic for providing actions at the true frame rate needs to be handled. This is usually done by an environment's frame skipping logic.

Some environments simply allow for no action at all. In that case, nothing needs to be done, and we only need to care about supplying actions at the effective frame rate. In other cases, the environment requires actions at the true frame rate. If the actions do not have a cumulative effect, one can safely repeat the action on the skipped frames. Mouse clicks in Dota 2 have this property: it does not matter how many redundant clicks a player makes before an action is actually executed. However, if actions are cumulative, they may interfere with one another. For example, throwing a banana in MarioKart [84] is cumulative: bananas are precious resources that should not be wasted through repeated actions. A safe option is to supply inactions (idle/null actions) in between skipped frames.

If FPA is too low for a game, an agent becomes *hyperactive*, and its rapid actions may compete with each other. It will exhibit a form of Brownian motion—a random walk averaged over many contributing actions. Even when the state frame skip frequency is ideal, FPA can still be too low.

One remedy to make the effective FPA higher is to use action skipping on top of state frame skipping. To get an effective FPA of 5 on top of state frame skip frequency of 4, an action has to skip 5 effective frames before it changes. The same methods of constant and stochastic frame skipping can be reapplied for actions as well. Then, relative to the true frame rate under the hood, state gets rendered every 4 true frames, and action gets applied every $5 \times 4 = 20$ true frames.

By analogy, if action skipping addresses *agent hyperactivity*, then frame skipping for states addresses *agent hypersensitivity*. Without frame skipping, an agent will train on states that vary little, which means it has to be sensitive to small changes. If frame skipping is suddenly introduced after training, the successive state changes will be too large for the agent—it will be hypersensitive.

To conclude, frame skipping can be done for states with either constant or stochastic skipping. This introduces a difference between true and effective frame rates, and the underlying environment stepping logic may need special handling. Frame skipping can also be applied to actions.

14.6 Summary

In this chapter, we looked at some important properties of states and the various forms they can take, such as a vector or an image. We also introduced the distinction between a raw state and a designed state.

We should consider if the raw state extracted from the world contains the complete set of information needed to solve the problem. This can then be used to design state representations which are a set of handpicked information we consider to be useful. There are a number of important factors when designing a state—most notably their complexity, completeness, and information loss. For usability, states should have low computational complexity. We also looked at some potential pitfalls to be aware of so that a state representation does not lose information crucial for solving a problem.

Finally, we looked at some common methods for preprocessing states such as standardization for numerical data, downsizing, grayscaling, and normalizing for image data, and frame-skipping and stacking for temporal data.

15

Actions

An action is an output from an agent that changes an environment by causing it to transition into the next state. A state is perceived; an action is actuated.

Action design is important because it gives an agent the ability to change its environment. How actions are designed affects whether the control of a system is easy or hard, and therefore directly impacts the difficulty of the problem. A particular control design may make sense to one person but not another. Fortunately, there often exist multiple ways to perform the same action. For example, the transmission of a car can be controlled manually or automatically, but people usually find automatic transmission easier to use.

Many of the lessons from Chapter 14 also apply to action design. This chapter is organized similarly. First, we give some examples of actions and talk about general design principles. We then consider action completeness and complexity.

15.1 Examples of Actions

Actions are also commonly called "controls" in our daily lives—think a TV remote control. They can come in various forms, from the familiar to the unexpected. As long as something can produce changes in an environment, it is considered an action. Game controllers and musical instruments are some of the most familiar examples of controls. The physical movements of our body are another one. The movement of a robotic arm inside a simulation is a virtual action.

On the less familiar side, a voice command to a digital assistant is an action which causes it to carry out tasks. A cat purring is an action to get attention of its human. A magnetic field can exert force to act on charged particles. Essentially, actions can come in any form, as long as it is information that can be transmitted to produce changes in a system.

Real-world environments are often complex, and actions can be as well. For example, hand manipulation is a complex form of control involving many muscles, precise coordination, and dexterous responses to an environment. We humans spend many years learning to master this while growing up. In simulated environments, actions are often simplified. For example, a robotic hand may have up to tens of degrees of freedom. This is a far cry from the complexity of a human hand, but it is not necessarily disadvantageous.

Similar to states, actions can be represented as numbers organized into any suitable data structures. They need to be designed to properly represent information necessary for an algorithm to use. This, too, is feature engineering, and can benefit from thoughtful design principles.

An action a is an element of an action space $\mathcal{A}$ which defines all the possible actions an environment can receive. Actions can be discrete and numbered with integer values, such as the buttons with floor numbers inside an elevator, or continuous with real values, such as the gas pedal of a car. They can also be a mixture of discrete and continuous values, such as a kettle with a power button (discrete) and a temperature knob (continuous).[1] An action can have more than one element (dimension), and each element may be of any cardinality (discrete or continuous).

For convenience and compatibility with standard computing libraries, actions are also encoded as tensors with a single data type (`int`, `float`). They can come in any ranks and shapes:

- Scalar (rank-0 tensor): temperature knob

- Vector (rank-1 tensor): piano keys

- Matrix (rank-2 tensor): calculator buttons

It is important to note the distinction between dimension and cardinality. A temperature knob has only 1 element, and hence 1 dimension, but its value is continuous, so its cardinality is $|\mathbb{R}^1|$. A piano has 88 keys and each can coarsely be considered binary (pressed or not pressed), so the cardinality of a piano's action space is 2^{88}. The rank and shape of an action tensor is merely how the elements get arranged into a tensor.

Most controls that we can immediately interact with only have up to rank-2. Control knobs, telephone, keyboard, and piano are rank-1 tensor actions. A DJ's music synthesizer and a smartphone's multitouch are rank-2 tensors, as is a shower knob, where usually there is one handle that can be tilted to control the water volume and rotated to control the water temperature.

Rank-3 tensor actions are less common but not completely absent. One example is a virtual reality controller that allows motion-capture in 3D space. Or, imagine a warehouse with many lockers positioned in a 3D grid, their doors controllable through a computer, so these virtual lock/unlock buttons form a 3D layout.

An action can also be a combination of tensors. A kettle can be controlled with a button that can be pressed to turn it on and a dial to set the temperature. A DJ controller is an example with a rich set of buttons, dials, sliders, and rotating platters. A computer game typically requires combined outputs, such as keyboard presses and mouse movements. Driving a car also involves a lot of controls such as a gas pedal, break, steering wheel, gear shift, light indicator, and so on.

---

1. We can argue that everything in the real world is actually discrete with some minimum granularity, but we choose to conceptually treat certain things as continuous regardless.

When actions are represented with multiple differently shaped tensors, this requires a neural network to have separate output layers. These distinct tensors are considered as subactions, which together form a combined action.

Even though an agent produces actions, they are defined by the environment that determines which actions are valid. An agent has to accept the states and actions as defined by the environment, although it can choose to preprocess them for its own usage, as long as the inputs to the environment have the correct final format.

There are, broadly, three ways to design actions—singular, singular-combination, or multiple. Let's look at some examples.

In simple environments, control is normally *singular*. The action is a rank-0 tensor (scalar), so an agent can only do one thing at a time. In CartPole, the available actions are to move either left or right, but an agent can only choose one option at a time.

However, this is not always the case. The retro Atari game controller supports action combinations, for example a button press to shoot and a joystick flip to move in a game. When designing an environment, these combinations can be implemented by making them appear as a single action to an agent. This can be described as a *singular combination*. Practically, this is achieved by fully enumerating all the possible combinations and mapping them to a list of integers. This design makes it easier to construct a policy network since only one output layer is needed. At each time step, an agent would pick one of the integers to perform. When the integer gets passed into an environment, it gets mapped back to the button–joystick combination.

Sometimes, singular combinations make the control problem harder. This happens when the set of combinations is too big. In robotics, agents often need to simultaneously control multiple torques or joint angles. These are represented as distinct real numbers. Fully enumerating these combinations requires an unnecessarily large set of numbers. In these cases, we keep the dimensions separate so that an action consists of *multiple* subactions, one for each dimension.

Actions in RL are designed mainly for machines or software to use—but we can still take inspiration from the variety and ingenuity of controls designed for humans. A number of examples are given in Section 15.5. The core design principle to take from these is that a control should be familiar and intuitive to users, since it helps them understand the effects of their actions better. For both hardware and software control design, it is helpful if the control is easy to understand and thus more straightforward to debug. Also, if a control is intuitive, software can potentially hand off control to a trained human for a manual override. This feature is particularly useful in autopilot systems, self-driving cars, and factory machines.

We as humans control a lot of things in our daily lives—these can serve as both good and bad examples of action design. In general, control design falls under the broader category of user interface (UI), which pertains to the designing of interactions between a user and a system. Good user interfaces should be effective and easy to use. Poorly designed controls can make a task harder, more error-prone, and sometimes dangerous.

15.2   Action Completeness

When constructing an action space we need to ensure that it provides sufficiently diverse and precise control to solve a problem—that it is *complete*. Does it allow us to control everything we need to control?

A useful starting point is to consider what we as humans would use to control a system to solve a problem. Then, consider what degree of precision and range of control is required. For example, industrial robots may need controls that are precise to within a fraction of a degree but do not need to move very far, whereas a human steering a car needs precision to only a few degrees, but cars need to be able to travel large distances.

We can take inspiration from humans—for example, by looking at video game design—when deciding *what* needs to be controlled. However, *how* an agent controls a system may be very different. For example, a machine can control multiple things simultaneously and very precisely—something humans find hard to do. We just gave an example of how humans and agents might control a robotics system differently.

Video games have some of the best and richest control designs. This is not that surprising given the variety of games that exist and how many of them mimic real-world scenarios. Typically, the control design process goes like this.

First, from the game dynamics, identify the elements that need to be controllable for a player to achieve an objective. It helps to have a theoretical model of the game, usually in the form of a flowchart describing all the game scenarios. Perform a sanity check to ensure that the identified elements and their intended actions are correct, at least in theory. This ensures that the actions are completely specified. Once the elements have been identified, figure out the ways to control them. If the game mimics reality, this should be relatively straightforward as the controls can also mimic their real-life counterparts. Otherwise, there is some designing to do.

If the control design is feasible, the next factors to consider are intuitiveness and efficiency. Not only do they help create a good gaming experience, but they also affect the difficulty of the game. Badly designed interfaces can make a task much harder than it should be. A design should strike a balance between conciseness and verbosity. Suppose there are 100 distinct actions in a game. One could have 100 distinct buttons for each one—but this is too verbose. One could also have 2 dials with 10 options each, their combinations mapped to the 100 actions—but this is too concise and unintuitive. If the actions have a natural categorization scheme—for example, a set of attacks, a set of spells, and a set of motion primitives such as moving left or right—then it is more natural to divide the controls into these categories. Within each category, one can then use a more compact design of a few keys, one for each element in the category.

Finally, when the control design is done and implemented, a designer needs to test it. Check if the set of actions achievable with the design is indeed complete by comparing and verifying them with the theoretical schema used for the implementation. Next, write a set of unit tests. Verify that it actually works and does not crash the game. Often, unit tests also check that the output values are within the prescribed range, because extreme values may cause unexpected behaviors. To verify action completeness, check that the design does not miss any necessary actions or produce extraneous actions that were not originally intended. Usually, the entire design and testing process goes through several iterations, improving and fine-tuning the design until it is acceptable for release.

The same process used in game design can also be useful and relevant for nongaming applications. It involves asking several questions. First, given an environment, what do we want an agent to do? This is largely answered when the objective of the environment is defined, and it helps provide a direction for listing a complete set of actions. Second, how can the environment be affected by the agent? What are the elements an agent should control? What about the elements an agent *cannot* control? These pertain to identifying the categories of actions that should exist. Third, how would an agent control them? This determines the possible design schemas for the identified actions and suggests how actions can be encoded intuitively and effectively. The implemented control design should then be tested similarly.

Take an example from robotics. Suppose the task is to pick up an object. A robotic arm has three axes of motion, thus an action would have three dimensions, one for each axis. The arm can move freely toward an object, but it does not have a way to pick it up. This action design is incomplete—it cannot perform the task. To fix this, we can attach a gripper to the end of the arm to pick things up. The final working control has four dimensions: three to move the arm and one for the gripper. Now the robotic arm can perform a complete set of intended actions to achieve its objective.

Suppose we wish to create an interface for controlling the robotic arm. What would be a good design? How might the interface differ if a machine or a human were controlling the robot? One option is for the actions to be represented as four numbers, corresponding to the three axes and one gripper. This is the easiest design for a machine to control. However, this would not be very intuitive or easy for a human. They would have to first become familiar with how the numbers map to the actual states of the robotic arm, not to mention typing the individual numbers would be quite slow. A better design for a human would include three turnable dials, mapped to the rotation of the axes, and one slider that tightens and releases the gripper.

After deciding on an action design, we can identify the appropriate data types to encode an action with the right ranges. If a control dimension is discrete, it can be turned into a button or a discrete dial, and correspondingly be encoded as an integer. If a control dimension is continuous, it can be turned into a continuous dial or a slider, and be encoded as a real number.

It is important to strike a balance between conciseness and the expressiveness of an action space design. If it is too small, an agent may not be able to control a system precisely enough. In the worst case, it will not be capable of performing the desired task at all. If the action space is too large or too complex, learning to control the system becomes much harder. In the next section we look at some techniques to manage action complexity.

15.3 Action Complexity

Let's now discuss a number of strategies for dealing with action complexities. These strategies include combining or splitting actions, using relative actions, discretizing continuous actions, and taking advantage of invariance in an environment.

One of the ways that humans deal with complex control is by combining low-level actions into a single high-level action.

A piano has 88 keys; to master it takes a lifetime of practice. Even with that many keys to control, when playing we do not focus on one key at a time because our brains lack the capacity to do so. Focusing on individual keys independently is also inefficient—it is much easier to organize sequences of keys into larger patterns. Piano music is written and played in chords, scales, and intervals.

Computer games such as Dota 2 and StarCraft have a lot of components and a vast strategy space; learning to play such a game at professional level takes many years of screen time. A game typically has many command keys to control units and their actions. Skilled players don't play at the level of individual actions; instead, they make use of command hotkeys, key combinations, and repeatable macro strategies. With practice, these get encoded into their muscle memory as they find more shortcuts to reduce the action complexity by reorganizing actions into higher-level patterns.

Effectively, forming higher-level patterns is equivalent to creating a control scheme using the original controls—just as chords are simpler control schemes composed from individual piano keys. This technique is a form of *meta control*, and humans do it all the time. Presently, we do not yet know how to make RL agents autonomously design their own control schemes. Therefore, we have to do the meta control for them—we put ourselves in their shoes and design these patterns from our perspective.

Sometimes, actions can be represented more simply as combinations of multiple subactions instead of a single complex action.

For example, consider a shooting game in which a player aims on a screen of 84 by 84 pixels. When designing the "aim" action, we have a choice to represent it in 1D or 2D. Sampling an action in 2D will draw from two distributions, each with a cardinality of 84. If this is bijected into 1D, it will have a cardinality of $84 \times 84 = 7096$ instead. In this case, sampling an action from 1D will draw from a single distribution that is very wide and sparse. Sparsity can complicate agent exploration and artificially make the problem even harder. Imagine being given a row of 7,096 distinct buttons to choose from—a player is likely to end up learning and using just a few while ignoring the rest. Sampling from 2D is much more manageable in comparison.

If a problem's natural control has multiple dimensions, such as a chess board or a game console, we need to find a balance between conciseness and verbosity when designing its action. We can either keep all the dimensions distinct or biject all of them into one dimension. Having too many dimensions increases the complexity of control, since an agent would have to explore and learn to control these separate subactions in one action. However, we also saw how splitting actions into multiple dimension can be an effective way to reduce the cardinality of the action space.

As a general guideline, things such as key combinations are better encoded as unique actions because it makes them easier to discover, especially if a combination involves a long chain of subactions.

We also saw that the Atari game controller can be bijected into an 1D vector mapped to all the possible button-joystick combinations.

Doing so may help in some scenarios, but it is not always beneficial—as we saw in the chess example where reducing the piece movements from 2D to 1D can make the game much harder. In other cases, bijection to 1D blows up the action space so much that it is simply impractical. If we take the full screen resolution from a modern video game with 1920×1080 pixels and biject it to 1D, this has a cardinality of 2,073,600.

A rule of thumb is to consider the sparsity and the information loss when bijecting a control to a lower dimension than the original. If bijection loses some crucial information or metainformation, such as the spatiality of the control, we should avoid that. Since bijecting to a lower dimension also increases its cardinality, the control sampling from that dimension will suddenly become very sparse.

Another factor to consider when it comes to complexity reduction is that of absolute versus relative control. In Dota 2, an agent can control many units over a vast game map. When designing the control to move units around, using the absolute x, y coordinates makes the problem quite impossible to solve, simply because the map is huge. A better control design is to allow the agent to first select a unit, get its current position, then choose a limited relative x, y offset to apply to it. This was used by the OpenAI Dota 2 agent [104] to reduce the cardinality of movement actions by orders of magnitude. It is also applicable to any action dimensions which are huge but have a natural ordering of values, such as a scale of values. Using a relative scale can shrink the cardinality of an action space by so much that it makes an intractable problem more approachable.

An advantage of this approach is that the relative x, y offset on a unit is applicable wherever it is, so this control design has translational symmetry. As soon as an agent learns to apply a useful movement maneuver, it can apply it to a unit anywhere on the map. When the same maneuver is combined with other subactions under different scenarios, they effectively become composable, and we get diverse actions for free by learning multiple simpler subactions.

More importantly, relative control is possible only because of the nature of the problem—locality. Since the movement control of a unit is only relevant to its neighborhood, moving the unit is a local problem and relative control can be used. Its disadvantage, however, is that it is blind to any global strategies tied to the terrain and map which are nonlocal. To solve the nonlocal aspect of a problem, global context and additional information must be restored.

To simplify continuous control, it can be discretized. When discretizing a continuous space, we need to think about the resolution of dividing the space—that is, how large is the "pixel" when the continuous space is forced into a grid. If it is too coarse, the agent will struggle to provide a faithful approximation; if it is too fine, the problem may become computationally intractable. Discretization must be done with care so as to not produce an action space with too high cardinality.

Another potential issue is the introduction of artificial boundaries in an otherwise continuous space. Suppose a continuous action with the range 0 to 2 is discretized into integers 0, 1, 2. Then, is it justified enough that the value 1.5 gets discretized to 2 by rounding up? If the resolution used for discretization is too coarse, we risk losing some precision and sensitivity in the discretized actions.

We humans use our intuition about a problem and our adaptivity to learn, test, and adjust the sensitivity of our controls to achieve balance between precision and efficiency. We understand how large the temperature increment in a thermostat should be, or how sensitive the volume knob on a speaker. Another major difference between machines and humans is reaction time. Machines can act extremely fast, so we may need to rate limit an agent to act once every N time steps to prevent it from becoming hyperactive. Otherwise, rapidly changing actions—counteracting the effects of preceding actions in a short time scale—may make the overall action random and jittery. Atari games are typically sampled with a frame skip of 4, so that a given action is repeated for all the skipped frames when stepping through the true game frames internally. We can also imagine letting an agent adaptively choose its ideal frame skip frequency by judging on the scenario. Humans already do this—for instance, when we speed up a Tetris game when we are ready to rapidly drop a block.

One of the most useful complexity reduction techniques, generally applicable to actions and states, is reducing by symmetry. For chess, an agent does not have to learn to play both sides separately. If it is in the position of the second player, it only needs to rotate the board (with absolute coordinates) and apply the same learned policy. This way, no matter which side the agent is on, it uses the same standardized coordinates to play. Symmetries can be spatial or temporal. Common types of symmetry include translational, rotational, reflectional, helical (rotation plus shift), and so on; all of them can be described as functional transformations. Once identified, transformations can be applied to states and actions to reduce the cardinalities of state and action spaces by orders of magnitude.

Quite notably in RL, there is often an asymmetric relationship between states and actions. The state space is usually much bigger and more complex than the action space. State tensors typically have more elements than action tensors, and often exhibit a greater range of variability. For instance, an Atari Pong image state (after preprocessing) has $84 \times 84 = 7096$ pixels, and each pixel can take one of 256 values, making the cardinality of the state space 256^{7096}. In contrast, the action has one dimension and can take one of four values, so the cardinality of the action space[2] is $4^1 = 4$.

When the state space is large with huge variations and the action space is small in comparison, an agent needs to learn a many-to-one function in which many states are mapped to the same action. This larger state space contains a lot of information to help select within the relatively small set of actions. In contrast, if the opposite were true, then a network would need to learn a one-to-many function in which one state maps to many potential actions—in this scenario, there may not be sufficient information supplied by a state to choose between actions.

Suppose a state tensor s carries n_s bits of information and an action tensor a carries n_a bits. If correctly determining one action bit requires one bit of information from a state, then, to fully distinguish between all possible values of a, we need at least $n_s = n_a$. If $n_s < n_a$, we will not be able do this, so some values of a will be underspecified.

---

2. The Pong actions in OpenAI Gym are: 0 (no-op), 1 (fire), 2 (up), and 3 (down).

For Atari Pong, the task of generating one out of four possible action values given a large state space is well determined, and there is sufficient information in states for an algorithm to learn a good policy. Imagine a reversed setup where the task is to produce an image given only one out of four possible action values. Generating the full variety of images we experience when playing Pong would then be hard to do.

Finally, when approaching a new problem, start with the simplest action design (the same goes for state). It is helpful for the first action design to be restricted so we can focus on the simplest aspects of the problem. Simplified problems can be very useful for building up a solution gradually. If the initial design looks promising and an agent can learn to solve the simplified version, then complexity can be introduced gradually to make the problem more realistic and closer to the complete version. Along the way, gradual design progression will also help us understand more about the nature of the problem and how an agent is learning to solve it.

The methods for reducing complexity are mostly relevant to actions, but they may also be applied to states when suitable. To summarize, here are our guidelines for dealing with complexity in action design:

1. **Biject to lower dimensions, or split to more dimensions:** Biject actions to 1D to help discover complex subaction combinations; split action dimensions to manage cardinality.

2. **Switch between absolute and relative:** Simplify by taking advantage of a relative scale for local controls; use absolute scale for global controls.

3. **Discretize:** Try to stay close to the original nature of a control, but discretize to simplify while making sure the resolution is sufficient.

4. **Reduce by symmetry:** Try to find symmetry in actions and apply it to reduce the action space.

5. **Check state-to-action-size ratio:** As a sanity check, the action space should not be more complex than the state space; generally, it should be significantly smaller.

6. **Start simple:** Start from the simplest action design, then gradually add complexity.

15.4 Summary

This chapter started with control design for humans as a source of inspiration and compared it with action design for agents. We also considered the completeness and complexity of actions. In particular, good action design should allow agents to efficiently control all the relevant components in an environment and not make the problem unnecessarily hard. Finally, we gave a set of tips to reduce complexity in action design.

15.5 Further Reading: Action Design in Everyday Things

This section contains a whimsical collection of interesting action designs for humans and is intended to be a source of inspiration.

Action design for humans, more commonly referred to as user interface (UI) design, is a vast and diverse discipline spanning many domains from industrial product design to gaming and, more recently, web and app design. Although the term was coined more recently, interface design has existed throughout the history of humanity, from the first prehistoric stone axe our ancestors made to the smartphones we hold today. It has always influenced how we interact with our environments. For inspiration on good interface design, look no further than musical instruments and games that are ubiquitous in human societies.

Musical instruments are essentially control devices which interact with air to produce rich states in the form of sound through plucking, blowing, or hammering, They need to be meticulously crafted and carefully tuned to produce good sounds. Besides the sound quality, the maker of an instrument also needs to think about the users—for example, their hand size, strength, and finger span all matter. But the instruments are only as good as their users. A top class violinist would play a basic modern violin better than a beginner would play the best Stradivarius (violins made in the 1700s by the Stradivari family and still considered the best in the world) whereas a brilliant musician on such an instrument can produce breathtaking music of great emotion and virtuosity.

Consider classical keyboard instruments which produce sound through a column of air (organ), a plucked string (harpsichord), or a hammered one (piano). Various organ stops, harpsichord registrations, and piano pedals also alter the sound together with the precise touch applied to the keyboard. We have seen that an action for a piano can be simplified to 88 integers. However, this is not sufficient to train a robot to properly play a piano mechanically. In reality, each piano key can be played with varying pressure to create a *piano* (soft) or a *forte* (loud) note. Additionally, to modify sound, a piano has three foot pedals: *soft*, *sostenuto*, and a *damper*. Its controls interact in complex ways to produce rich notes, so modeling the actions and the states (sounds) a piano produces would be a difficult task. Nonetheless, this is possible and has already been done with digital pianos, although they still sound different from real ones. To train a piano-playing robot, a first attempt could be to repurpose the software of a digital piano into a virtual environment for training before letting the robot train on (and potentially wreck) an expensive piano.

New musical instruments are still being invented. Modern musical genres such as electronic dance music and techno are known for breaking the mold and creating new sounds with the help of modern technology. Among these newly created instruments, one notable example is a new type of keyboard known as the *Seaboard* [116]. It evolves the piano into the realm of continuous control. Instead of having disjoint keys, the Seaboard has a single wavy surface which resembles the contour of a piano's layout. Touching any point on the surface will produce a sound from one of its many software presets (guitar, strings, etc.). Furthermore, its responsive surface recognizes five dimensions of touch: strike, press, lift, glide, slide. To accommodate these new control dimensions, the Seaboard maker, ROLI, also introduced new notations for its sheet music. Overall, with a two-dimensional surface, five dimensions of touch, and one more for sound presets, this instrument effectively has eight dimensions: seven continuous and one discrete. To get a glimpse of it in action, check out some of the videos on YouTube or on its website `https://roli.com/products/blocks/seaboard-block`.

One other great source of inspiration for control design is games. Games have been present in human societies for a long time, growing together with the available technology. Every generation of games has their own medium, design challenges, and innovations, and reflects the technology of its own era. When wood tiling became commonplace, the Chinese created dominoes. With the availability of paper, playing cards could be made. Pre-computer-era games have physical game pieces to control or interact with, such as tiles, cards, dices, chess pieces, marbles, sticks, and so on.

During the early computing age, electronic games were popularized by arcade machines, most notably Atari and Sega. These machines render images on a screen, which correspond to the states in RL. Their controls are physical buttons and a joystick, which correspond to the actions. Arcade designers not only had to design the games—they also had to create the necessary control interfaces that suited them. Sometimes, this meant inventing an entirely new control interface besides the usual joystick and buttons. An arcade center these days still showcases many of these early innovations. Shooting games have plastic guns or joysticks which can aim at targets on screen and shoot. Some ride-and-shoot games such as the Jurassic Park 1994 Sega additionally have motion seats that move when players are chased by dinosaurs on screen. A typical driving arcade machine has a steering wheel, foot pedals, and a gear shift. Dance Dance Revolution has a floor mat which players can step on to match the rhythmic arrows on screen to the music. Other arcade machines have unique controls made specifically for their games, such as a bow-and-arrow, hammer, claw machine, and so on.

The portability of electronic gaming technology gave rise to console games. Most of these consoles inherited controls from their predecessors, with two buttons, but the joystick from arcade games was replaced by four distinct arrow buttons. As console games became popular, makers such as Sony and Nintendo started introducing new control units to their devices to give the familiar forms we see today—four buttons on each side, with the additional left/right buttons in the upper corner. Modern console systems today, such as PSP and Xbox, include a joystick to bring back richer directional control. More advanced consoles such as the Wii and Nintendo Switch also feature gyroscopic controls that detect movement in 3D space.

When personal computers became mainstream, computer games also proliferated, and control design quickly expanded to the keyboard and mouse. Simpler games typically use the arrow keys along with two other keys to mimic the joystick and two buttons from early consoles. The inclusion of mouse movement and click opened up new possibilities, such as camera panning on top of player movements. This made for more intuitive first-person shooter games—such as Doom where the arrow keys are used to move the player around and the mouse is used to pan the camera, aim, and shoot. As games grew more complex, so did their actions. Multiple keys could be pressed in combination to produce new combo moves. Actions could also be overloaded depending on the game context. In StarCraft and Dota 2, there are tens to hundreds of objects to control, but humans only have so many fingers. Therefore, the game controls are designed to be generic and applicable across different game contexts and objects. Even then, playing any of these games requires nearly twenty distinct keys. Translating these complex control systems into RL environments is challenging.

The invention of smartphones created another new media for games, and the mobile gaming industry was born. Game states and controls moved to a small touch screen where designers are free to create whatever virtual interfaces they desire. Some smartphones also include gyroscopic sensors, which car racing games take advantage of by treating the entire smartphone as a steering wheel.

Now, we are at a new frontier of entertainment technology: virtual reality (VR). Primitive motion controllers have already been designed to allow users to perform actions inside an immersive spatial environment. VR platforms such as Oculus [97] and HTC Vive [55] use handheld consoles with motion sensors. They can also use a Leap Motion [69] vision-based sensor to track hand and finger movements for a more intricate and intuitive control experience. VR gloves are another option for hand tracking. These VR controllers can be used to create and manipulate virtual objects in space. Artists also use them to create stunning 3D virtual sculptures not possible in the real world. The sculptures are viewable by others through a screen or a headset that connects to the same virtual reality.

Another truly impressive but lesser known control technology is the neural interface wristband by CTRL-Labs [29]. This is a noninvasive wristband that detects the neural signals sent from a user's brain to the hand, then reconstructs the corresponding hand and finger movements using those signals. This sounds straight out of science fiction, but they have demonstrated the wristband by using it to play Atari Asteroid. At the time of writing, the wristband is still in active development.

Apart from music and gaming, many more creative control designs can be found at interactive modern art installations. Actions are conveyed through unusual means to trigger these installations using shadow, light, motion gestures, or sound. Artist Daniel Rozin [31] specializes in creating interactive mirrors that use materials such as black and white tiles, troll dolls, or toy penguins which rotate on a large grid. These objects are essentially the "pixels" of a physical "screen." A nearby infrared camera captures a person's silhouette, then reflects it back to them on the grid like a mirror. In this creative example, a person's moving silhouette is used as an action to control a grid of cute and colorful toys.

Last but not least, common daily objects we interact with are also full of design inspirations for actions. We are used to the typical control interfaces such as buttons, dials, sliders, switches, and levers. These are usually mechanical, although virtual interfaces tend to mimic them as well. As an in-depth reading about control interface design, we highly recommend the book *The Design of Everyday Things* by Donald Norman [94].

16

Rewards

This short chapter looks at reward design. We discuss the role of rewards in an RL problem and some important design choices. In particular, we consider the scale, magnitude, frequency, and potential for exploitation when designing a reward signal. The chapter ends with a set of simple design guidelines.

16.1   The Role of Rewards

Reward signals define the objective that an agent should maximize. A reward is a scalar from an environment assigning credit to a particular transition s, a, s' that has happened due to an agent's action a.

Reward design is one of the fundamental problems in RL, and it is known to be difficult for several reasons. First, it takes deep knowledge of the environment to have an intuition about proper credit assignment—that is, judging which transitions are good (positive reward), neutral (zero reward), or bad (negative reward). Even if we have decided on the sign of a reward, we still need to choose its magnitude.

If one transition is assigned a reward of $+1$ and another is assigned a reward of $+10$, we can roughly say that the latter is 10 times more important. However, it is often unclear how these scales should be determined. Since an agent that learns by using rewards as its reinforcing signal takes them quite literally, reward design must be literal as well. Furthermore, an agent may learn to abuse a reward by finding an unexpected strategy to exploit it without producing the intended behavior. As a result, reward design may need frequent tuning—and thus a lot of manual effort—to get the agent to behave correctly.

Humans tend to have an intuitive sense when it comes to judging if their actions contribute to an objective. This kind of implicit credit-assignment ability is built from experience and knowledge. It is a good starting point for designing rewards to encourage agent behaviors.

Reward is the feedback signal to inform an agent how well or badly it is doing. An agent typically learns from scratch without any prior knowledge or common sense, so there are very few constraints on the actions that it explores. A reward signal which grades only a task's outcome but not how the task was performed does not constrain the kinds of behaviors the agent can exhibit, no matter how weird they may be. This is because a solution to a problem is often not unique—there exist many paths to multiple solutions. From a human viewpoint, however, these weird behaviors are not desirable and are considered buggy.

We can attempt to fix this by placing some constraints on the agent. However, even serious restrictions on the freedom of action may not be enough. Consider how our muscular constraints help us learn to walk optimally—but we can also walk strangely if we want to. The alternative is reward design. In the same way as humans can walk properly or strangely depending on their objective at the moment, we can design rewards to encourage the desired behavior of an agent—at least in theory. If we were to faithfully reproduce the proper reward signal for human-like walking, we can imagine it being quite complex given how many components have to function properly to achieve this task.

To design a good reward signal, we need to identify which behaviors are desired, then assign rewards to them accordingly—all while being careful to not exclude other possible good actions. Then, test and evaluate agents to check that the reward signal we designed was acceptable. For trivial toy problems, this is doable. However, it is unclear if this is possible or practical for environments that are far more complex.

Regardless, well-designed reward signals for specific tasks can still take us pretty far. This was demonstrated by recent breakthroughs in RL such as OpenAI's Dota 2 [104] and robotic hand manipulation [101]—in which the reward functions were carefully tuned by humans and agents were able to accomplish impressive results. The reward design was an important part of successful agent learning. These results suggest that the complexity threshold at which manual reward design becomes inadmissible is quite high. Here's a natural question to ask: is there any problem that we cannot design a good reward signal for? If the answer is no, then designing a good reward signal will be possible for a task of any complexity, even though it might be difficult and time-consuming. With that said, let's look at some practical reward design guidelines.

16.2   Reward Design Guidelines

A reward signal can be dense or sparse. A sparse reward is one which produces a neutral reward signal (usually $r = 0$) for most of the time steps, and a positive and negative reward only when the environment terminates or the agent does something of crucial importance. A dense reward is the opposite: it provides a lot of nonneutral reward signals indicating whether the last action was good or bad, so that in most time steps an agent will receive a positive or negative reward.

The correspondence of a reward's value to the notion of good, neutral, or bad is relative—that is, the numerical scale for rewards is a design choice. This is also why it is justified to standardize rewards during agent training. One can design an environment where all the reward values are negative, with bad rewards being more negative than good rewards. Since an agent always maximizes the objective, reward values still need to be ordered so that better rewards have higher values.

Although not necessary, it makes good mathematical sense to set neutral rewards to 0, bad rewards to negative, and good rewards to positive. This design is easy to reason with, while it also possesses nice mathematical properties. For instance, if the scale of reward is centered at 0, one can easily rescale it symmetrically on both the negative and positive sides by multiplying with a scalar.

Reward is defined as $r_t = \mathcal{R}(s, a, s')$, so the first step of reward design is to figure out what constitutes good or bad transitions within the environment. Since a transition consists of an action a causing transition from state s to s', it helps to systematically enumerate all possible transitions. However, in complex environments there may be too many transitions to enumerate, so we need smarter reward design methods.

If possible, classify transitions by rules into good or bad groups, then assign rewards using these rules. Better still, in many tasks it is possible to simply assign credit based on the state s' that is transitioned into without having to consider the preceding action. For example, CartPole assigns reward of 0.1 for all the states where the pole does not fall over, regardless of the actions performed to keep it upright. Alternatively, rewards can be given based only on the action. For example, in OpenAI's LunarLander environment, each action of firing the main engine is given a small negative reward as its cost.

Fortunately, rewards are ubiquitous in games, although there they go by a different name—game score. Score keeping is a universal feature of games because there is always a winner or tasks to complete. The scores can be provided in an explicit numerical form, usually displayed on a screen, or in implicit nonnumerical form such as a win/loss declaration. Once again, we can look to games for inspiration and techniques for reward design.

The simplest form of reward is a binary win or loss, which we can encode as 1 and 0, respectively. Chess is one such example. Additionally, when playing multiple rounds of such a game, the average reward nicely translates to the winning probability. For a role-playing narrative game, usually there is no score but we can still attach a binary score for advancing through every stage, so there is an incentive to complete the game.

Another form of reward is a single scalar value that is gradually increased as a player collects more points. In many games, there are goals to reach, objects to collect, and stages to pass. Each of these goals or objects is assigned a score. As a game progresses, the score gets accumulated to an ultimate score that ranks the success of each player. Games with simple to medium complexity display these cumulative rewards, because it is still practical to assign scores to all the relevant game elements while making sure their sum reflects the final game objective correctly.

Lastly, a larger and much more complex game may also track multiple auxiliary game scores, but these do not necessarily add to the ultimate game objective. Real-time strategy games like StarCraft and Command & Conquer track scores including buildings, research, resources, and units, but these do not necessarily correspond to the final game outcome. In Dota 2, auxiliary scores such as last hits, gold, and experience gains are closely tracked throughout the game—but in the end, the team that destroys the enemy's throne wins. These auxiliary scores often help narrate progress in a long-running game by showing the advantages of one side over the other, and they are indicative of the final outcome. However, favorable indication does not always guarantee victory, as a player with low auxiliary scores can still win the game. Therefore, auxiliary scores are a set of "rewards" disjoint from the game objective. Despite this, they are still useful to serve as actual reward signals since they can help an agent learn. OpenAI Five [104] uses a combination of auxiliary scores and the final objective as the reward signal for Dota 2.

For win/loss games such as chess, it is hard to design a good intermediate reward because, with the astronomical number of possible configurations, it is objectively hard to determine how good a board configuration is. In this case, a reward is only given at the end of a game when the winner is known. The end reward is simply 1 for the winner and 0 for the loser, and the intermediate reward is 0. This reward signal is sparse.

This begs a question: when a task is defined and we know the final desired outcome that can be assigned and rewarded easily, why don't we just stick with a sparse reward, as in chess?

There is a tradeoff between sparse and dense rewards. Although a sparse reward is easy to specify, it is much harder to learn from because there is much less feedback from the environment. An agent has to wait until a task terminates to get a reward signal, but even then it has no easy way of telling which actions in the intermediate steps were good or bad. Sparse rewards make a problem very sample-inefficient, so an agent will require orders of magnitude more examples to learn from. Sometimes, reward sparsity may even make the problem unsolvable because the agent receives so little feedback that it is unable to discover a sequence of good actions. In contrast, with dense rewards, although intermediate rewards may be difficult to specify, the feedback from the environment is immediate so an agent will get signals to learn from more often.

A useful trick is to combine sparse and dense rewards and vary their weights over time to gradually switch from dense to sparse reward. Let's define the *combined reward* in Equation 16.1.

$$r = \delta \cdot r_{\text{dense}} + r_{\text{sparse}}, \quad \text{where } \delta = 1.0 \rightarrow 0.0 \tag{16.1}$$

We gradually decay the coefficient δ from 1.0 to 0.0 over the course of agent training. A small design detail is to exclude the end reward from r_{dense}, since we do not wish to double-count it.

Having dense rewards during the early phase of training can help an agent with exploration by giving it a lot of feedback. Suppose, in a robotic task, an agent's goal is to walk to a flag on an open plane. The end reward is easy: 1 for reaching the flag and -1 for failing when the episode ends. Let the agent's distance to the flag be $d(\text{agent}, \text{flag})$. Then, a useful dense intermediate reward could be the negative distance, $r_{\text{dense}} = -d(\text{agent}, \text{flag})$. In the beginning, this dense reward helps teach the agent that the movements it makes change its distance to the flag, and that minimizing that distance is good for the objective. From this, it learns a distance-minimizing policy. After some training, we can remove the training wheels by decaying δ to 0.0. By the time r_{dense} is muted, the same policy will still be able to function properly using only the sparse reward.

To appreciate how crucial the dense reward may be, just imagine the same task but with only the sparse reward. The chance of an agent ever reaching the flag by performing random walks on a vast 2D plane is extremely small. Most of the time, it is going to fail. Even if on rare occasions it succeeds, there will be too few successful examples for it to learn from, let alone to discover the concept of distance minimization. The chance of the agent learning to solve the problem, even if given plenty of time, is small.

Another advanced technique used to address the sparse reward issue is *reward redistribution*. The idea is to take the end reward, split it up, and redistribute some of it to credit significant events in the intermediate steps. If such significant events are known to the reward designer, this is relatively straightforward, but it may not always be easy to identify them. One solution is to estimate them by collecting many trajectories, identifying common patterns, and correlating them with the final rewards. This is a form of auto-credit assignment. An example of this is RUDDER [8] developed by the LIT AI Lab.

The converse of reward redistribution is *reward delay*, in which all the reward signals are withheld for a number of time steps. An example of this happens when we skip frames. It is important that the rewards from the skipped frames are not lost—the total reward should remain equivalent to that of the original environment. We do this by storing the rewards from the intermediate frames, then summing them to produce the reward for the next sampled frame. Summing also ensures that the reward signal has a nice linear property of working for any frame-skipping frequency without changing the objective.

Something to consider when designing a reward signal is its distribution profile. In many algorithms, the reward is used in the computation of loss. Having a large reward magnitude can make the loss huge and cause the gradient to explode. When creating a reward function, avoid using extreme values. Overall, it is beneficial to shape the reward signal to have a healthy statistical profile—standardized, with zero mean, and no extreme values. Ideally, rewards should be assigned based on reasons that are simple and easy to understand. Overly complicated reward design not only takes time and effort but also makes the environment and the agent difficult to debug—while there is no guarantee that it will function significantly better than a simpler one. A complicated reward signal is often the result of being too focused on some scenarios, so it is unlikely to generalize well to variations in the environment.

Another thing to be aware of when designing a reward signal is *reward farming* or *reward hacking*. In a sufficiently complex environment, it is hard to anticipate all the possible scenarios. In video games, it is considered a bug if a player finds an exploit or hack and then abuses it repeatedly to get extremely large rewards—even if it is permissible within the game. This is what happened when an evolution-strategy-based agent created by a team of researchers from the University of Freiburg managed to find a bug in the Atari Qbert game [23]. Their agent performed a specific sequence of moves which triggered a bonus animation that kept increasing the game points without bound. The video can be found on YouTube as "Canonical ES finds a bug in Qbert (Full)," at https://youtu.be/meE5aaRJOZs [22].

In video games, the result of reward hacking may be funny and amusing—but in real-world applications, this could potentially be harmful with serious implications. If an RL system controlling industrial hardware encounters an exploit with a runaway process, it may end up destroying some expensive equipment or injuring people. Since credit assignment is closely related to specifying and controlling the behavior of an agent, it is also a major subject of research in AI safety. A good introduction can be found in the paper "Concrete Problems in AI Safety" [4]. Environments should be designed and agents trained responsibly to avoid negative side effects, prevent reward hacking, ensure oversight, encourage safe exploration, and ensure robustness when an RL system is deployed in the real world.

When reward hacking occurs, we consider the reward signal to be faulty [100]. Then, the designer must act to patch the bug in the environment or redesign part of the faulty reward signal. There is no sure way to anticipate where reward hacking could happen; we have to rely on observations in a test environment to discover it. One way to do so is to record all the rewards obtained during training and analyze them. Compute the mean, mode, standard deviation, then scan for abnormal and extreme values. If any extreme reward values are found, identify the relevant scenarios and manually inspect them to see how an agent behaved to produce these abnormal reward values. We can also save video replays of these scenarios for easier debugging, or just watch the environment live provided there are ways to reproduce the buggy scenarios.

We have covered quite some ground in reward design. To summarize, these are the factors to consider when designing a reward signal:

1. **Use good, neutral, bad reward values:** A good starting point is to use positive values for good, zero for neutral, and negative for bad. Pay attention to scale, avoid extreme values.

2. **Choose sparse or dense reward signal:** Sparse rewards are easy to design but often make a problem much harder; dense rewards are hard to design but give agents much more feedback.

3. **Watch for reward hacking and safety:** Constantly evaluate agents and environments to ensure reward hacking is not taking place. Agent training and environment design should be done responsibly to ensure the safety of a deployed system.

A reward signal can be seen as a proxy for transferring human prior knowledge, expectations, and common sense about a task to an agent—which has none of these. The way RL is currently set up, an agent does not understand or see a task the same way we humans do. Its only goal is to maximize the objective. All its behaviors emerge from the reward signal. To encourage certain behavior, we have to figure out how to assign rewards in such a way that they emerge as a side effect of maximizing the objective. However, reward design may not always be perfect, and an agent may misunderstand our intentions and fail to solve the problem the way we want it to even though it is still maximizing the total reward. That's why human domain expertise is required to design a good reward signal.

16.3   Summary

In this chapter on reward design, we discussed the tradeoff between sparse and dense reward signals and the importance of the reward scale. A carefully designed reward function can be very effective, as shown by OpenAI's Dota 2 results. A good reward signal should not be too generic or too specific, and should encourage desired behaviors from an agent. However, unexpected behaviors may emerge from a faulty reward design. This is known as reward hacking, and it can pose risks to a deployed system. Therefore, we should be mindful when deploying an RL system to ensure safety.

17

Transition Function

Now that we have looked at states, actions, and rewards, the last component necessary to make a functioning RL environment is a transition function, also known as a model.

The model of an environment can be programmed or learned. Programmable rules are common, and they can yield environments with various levels of complexity. Chess is perfectly described by a simple set of rules. Robot simulations approximate a robot's dynamics and its surroundings. Modern computer games can be very complex, but they are still built using programmed game engines.

However, when modeling problems that cannot be efficiently programmed, a model of an environment can be learned instead. For example, contact dynamics in robotics is difficult to model with programmable rules, so an alternative is to try to learn it from real-world observations. For applied problems where the states and actions are abstract quantities that are difficult to understand and model but for which a lot of transition data is available, a transition function may be learned instead. An environment could also have a hybrid model that is partly programmed and partly learned.

This chapter presents some guidelines for checking the feasibility of building a transition function and for evaluating how closely it approximates the real problem.

17.1 Feasibility Checks

Recall that a transition function is defined as $P(s_{t+1} \mid s_t, a_t)$. It has the Markov property, which means that the transition is fully determined by the current state and action. In theory, we have to consider if a model can be built in this form. In practice, we first consider if we can conceivably build the model using rules, a physics engine, a game engine, or data.

This section provides some feasibility checks to satisfy before building a transition function. There are a few things to consider:

1. **Programmable vs. learnable:** Can one build an RL environment without using data, by figuring out and programming the transition rules? Can the problem be fully described by a set of rules? Examples are board games such as chess and physical systems such as robots. If it is not possible or practical, then the model can only be learned from data.

2. **Data completeness:** If the model needs to be learned from data, is there sufficient data available? That is, is the data representative enough? If not, is it possible to gather more data or make up for it? Is all the data fully observable? If not, the model may be inaccurate; in that case, what is an acceptable threshold of error?

3. **Cost of data:** Sometimes, generating data can be costly. The process may take a long time, or cost a lot of money, because collecting real-world data involves long process cycles and expensive assets. For instance, a real robot moves more slowly compared to a simulation and is expensive—but creating a realistic model may require first collecting data from actual robot movements.

4. **Data sample vs. sample efficiency:** Deep RL still has low sample efficiency and poor generalizability. This means that a model of the problem needs to have high fidelity. This, in turn, requires a lot of data to build, and will add to the cost of learning the model. Even if a transition function is programmable, it may still take a lot of time and effort to produce a realistic model. For example, video games have some of the most complex programmable transition functions and can cost millions of dollars to produce.

5. **Offline vs. online:** When data is gathered in isolation from an actual RL agent, it is considered offline. If a model is built with offline data, will it be sufficient to account for the effects of interactions with an agent? For example, a learning agent may explore new parts of the state space, thereby requiring new data to fill in the gap in the model. This requires an online approach—that is, deploying the agent to interact with the actual problem to gather more data. Is this possible?

6. **Training vs. production** (related to the previous point): An agent that is trained using a learned model needs to be evaluated against the actual problem before it can be used. Is it safe to test an agent in production? How can we ensure that the behavior is within reasonable bounds? If unexpected behavior occurs in production, what is the potential financial cost?

If these feasibility checks pass, then we may proceed with constructing a transition function. When building a model, there are generally a few problem characteristics to consider. These determine which methods are appropriate.

1. **Deterministic problems with known transition rules**—for example, chess. We use the known rules to build a deterministic mapping function, for example using a stored dictionary. This can be written as $s_{t+1} \sim P(s_{t+1} \mid s_t, a_t) = 1$ or, equivalently, as a direct function where $s_{t+1} = f_{\text{deterministic}}(s_t, a_t)$. When building a model, it is convenient to make use of existing open source engines or commercial tools. There are many excellent physics or game engines such as Box2D [17], PyBullet [19], Unity [138], and Unreal Engine [139] that have been used to build a number of RL environments, from simple 2D toy problems to a highly realistic driving simulator.

2. **Stochastic (nondeterministic) problems with known dynamics**—for example, a realistic robotic simulation. Here, parts of the dynamics are inherently stochastic, while the rest is composed of a deterministic dynamic with added random

noise. For example, a physical system can be modeled with deterministic rules—but to make it more realistic, it is common to account for random noise such as friction, jitter, or sensor noise. In this case, the transition model has the form $s_{t+1} \sim P(s_{t+1} \mid s_t, a_t)$.

3. **Stochastic problems with unknown dynamics**—for example, complex inventory management or sales optimization with many unobservable or unpredictable components. Since the dynamics is unknown, we have to learn them from data. Collect all the available data in the form $\ldots, s_t, a_t, s_{t+1}, a_{t+1}, \ldots$ and build a histogram to capture the frequencies of s_{t+1} given s_t, a_t. Then, fit the histogram with a distribution type, such as Gaussian, Beta, Bernoulli, etc. to obtain a probability distribution of the form $P(s_{t+1} \mid s_t, a_t)$. This is the learned model. The entire process can be turned into a supervised learning task to learn the probability distribution from data, with s_t, a_t as inputs and s_{t+1} as target outputs.

4. **Problems that do not obey the Markov property**—for example, complex video games. In this situation, longer time horizons are required to fully determine transitions. There are two common strategies to deal with this. First, if the transition function is programmable, focus on building a realistic model that is not necessarily Markov, then decide if the states exposed to an agent should be Markov. If it is important that they are Markov, this may require redesigning the state to include sufficient history. Alternatively, states can be simpler; then the problem for an agent becomes a partially observable MDP. If we are learning a transition function, we don't have this luxury since the training data s_t, a_t needs to contain sufficient information to fully learn the next transition. The main strategy here is to redefine the state to be Markov.

Once we have built a model, how do we check that it is a sufficiently realistic representation of a problem? This leads us to the next section.

17.2 Reality Check

Any model approximating real-world phenomena is likely imperfect. We therefore need methods to evaluate how good our approximation is. In this section, we first discuss some sources of model error, then discuss KL divergence as a way to quantify the error.

We can identify two main reasons that may cause a model to be imperfect.

The first case is when it might not be feasible to completely simulate every aspect of a problem, so simplifications have to be made. For example, simulation of a robotic arm might not account for friction, jitters, thermal expansion, and impact-induced deformations of its physical parts that occur in the real world. Some data is simply not available in practice. For example, take movie recommendations; it would be useful to know which genres a person likes, but this cannot be known directly. It can only be inferred from the previous movies they watched.

The second case is due to the limit of exploration when using learned transition functions. The problem in this case is that some transitions might not be visited until an algorithm is deployed to interact with the environment. This happens when the state space is so large that it is impractical to learn a good model for all the transitions. Instead, we typically focus on learning a good model for the transitions an agent is likely to encounter. Of course if the model fails to account for transitions that an agent encounters in production, then it may produce inaccurate transitions—but this does not mean that an agent cannot be trained on a limited model.

A model can be iteratively learned from data as follows. First, collect a subset of data from the real world and use it to train a model. This model will approximate reality with some error. We can then train an agent, deploy it to production, collect more transition data, and retrain to improve the model. We iterate this until the error is reduced to an acceptable threshold.

Now, we need a notion of error between a learned model and the problem it approximates. Let's define the transition function for training versus production respectively as $P_{\text{train}}(s' \mid s, a)$ and $P_{\text{prod}}(s' \mid s, a)$. We now have two probability distributions so we can measure the difference between them using standard methods.

The Kullback-Leibler (KL) divergence[1] is a widely used method to measure how much one probability distribution diverges from another. Suppose we are given two distributions $p(s), q(s)$ of the random variable, say $s \in \mathcal{S}$. Let $p(s)$ be the ground truth distribution and $q(s)$ be its approximation. We can determine how much $q(s)$ diverges from the ground truth $p(s)$ using the KL divergence.

The KL divergence for a discrete variable is shown in Equation 17.1.

$$KL\big(p(s) \,||\, q(s)\big) = \sum_{s \in \mathcal{S}} p(s) \log \frac{p(s)}{q(s)} \tag{17.1}$$

The generalization to a continuous variable is straightforward by turning the discrete sum into a continuous integral, as shown in Equation 17.2.

$$KL\big(p(s) \,||\, q(s)\big) = \int_{-\infty}^{\infty} p(s) \log \frac{p(s)}{q(s)} ds \tag{17.2}$$

The KL divergence is a non-negative number. When it is 0, the approximate distribution q does not diverge from the ground truth distribution p—that is, the two distributions are equal. The larger the KL divergence is, the greater the divergence of q from p is. It is also an asymmetric metric—that is, $KL(p \,||\, q) \neq KL(q \,||\, p)$ in general. Because of its desirable properties, KL is also used in a number of RL algorithms to measure divergence in policy iterations, as we saw in Chapter 7.

KL can be interpreted as the information loss when using $q(s)$ to approximate the reality $p(s)$. In our case, the reality is $P_{\text{prod}}(s' \mid s, a)$ from production, and the approximation is $P_{\text{train}}(s' \mid s, a)$ from training. Additionally, P_{prod} and P_{train} are conditional probabilities, but we can simply calculate KL for each specific instance of the conditional variables. Let $p = P_{\text{prod}}$, $q = P_{\text{train}}$, and the $KL_{s,a}$ between them is written in Equation 17.3.

---

1. KL divergence is also known as *relative entropy*.

$$KL_{s,a}\big(P_{\text{prod}}(s' \mid s, a) \mid\mid P_{\text{train}}(s' \mid s, a)\big)$$
$$= \sum_{s' \in \mathcal{S}} P_{\text{prod}}(s' \mid s, a) \log \frac{P_{\text{prod}}(s' \mid s, a)}{P_{\text{train}}(s' \mid s, a)} \qquad (17.3)$$

This is written for the discrete case. For continuous variables, simply convert the sum into an integral as appropriate.

Equation 17.3 applies to a single (s, a) pair. However, we want to estimate the KL for the entire model over all (s, a) pairs. In practice, we do this using a technique often seen in this book—Monte Carlo sampling.

To use this to improve a model, calculate and keep track of the KL during every iterations of model training and deployment to ensure that P_{train} does not diverge too far from P_{prod}. Over multiple training iterations, we should aim to reduce the KL to an acceptable threshold.

In this chapter, we set out to build a model $P(s' \mid s, a)$ for an environment with the requirement that it is realistic. Now armed with a tool to perform a quite literal *reality check*, we can ask more practical questions. What is the distribution of data available for training versus for production, and what are the differences? How will the gap between training and production converge? These questions matter especially in industrial applications where data is often limited and difficult to obtain, so it may only represent some subset of the actual problem's full transition distribution. The available data will affect the quality of the model, which in turn affects the learning of an RL algorithm. For RL algorithms to be useful outside of training, we need them to generalize beyond the training data when deployed to production. If the gap between training and production data is too large, the agent may fail outside of the training set, so we need to iteratively improve the model to close the gap.

17.3 Summary

This chapter looked at transition functions, also known as models of environments. A model can be programmed with rules or learned from data. We presented a list for checking the feasibility of programming or learning a model. Then, we looked at different forms a transition function may take. Finally, we presented the KL divergence as a method for measuring the error between a constructed model and the real transition distribution.

Epilogue

This book began by formulating an RL problem as an MDP. Parts I and II introduced the main families of deep RL algorithms that can be used to solve MDPs—policy-based, value-based, and combined methods. Part III focused on the practicalities of training agents, covering topics such as debugging, neural network architecture, and hardware. We also included a deep RL almanac containing information about hyperparameters and algorithm performance for some classic control and Atari environments from OpenAI Gym.

It was fitting to end the book by taking a look at environment design since this is an important part of using deep RL in practice. Without environments, there is nothing for an agent to solve. Environment design is a large and interesting topic, so we were only able to touch briefly on some of the important ideas. Part IV should be understood as a set of high-level guidelines, not a detailed and in-depth review of the topic.

We hope this book has served as a useful introduction to deep RL, and has conveyed some of the excitement, curiosity, and appreciation we feel for studying and participating in this field. We also hope that it has stimulated your interest and you are curious to learn more. With this in mind, we end the book by briefly mentioning a number of open research questions and, where relevant, providing pointers to recent work in these areas. This is not a complete list but is a starting point for an endlessly interesting and rapidly changing field of research.

Reproducibility   Currently, deep RL algorithms are known to be unstable, sensitive to hyperparameters, and for having high variance in performance. This makes results hard to reproduce. The "Deep Reinforcement Learning that Matters" paper by Henderson et al. [48] contains an excellent analysis of these issues and proposes some potential remedies. One of these is to use a more reproducible workflow which this book and its companion library, SLM Lab, have tried to encourage.

Reality Gap   This is also known as the simulation-to-reality (sim-to-real) transfer problem. It is often difficult to train a deep RL agent in the real world because of cost, time, and safety. Often, we train an agent in a simulation and deploy it in the real world. Unfortunately, it is very difficult to model the real world accurately in a simulation—this is what is called a reality gap. This represents a domain transfer problem in which an agent is trained on a data distribution different from the test data.

One common approach to deal with this problem is by adding random noise to the simulation during training. "Learning Dexterous In-Hand Manipulation" by OpenAI [98] does this by randomizing the physical properties of the simulation such as object mass, color, and friction.

Meta- and Multitask Learning   One limitation of the algorithms in this book is that they learn from scratch for each task, which is very inefficient. Naturally, many tasks are related. For example, competitive swimmers often compete in multiple swimming styles because the techniques are closely related. When learning a new style, they do not learn how to swim again from scratch. More generally, humans learn to control their bodies when growing up, and apply this knowledge to learn many different physical skills.

Metalearning approaches this problem by learning how to learn. The algorithms are designed to learn how to learn a new task efficiently after being trained on a set of related learning tasks. An example of this "Model-Agnostic Meta-Learning for Fast Adaptation of Deep Networks" by Finn et al. [40].

Multitask learning is concerned with learning multiple tasks more efficiently by learning them jointly. The Distral algorithm by Teh et al. [134] and the Actor-Mimic algorithm by Parisotto et al. [110] are examples of this approach.

Multiagent Problems   It is natural to apply RL to multiagent problems. OpenAI Five [104] is an example, where five separate agents were trained using the PPO algorithm to play the Dota 2 multiplayer game. Simply by tuning the coefficients which balanced the team and individual rewards, authors saw cooperative behavior emerge among the agents. DeepMind's FTW algorithm [56] played the multiplayer game Quake by using population-based training and deep RL where each agent's objective was to maximize the probability of its team winning.

Sample Efficiency   The sample efficiency of deep RL algorithms is a significant obstacle to applying them to real-world problems. One way to tackle this is to incorporate environment models. The MB-MPO [24] algorithm by Clavera et al. and the SimPLe [62] algorithm by Kaiser et al. are two recent examples.

Hindsight Experience Replay (HER) [6] is another alternative. It was motivated by the idea that humans are good at learning from failed attempts at a task as well as successful ones. In the HER algorithm, trajectories are given new rewards which assume that what an agent did in an episode was what it was supposed to do. This helps an agent learn about the environment when rewards are sparse, improving sample efficiency.

Generalization   Deep RL algorithms still have poor generalizability. They are often trained and tested on the same environments, which makes them susceptible to overfitting. For example, "Natural Environment Benchmarks for Reinforcement Learning" by Zhang et al. [152] showed that simply by adding image noise to some Atari games, a trained agent can completely fail. To remedy this problem, they modified the Atari environments by embedding videos in the game background and used these to train the agents.

In the previous example, the underlying task remained the same even as variations were introduced into the environment. However, an agent should also be able to generalize to unseen but related tasks. To test for this, an environment can be made to progressively generate new but related tasks. Two examples are the game Obstacle Tower [60] with generative elements and levels, and the Animal-AI Olympics environment [7] with a disjoint set of training and evaluation tasks.

Exploration and Reward Shaping   It is challenging to train deep RL agents in environments with sparse rewards because the environment provides little information about which actions are desirable. When exploring an environment, it is difficult for agents to discover useful actions and they often get stuck in local minima.

It is often possible to design additional rewards which encourage behavior that will help solve the task. For example, in the BipedalWalker environment [18], instead of giving an agent a reward only when it succeeds in reaching the far end, rewards are given for moving forward and penalties are given for applying motor torque and falling over. These dense rewards encourage the agent to progress forward efficiently.

However, designing rewards is time-consuming as rewards are often problem-specific. One way to address this problem is to give an agent an intrinsic reward which motivates it to explore novel states and develop new skills. This is analogous to rewarding an agent for curiosity. "Curiosity-Driven Exploration by Self-Supervised Prediction" by Pathak et al. [111] is a recent example.

The Go-Explore algorithm by Ecoffet et al. [36] takes a different approach. It was motivated by the idea that exploration could be more effective if it started from promising states instead of from the beginning of an episode. To implement this, training is split into an exploration phase and an imitation phase. In the exploration phase, a Go-Explore agent explores the environment randomly and remembers interesting states and the trajectories that led up to them. In the imitation phase, it does not explore from scratch but iteratively from the stored states.

Deep Reinforcement Learning Timeline

- 1947: Monte Carlo Sampling
- 1958: Perceptron
- 1959: Temporal Difference Learning
- 1983: ASE-ALE—the first Actor-Critic algorithm
- 1986: Backpropagation algorithm
- 1989: CNNs
- 1989: Q-Learning
- 1991: TD-Gammon
- 1992: REINFORCE
- 1992: Experience Replay
- 1994: SARSA
- 1999: Nvidia invents the GPU
- 2007: CUDA released
- 2012: Arcade Learning Environment (ALE)
- 2013: DQN
- 2015 Feb: DQN human-level control in Atari
- 2015 Feb: TRPO
- 2015 Jun: Generalized Advantage Estimation
- 2015 Sep: Deep Deterministic Policy Gradient (DDPG) [81]
- 2015 Sep: Double DQN
- 2015 Nov: Dueling DQN [144]
- 2015 Nov: Prioritized Experience Replay
- 2015 Nov: TensorFlow

- 2016 Feb: A3C
- 2016 Mar: AlphaGo beats Lee Sedol 4-1
- 2016 Jun: OpenAI Gym
- 2016 Jun: Generative Adversarial Imitation Learning (GAIL) [51]
- 2016 Oct: PyTorch
- 2017 Mar: Model-Agnostic Meta-Learning (MAML) [40]
- 2017 Jul: Distributional RL [13]
- 2017 Jul: PPO
- 2017 Aug: OpenAI Dota 2 1:1
- 2017 Aug: Intrinsic Curiosity Module (ICM) [111]
- 2017 Oct: Rainbow [49]
- 2017 Dec: AlphaZer [126]
- 2018 Jan: Soft Actor-Critic (SAC) [47]
- 2018 Feb: IMPALA [37]
- 2018 Jun: Qt-Opt [64]
- 2018 Nov: Go-Explore solves Montezuma's Revenge [36]
- 2018 Dec: AlphaZero becomes the strongest player in history for chess, Go, and Shogi
- 2018 Dec: AlphaStar [3] defeats one of the world strongest players in the game of StarCraft II
- 2019 Apr: OpenAI Five defeats world champions at Dota 2
- 2019 May: FTW Quake III Arena Capture the Flag [56]

B

Example Environments

Deep RL today enjoys a great selection of RL environments offered through a number of Python libraries. Some of these are listed below for reference.

1. Animal-AI Olympics [7] https://github.com/beyretb/AnimalAI-Olympics: an AI competition with tests inspired by animal cognition.

2. Deepdrive [115] https://github.com/deepdrive/deepdrive: end-to-end simulation for self-driving cars.

3. DeepMind Lab [12] https://github.com/deepmind/lab: a suite of challenging 3D navigation and puzzle-solving tasks.

4. DeepMind PySC2 [142] https://github.com/deepmind/pysc2: StarCraft II environment.

5. Gibson Environments [151] https://github.com/StanfordVL/GibsonEnv: real-world perception for embodied agents.

6. Holodeck [46] https://github.com/BYU-PCCL/holodeck: high-fidelity simulations created with the Unreal Engine 4.

7. Microsoft Malmö [57] https://github.com/Microsoft/malmo: Minecraft environments.

8. MuJoCo [136] http://www.mujoco.org/: physics engine with robotics simulations.

9. OpenAI Coinrun [25] https://github.com/openai/coinrun: custom environment created to quantify generalization in RL.

10. OpenAI Gym [18] https://github.com/openai/gym: a huge selection of classic control, Box2D, robotics, and Atari environments.

11. OpenAI Retro [108] https://github.com/openai/retro: retro games including Atari, NEC, Nintendo, and Sega.

12. OpenAI Roboschool [109] https://github.com/openai/roboschool: robotics environments tuned for research.

13. Stanford osim-RL [129] https://github.com/stanfordnmbl/osim-rl: musculoskeletal RL environment.

14. Unity ML-Agents [59] `https://github.com/Unity-Technologies/ml-agents`: a set of environments created with the Unity game engine.

15. Unity Obstacle Tower [60] `https://github.com/Unity-Technologies /obstacle-tower-env`: a procedurally generated environment consisting of multiple floors to be solved by a learning agent.

16. VizDoom [150] `https://github.com/mwydmuch/ViZDoom`: VizDoom game simulator, usable with OpenAI Gym.

In this book, we use a number of environments from OpenAI Gym. These include some easy-to-moderate discrete environments `CartPole-v0`, `MountainCar-v0`, `LunarLander-v2` and a continuous environment `Pendulum-v0`. For harder environments, some Atari games such as `PongNoFrameskip-v4` and `BreakoutNoFrameskip-v4` are used.

B.1   Discrete Environments

The discrete-control environments available in OpenAI Gym include easy-to-moderate environments `CartPole-v0`, `MountainCar-v0`, and `LunarLander-v2`. Harder environments are some Atari games `PongNoFrameskip-v4` and `BreakoutNoFrameskip-v4`. This section provides detailed descriptions of these environments; some information is referenced from the original OpenAI Gym documentation Wiki.

B.1.1   CartPole-v0

Figure B.1   The `CartPole-v0` environment. The objective is to balance the pole for 200 time steps.

This is the simplest toy problem in OpenAI Gym, and it is commonly used to debug algorithms. It was originally described by Barto, Sutton, and Anderson [11]. A pole is attached to a cart that can be moved along a frictionless track.

1. **Objective:** Keep the pole upright for 200 time steps.

2. **State:** An array of length 4: [cart position, cart velocity, pole angle, pole angular velocity]. For example, $[-0.03474355, 0.03248249, -0.03100749, 0.03614301]$.

3. **Action:** An integer within $\{0, 1\}$ to move the cart left or right. For example, 0 to move left.

4. **Reward:** $+1$ for every time step the pole remains upright.

5. **Termination:** When the pole falls over (12 degrees from vertical), or the cart moves out of the screen, or a maximum of 200 time steps is reached.

6. **Solution:** Average total reward of 195.0 over 100 consecutive episodes.

B.1.2   MountainCar-v0

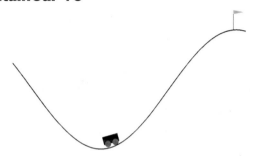

Figure B.2   The MountainCar-v0 environment. The objective is to swing the car left and right to reach the hilltop in the shortest amount of time.

This is a sparse-reward problem originally proposed by Andrew Moore [91]. The goal is to strategically "swing" an underpowered car to the top of a hill indicated with a flag.

1. **Objective:** Swing the car up to the flag.

2. **State:** An array of length 2: [car position, car velocity]. For example, $[-0.59025158, 0.]$.

3. **Action:** An integer within $\{0, 1, 2\}$ to push left, stay still, or push right. For example, 0 to push left.

4. **Reward:** -1 for every time step, until the car reaches the hilltop.

5. **Termination:** When the car reaches the hilltop, or after 200 maximum time steps.

6. **Solution:** Average total reward of -110 over 100 consecutive episodes.

B.1.3   LunarLander-v2

This is harder control problem where an agent has to steer a lander and land it without crashing. The fuel is infinite. The landing pad is always at the center, indicated by two flags.

1. **Objective:** Land the lander without crashing fuel. Solution total reward is $+200$.

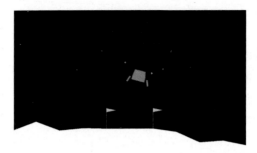

Figure B.3 The LunarLander-v2 environment. The objective is to steer and land the lander between the flags using minimal fuel, without crashing.

2. **State:** An array of length 8: [x-position, y-position, x-velocity, y-velocity, lander angle, lander angular velocity, left leg ground contact, right leg ground contact]. For example, $[-0.00550737, 0.94806147, -0.55786095, 0.49652665, 0.00638856, 0.12636393, 0., 0.]$.

3. **Action:** An integer within $\{0, 1, 2, 3\}$ to fire no engine, fire left engine, fire main engine, or fire right engine. For example, 2 to fire main engine.

4. **Reward:** -100 for crashing, -0.3 per time step when firing main engine, $+100$ to $+140$ for landing, $+10$ for each leg ground contact.

5. **Termination:** When the lander lands or crashes, or after 1000 maximum time steps.

6. **Solution:** Average total reward of 200.0 over 100 consecutive episodes.

B.1.4 PongNoFrameskip-v4

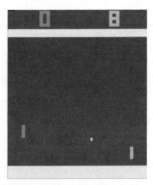

Figure B.4 The PongNoFrameskip-v4 environment. The main objective is to beat the programmed opponent on the left.

This is an image-based Atari game that consists of a ball, a left paddle controlled by a program, and a right paddle controlled by an agent. The goal is to catch the ball and make the opponent miss the ball. The game goes on for 21 rounds.

1. **Objective:** Maximize the game score, with a maximum of +21.
2. **State:** An RGB image tensor of shape $(210, 160, 3)$.
3. **Action:** An integer within $\{0, 1, 2, 3, 4, 5\}$ to control an emulated game console.
4. **Reward:** -1 if agent misses the ball, $+1$ if opponent misses the ball. The game goes on for 21 rounds.
5. **Termination:** After 21 rounds.
6. **Solution:** Maximize the average score over 100 consecutive episodes. A perfect score of +21 is possible.

B.1.5   BreakoutNoFrameskip-v4

Figure B.5   The BreakoutNoFrameskip-v4 environment. The main objective is to destroy all the bricks.

This is an image-based Atari game that consists of a ball, a bottom paddle controlled by an agent, and bricks. The goal is to destroy all the bricks by bouncing the ball. A game life is lost every time the ball falls off the screen from the bottom.

1. **Objective:** Maximize the game score.
2. **State:** An RGB image tensor of shape $(210, 160, 3)$.
3. **Action:** An integer within $\{0, 1, 2, 3\}$ to control an emulated game console.
4. **Reward:** Determined by the game logic.
5. **Termination:** After all game lives are lost.
6. **Solution:** Maximize the average score over 100 consecutive episodes.

B.2   Continuous Environments

The continuous-control environments in OpenAI Gym include robotics control problems `Pendulum-v0` and `BipedalWalker-v2`. This section provides detailed descriptions of these environments; some information is referenced from the original OpenAI Gym documentation Wiki.

B.2.1   Pendulum-v0

Figure B.6   The `Pendulum-v0` environment. The objective is to swing up an inverted pendulum and keep it standing.

This is a continuous-control problem where an agent applies torque to swing a frictionless inverted pendulum up, and keep it standing.

1. **Objective:** Swing and keep the pendulum standing up.
2. **State:** An array of length 3 with the joint angle θ and its angular velocity: $[\cos \theta, \sin \theta, \frac{d\theta}{dt}]$. For example, $[0.91450008, -0.40458573, 0.85436913]$.
3. **Action:** A floating-point number in interval $[-2.0, 2.0]$ to apply torque to joint. For example, 0.0 to apply no torque.
4. **Reward:** Equation $-(\theta^2 + 0.1\frac{d\theta}{dt}^2 + 0.001\text{torque}^2)$.
5. **Termination:** After 200 maximum time steps.
6. **Solution:** Maximize the average total reward over 100 consecutive episodes.

B.2.2   BipedalWalker-v2

This is a continuous-control problem where an agent uses a robot's lidar sensor to sense its surroundings and move to the right without falling.

1. **Objective:** Walk to the right without falling.
2. **State:** An array of length 24: [hull angle, hull angular velocity, x-velocity, y-velocity, hip 1 joint angle, hip 1 joint speed, knee 1 joint angle, knee 1 joint speed, leg 1

Figure B.7   The BipedalWalker-v2 environment. The objective is to move
the agent forward to the right without falling.

ground contact, hip 2 joint angle, hip 2 joint speed, knee 2 joint angle, knee 2 joint
speed, leg 2 ground contact, . . ., 10 lidar readings]. For example, [2.74561788e−03,
1.18099805e−05, −1.53996013e−03, −1.60000777e−02, . . ., 7.09147751e−01,
8.85930359e−01, 1.00000000e+00, 1.00000000e+00].

3. **Action:** A vector of four floating-point numbers in interval $[-1.0, 1.0]$: [hip 1
torque and velocity, knee 1 torque and velocity, hip 2 torque and velocity, knee 2
torque and velocity]. For example,
[0.09762701, 0.43037874, 0.20552675, 0.08976637].

4. **Reward:** Reward for moving forward to the right for up to +300 in total; −100 if
the robot falls.

5. **Termination:** When the robot body touches the ground or reaches the far right
side, or after 1600 maximum time steps.

6. **Solution:** Average total reward of 300 over 100 consecutive episodes.

References

[1]   Abadi, M., Agarwal, A., Barham, P., Brevdo, E., Chen, Z., Citro, C.,
      Corrado, G. S., et al. "TensorFlow: Large-Scale Machine Learning on
      Heterogeneous Distributed Systems." Software available from tensorflow.org. 2015.
      ARXIV: 1603.04467.

[2]   Achiam, J., Held, D., Tamar, A., and Abbeel, P. "Constrained Policy
      Optimization." 2017. ARXIV: 1705.10528.

[3]   AlphaStar Team. "AlphaStar: Mastering the Real-Time Strategy Game StarCraft
      II." 2019. URL: https://deepmind.com/blog/alphastar-mastering-real-time-
      strategy-game-starcraft-ii.

[4]   Amodei, D., Olah, C., Steinhardt, J., Christiano, P., Schulman, J., and Mané, D.
      "Concrete Problems in AI Safety." 2016. ARXIV: 1606.06565.

[5]   Anderson, H. L. "Metropolis, Monte Carlo, and the MANIAC." In: *Los Alamos
      Science* 14 (1986). URL:
      http://library.lanl.gov/cgi-bin/getfile?00326886.pdf.

[6]   Andrychowicz, M., Wolski, F., Ray, A., Schneider, J., Fong, R., Welinder, P.,
      McGrew, B., Tobin, J., Abbeel, P., and Zaremba, W. "Hindsight Experience
      Replay." 2017. ARXIV: 1707.01495.

[7]   Animal-AI Olympics. URL: https://github.com/beyretb/AnimalAI-Olympics.

[8]   Arjona-Medina, J. A., Gillhofer, M., Widrich, M., Unterthiner, T.,
      Brandstetter, J., and Hochreiter, S. "RUDDER: Return Decomposition for
      Delayed Rewards." 2018. ARXIV: 1806.07857.

[9]   Baird, L. C. *Advantage Updating*. Tech. rep. Wright-Patterson Air Force Base, OH,
      1993.

[10] Bakker, B. "Reinforcement Learning with Long Short-Term Memory." In:
      Advances in Neural Information Processing Systems 14 (NeurIPS 2001). Ed. by
      Dietterich, T. G., Becker, S., and Ghahramani, Z. MIT Press, 2002,
      pp. 1475–1482. URL: http://papers.nips.cc/paper/1953-reinforcement-
      learning-with-long-short-term-memory.pdf.

[11] Barto, A. G., Sutton, R. S., and Anderson, C. W. "Neuronlike Adaptive Elements
      That Can Solve Difficult Learning Control Problems." In: *IEEE Transactions on
      Systems, Man, & Cybernetics* 13.5 (1983), pp. 834–846. URL:
      https://ieeexplore.ieee.org/abstract/document/6313077.

[12] Beattie, C., Leibo, J. Z., Teplyashin, D., Ward, T., Wainwright, M., Küttler, H.,
      Lefrancq, A., et al. "DeepMind Lab." 2016. ARXIV: 1612.03801.

[13]   Bellemare, M. G., Dabney, W., and Munos, R. "A Distributional Perspective on Reinforcement Learning." 2017. ARXIV: 1707.06887.

[14]   Bellemare, M. G., Naddaf, Y., Veness, J., and Bowling, M. "The Arcade Learning Environment: An Evaluation Platform for General Agents." In: *Journal of Artificial Intelligence Research* 47 (June 2013), pp. 253–279. ARXIV: 1207.4708.

[15]   Bellman, R. "A Markovian Decision Process." In: *Indiana University Mathematics Journal* 6.5 (1957), pp. 679–684. ISSN: 0022-2518. URL: https://www.jstor.org/stable/24900506.

[16]   Bellman, R. "The Theory of Dynamic Programming." In: *Bulletin of the American Mathematical Society* 60.6 (1954). URL: https://projecteuclid.org/euclid.bams/1183519147.

[17]   Box2D. 2006. URL: https://github.com/erincatto/box2d.

[18]   Brockman, G., Cheung, V., Pettersson, L., Schneider, J., Schulman, J., Tang, J., and Zaremba, W. "OpenAI Gym." 2016. ARXIV: 1606.01540.

[19]   Bullet Physics SDK. URL: https://github.com/bulletphysics/bullet3.

[20]   Cho, K. "Natural Language Understanding with Distributed Representation." 2015. ARXIV: 1511.07916.

[21]   Cho, K., van Merrienboer, B., Gulçehre, Ç., Bahdanau, D., Bougares, F., Schwenk, H., and Bengio, Y. "Learning Phrase Representations Using RNN Encoder-Decoder for Statistical Machine Translation." 2014. ARXIV: 1406.1078.

[22]   Chrabaszcz, P. "Canonical ES Finds a Bug in Qbert (Full)." YouTube video, 13:54. 2018. URL: https://youtu.be/meE5aaRJOZs.

[23]   Chrabaszcz, P., Loshchilov, I., and Hutter, F. "Back to Basics: Benchmarking Canonical Evolution Strategies for Playing Atari." 2018. ARXIV: 1802.08842.

[24]   Clavera, I., Rothfuss, J., Schulman, J., Fujita, Y., Asfour, T., and Abbeel, P. "Model-Based Reinforcement Learning via Meta-Policy Optimization." 2018. ARXIV: 1809.05214.

[25]   Cobbe, K., Klimov, O., Hesse, C., Kim, T., and Schulman, J. "Quantifying Generalization in Reinforcement Learning." 2018. ARXIV: 1812.02341.

[26]   Codacy. URL: https://www.codacy.com.

[27]   Code Climate. URL: https://codeclimate.com.

[28]   Cox, D. and Dean, T. "Neural Networks and Neuroscience-Inspired Computer Vision." In: *Current Biology* 24 (2014). Computational Neuroscience, pp. 921–929. DOI: 10.1016/j.cub.2014.08.026.

[29]   CTRL-Labs. URL: https://www.ctrl-labs.com.

[30]   Cun, Y. L., Denker, J. S., and Solla, S. A. "Optimal Brain Damage." In: *Advances in Neural Information Processing Systems 2*. Ed. by Touretzky, D. S. San Francisco, CA, USA: Morgan Kaufmann Publishers Inc., 1990, pp. 598–605. ISBN: 1-55860-100-7. URL: http://dl.acm.org/citation.cfm?id=109230.109298.

[31] Daniel Rozin Interactive Art. URL: http://www.smoothware.com/danny.

[32] Deng, J., Dong, W., Socher, R., Li, L.-J., Li, K., and Fei-Fei, L. "ImageNet: A Large-Scale Hierarchical Image Database." In: *IEEE Conference on Computer Vision and Pattern Recognition, CVPR09*. IEEE, 2009, pp. 248–255.

[33] Dettmers, T. "A Full Hardware Guide to Deep Learning." 2018. URL: https://timdettmers.com/2018/12/16/deep-learning-hardware-guide.

[34] Dreyfus, S. "Richard Bellman on the Birth of Dynamic Programming." In: *Operations Research* 50.1 (2002), pp. 48–51. DOI: 10.1287/opre.50.1.48.17791.

[35] Duan, Y., Chen, X., Houthooft, R., Schulman, J., and Abbeel, P. "Benchmarking Deep Reinforcement Learning for Continuous Control." 2016. ARXIV: 1604.06778.

[36] Ecoffet, A., Huizinga, J., Lehman, J., Stanley, K. O., and Clune, J. "Go-Explore: A New Approach for Hard-Exploration Problems." 2019. ARXIV: 1901.10995.

[37] Espeholt, L., Soyer, H., Munos, R., Simonyan, K., Mnih, V., Ward, T., Doron, Y., et al. "IMPALA: Scalable Distributed Deep-RL with Importance Weighted Actor-Learner Architectures." 2018. ARXIV: 1802.01561.

[38] Fazel, M., Ge, R., Kakade, S. M., and Mesbahi, M. "Global Convergence of Policy Gradient Methods for the Linear Quadratic Regulator." 2018. ARXIV: 1801.05039.

[39] Fei-Fei, L., Johnson, J., and Yeung, S. "Lecture 14: Reinforcement Learning." In: *CS231n: Convolutional Neural Networks for Visual Recognition, Spring 2017*. Stanford University, 2017. URL: http://cs231n.stanford.edu/slides/2017/cs231n_2017_lecture14.pdf.

[40] Finn, C., Abbeel, P., and Levine, S. "Model-Agnostic Meta-Learning for Fast Adaptation of Deep Networks." 2017. ARXIV: 1703.03400.

[41] Frankle, J. and Carbin, M. "The Lottery Ticket Hypothesis: Finding Sparse, Trainable Neural Networks." 2018. ARXIV: 1803.03635.

[42] Fujimoto, S., van Hoof, H., and Meger, D. "Addressing Function Approximation Error in Actor-Critic Methods." 2018. ARXIV: 1802.09477.

[43] Fukushima, K. "Neocognitron: A Self-Organizing Neural Network Model for a Mechanism of Pattern Recognition Unaffected by Shift in Position." In: *Biological Cybernetics* 36 (1980), pp. 193–202. URL: https://www.rctn.org/bruno/public/papers/Fukushima1980.pdf.

[44] Glances—An Eye on Your System. URL: https://github.com/nicolargo/glances.

[45] Goodfellow, I., Bengio, Y., and Courville, A. *Deep Learning*. MIT Press, 2016. URL: http://www.deeplearningbook.org.

[46] Greaves, J., Robinson, M., Walton, N., Mortensen, M., Pottorff, R., Christopherson, C., Hancock, D., and Wingate, D. "Holodeck—A High Fidelity Simulator for Reinforcement Learning." 2018. URL: https://github.com/byu-pccl/holodeck.

[47] Haarnoja, T., Zhou, A., Abbeel, P., and Levine, S. "Soft Actor-Critic: Off-Policy Maximum Entropy Deep Reinforcement Learning with a Stochastic Actor." 2018. ARXIV: 1801.01290.

[48] Henderson, P., Islam, R., Bachman, P., Pineau, J., Precup, D., and Meger, D. "Deep Reinforcement Learning That Matters." 2017. ARXIV: 1709.06560.

[49] Hessel, M., Modayil, J., van Hasselt, H., Schaul, T., Ostrovski, G., Dabney, W., Horgan, D., Piot, B., Azar, M. G., and Silver, D. "Rainbow: Combining Improvements in Deep Reinforcement Learning." 2017. ARXIV: 1710.02298.

[50] Hinton, G. "Lecture 6a: Overview of Mini-Batch Gradient Descent." In: *CSC321: Neural Networks for Machine Learning*. University of Toronto, 2014. URL: http://www.cs.toronto.edu/~tijmen/csc321/slides/lecture_slides_lec6.pdf.

[51] Ho, J. and Ermon, S. "Generative Adversarial Imitation Learning." 2016. ARXIV: 1606.03476.

[52] Hochreiter, S. and Schmidhuber, J. "Long Short-Term Memory." In: *Neural Computation* 9.8 (Nov. 1997), pp. 1735–1780. ISSN: 0899-7667. DOI: 10.1162/neco.1997.9.8.1735.

[53] Hofstadter, D. R. *Gödel, Escher, Bach: An Eternal Golden Braid*. New York: Vintage Books, 1980. ISBN: 0-394-74502-7.

[54] Horgan, D., Quan, J., Budden, D., Barth-Maron, G., Hessel, M., van Hasselt, H., and Silver, D. "Distributed Prioritized Experience Replay." 2018. ARXIV: 1803.00933.

[55] HTC Vive. URL: https://www.vive.com/us.

[56] Jaderberg, M., Czarnecki, W. M., Dunning, I., Marris, L., Lever, G., Castañeda, A. G., Beattie, C., et al. "Human-Level Performance in 3D Multiplayer Games with Population-Based Reinforcement Learning." In: *Science* 364.6443 (2019), pp. 859–865. ISSN: 0036-8075. DOI: 10.1126/science.aau6249.

[57] Johnson, M., Hofmann, K., Hutton, T., and Bignell, D. "The Malmo Platform for Artificial Intelligence Experimentation." In: *IJCAI'16 Proceedings of the Twenty-Fifth International Joint Conference on Artificial Intelligence*. New York, USA: AAAI Press, 2016, pp. 4246–4247. ISBN: 978-1-57735-770-4. URL: http://dl.acm.org/citation.cfm?id=3061053.3061259.

[58] Jouppi, N. "Google Supercharges Machine Learning Tasks with TPU Custom Chip." Google Blog. 2016. URL: https://cloudplatform.googleblog.com/2016/05/Google-supercharges-machine-learning-tasks-with-custom-chip.html.

[59] Juliani, A., Berges, V.-P., Vckay, E., Gao, Y., Henry, H., Mattar, M., and Lange, D. "Unity: A General Platform for Intelligent Agents." 2018. ARXIV: 1809.02627.

[60] Juliani, A., Khalifa, A., Berges, V., Harper, J., Henry, H., Crespi, A., Togelius, J., and Lange, D. "Obstacle Tower: A Generalization Challenge in Vision, Control, and Planning." 2019. ARXIV: 1902.01378.

[61]   Kaelbling, L. P., Littman, M. L., and Moore, A. P. "Reinforcement Learning: A Survey." In: *Journal of Artificial Intelligence Research* 4 (1996), pp. 237–285. URL: http://people.csail.mit.edu/lpk/papers/rl-survey.ps.

[62]   Kaiser, L., Babaeizadeh, M., Milos, P., Osinski, B., Campbell, R. H., Czechowski, K., Erhan, D., et al. "Model-Based Reinforcement Learning for Atari." 2019. ARXIV: 1903.00374.

[63]   Kakade, S. "A Natural Policy Gradient." In: *NeurIPS'11 Proceedings of the 14th International Conference on Neural Information Processing Systems: Natural and Synthetic.* Cambridge, MA, USA: MIT Press, 2001, pp. 1531–1538. URL: http://dl.acm.org/citation.cfm?id=2980539.2980738.

[64]   Kalashnikov, D., Irpan, A., Pastor, P., Ibarz, J., Herzog, A., Jang, E., Quillen, D., et al. "QT-Opt: Scalable Deep Reinforcement Learning for Vision-Based Robotic Manipulation." 2018. ARXIV: 1806.10293.

[65]   Kapturowski, S., Ostrovski, G., Quan, J., Munos, R., and Dabney, W. "Recurrent Experience Replay in Distributed Reinforcement Learning." In: *International Conference on Learning Representations.* 2019. URL: https://openreview.net/forum?id=r1lyTjAqYX.

[66]   Karpathy, A. "The Unreasonable Effectiveness of Recurrent Neural Networks." 2015. URL: http://karpathy.github.io/2015/05/21/rnn-effectiveness.

[67]   Keng, W. L. and Graesser, L. "SLM-Lab." 2017. URL: https://github.com/kengz/SLM-Lab.

[68]   Kingma, D. P. and Ba, J. "Adam: A Method for Stochastic Optimization." 2014. ARXIV: 1412.6980.

[69]   Leap Motion. URL: https://www.leapmotion.com/technology.

[70]   LeCun, Y., Boser, B., Denker, J. S., Henderson, D., Howard, R. E., Hubbard, W., and Jackel, L. D. "Backpropagation Applied to Handwritten Zip Code Recognition." In: *Neural Computation* 1 (1989), pp. 541–551. URL: http://yann.lecun.com/exdb/publis/pdf/lecun-89e.pdf.

[71]   LeCun, Y. "Generalization and Network Design Strategies." In: *Connectionism in Perspective.* Ed. by Pfeifer, R., Schreter, Z., Fogelman, F., and Steels, L. Elsevier, 1989.

[72]   LeCun, Y. "Week 10, Unsupervised Learning Part 1." In: *DS-GA-1008: Deep Learning, NYU.* 2017. URL: https://cilvr.cs.nyu.edu/lib/exe/fetch.php?media=deeplearning:2017:007-unsup01.pdf.

[73]   LeCun, Y., Cortes, C., and Burges, C. J. "The MNIST Database of Handwritten Digits." 2010. URL: http://yann.lecun.com/exdb/mnist.

[74]   Levine, S. "Sep 6: Policy Gradients Introduction, Lecture 4." In: *CS 294: Deep Reinforcement Learning, Fall 2017.* UC Berkeley, 2017. URL: http://rail.eecs.berkeley.edu/deeprlcourse-fa17/index.html#lectures.

[75]   Levine, S. "Sep 11: Actor-Critic Introduction, Lecture 5." In: *CS 294: Deep Reinforcement Learning, Fall 2017*. UC Berkeley, 2017. URL: http://rail.eecs.berkeley.edu/deeprlcourse-fa17/index.html#lectures.

[76]   Levine, S. "Sep 13: Value Functions Introduction, Lecture 6." In: *CS 294: Deep Reinforcement Learning, Fall 2017*. UC Berkeley, 2017. URL: http://rail.eecs.berkeley.edu/deeprlcourse-fa17/index.html#lectures.

[77]   Levine, S. "Sep 18: Advanced Q-Learning Algorithms, Lecture 7." In: *CS 294: Deep Reinforcement Learning, Fall 2017*. UC Berkeley, 2017. URL: http://rail.eecs.berkeley.edu/deeprlcourse-fa17/index.html#lectures.

[78]   Levine, S. and Achiam, J. "Oct 11: Advanced Policy Gradients, Lecture 13." In: *CS 294: Deep Reinforcement Learning, Fall 2017*. UC Berkeley, 2017. URL: http://rail.eecs.berkeley.edu/deeprlcourse-fa17/index.html#lectures.

[79]   Li, W. and Todorov, E. "Iterative Linear Quadratic Regulator Design for Nonlinear Biological Movement Systems." In: *Proceedings of the 1st International Conference on Informatics in Control, Automation and Robotics (ICINCO 1)*. Ed. by Araújo, H., Vieira, A., Braz, J., Encarnação, B., and Carvalho, M. INSTICC Press, 2004, pp. 222–229. ISBN: 972-8865-12-0.

[80]   LIGO. "Gravitational Waves Detected 100 Years after Einstein's Prediction." 2016. URL: https://www.ligo.caltech.edu/news/ligo20160211.

[81]   Lillicrap, T. P., Hunt, J. J., Pritzel, A., Heess, N., Erez, T., Tassa, Y., Silver, D., and Wierstra, D. "Continuous Control with Deep Reinforcement Learning." 2015. ARXIV: 1509.02971.

[82]   Lin, L.-J. "Self-Improving Reactive Agents Based on Reinforcement Learning, Planning and Teaching." In: *Machine Learning* 8 (1992), pp. 293–321. URL: http://www.incompleteideas.net/lin-92.pdf.

[83]   Mania, H., Guy, A., and Recht, B. "Simple Random Search Provides a Competitive Approach to Reinforcement Learning." 2018. ARXIV: 1803.07055.

[84]   MarioKart 8. URL: https://mariokart8.nintendo.com.

[85]   Metropolis, N. "The Beginning of the Monte Carlo Method." In: *Los Alamos Science*. Special Issue. 1987. URL: http://library.lanl.gov/cgi-bin/getfile?00326866.pdf.

[86]   Microsoft Research. "Policy Gradient Methods: Tutorial and New Frontiers." YouTube video, 1:09:19. 2017. URL: https://youtu.be/y4ci8whvS1E.

[87]   Mnih, V., Badia, A. P., Mirza, M., Graves, A., Harley, T., Lillicrap, T. P., Silver, D., and Kavukcuoglu, K. "Asynchronous Methods for Deep Reinforcement Learning." In: *ICML'16 Proceedings of the 33rd International Conference on International Conference on Machine Learning–Volume 48*. New York, NY, USA: JMLR.org, 2016, pp. 1928–1937. URL: http://dl.acm.org/citation.cfm?id=3045390.3045594.

[88]   Mnih, V., Kavukcuoglu, K., Silver, D., Graves, A., Antonoglou, I., Wierstra, D., and Riedmiller, M. A. "Playing Atari with Deep Reinforcement Learning." 2013. ARXIV: 1312.5602.

[89]   Mnih, V., Kavukcuoglu, K., Silver, D., Rusu, A. A., Veness, J., Bellemare, M. G., Graves, A., et al. "Human-Level Control through Deep Reinforcement Learning." In: *Nature* 518.7540 (Feb. 2015), pp. 529–533. ISSN: 00280836. URL: http://dx.doi.org/10.1038/nature14236.

[90]   Molchanov, P., Tyree, S., Karras, T., Aila, T., and Kautz, J. "Pruning Convolutional Neural Networks for Resource Efficient Inference." 2016. ARXIV: 1611.06440.

[91]   Moore, A. W. *Efficient Memory-Based Learning for Robot Control*. Tech. rep. University of Cambridge, 1990.

[92]   Nielsen, M. *Neural Networks and Deep Learning*. Determination Press, 2015.

[93]   Niu, F., Recht, B., Re, C., and Wright, S. J. "HOGWILD!: A Lock-Free Approach to Parallelizing Stochastic Gradient Descent." In: *NeurIPS'11 Proceedings of the 24th International Conference on Neural Information Processing Systems*. USA: Curran Associates Inc., 2011, pp. 693–701. ISBN: 978-1-61839-599-3. URL: http://dl.acm.org/citation.cfm?id=2986459.2986537.

[94]   Norman, D. A. *The Design of Everyday Things*. New York, NY, USA: Basic Books, Inc., 2002. ISBN: 9780465067107.

[95]   Nvidia. "NVIDIA Launches the World's First Graphics Processing Unit: GeForce 256." 1999. URL: https://www.nvidia.com/object/IO_20020111_5424.html.

[96]   NVIDIA. "NVIDIA Unveils CUDA–The GPU Computing Revolution Begins." 2006. URL: https://www.nvidia.com/object/IO_37226.html.

[97]   Oculus. URL: https://www.oculus.com.

[98]   OpenAI, Andrychowicz, M., Baker, B., Chociej, M., Józefowicz, R., McGrew, B., Pachocki, J., et al. "Learning Dexterous In-Hand Manipulation." 2018. ARXIV: 1808.00177.

[99]   OpenAI Baselines. URL: https://github.com/openai/baselines.

[100] OpenAI Blog. "Faulty Reward Functions in the Wild." 2016. URL: https://blog.openai.com/faulty-reward-functions.

[101] OpenAI Blog. "Learning Dexterity." 2018. URL: https://blog.openai.com/learning-dexterity.

[102] OpenAI Blog. "More on Dota 2." 2017. URL: https://blog.openai.com/more-on-dota-2.

[103] OpenAI Blog. "OpenAI Baselines: DQN." 2017. URL: https://blog.openai.com/openai-baselines-dqn.

[104] OpenAI Blog. "OpenAI Five." 2018. URL: https://blog.openai.com/openai-five.

[105] OpenAI Blog. "OpenAI Five Benchmark: Results." 2018. URL: https://blog.openai.com/openai-five-benchmark-results.

[106] OpenAI Blog. "Proximal Policy Optimization." 2017. URL: https://blog.openai.com/openai-baselines-ppo.

[107]   OpenAI Five. URL: https://openai.com/five.

[108]   OpenAI Retro. URL: https://github.com/openai/retro.

[109]   OpenAI Roboschool. 2017. URL: https://github.com/openai/roboschool.

[110]   Parisotto, E., Ba, L. J., and Salakhutdinov, R. "Actor-Mimic: Deep Multitask and Transfer Reinforcement Learning." In: *4th International Conference on Learning Representations, ICLR 2016, San Juan, Puerto Rico, May 2–4, 2016, Conference Track Proceedings*. 2016. ARXIV: 1511.06342.

[111]   Pathak, D., Agrawal, P., Efros, A. A., and Darrell, T. "Curiosity-Driven Exploration by Self-Supervised Prediction." In: *ICML*. 2017.

[112]   Peters, J. and Schaal, S. "Reinforcement Learning of Motor Skills with Policy Gradients." In: *Neural Networks* 21.4 (May 2008), pp. 682–697.

[113]   Peters, J. and Schaal, S. "Natural Actor-Critic." In: *Neurocomputing* 71.7–9 (Mar. 2008), pp. 1180–1190. ISSN: 0925-2312. DOI: 10.1016/j.neucom.2007.11.026.

[114]   PyTorch. 2018. URL: https://github.com/pytorch/pytorch.

[115]   Quiter, C. and Ernst, M. "deepdrive/deepdrive: 2.0." Mar. 2018. DOI: 10.5281/zenodo.1248998.

[116]   ROLI. Seaboard: The future of the keyboard. URL: https://roli.com/products/seaboard.

[117]   Rumelhart, D. E., Hinton, G. E., and Williams, R. J. "Learning Representations by Back-Propagating Errors." In: *Nature* 323 (Oct. 1986), pp. 533–536. DOI: 10.1038/323533a0.

[118]   Rummery, G. A. and Niranjan, M. *On-Line Q-Learning Using Connectionist Systems*. Tech. rep. University of Cambridge, 1994.

[119]   Samuel, A. L. "Some Studies in Machine Learning Using the Game of Checkers." In: *IBM Journal of Research and Development* 3.3 (July 1959), pp. 210–229. ISSN: 0018-8646. DOI: 10.1147/rd.33.0210.

[120]   Samuel, A. L. "Some Studies in Machine Learning Using the Game of Checkers. II–Recent Progress." In: *IBM Journal of Research and Development* 11.6 (Nov. 1967), pp. 601–617. ISSN: 0018-8646. DOI: 10.1147/rd.116.0601.

[121]   Schaul, T., Quan, J., Antonoglou, I., and Silver, D. "Prioritized Experience Replay." 2015. ARXIV: 1511.05952.

[122]   Schulman, J., Levine, S., Moritz, P., Jordan, M. I., and Abbeel, P. "Trust Region Policy Optimization." 2015. ARXIV: 1502.05477.

[123]   Schulman, J., Moritz, P., Levine, S., Jordan, M. I., and Abbeel, P. "High-Dimensional Continuous Control Using Generalized Advantage Estimation." 2015. ARXIV: 1506.02438.

[124]   Schulman, J., Wolski, F., Dhariwal, P., Radford, A., and Klimov, O. "Proximal Policy Optimization Algorithms." 2017. ARXIV: 1707.06347.

[125] Silver, D., Huang, A., Maddison, C. J., Guez, A., Sifre, L., Van Den Driessche, G., Schrittwieser, J., Antonoglou, I., Panneershelvam, V., Lanctot, M., et al. "Mastering the Game of Go with Deep Neural Networks and Tree Search." In: *Nature* 529.7587 (2016), pp. 484–489.

[126] Silver, D., Hubert, T., Schrittwieser, J., Antonoglou, I., Lai, M., Guez, A., Lanctot, M., Sifre, L., Kumaran, D., Graepel, T., et al. "Mastering Chess and Shogi by Self-Play with a General Reinforcement Learning Algorithm." 2017. ARXIV: 1712.01815.

[127] Silver, D., Schrittwieser, J., Simonyan, K., Antonoglou, I., Huang, A., Guez, A., Hubert, T., Baker, L., Lai, M., Bolton, A., et al. "Mastering the Game of Go without Human Knowledge." In: *Nature* 550.7676 (2017), p. 354.

[128] Smith, J. E. and Winkler, R. L. "The Optimizer's Curse: Skepticism and Postdecision Surprise in Decision Analysis." In: *Management Science* 52.3 (2006), pp. 311–322. URL: http://dblp.uni-trier.de/db/journals/mansci/mansci52.html#SmithW06.

[129] Stanford osim-RL. URL: https://github.com/stanfordnmbl/osim-rl.

[130] Sutton, R. S. "Dyna, an Integrated Architecture for Learning, Planning, and Reacting." In: *ACM SIGART Bulletin* 2.4 (July 1991), pp. 160–163. ISSN: 0163-5719. DOI: 10.1145/122344.122377.

[131] Sutton, R. S. "Learning to Predict by the Methods of Temporal Differences." In: *Machine Learning* 3.1 (1988), pp. 9–44.

[132] Sutton, R. S. and Barto, A. G. *Reinforcement Learning: An Introduction*. Second ed. The MIT Press, 2018. URL: https://web.stanford.edu/class/psych209/Readings/SuttonBartoIPRLBook2ndEd.pdf.

[133] Sutton, R. S., McAllester, D., Singh, S., and Mansour, Y. "Policy Gradient Methods for Reinforcement Learning with Function Approximation." In: *NeurIPS'99 Proceedings of the 12th International Conference on Neural Information Processing Systems*. Cambridge, MA, USA: MIT Press, 1999, pp. 1057–1063. URL: http://dl.acm.org/citation.cfm?id=3009657.3009806.

[134] Teh, Y. W., Bapst, V., Czarnecki, W. M., Quan, J., Kirkpatrick, J., Hadsell, R., Heess, N., and Pascanu, R. "Distral: Robust Multitask Reinforcement Learning." 2017. ARXIV: 1707.04175.

[135] Tesauro, G. "Temporal Difference Learning and TD-Gammon." In: *Communications of the ACM* 38.3 (Mar. 1995), pp. 58–68. ISSN: 0001-0782. DOI: 10.1145/203330.203343.

[136] Todorov, E., Erez, T., and Tassa, Y. "MuJoCo: A Physics Engine for Model-Based Control." In: *IROS*. IEEE, 2012, pp. 5026–5033. ISBN: 978-1-4673-1737-5. URL: http://dblp.uni-trier.de/db/conf/iros/iros2012.html#TodorovET12.

[137] Tsitsiklis, J. N. and Van Roy, B. "An Analysis of Temporal-Difference Learning with Function Approximation." In: *IEEE Transactions on Automatic Control* 42.5 (1997). URL: http://www.mit.edu/~jnt/Papers/J063-97-bvr-td.pdf.

[138] Unity. URL: https://unity3d.com.

[139] Unreal Engine. URL: https://www.unrealengine.com.

[140] van Hasselt, H. "Double Q-Learning." In: *Advances in Neural Information Processing Systems 23*. Ed. by Lafferty, J. D. et al. Curran Associates, 2010, pp. 2613–2621. URL: http://papers.nips.cc/paper/3964-double-q-learning.pdf.

[141] van Hasselt, H., Guez, A., and Silver, D. "Deep Reinforcement Learning with Double Q-Learning." 2015. ARXIV: 1509.06461.

[142] Vinyals, O., Ewalds, T., Bartunov, S., Georgiev, P., Vezhnevets, A. S., Yeo, M., Makhzani, A., et al. "StarCraft II: A New Challenge for Reinforcement Learning." 2017. ARXIV: 1708.04782.

[143] Walt, S. v., Colbert, S. C., and Varoquaux, G. "The NumPy Array: A Structure for Efficient Numerical Computation." In: *Computing in Science and Engineering* 13.2 (Mar. 2011), pp. 22–30. ISSN: 1521-9615. DOI: 10.1109/MCSE.2011.37.

[144] Wang, Z., Schaul, T., Hessel, M., van Hasselt, H., Lanctot, M., and Freitas, N. d. "Dueling Network Architectures for Deep Reinforcement Learning." 2015. ARXIV: 1511.06581.

[145] Watkins, C. J. C. H. "Learning from Delayed Rewards." PhD thesis. Cambridge, UK: King's College, May 1989. URL: http://www.cs.rhul.ac.uk/~chrisw/new_thesis.pdf.

[146] Widrow, B., Gupta, N. K., and Maitra, S. "Punish/Reward: Learning with a Critic in Adaptive Threshold Systems." In: *IEEE Transactions on Systems, Man, and Cybernetics* SMC-3.5 (Sept. 1973), pp. 455–465. ISSN: 0018-9472. DOI: 10.1109/TSMC.1973.4309272.

[147] Wierstra, D., Förster, A., Peters, J., and Schmidhuber, J. "Recurrent Policy Gradients." In: *Logic Journal of the IGPL* 18.5 (Oct. 2010), pp. 620–634.

[148] Williams, R. J. "Simple Statistical Gradient-Following Algorithms for Connectionist Reinforcement Learning." In: *Machine Learning* 8.3–4 (May 1992), pp. 229–256. ISSN: 0885-6125. DOI: 10.1007/BF00992696.

[149] Williams, R. J. and Peng, J. "Function Optimization Using Connectionist Reinforcement Learning algorithms." In: *Connection Science* 3.3 (1991), pp. 241–268.

[150] Wydmuch, M., Kempka, M., and Jaśkowski, W. "ViZDoom Competitions: Playing Doom from Pixels." In: *IEEE Transactions on Games* 11.3 (2018).

[151] Xia, F., R. Zamir, A., He, Z.-Y., Sax, A., Malik, J., and Savarese, S. "Gibson Env: Real-World Perception for Embodied Agents." In: *2018 IEEE/CVF Conference on Computer Vision and Pattern Recognition*. IEEE. 2018. ARXIV: 1808.10654.

[152] Zhang, A., Wu, Y., and Pineau, J. "Natural Environment Benchmarks for Reinforcement Learning." 2018. ARXIV: 1811.06032.

[153] Zhang, S. and Sutton, R. S. "A Deeper Look at Experience Replay." 2017. ARXIV: 1712.01275.

Index

Credits

Figure 1.1: Screenshot of CartPole-v0 © OpenAI.

Figure 1.3: Screenshot of CartPole © OpenAI; screenshot of Atari Breakout © 2018 Atari, Inc.; screenshot of BipedalWalker © OpenAI.

Figure 5.2: Screenshot of Pong © 2018 Atari, Inc.; screenshot of Qbert © 2019 Sony Pictures Digital Productions Inc.

Figure 10.3: Screenshot of Atari Pong © 2018 Atari, Inc.

Figure 12.1: Photos by Laura Graesser.

Figure 14.3: Screenshot of CartPole-v0 © OpenAI.

Figure 14.4: Screenshot of Original View, Algorithm View, Corrected View © OpenAI.

Figure 14.7: Screenshot of CartPole-v0 © OpenAI.

Figure B.1: Screenshot of CartPole-v0 © OpenAI.

Figure B.2: Screenshot of MountainCar-v0 © OpenAI.

Figure B.3: Screenshot of LunarLander-v2 © OpenAI.

Figure B.6: Screenshot of Pendulum-v0 © OpenAI.

Figure B.7: Screenshot of BipedalWalker-v2 © OpenAI.

Photo by Marvent/Shutterstock

VIDEO TRAINING FOR THE **IT PROFESSIONAL**

LEARN QUICKLY
Learn a new technology in just hours. Video training can teach more in less time, and material is generally easier to absorb and remember.

WATCH AND LEARN
Instructors demonstrate concepts so you see technology in action.

TEST YOURSELF
Our Complete Video Courses offer self-assessment quizzes throughout.

CONVENIENT
Most videos are streaming with an option to download lessons for offline viewing.

Learn more, browse our store, and watch free, sample lessons at
informit.com/video

Save 50%* off the list price of video courses with discount code **VIDBOB**

Photo by izusek/gettyimages

Register Your Product at informit.com/register

Access additional benefits and **save 35%** on your next purchase

- Automatically receive a coupon for 35% off your next purchase, valid for 30 days. Look for your code in your InformIT cart or the Manage Codes section of your account page.

- Download available product updates.

- Access bonus material if available.*

- Check the box to hear from us and receive exclusive offers on new editions and related products.

Registration benefits vary by product. Benefits will be listed on your account page under Registered Products.

InformIT.com—The Trusted Technology Learning Source

InformIT is the online home of information technology brands at Pearson, the world's foremost education company. At InformIT.com, you can:

- Shop our books, eBooks, software, and video training
- Take advantage of our special offers and promotions (informit.com/promotions)
- Sign up for special offers and content newsletter (informit.com/newsletters)
- Access thousands of free chapters and video lessons

Connect with InformIT—Visit informit.com/community

the trusted technology learning source

Addison-Wesley • Adobe Press • Cisco Press • Microsoft Press • Pearson IT Certification • Que • Sams • Peachpit Press

 Pearson